CHAPTER 71 ··· SURELY, IROHA ISSHIKI IS MADE OF SUGAR AND SPICE AND EVERYTHING NICE.

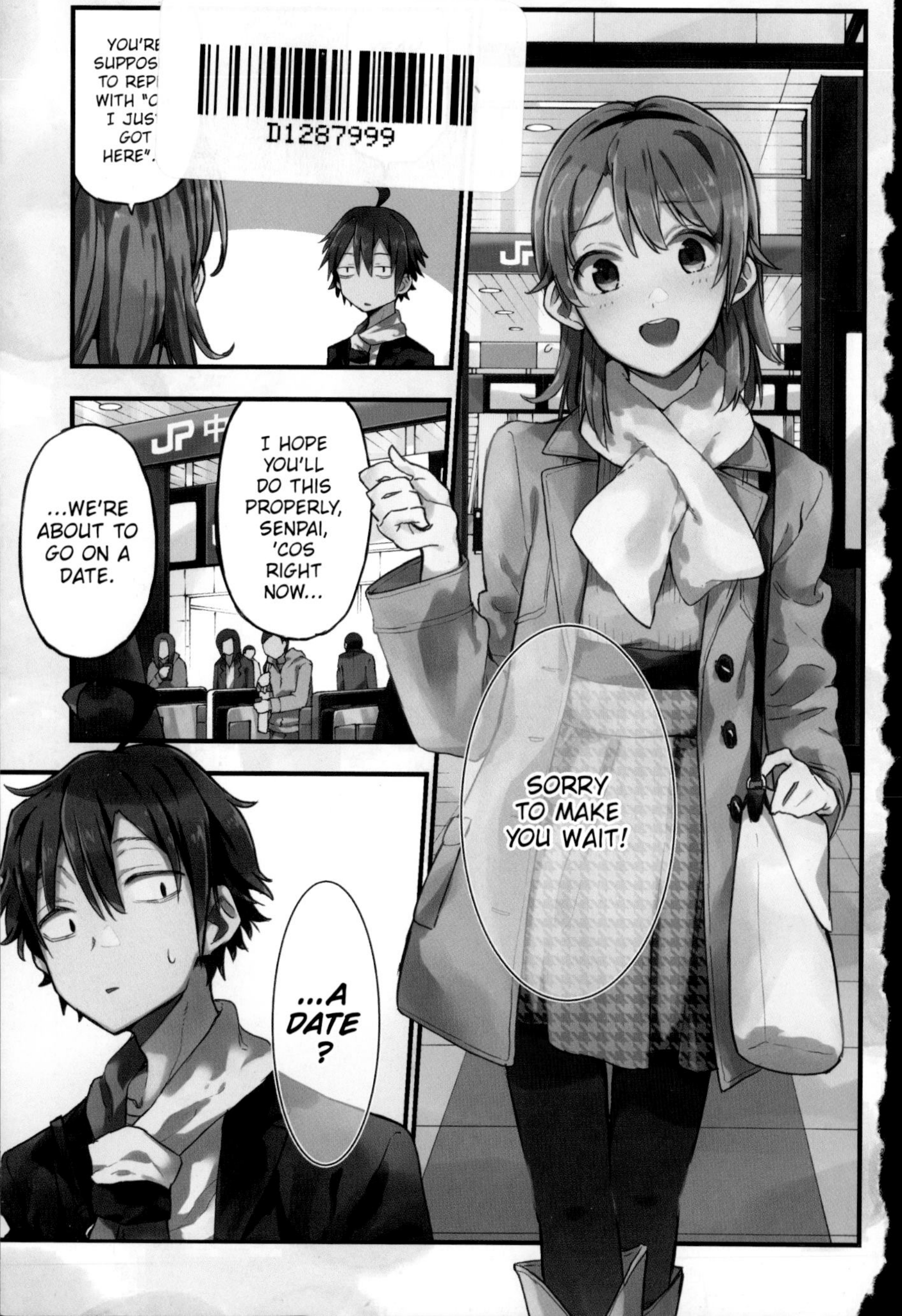

SORRY TO MAKE YOU WAIT!
YOU'RE SUPPOS TO REP WITH "O I JUST GOT HERE".
I HOPE YOU'LL DO THIS PROPERLY, SENPAI, 'COS RIGHT NOW...
...WE'RE ABOUT TO GO ON A DATE.
...A DATE?

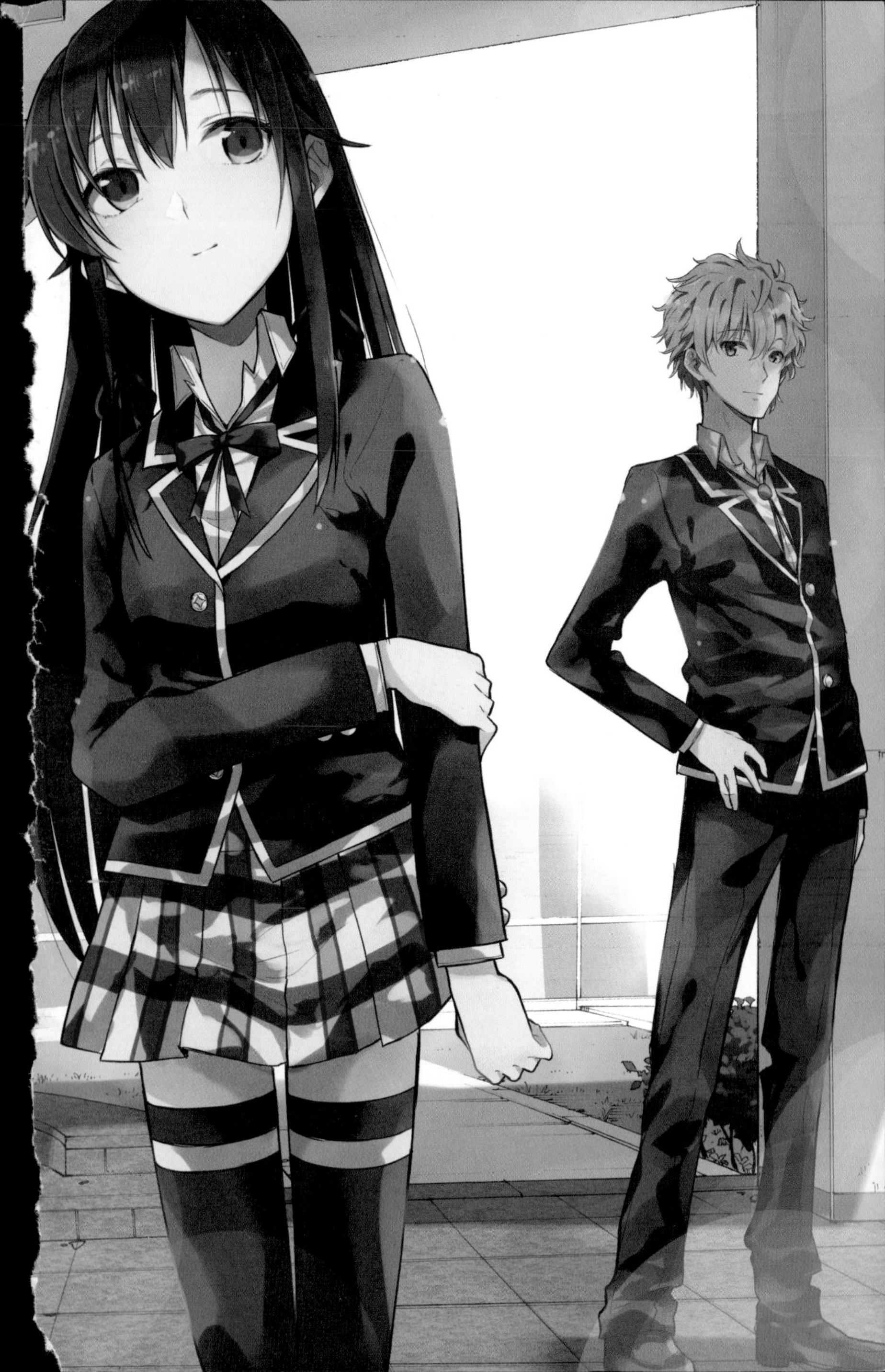

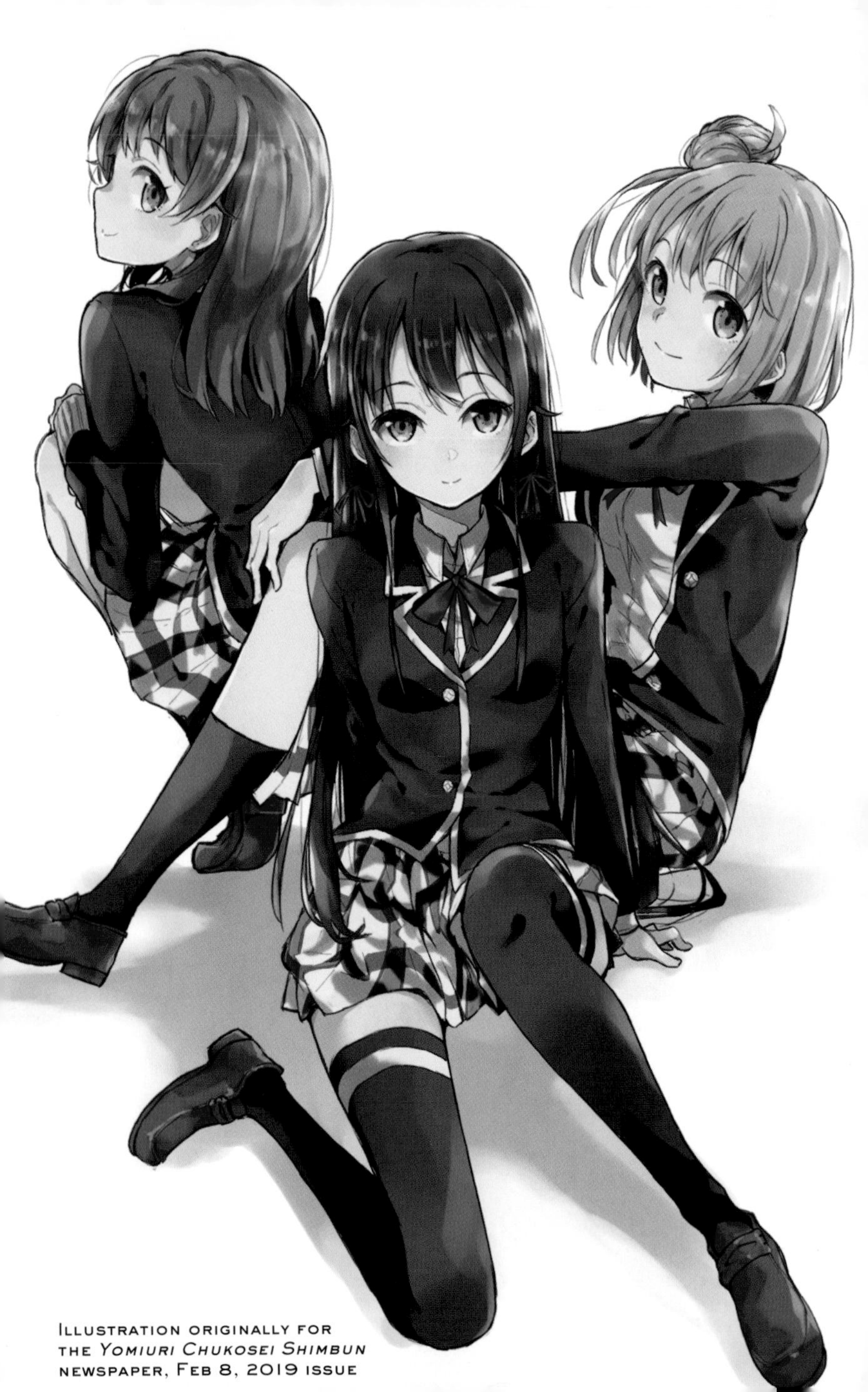

Illustration originally for
the *Yomiuri Chukosei Shimbun*
newspaper, Feb 8, 2019 issue

MY YOUTH ROMANTIC COMEDY is WRØNG, AS I EXPECTED @comic

13

▋Original Story
Wataru Watari
▋Art
Naomichi Io
▋Character Design
Ponkan⑧

MY YOUTH ROMANTIC COMEDY IS WRONG, AS I EXPECTED @COMIC

CHARACTERS + STORY SO FAR

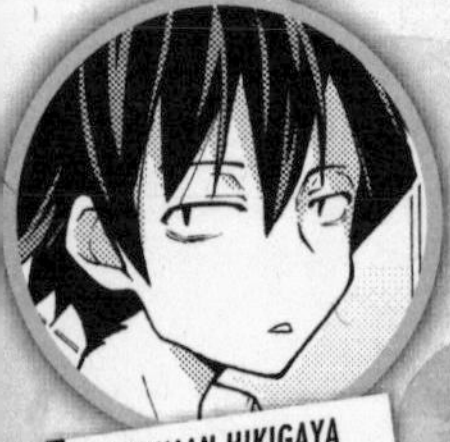

HACHIMAN HIKIGAYA

LONER AND A TWISTED HUMAN BEING. FORCED TO JOIN THE SERVICE CLUB. ASPIRES TO BE A HOUSEHUSBAND.

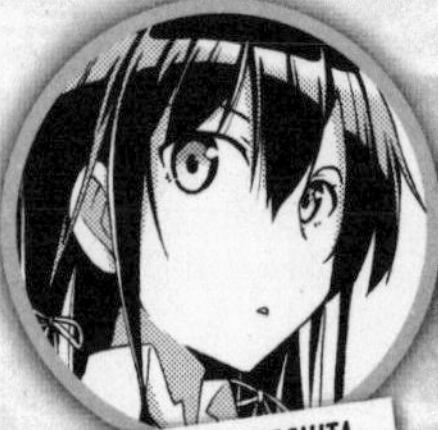

YUKINO YUKINOSHITA

PERFECT SUPERWOMAN WITH TOP GRADES AND FLAWLESS LOOKS, BUT HER PERSONALITY AND BOOBS ARE A LETDOWN. PRESIDENT OF THE SERVICE CLUB.

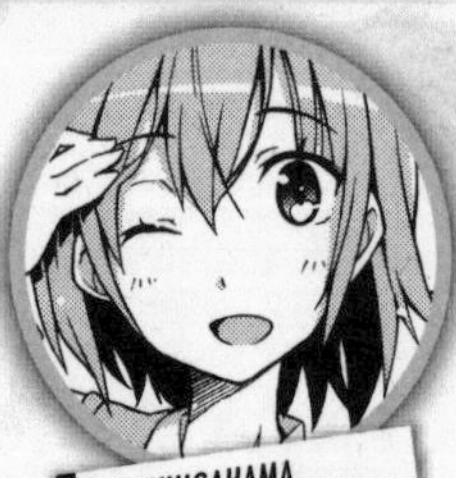

YUI YUIGAHAMA

LIGHT-BROWN HAIR, MINISKIRT, LARGE-BOOBED SLUTTY TYPE. BUT SHE'S ACTUALLY A VIRGIN!? MEMBER OF THE SERVICE CLUB.

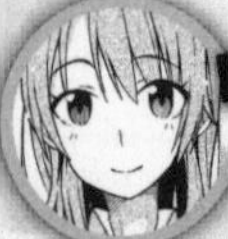

IROHA ISSHIKI

SOCCER CLUB ASSISTANT. FIRST-YEAR.

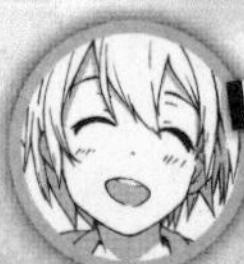

SAIKA TOTSUKA

THE SINGLE FLOWER BLOOMING IN THIS STORY. BUT...HAS A "PACKAGE."

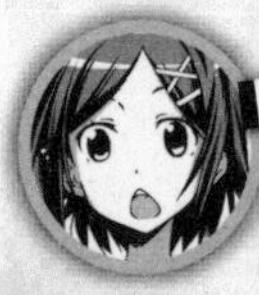

KOMACHI HIKIGAYA

HACHIMAN'S LITTLE SISTER. IN MIDDLE SCHOOL. EVERYTHING SHE DOES IS CALCULATED!?

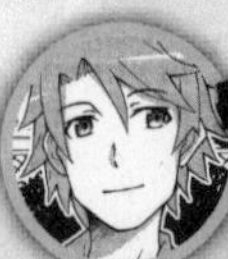

HAYATO HAYAMA

TOP RANKED IN THE SCHOOL CASTE. HANDSOME MEMBER OF THE SOCCER TEAM.

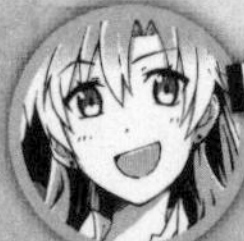

YUMIKO MIURA

THE HIGH EMPRESS NONE CAN OPPOSE.

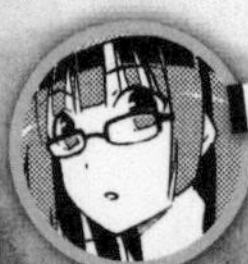

HINA EBINA

A MEMBER OF MIURA'S CLIQUE BUT A RAGING FUJOSHI ON THE INSIDE.

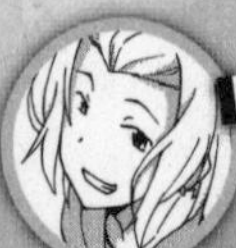

KAKERU TOBE

ALWAYS OVEREXCITED. MEMBER OF HAYAMA'S CLIQUE.

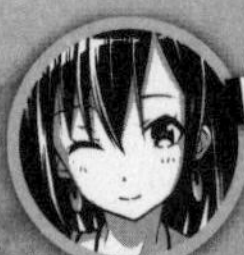

HARUNO YUKINOSHITA

YUKINO'S SISTER. UNIVERSITY UNDERGRADUATE. IS QUITE INTERESTED IN HACHIMAN.

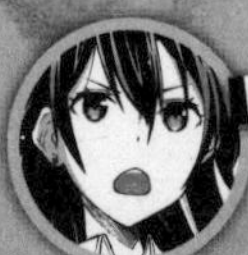

SHIZUKA HIRATSUKA

GUIDANCE COUNSELOR. ATTEMPTING TO FIX HACHIMAN BY FORCING HIM INTO THE SERVICE CLUB.

SO FAR

HACHIMAN'S LIFE HAS BEEN A FLURRY OF ACTIVITY, WHAT WITH GETTING ROPED INTO DOING IROHA'S BIDDING AND VISITING THE SHRINE AT NEW YEAR'S WITH KOMACHI. ONCE THE NEW YEAR HITS, HE WINDS UP GOING SHOPPING WITH YUI TO GET A BIRTHDAY PRESENT FOR YUKINON. BUT WHILE THEY'RE OUT ON THIS THING THAT FEELS JUST LIKE A DATE, THEY HAPPEN TO RUN INTO HARUNO YUKINOSHITA, AND THINGS START ROLLING IN AN UNEXPECTED DIRECTION...

—CONTENTS—

MADE IN COOPERATION WITH THE CHIBA CITY LOCATION SERVICE

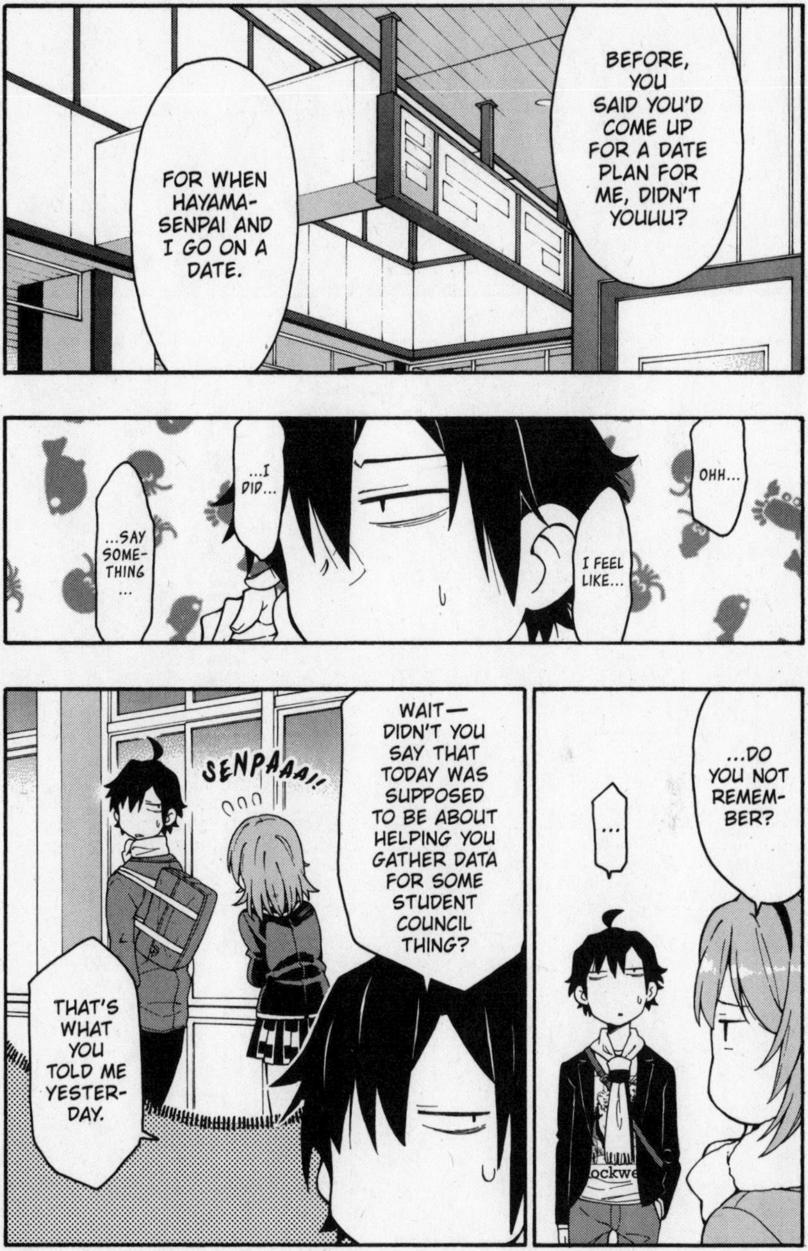
BEFORE, YOU SAID YOU'D COME UP FOR A DATE PLAN FOR ME, DIDN'T YOUUU?
FOR WHEN HAYAMA-SENPAI AND I GO ON A DATE.
OHH...
I FEEL LIKE...
...I DID...
...SAY SOME-THING...
...DO YOU NOT REMEMBER?
...
WAIT— DIDN'T YOU SAY THAT TODAY WAS SUPPOSED TO BE ABOUT HELPING YOU GATHER DATA FOR SOME STUDENT COUNCIL THING?
SENPAAAI!!
THAT'S WHAT YOU TOLD ME YESTER-DAY.

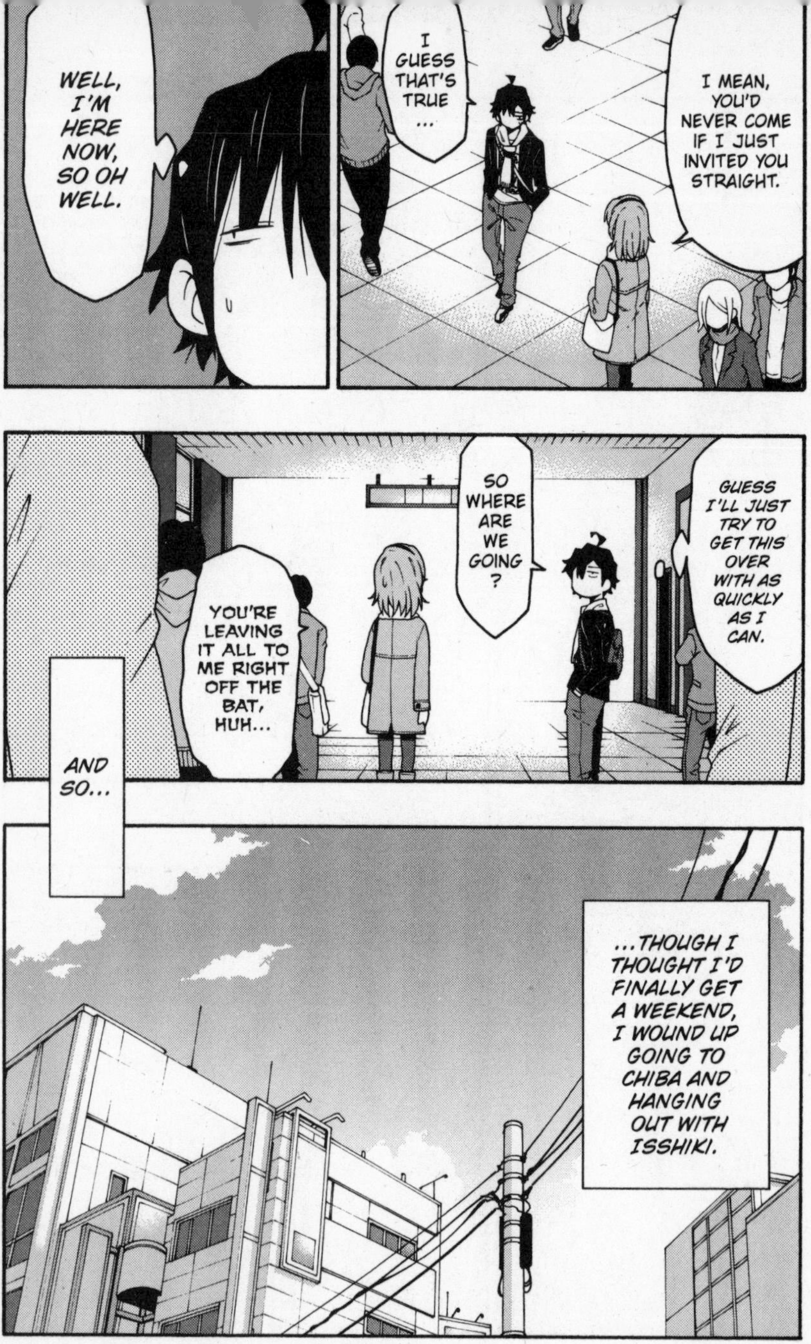
I MEAN, YOU'D NEVER COME IF I JUST INVITED YOU STRAIGHT.
I GUESS THAT'S TRUE...
WELL, I'M HERE NOW, SO OH WELL.
GUESS I'LL JUST TRY TO GET THIS OVER WITH AS QUICKLY AS I CAN.
SO WHERE ARE WE GOING?
YOU'RE LEAVING IT ALL TO ME RIGHT OFF THE BAT, HUH...
AND SO...
...THOUGH I THOUGHT I'D FINALLY GET A WEEKEND, I WOUND UP GOING TO CHIBA AND HANGING OUT WITH ISSHIKI.

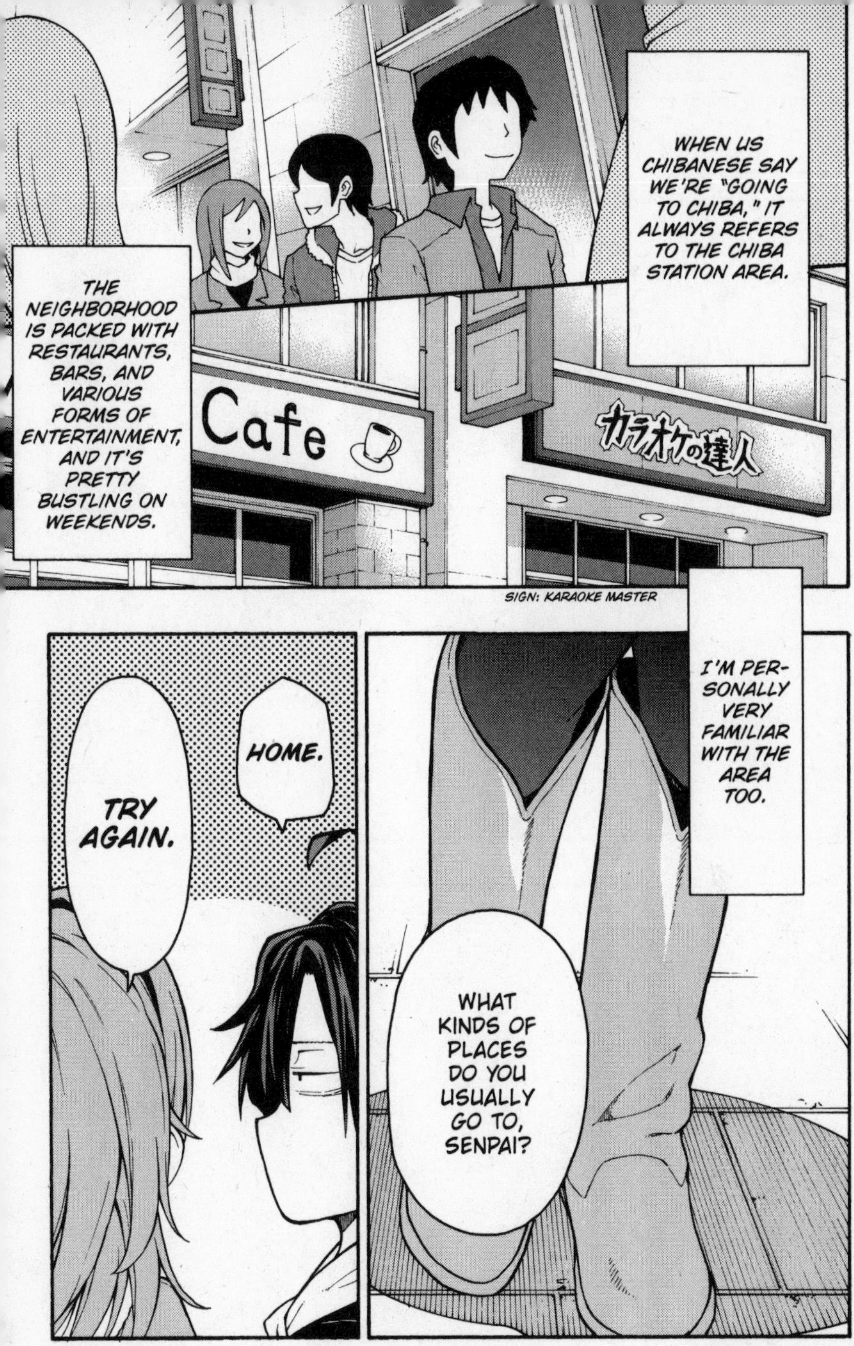
WHEN US CHIBANESE SAY WE'RE "GOING TO CHIBA," IT ALWAYS REFERS TO THE CHIBA STATION AREA.
THE NEIGHBORHOOD IS PACKED WITH RESTAURANTS, BARS, AND VARIOUS FORMS OF ENTERTAINMENT, AND IT'S PRETTY BUSTLING ON WEEKENDS.
カラオケの達人
Cafe
SIGN: KARAOKE MASTER
I'M PERSONALLY VERY FAMILIAR WITH THE AREA TOO.
WHAT KINDS OF PLACES DO YOU USUALLY GO TO, SENPAI?
HOME.
TRY AGAIN.

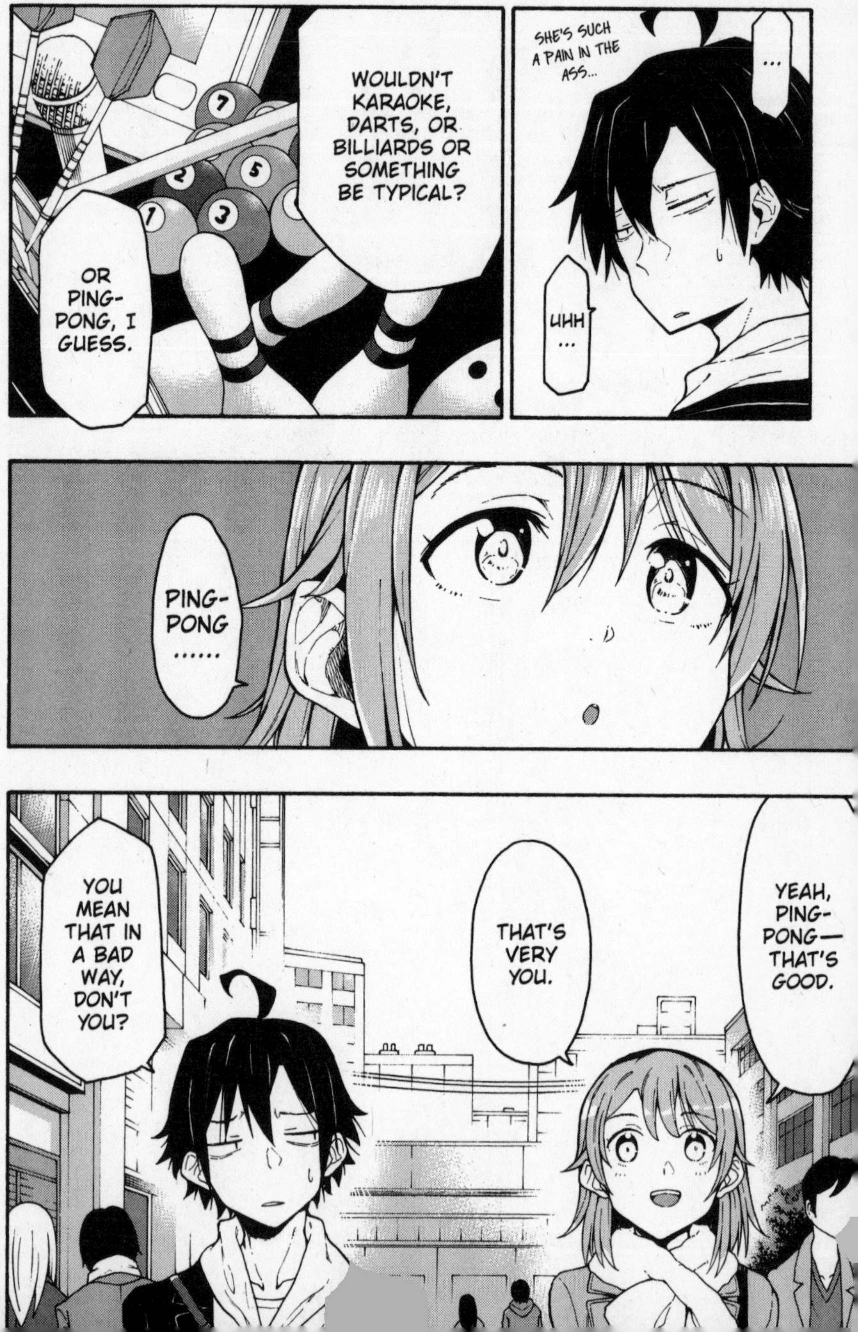
...
SHE'S SUCH A PAIN IN THE ASS...
UHH ...
WOULDN'T KARAOKE, DARTS, OR BILLIARDS OR SOMETHING BE TYPICAL?
OR PING-PONG, I GUESS.
PING-PONG ......
YEAH, PING-PONG—THAT'S GOOD.
THAT'S VERY YOU.
YOU MEAN THAT IN A BAD WAY, DON'T YOU?

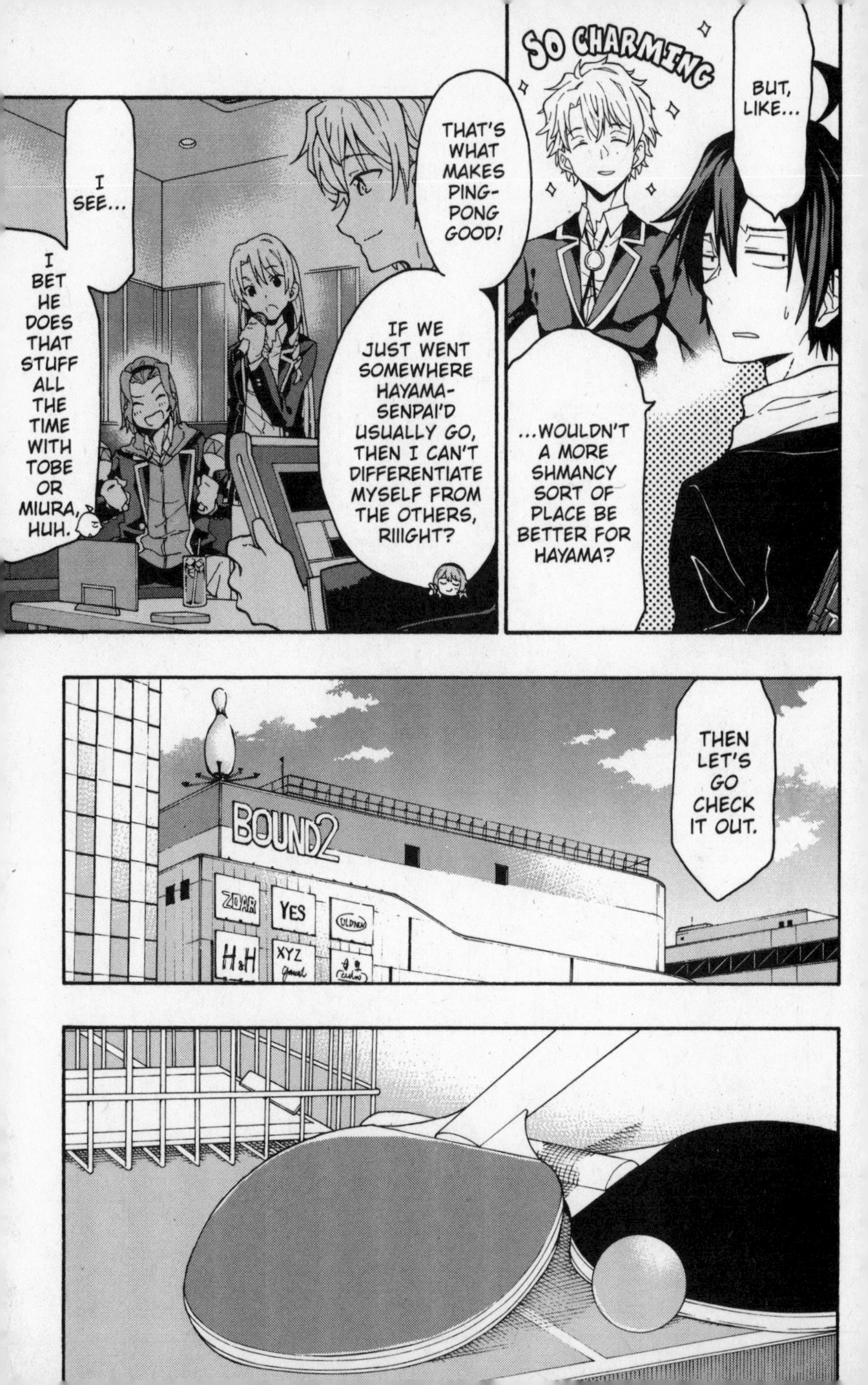
BUT, LIKE...
SO CHARMING
...WOULDN'T A MORE SHMANCY SORT OF PLACE BE BETTER FOR HAYAMA?
THAT'S WHAT MAKES PING-PONG GOOD!
IF WE JUST WENT SOMEWHERE HAYAMA-SENPAI'D USUALLY GO, THEN I CAN'T DIFFERENTIATE MYSELF FROM THE OTHERS, RIIIGHT?
I SEE...
I BET HE DOES THAT STUFF ALL THE TIME WITH TOBE OR MIURA, HUH.
THEN LET'S GO CHECK IT OUT.
BOUND2
ZOAR
YES
H&H
XYZ

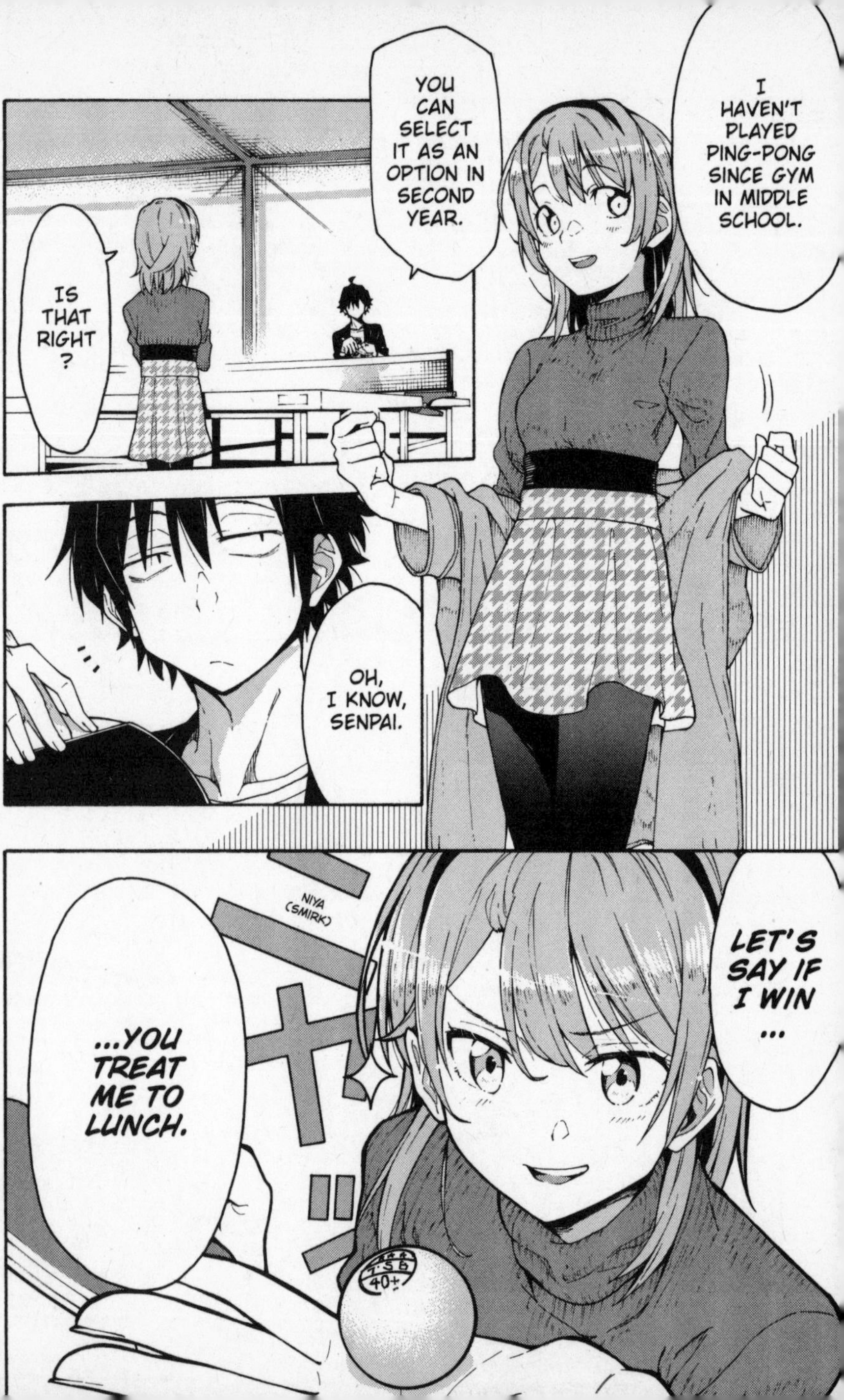
I HAVEN'T PLAYED PING-PONG SINCE GYM IN MIDDLE SCHOOL.
YOU CAN SELECT IT AS AN OPTION IN SECOND YEAR.
IS THAT RIGHT?
OH, I KNOW, SENPAI.
...
LET'S SAY IF I WIN...
NIYA (SMIRK)
...YOU TREAT ME TO LUNCH.

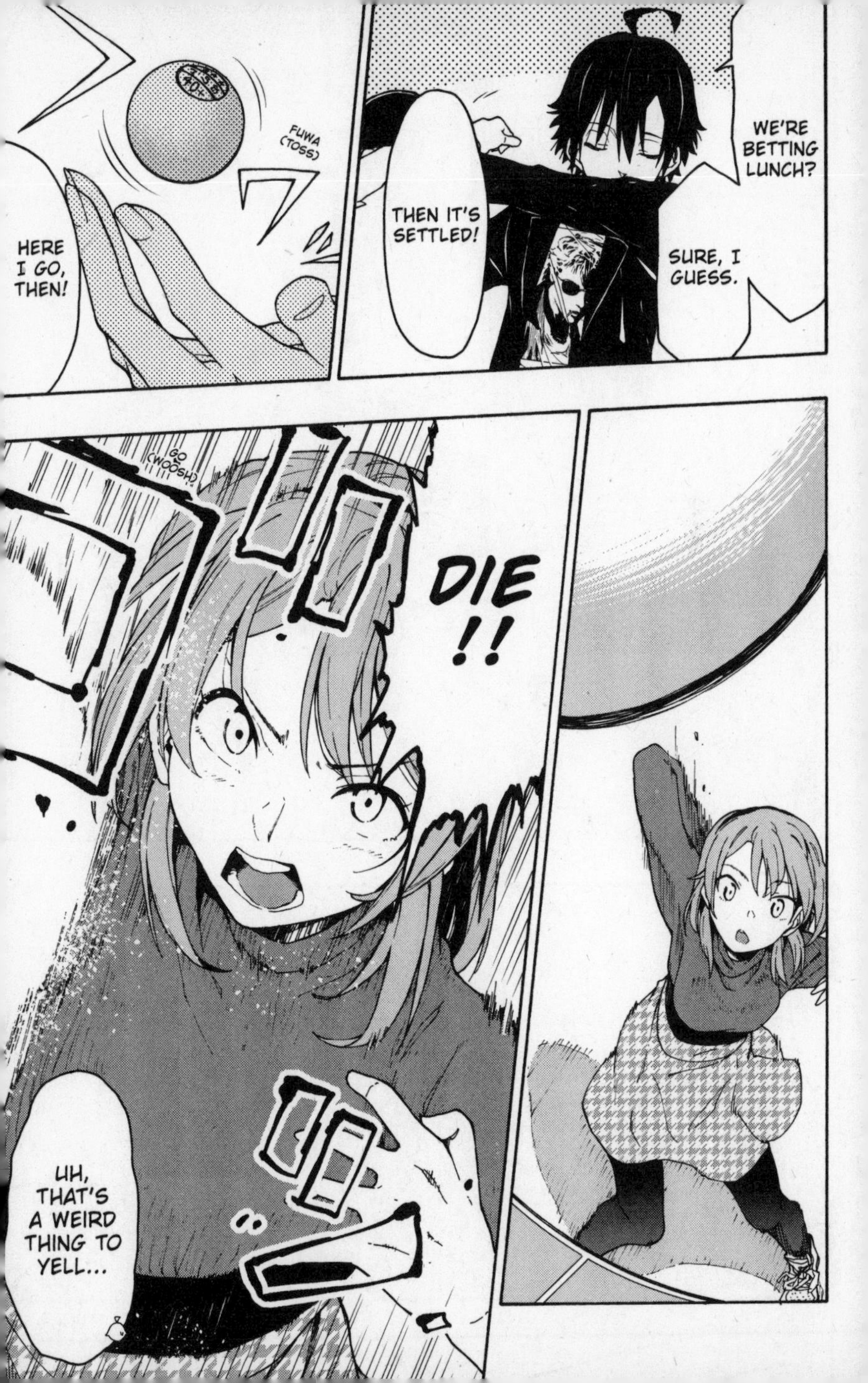
WE'RE BETTING LUNCH?
SURE, I GUESS.
THEN IT'S SETTLED!
FUWA (TOSS)
HERE I GO, THEN!
GO (WOOSH)
DIE!!
UH, THAT'S A WEIRD THING TO YELL...

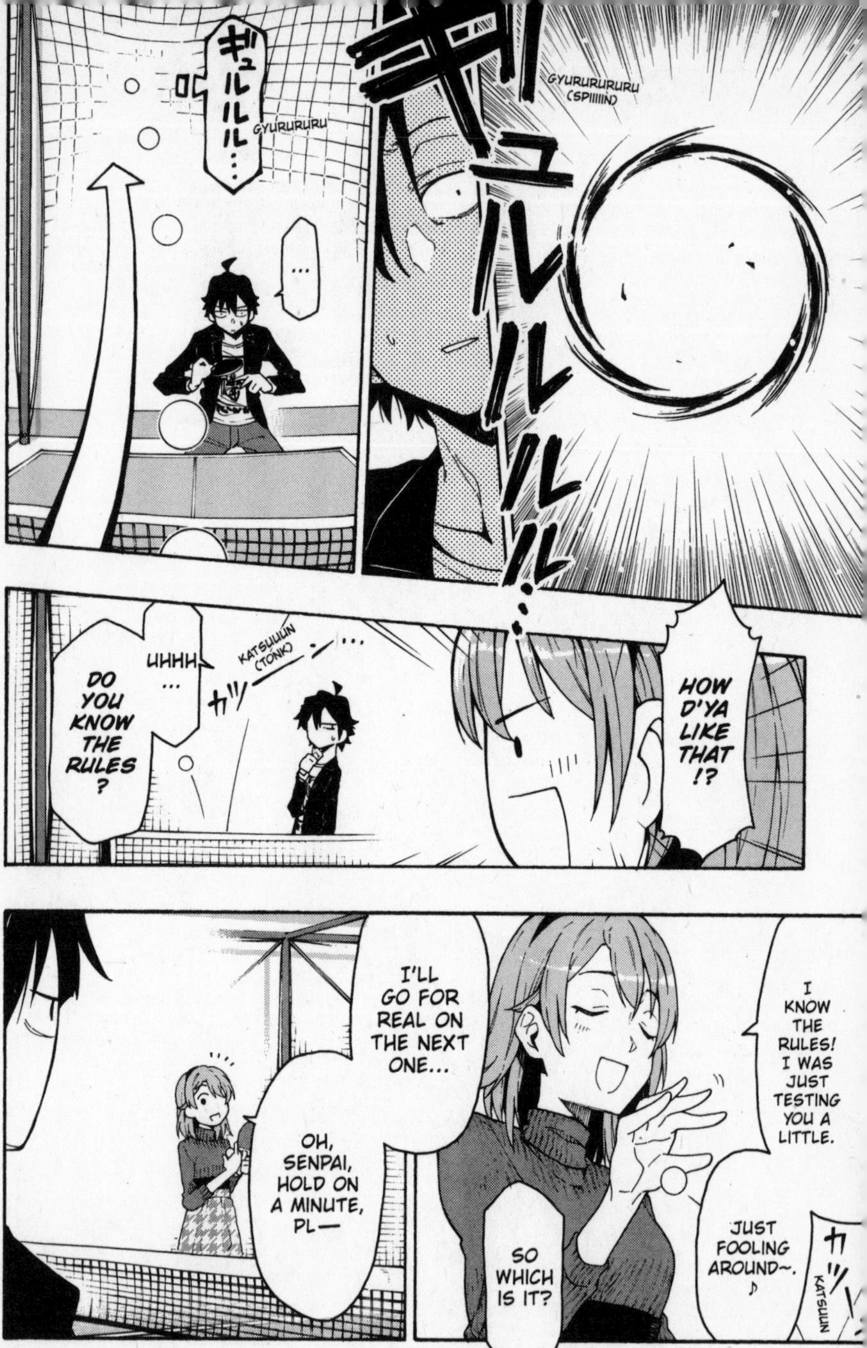
ギュルルルル…
GYURURURURU (SPIIIIN)
ギュルルルル…
GYURURURU
…
HOW D'YA LIKE THAT!?
KATSUUUN (TONK)
カツ
UHHH…
DO YOU KNOW THE RULES?
I KNOW THE RULES! I WAS JUST TESTING YOU A LITTLE.
JUST FOOLING AROUND~. ♪
カツ
KATSUUN
SO WHICH IS IT?
I'LL GO FOR REAL ON THE NEXT ONE…
OH, SENPAI, HOLD ON A MINUTE, PL—

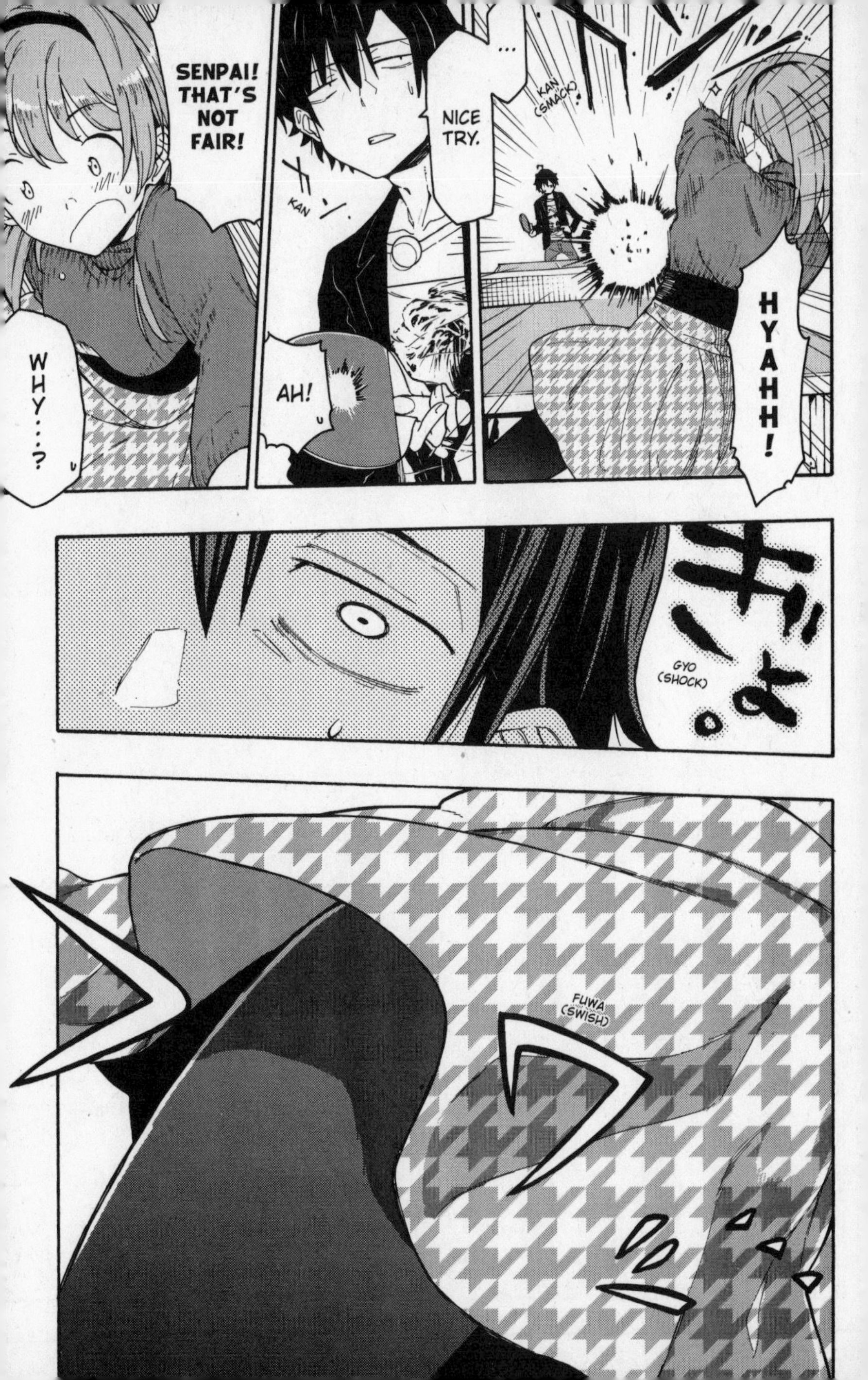
HYAHH!
KAN (SMACK)
...
NICE TRY.
KAN
AH!
SENPAI! THAT'S NOT FAIR!
WHY...?
GYO (SHOCK)
FUWA (SWISH)

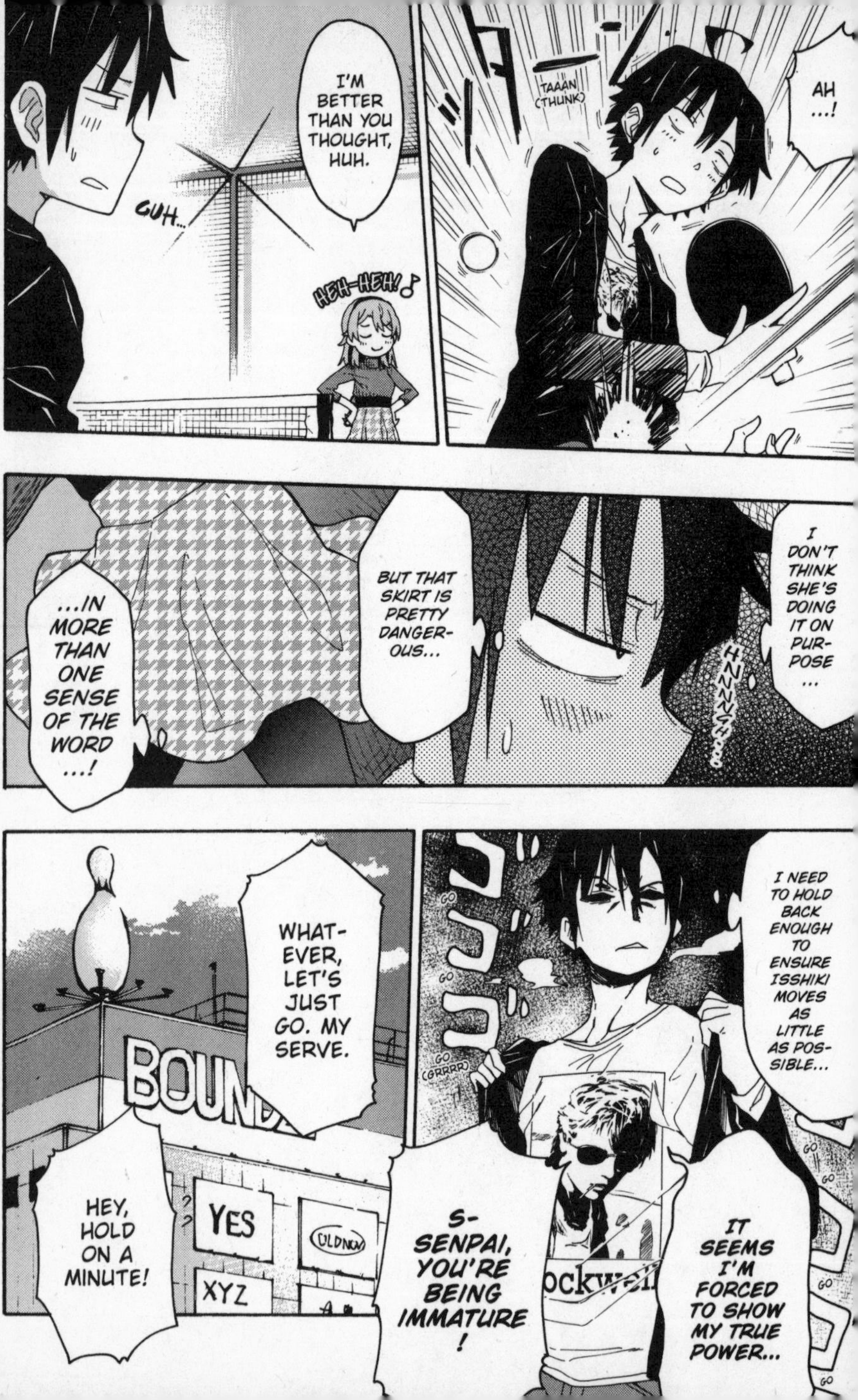
AH ...!
TAAAN (THUNK)
I'M BETTER THAN YOU THOUGHT, HUH.
GUH...
HEH-HEH! ♪
I DON'T THINK SHE'S DOING IT ON PURPOSE...
HNNNNGH...
BUT THAT SKIRT IS PRETTY DANGEROUS...
...IN MORE THAN ONE SENSE OF THE WORD...!
I NEED TO HOLD BACK ENOUGH TO ENSURE ISSHIKI MOVES AS LITTLE AS POSSIBLE...
GO GO GO (GRRRR)
IT SEEMS I'M FORCED TO SHOW MY TRUE POWER...
S-SENPAI, YOU'RE BEING IMMATURE!
WHATEVER, LET'S JUST GO. MY SERVE.
BOUN
YES
XYZ
HEY, HOLD ON A MINUTE!

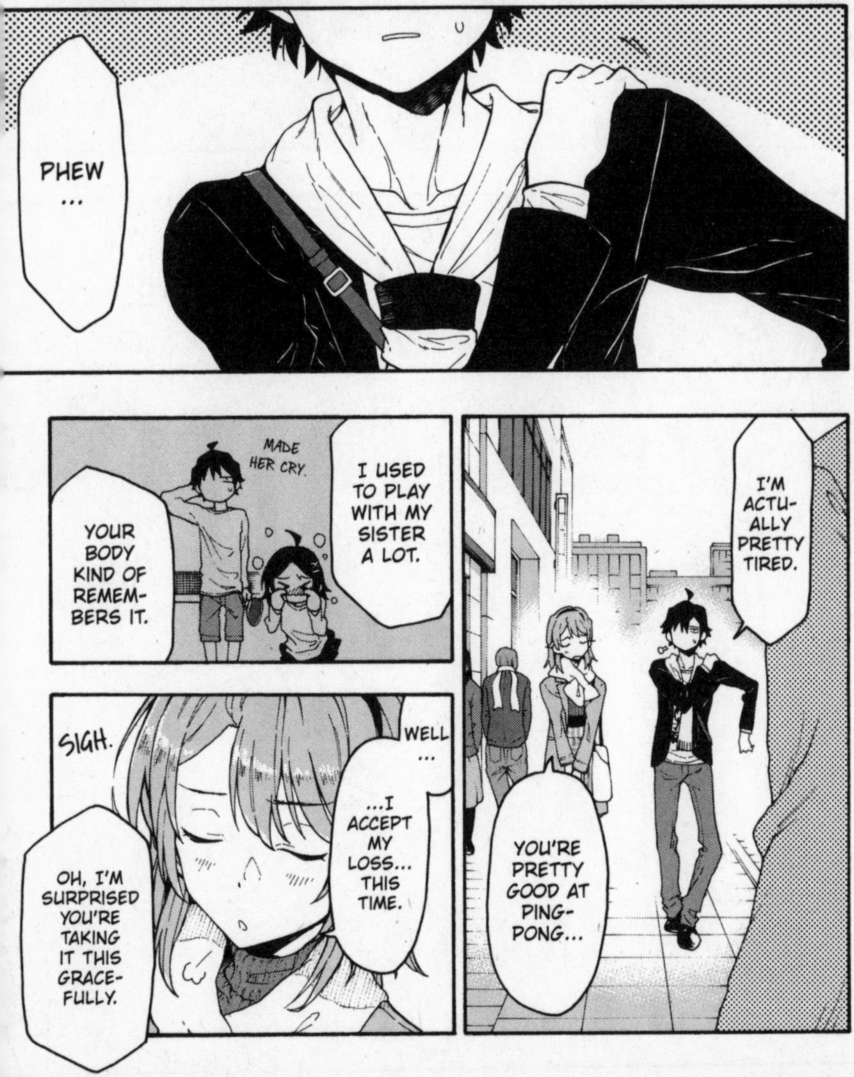
PHEW...
I'M ACTUALLY PRETTY TIRED.
YOU'RE PRETTY GOOD AT PING-PONG...
I USED TO PLAY WITH MY SISTER A LOT.
MADE HER CRY.
YOUR BODY KIND OF REMEMBERS IT.
WELL...
...I ACCEPT MY LOSS... THIS TIME.
SIGH.
OH, I'M SURPRISED YOU'RE TAKING IT THIS GRACEFULLY.

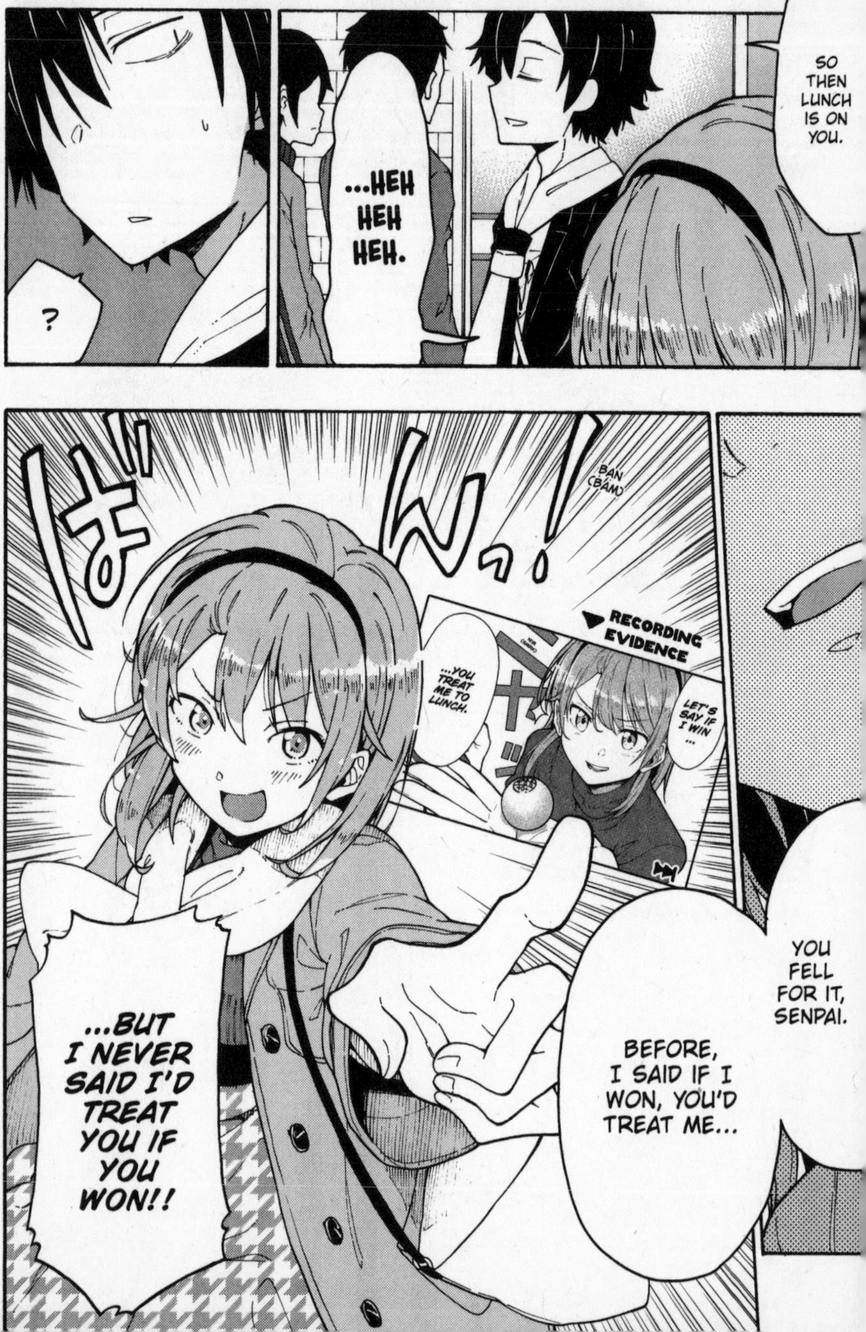
SO THEN LUNCH IS ON YOU.
...HEH HEH HEH.
?
YOU FELL FOR IT, SENPAI.
BAN (BAM)
RECORDING EVIDENCE
LET'S SAY IF I WIN...
...YOU TREAT ME TO LUNCH.
BEFORE, I SAID IF I WON, YOU'D TREAT ME...
...BUT I NEVER SAID I'D TREAT YOU IF YOU WON!!

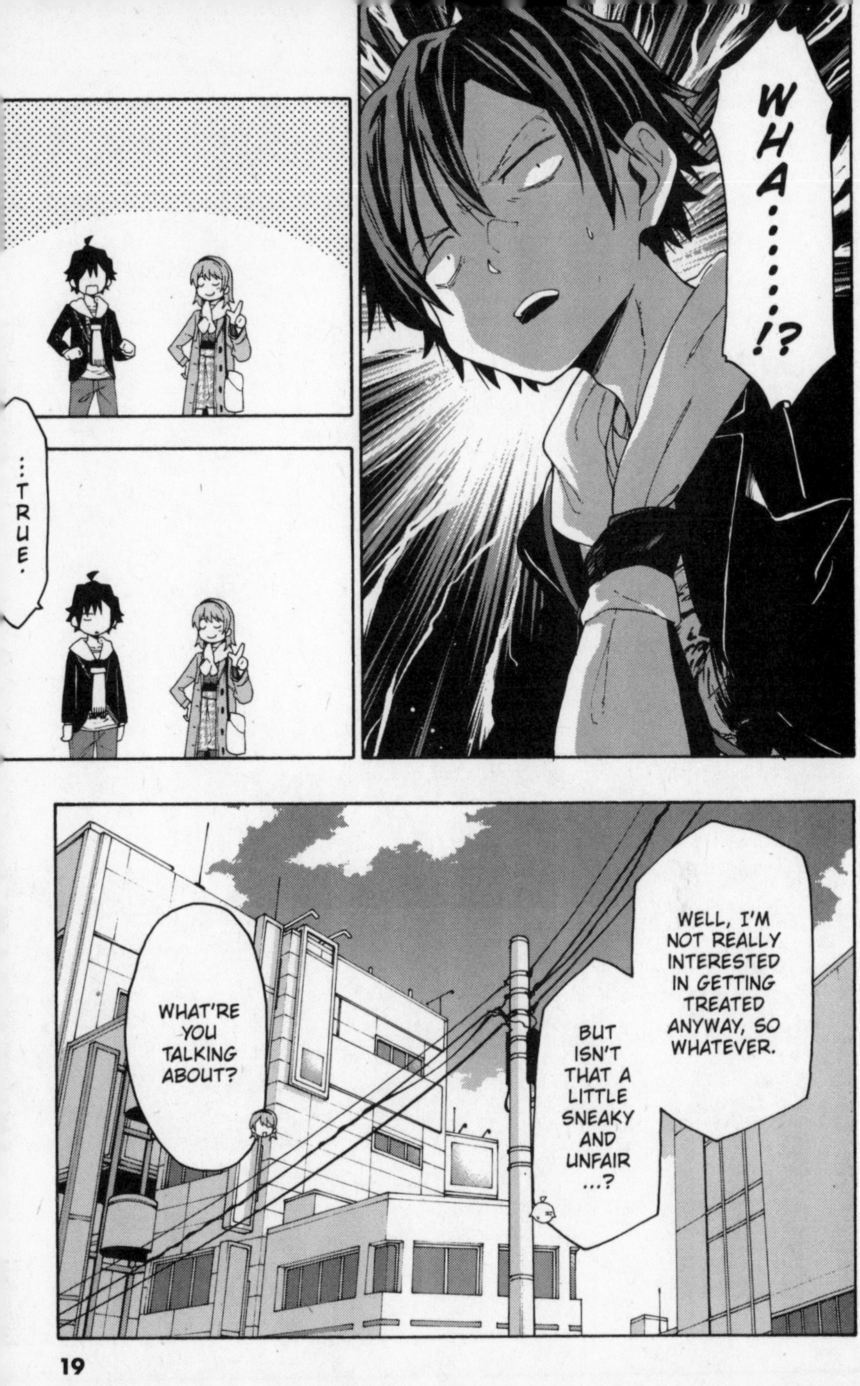
WHA......!?
...TRUE.
WELL, I'M NOT REALLY INTERESTED IN GETTING TREATED ANYWAY, SO WHATEVER.
BUT ISN'T THAT A LITTLE SNEAKY AND UNFAIR ...?
WHAT'RE YOU TALKING ABOUT?

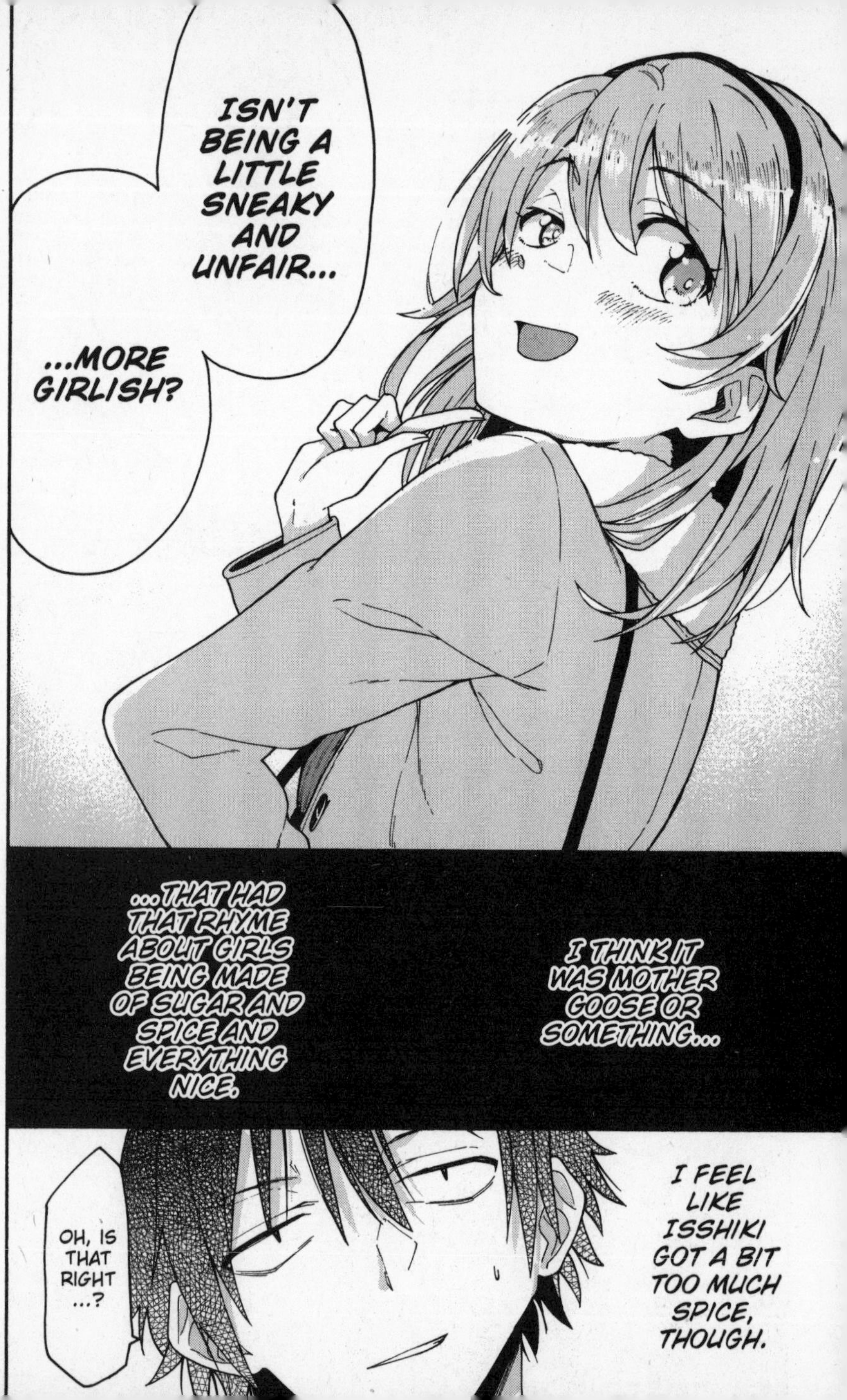
ISN'T BEING A LITTLE SNEAKY AND UNFAIR...
...MORE GIRLISH?
I THINK IT WAS MOTHER GOOSE OR SOMETHING...
...THAT HAD THAT RHYME ABOUT GIRLS BEING MADE OF SUGAR AND SPICE AND EVERYTHING NICE.
I FEEL LIKE ISSHIKI GOT A BIT TOO MUCH SPICE, THOUGH.
OH, IS THAT RIGHT ...?

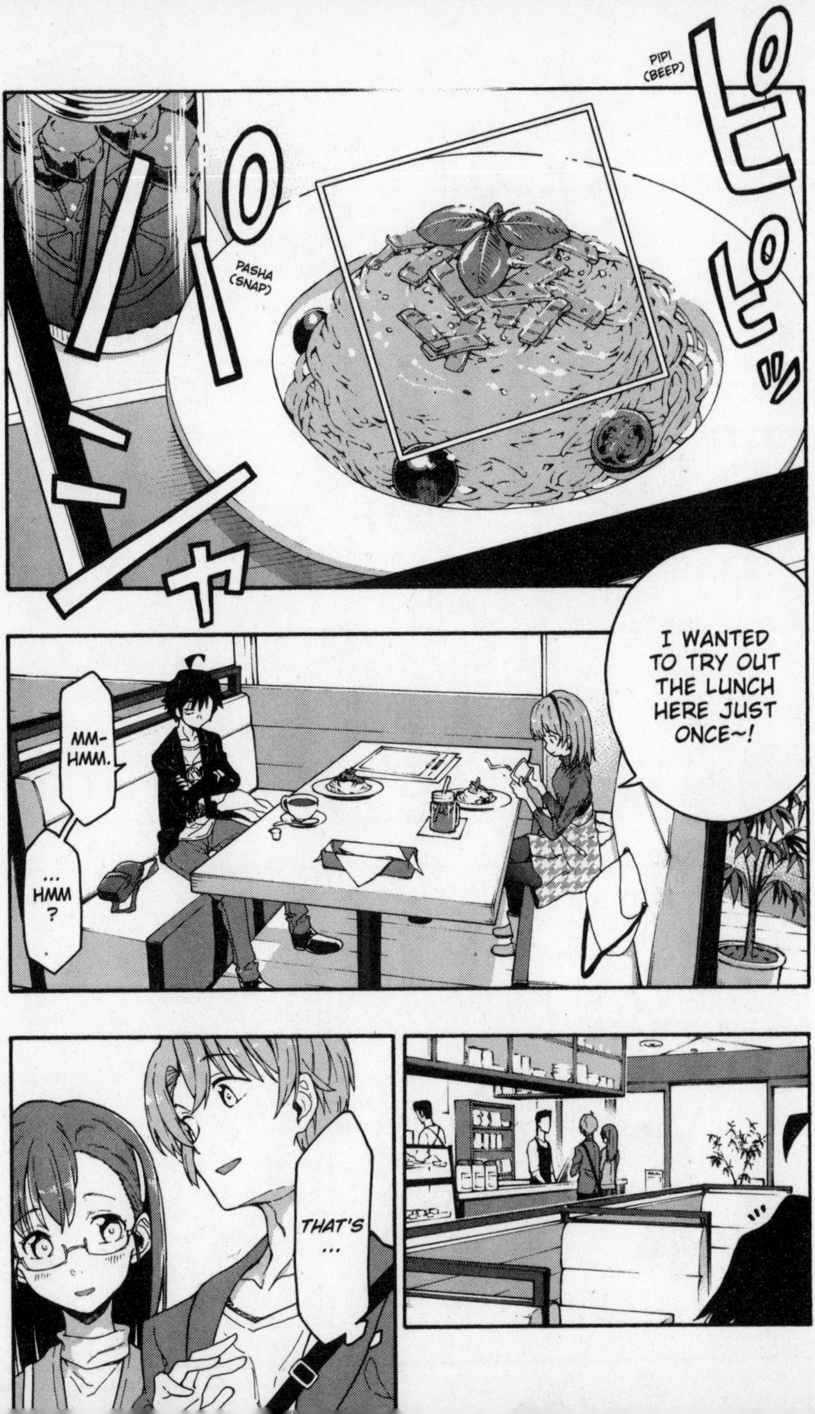
ピピッ
PIPI (BEEP)
パシャ
PASHA (SNAP)
I WANTED TO TRY OUT THE LUNCH HERE JUST ONCE~!
MM-HMM.
... HMM ?
...
THAT'S ...

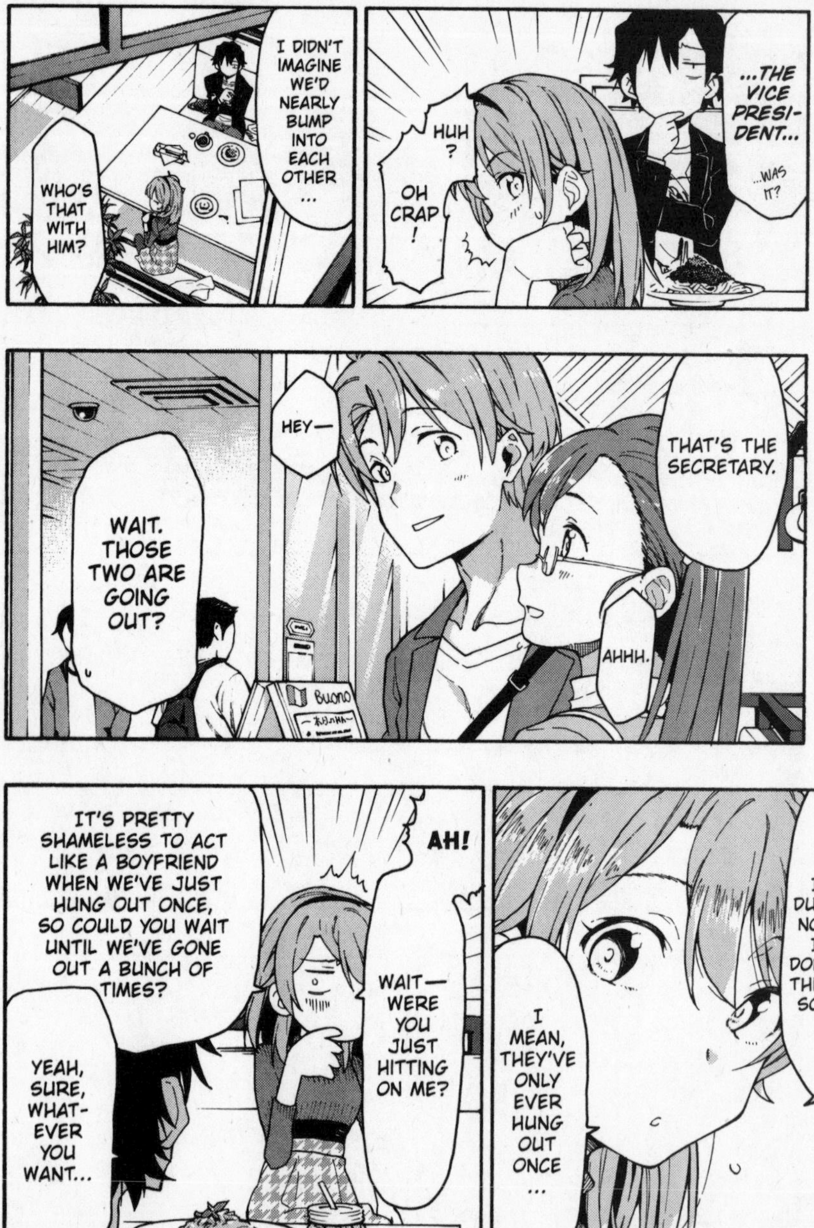
...THE VICE PRESIDENT...
...WAS IT?
HUH?
OH CRAP!
I DIDN'T IMAGINE WE'D NEARLY BUMP INTO EACH OTHER...
WHO'S THAT WITH HIM?
THAT'S THE SECRETARY.
AHHH.
HEY—
WAIT. THOSE TWO ARE GOING OUT?
Buono
I DUN-NO? I DON'T THINK SO?
I MEAN, THEY'VE ONLY EVER HUNG OUT ONCE...
AH!
WAIT—WERE YOU JUST HITTING ON ME?
IT'S PRETTY SHAMELESS TO ACT LIKE A BOYFRIEND WHEN WE'VE JUST HUNG OUT ONCE, SO COULD YOU WAIT UNTIL WE'VE GONE OUT A BUNCH OF TIMES?
YEAH, SURE, WHAT-EVER YOU WANT...

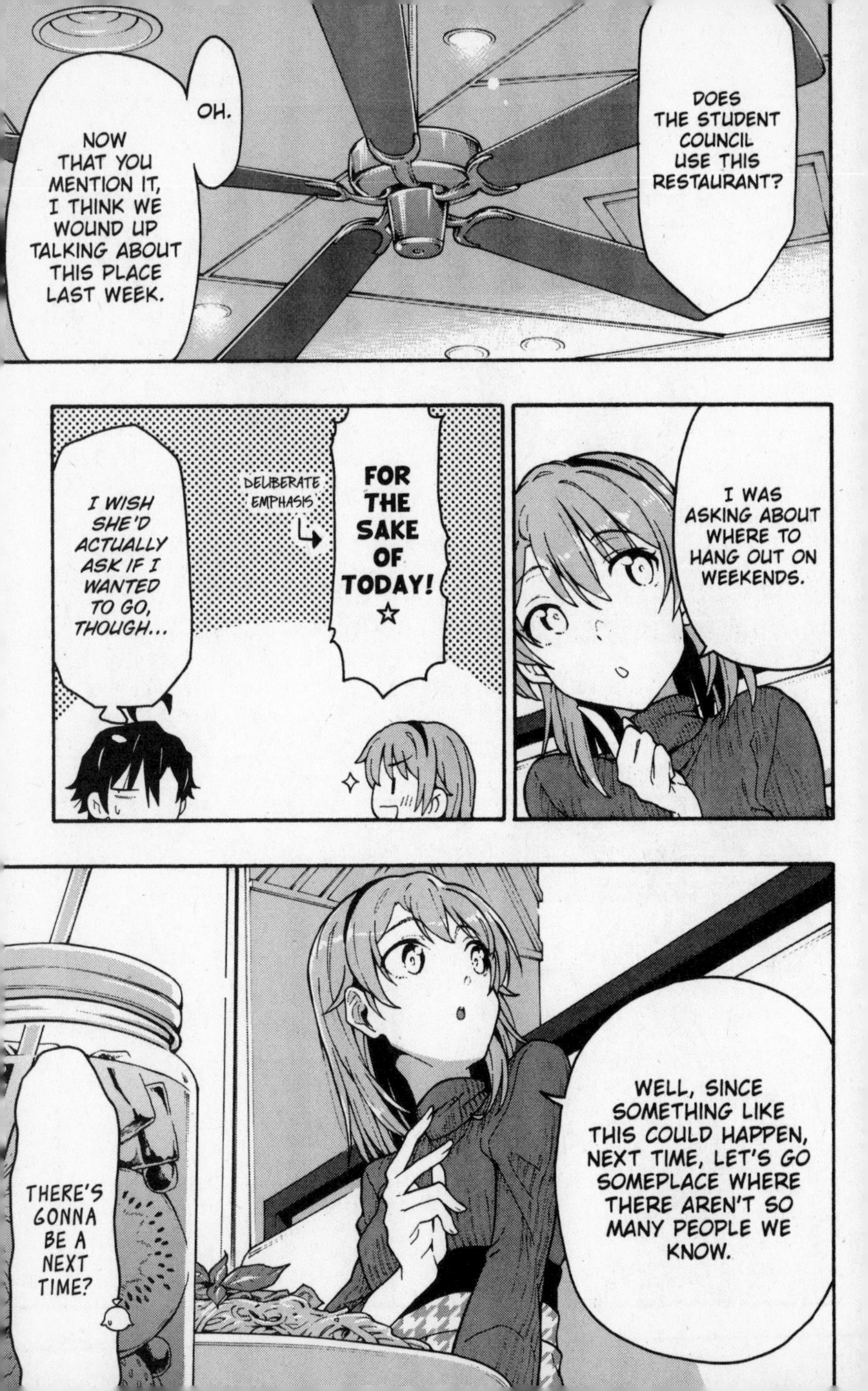
DOES THE STUDENT COUNCIL USE THIS RESTAURANT?
OH.
NOW THAT YOU MENTION IT, I THINK WE WOUND UP TALKING ABOUT THIS PLACE LAST WEEK.
I WAS ASKING ABOUT WHERE TO HANG OUT ON WEEKENDS.
FOR THE SAKE OF TODAY! ☆
DELIBERATE EMPHASIS
I WISH SHE'D ACTUALLY ASK IF I WANTED TO GO, THOUGH...
WELL, SINCE SOMETHING LIKE THIS COULD HAPPEN, NEXT TIME, LET'S GO SOMEPLACE WHERE THERE AREN'T SO MANY PEOPLE WE KNOW.
THERE'S GONNA BE A NEXT TIME?

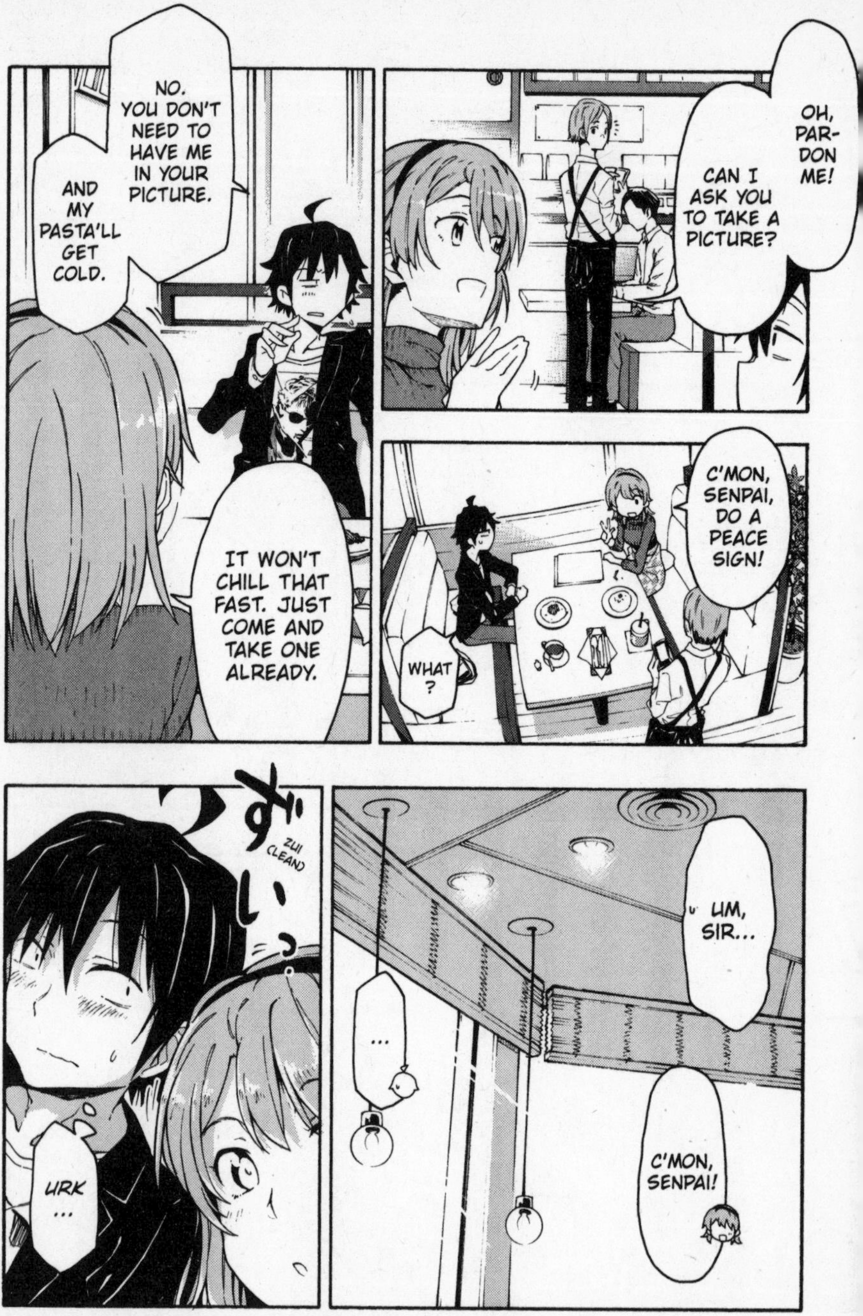
OH, PARDON ME!
CAN I ASK YOU TO TAKE A PICTURE?
C'MON, SENPAI, DO A PEACE SIGN!
WHAT?
NO. YOU DON'T NEED TO HAVE ME IN YOUR PICTURE.
AND MY PASTA'LL GET COLD.
IT WON'T CHILL THAT FAST. JUST COME AND TAKE ONE ALREADY.
UM, SIR...
...
C'MON, SENPAI!
ZUI (LEAN)
URK ...

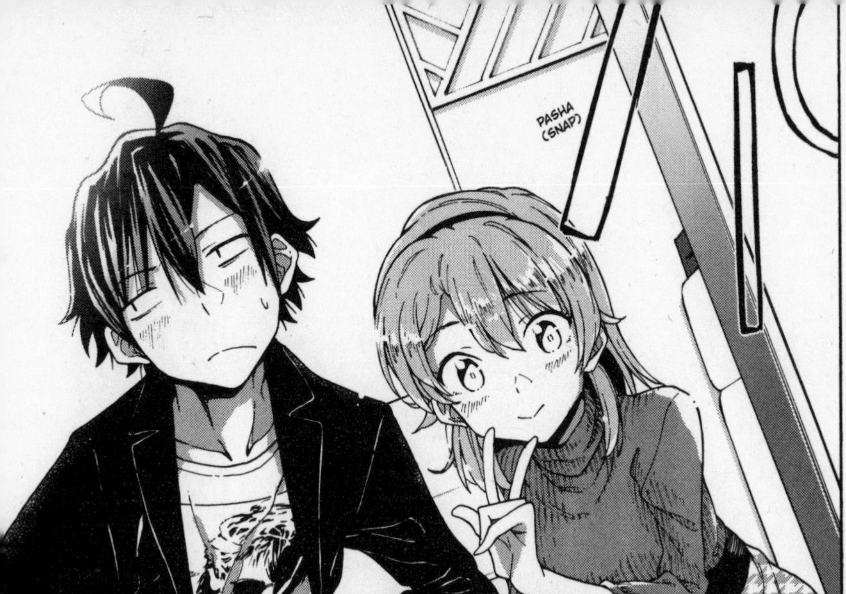
PASHA
(SNAP)
MENU

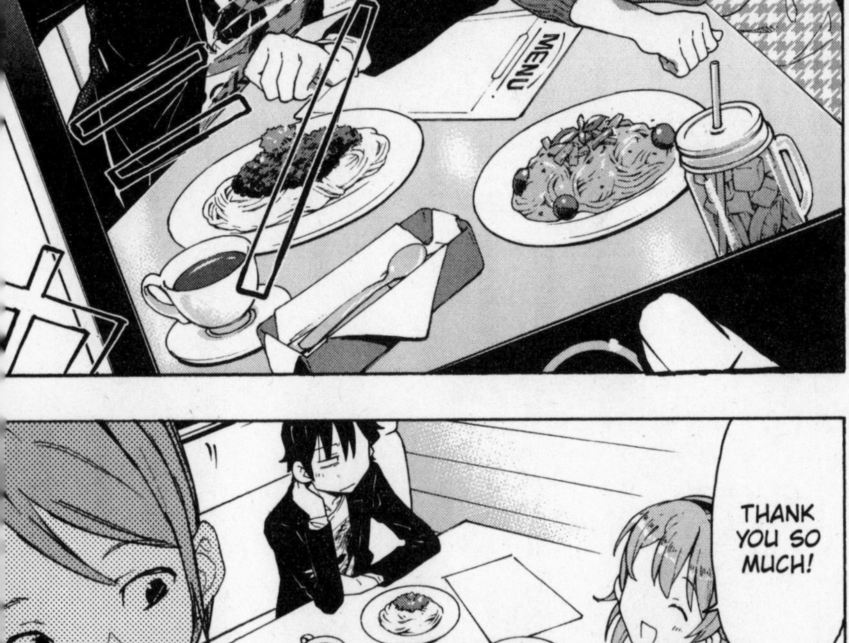
THANK YOU SO MUCH!

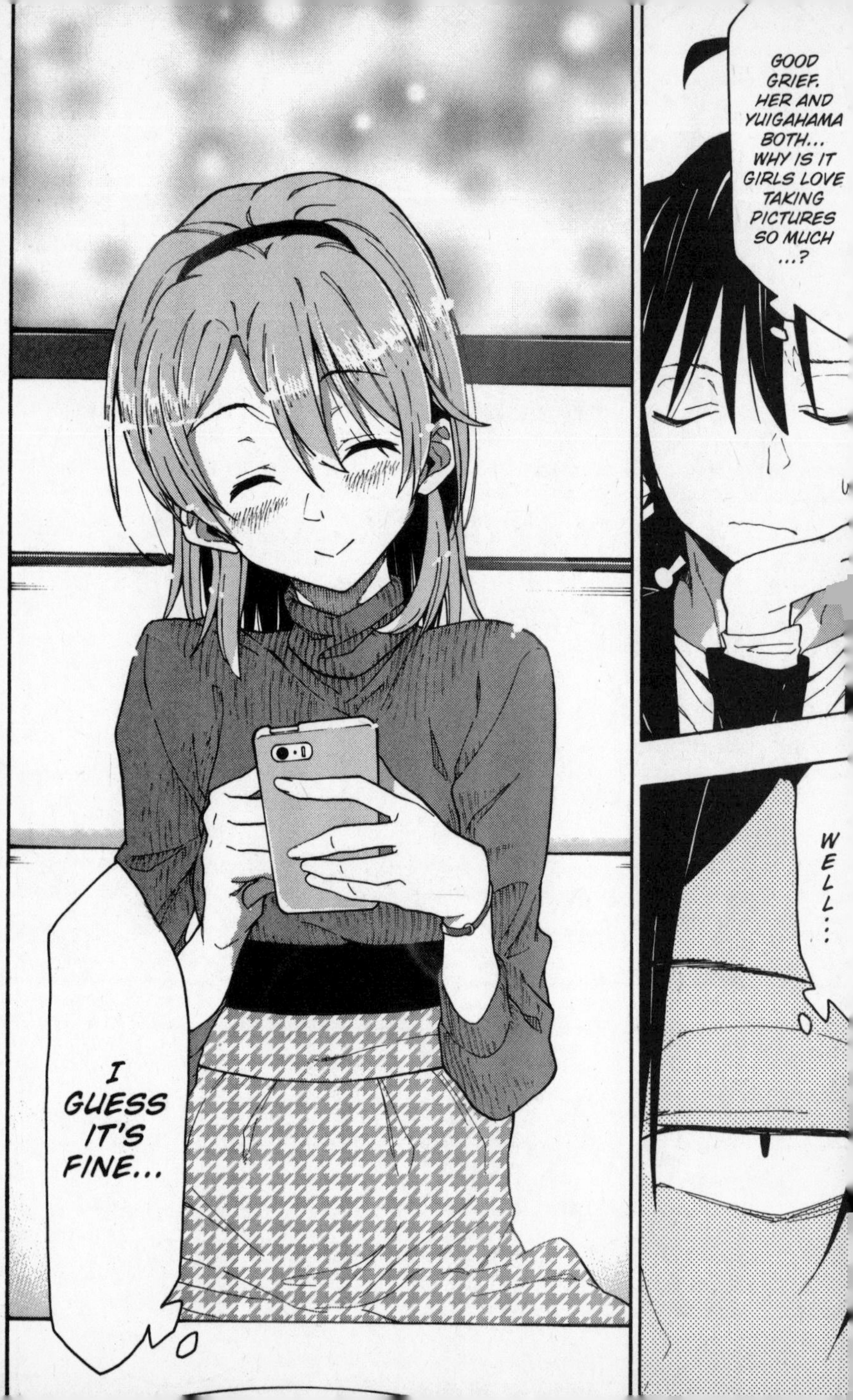
GOOD GRIEF. HER AND YUIGAHAMA BOTH... WHY IS IT GIRLS LOVE TAKING PICTURES SO MUCH ...?
WELL...
I GUESS IT'S FINE...

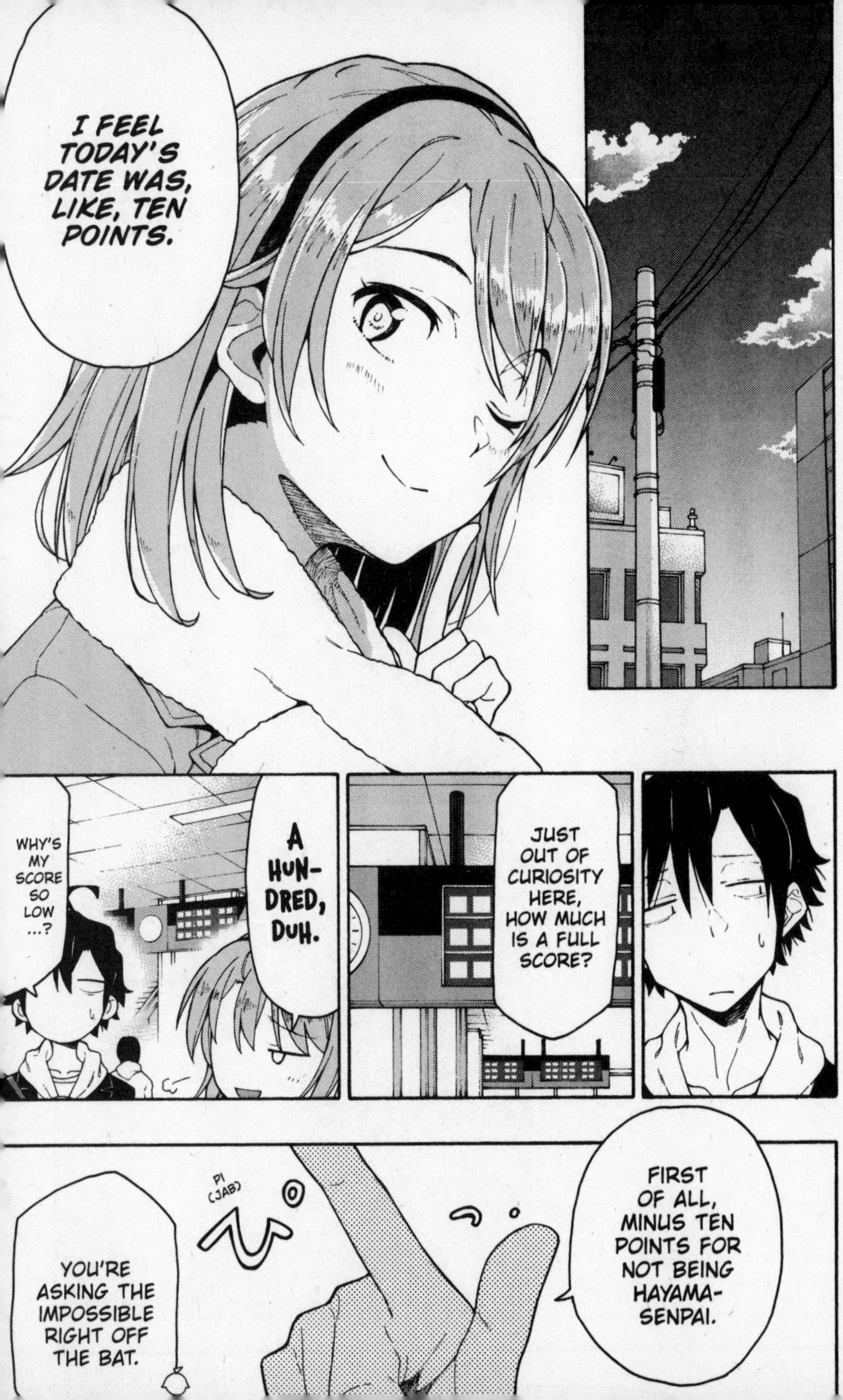
I FEEL TODAY'S DATE WAS, LIKE, TEN POINTS.
JUST OUT OF CURIOSITY HERE, HOW MUCH IS A FULL SCORE?
A HUN-DRED, DUH.
WHY'S MY SCORE SO LOW ...?
FIRST OF ALL, MINUS TEN POINTS FOR NOT BEING HAYAMA-SENPAI.
PI (JAB)
YOU'RE ASKING THE IMPOSSIBLE RIGHT OFF THE BAT.

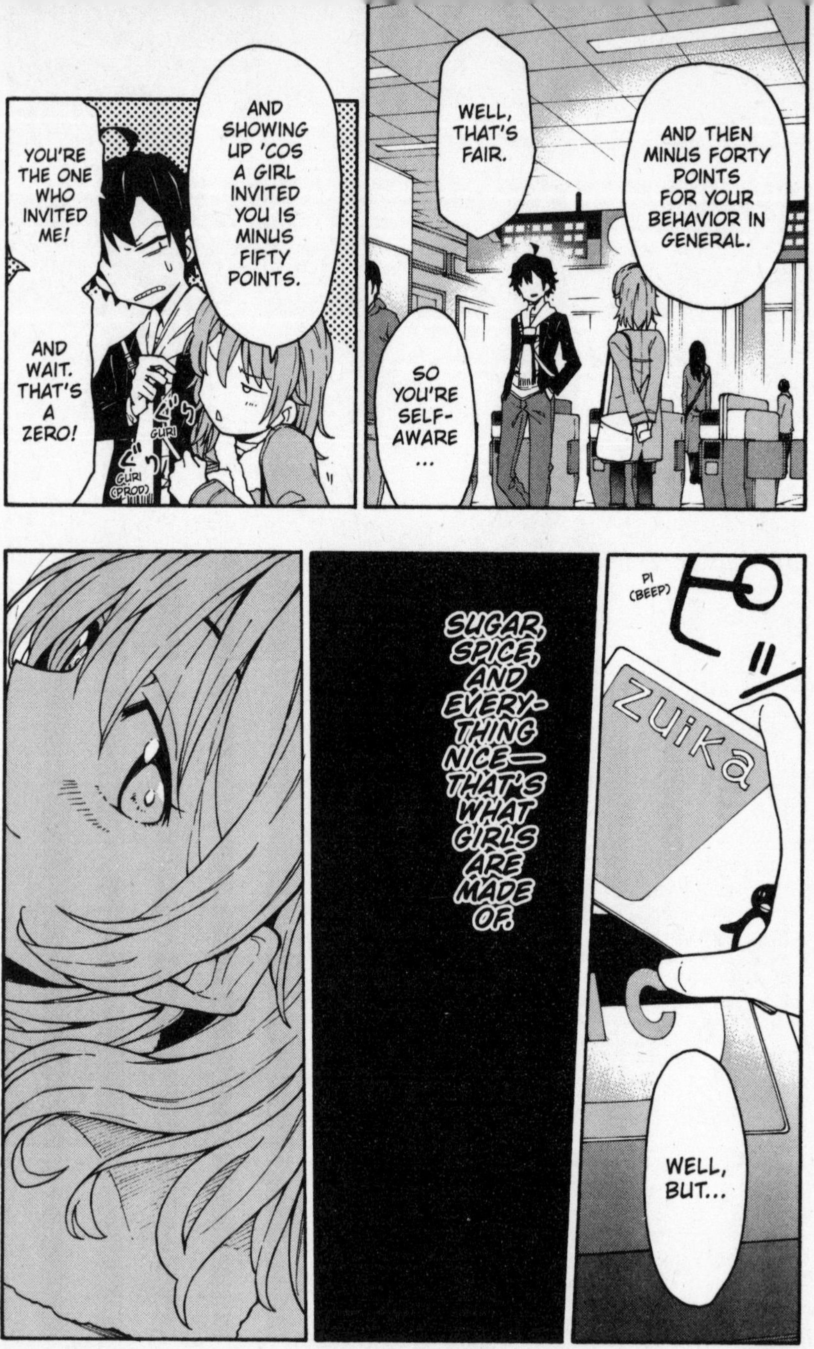
AND THEN MINUS FORTY POINTS FOR YOUR BEHAVIOR IN GENERAL.
WELL, THAT'S FAIR.
SO YOU'RE SELF-AWARE...
AND SHOWING UP 'COS A GIRL INVITED YOU IS MINUS FIFTY POINTS.
YOU'RE THE ONE WHO INVITED ME!
GURI
GURI (PROD)
AND WAIT. THAT'S A ZERO!
PI (BEEP)
Zuika
WELL, BUT...
SUGAR, SPICE, AND EVERYTHING NICE—THAT'S WHAT GIRLS ARE MADE OF.

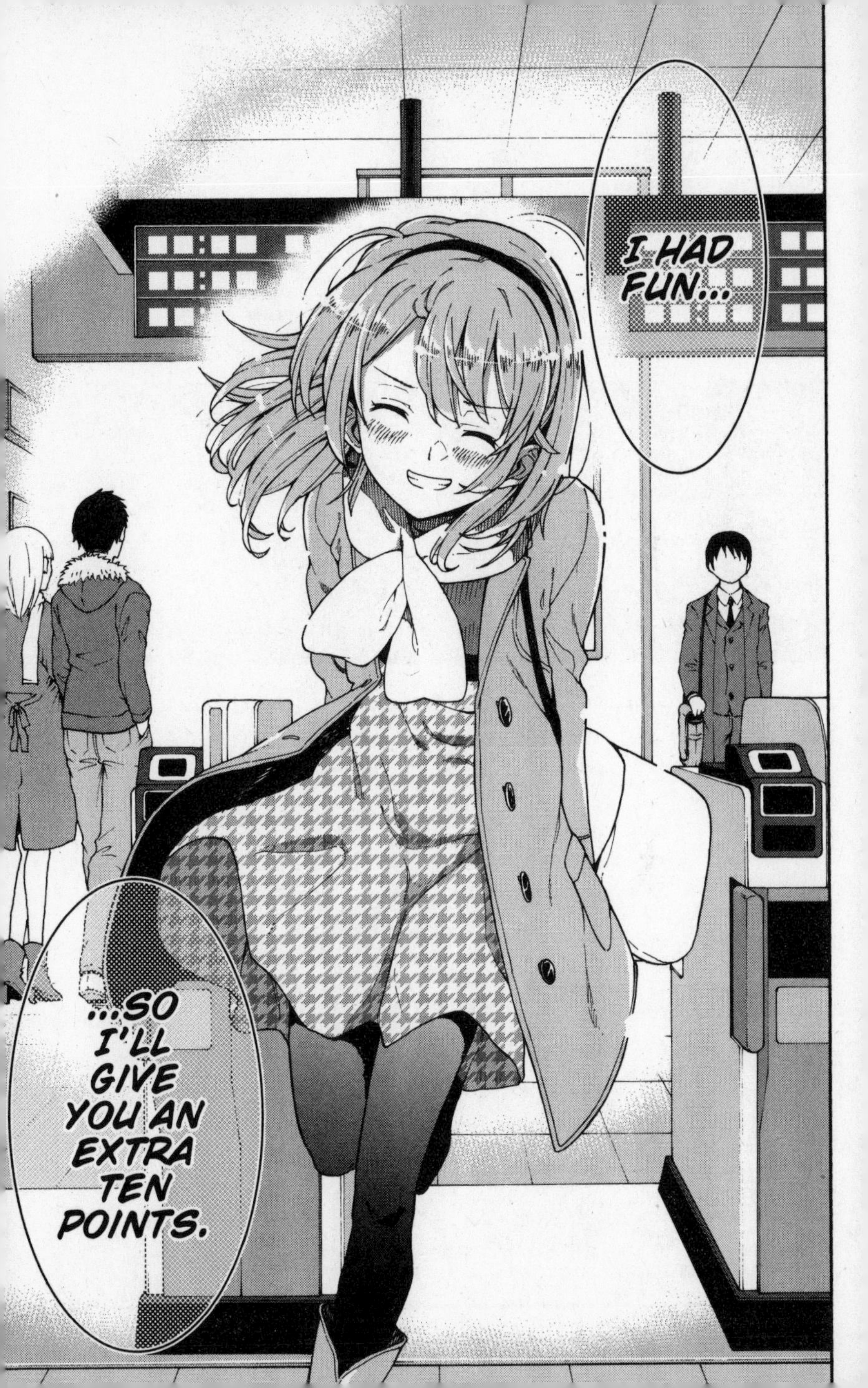
I HAD FUN...
...SO I'LL GIVE YOU AN EXTRA TEN POINTS.

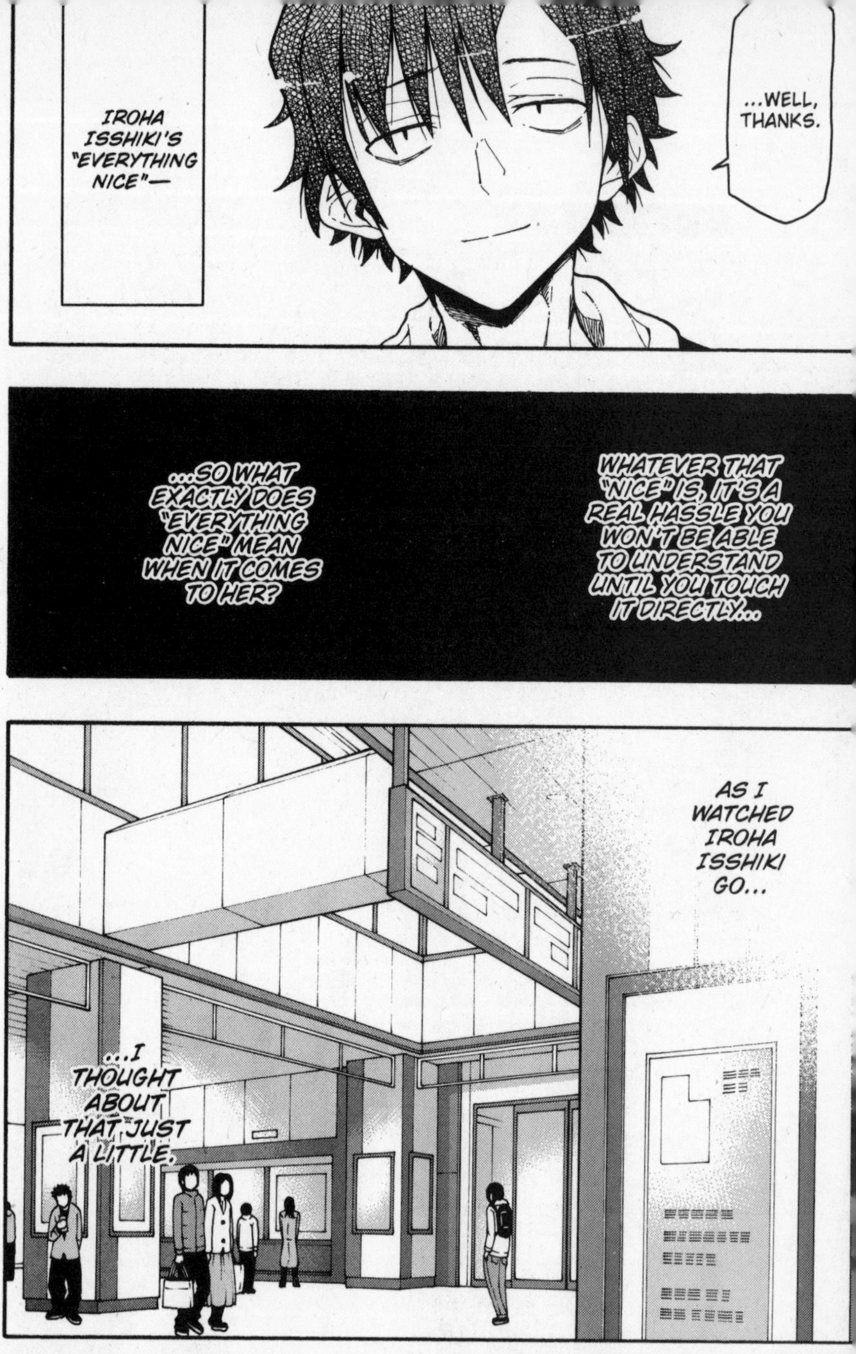
...WELL, THANKS.
IROHA ISSHIKI'S "EVERYTHING NICE"—
WHATEVER THAT "NICE" IS, IT'S A REAL HASSLE YOU WON'T BE ABLE TO UNDERSTAND UNTIL YOU TOUCH IT DIRECTLY...
...SO WHAT EXACTLY DOES "EVERYTHING NICE" MEAN WHEN IT COMES TO HER?
AS I WATCHED IROHA ISSHIKI GO...
...I THOUGHT ABOUT THAT JUST A LITTLE.

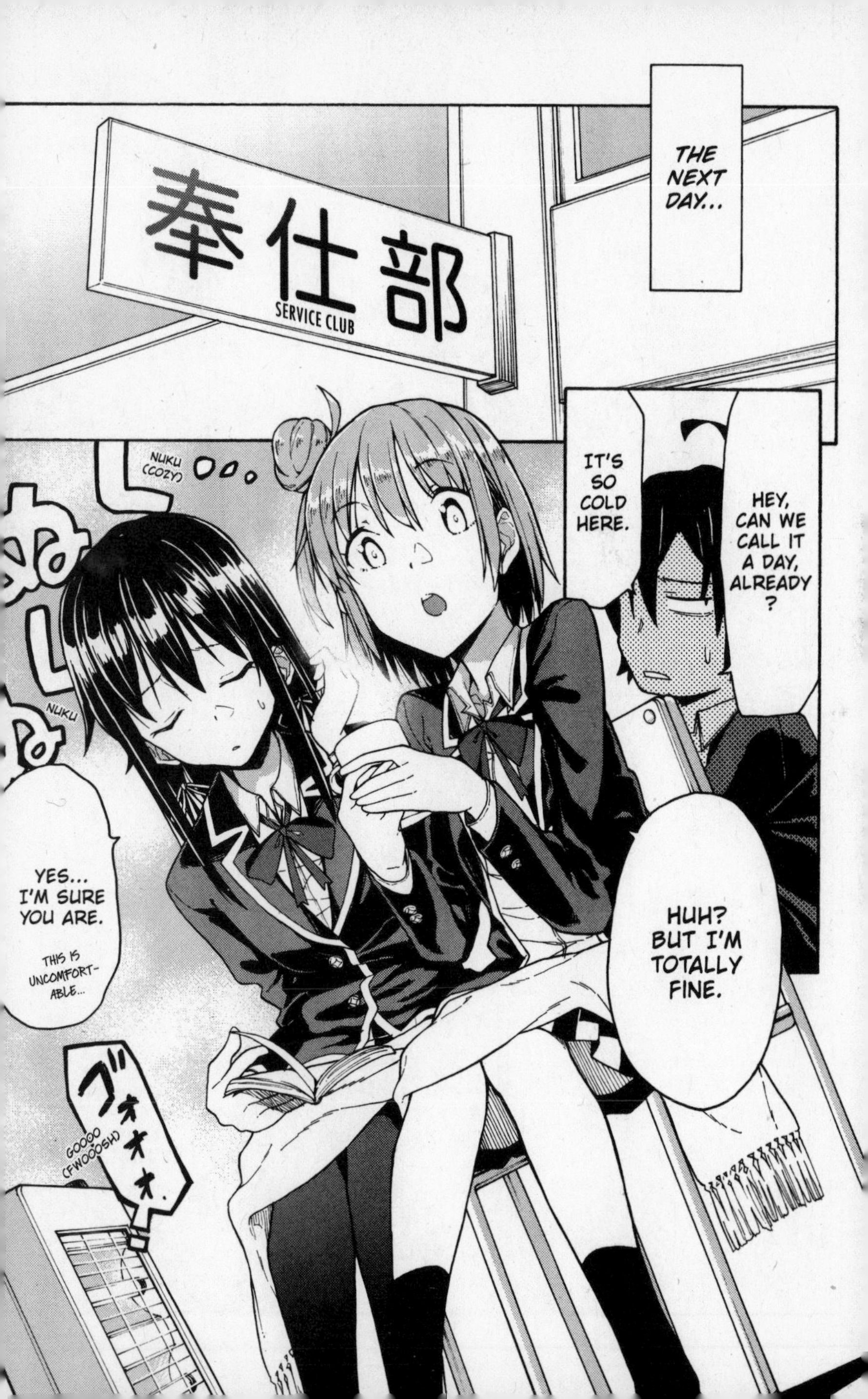
THE NEXT DAY...
奉仕部
SERVICE CLUB
HEY, CAN WE CALL IT A DAY, ALREADY?
IT'S SO COLD HERE.
HUH? BUT I'M TOTALLY FINE.
NUKU (COZY)
NUKU
YES... I'M SURE YOU ARE.
THIS IS UNCOMFORT-ABLE...
ゴォォォ
GOOOO (FWOOOSH)

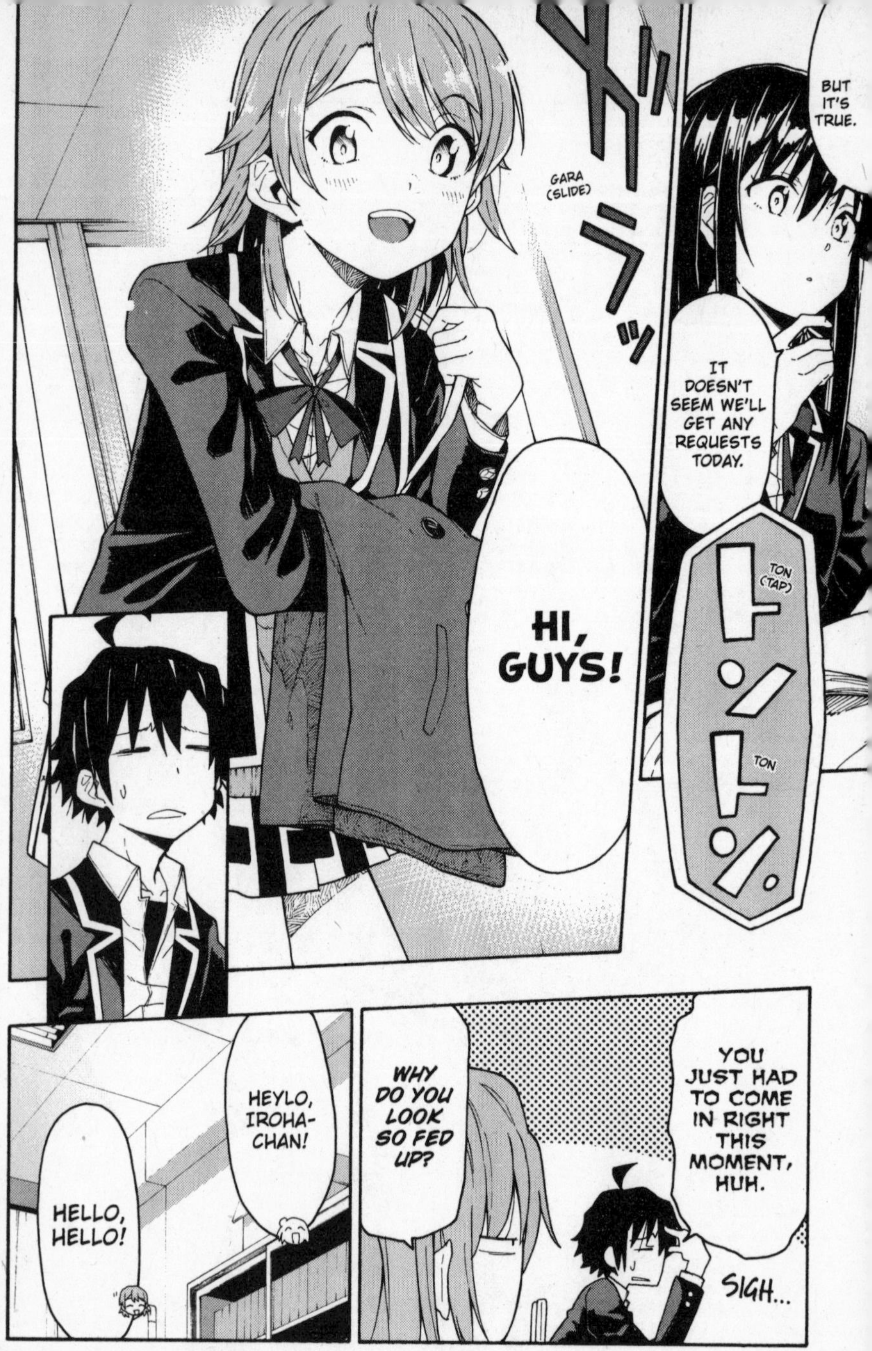
BUT IT'S TRUE.
IT DOESN'T SEEM WE'LL GET ANY REQUESTS TODAY.
TON (TAP)
TON
GARA (SLIDE)
HI, GUYS!
YOU JUST HAD TO COME IN RIGHT THIS MOMENT, HUH.
SIGH...
WHY DO YOU LOOK SO FED UP?
HEYLO, IROHA-CHAN!
HELLO, HELLO!

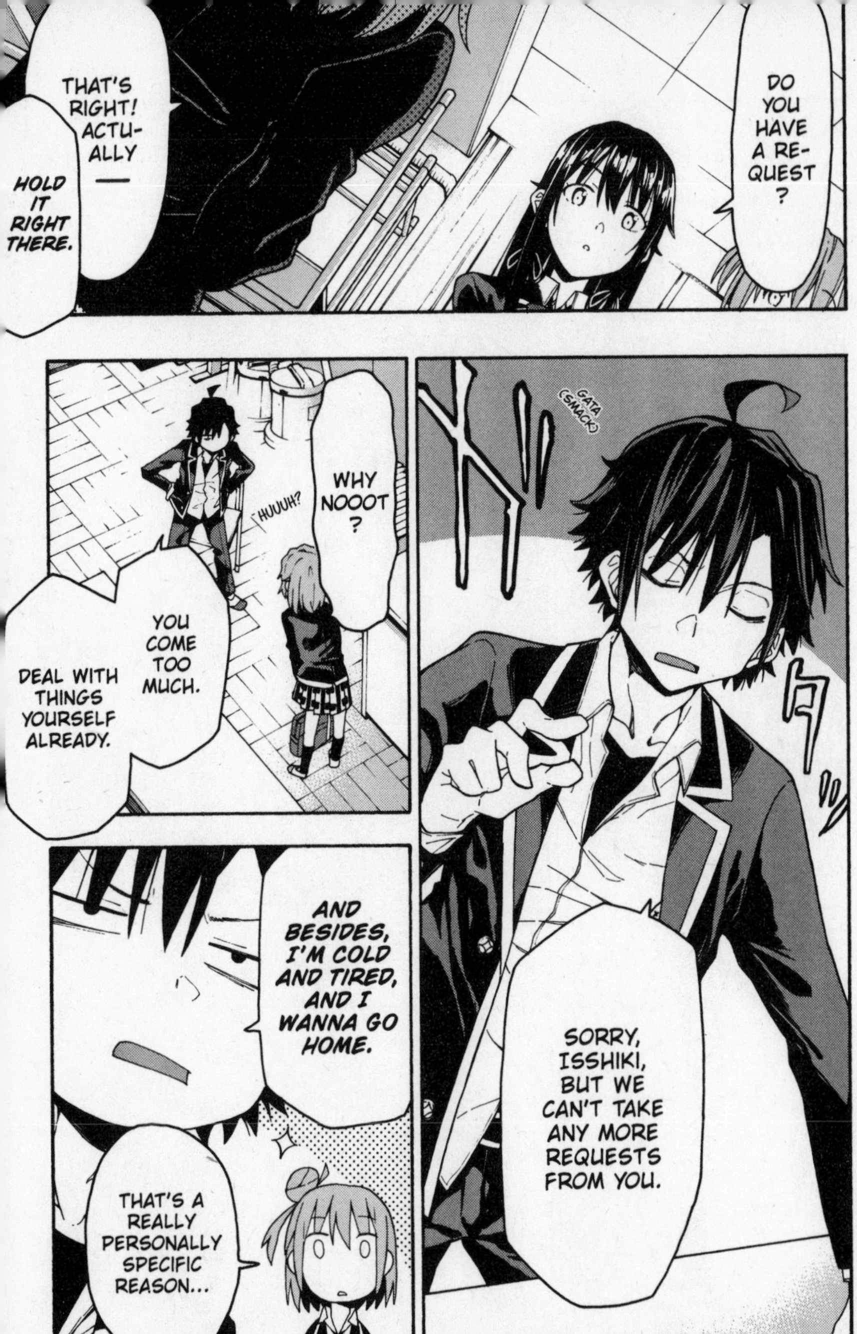
DO YOU HAVE A REQUEST?
THAT'S RIGHT! ACTUALLY—
HOLD IT RIGHT THERE.
GATA (SMACK)
SORRY, ISSHIKI, BUT WE CAN'T TAKE ANY MORE REQUESTS FROM YOU.
WHY NOOOT?
HUUUH?
YOU COME TOO MUCH.
DEAL WITH THINGS YOURSELF ALREADY.
AND BESIDES, I'M COLD AND TIRED, AND I WANNA GO HOME.
THAT'S A REALLY PERSONALLY SPECIFIC REASON...

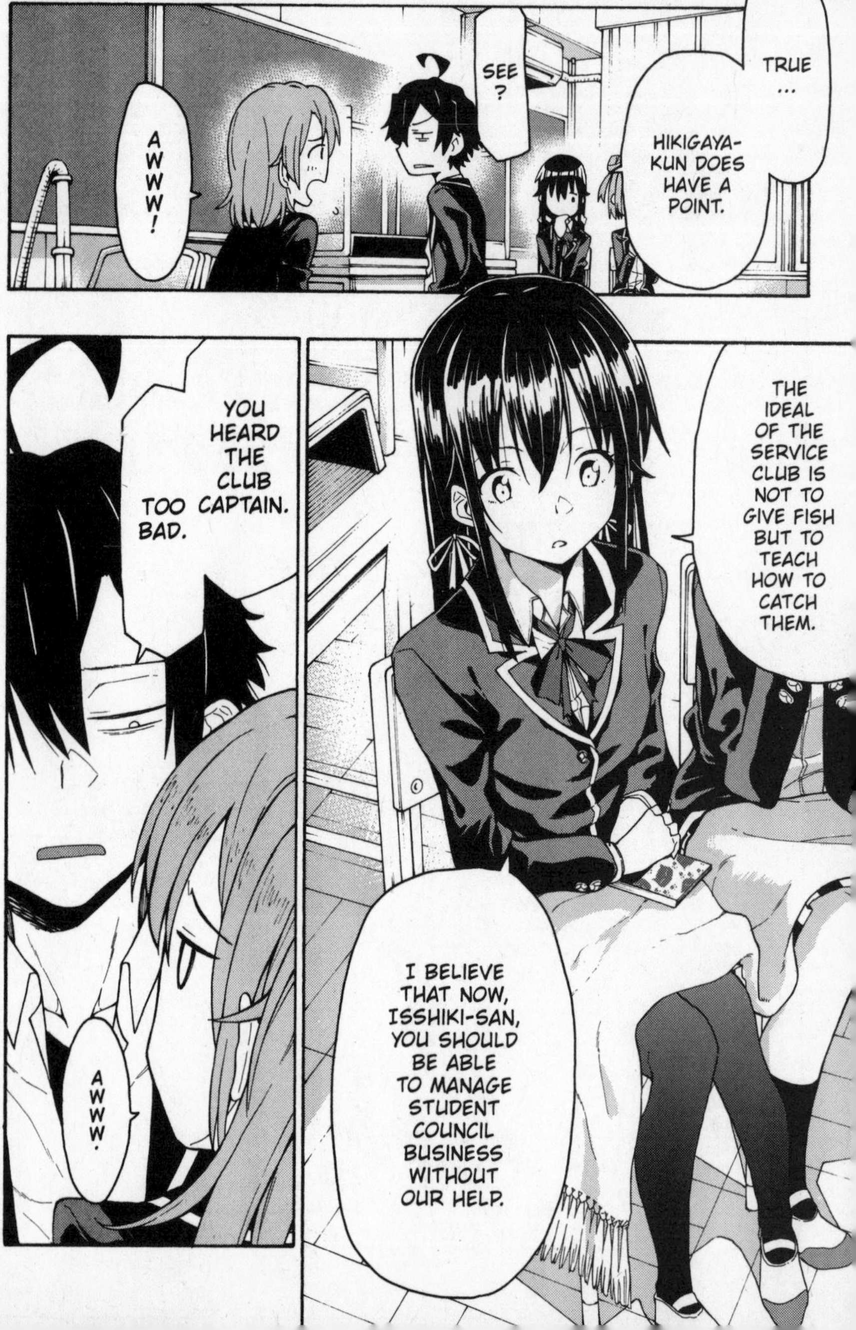
TRUE...
HIKIGAYA-KUN DOES HAVE A POINT.
SEE?
AWWW!
THE IDEAL OF THE SERVICE CLUB IS NOT TO GIVE FISH BUT TO TEACH HOW TO CATCH THEM.
I BELIEVE THAT NOW, ISSHIKI-SAN, YOU SHOULD BE ABLE TO MANAGE STUDENT COUNCIL BUSINESS WITHOUT OUR HELP.
YOU HEARD THE CLUB CAPTAIN. TOO BAD.
AWWW.

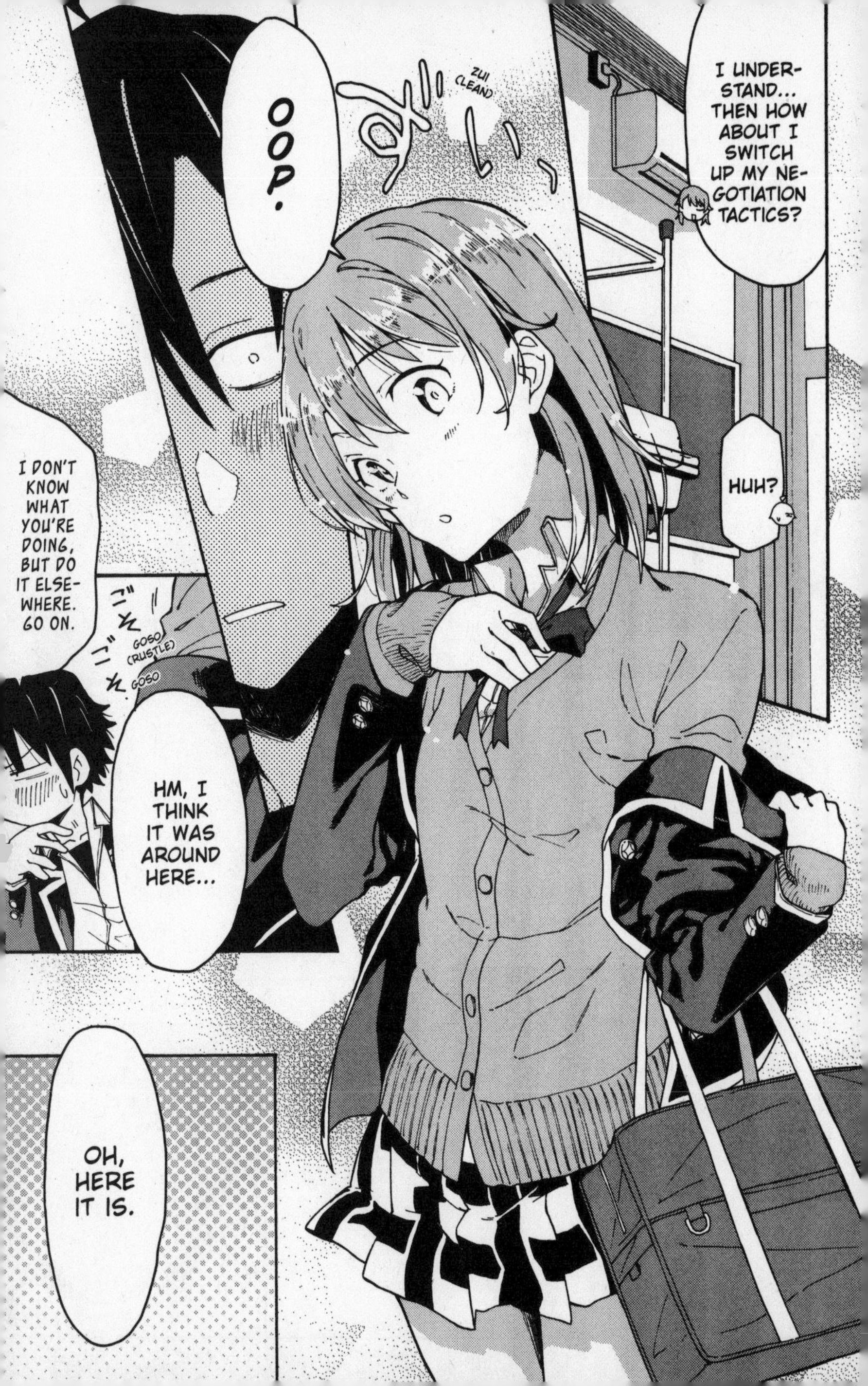
I UNDER-STAND... THEN HOW ABOUT I SWITCH UP MY NE-GOTIATION TACTICS?
ZUI (LEAN)
OOP.
HUH?
I DON'T KNOW WHAT YOU'RE DOING, BUT DO IT ELSE-WHERE. GO ON.
GOSO (RUSTLE) GOSO
HM, I THINK IT WAS AROUND HERE...
OH, HERE IT IS.

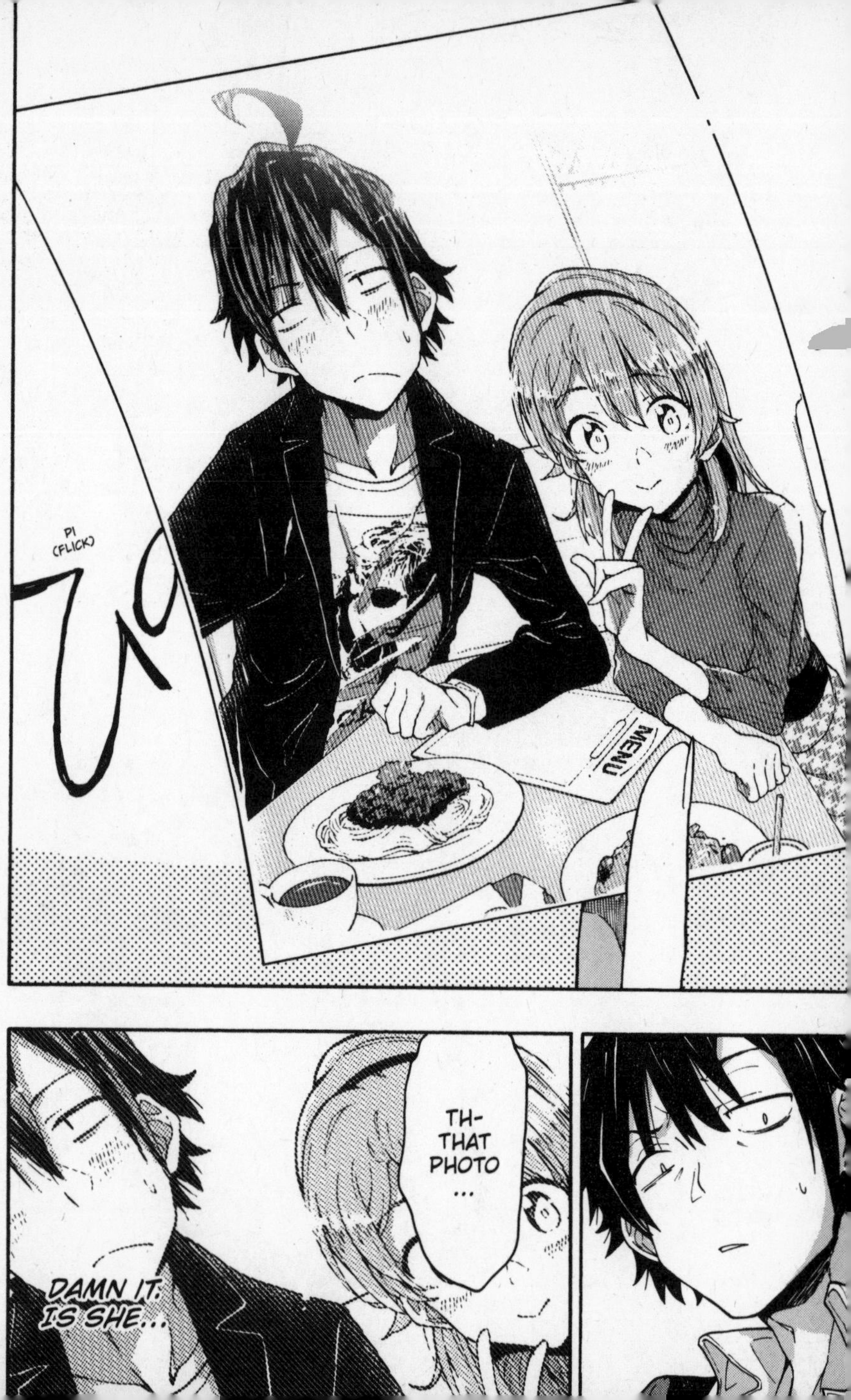
PI
(FLICK)
MENU
TH-THAT PHOTO...
DAMN IT. IS SHE...

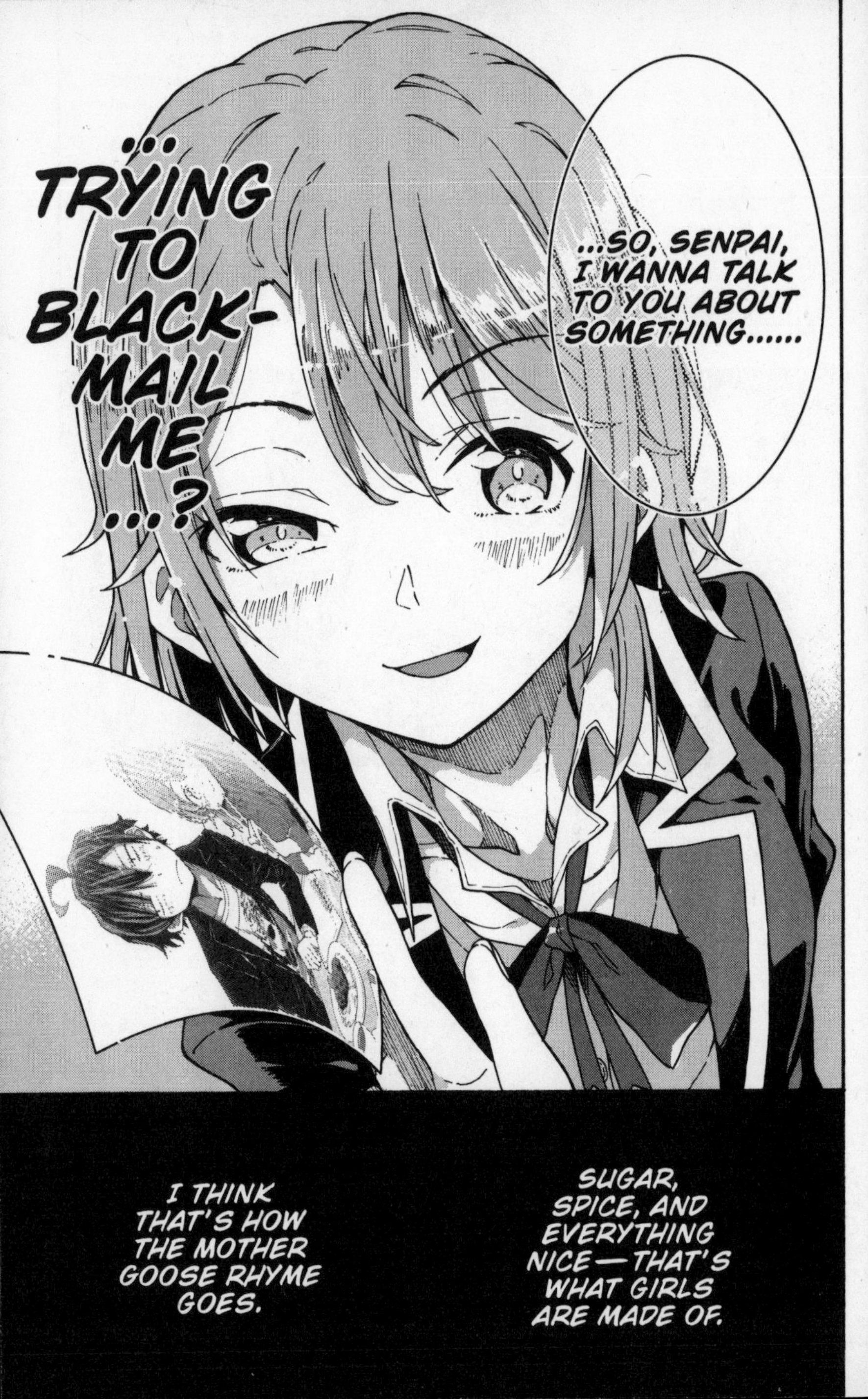
...SO, SENPAI, I WANNA TALK TO YOU ABOUT SOMETHING......
...TRYING TO BLACK-MAIL ME...?
SUGAR, SPICE, AND EVERYTHING NICE—THAT'S WHAT GIRLS ARE MADE OF.
I THINK THAT'S HOW THE MOTHER GOOSE RHYME GOES.

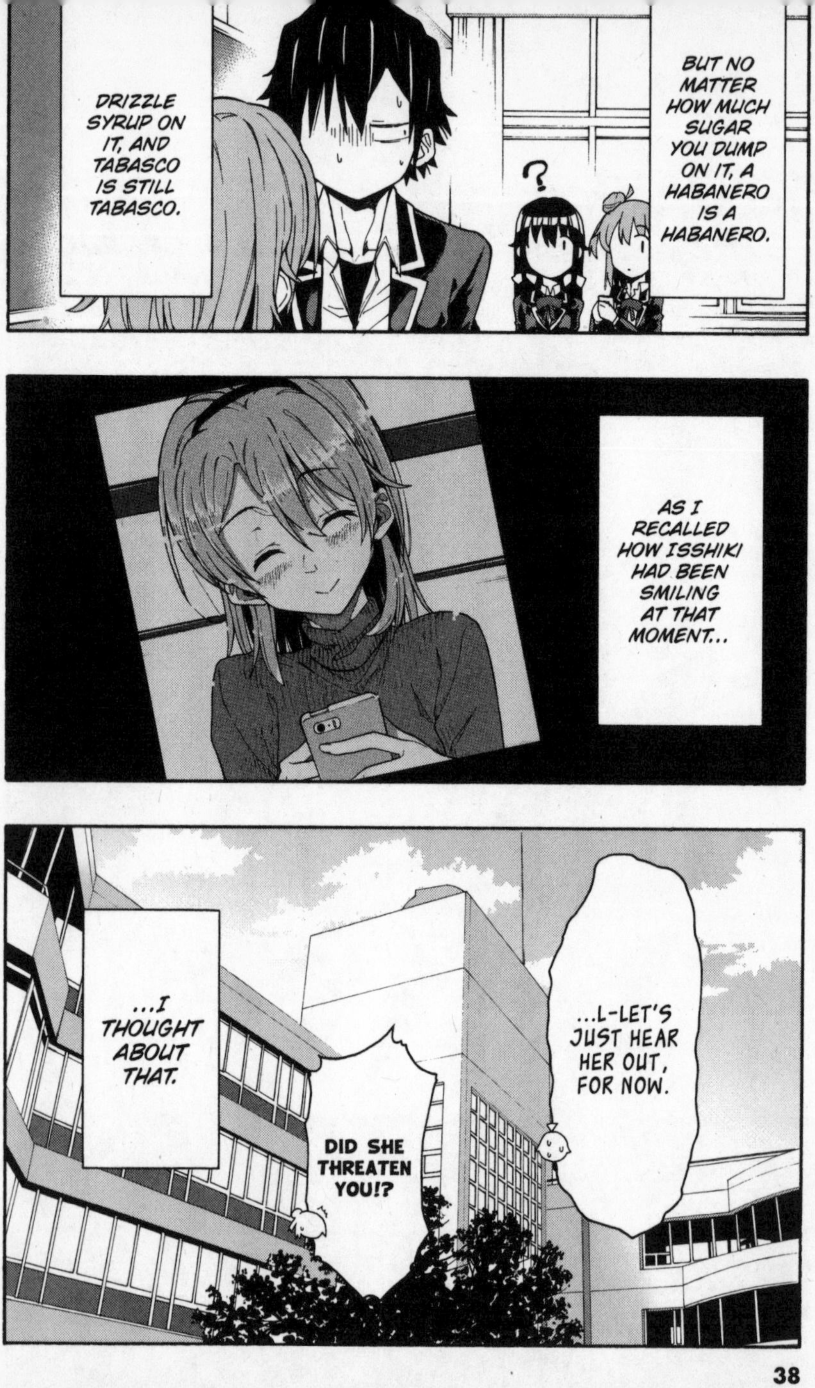
BUT NO MATTER HOW MUCH SUGAR YOU DUMP ON IT, A HABANERO IS A HABANERO.
DRIZZLE SYRUP ON IT, AND TABASCO IS STILL TABASCO.
AS I RECALLED HOW ISSHIKI HAD BEEN SMILING AT THAT MOMENT...
...L-LET'S JUST HEAR HER OUT, FOR NOW.
DID SHE THREATEN YOU!?
...I THOUGHT ABOUT THAT.

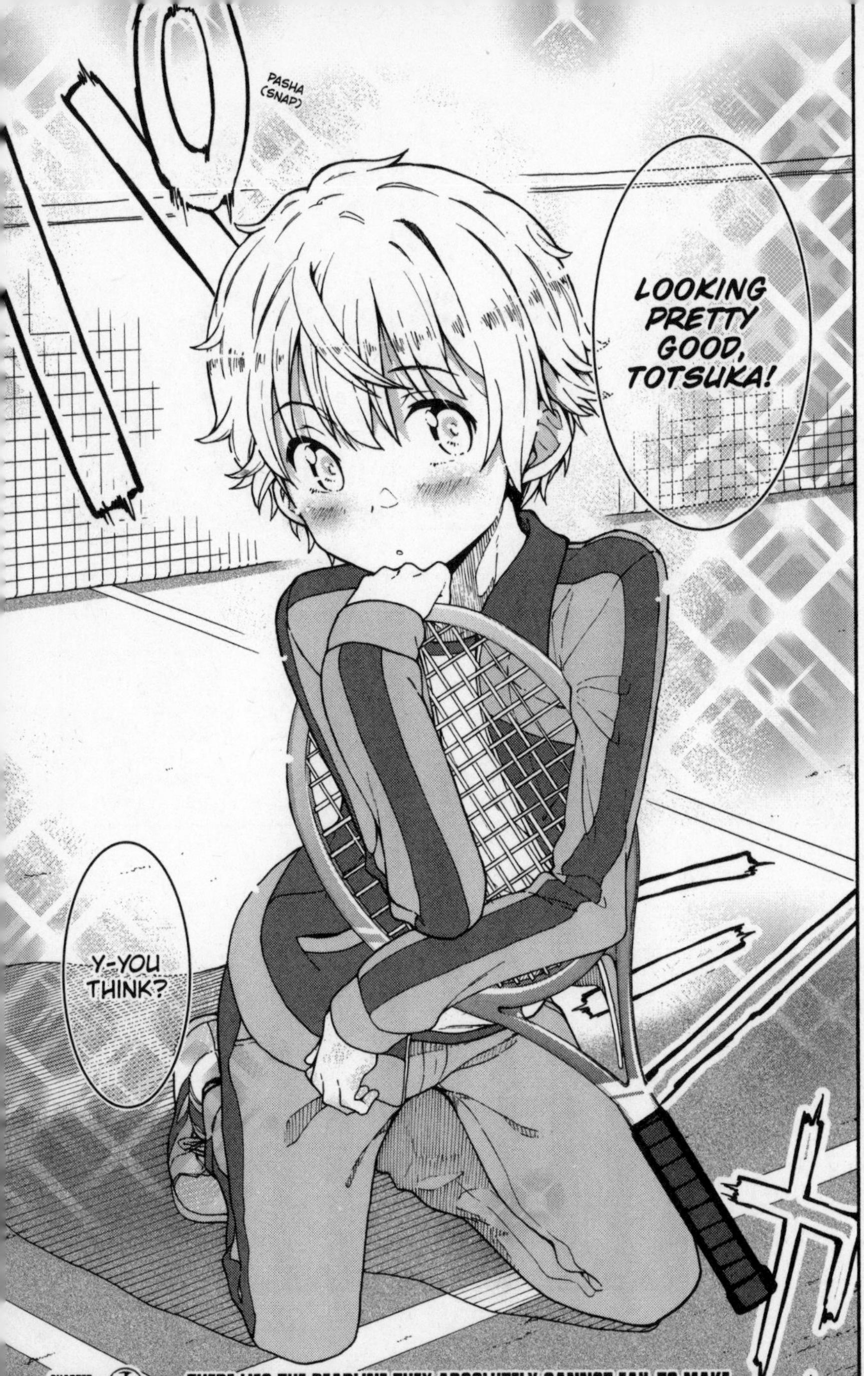
PASHA
(SNAP)
LOOKING PRETTY GOOD, TOTSUKA!
Y-YOU THINK?

CHAPTER 72 ... THERE LIES THE DEADLINE THEY ABSOLUTELY CANNOT FAIL TO MAKE.

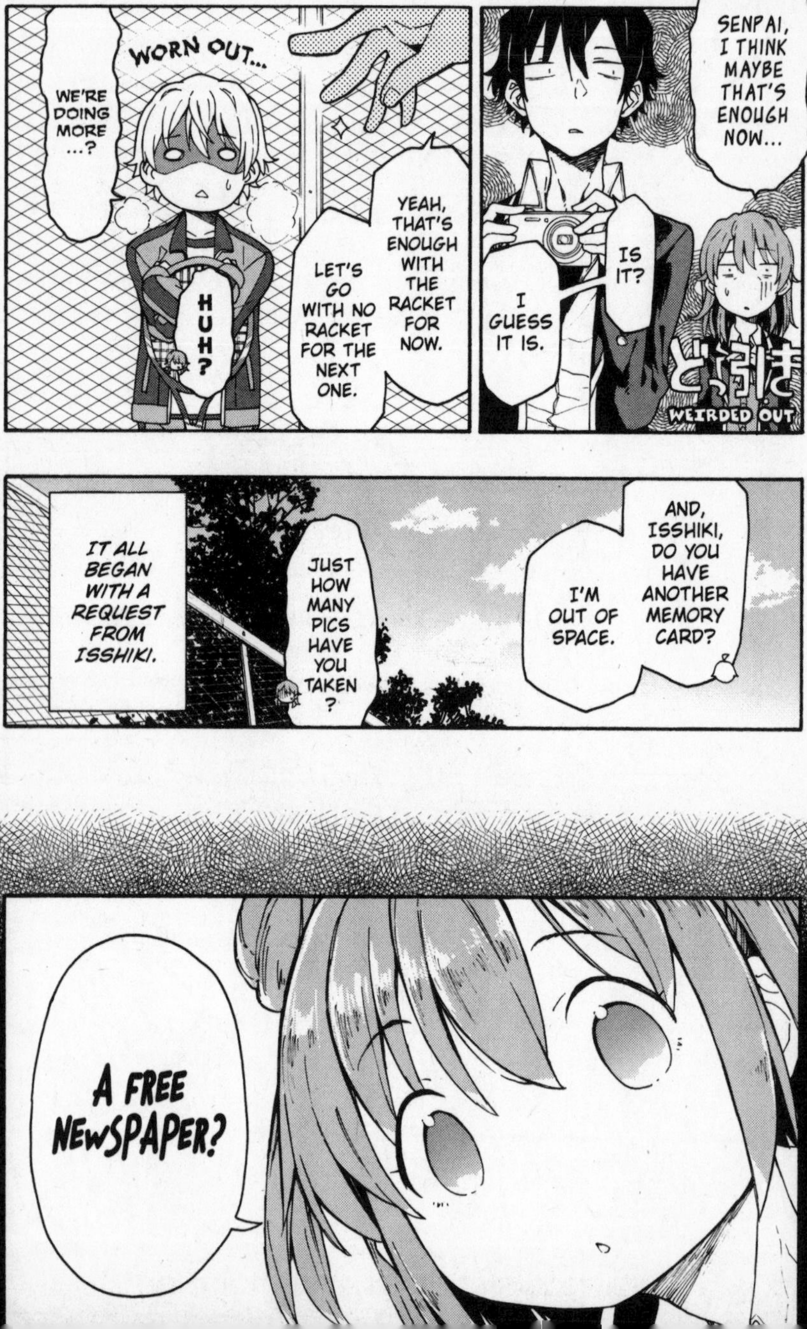
SENPAI, I THINK MAYBE THAT'S ENOUGH NOW...
IS IT?
I GUESS IT IS.
WEIRDED OUT
YEAH, THAT'S ENOUGH WITH THE RACKET FOR NOW.
LET'S GO WITH NO RACKET FOR THE NEXT ONE.
WORN OUT...
WE'RE DOING MORE ...?
HUH?
AND, ISSHIKI, DO YOU HAVE ANOTHER MEMORY CARD?
I'M OUT OF SPACE.
JUST HOW MANY PICS HAVE YOU TAKEN?
IT ALL BEGAN WITH A REQUEST FROM ISSHIKI.
A FREE NEWSPAPER?

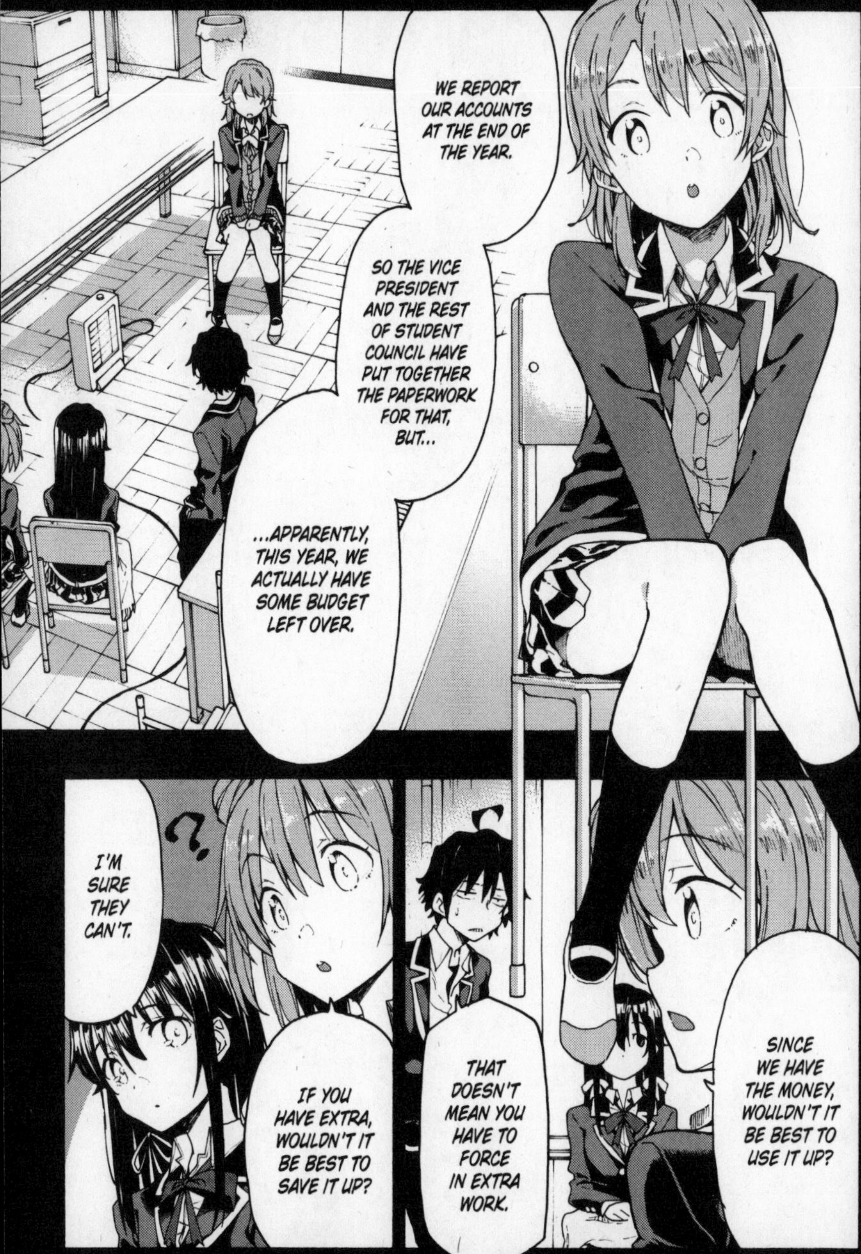
WE REPORT OUR ACCOUNTS AT THE END OF THE YEAR.
SO THE VICE PRESIDENT AND THE REST OF STUDENT COUNCIL HAVE PUT TOGETHER THE PAPERWORK FOR THAT, BUT...
...APPARENTLY, THIS YEAR, WE ACTUALLY HAVE SOME BUDGET LEFT OVER.
SINCE WE HAVE THE MONEY, WOULDN'T IT BE BEST TO USE IT UP?
THAT DOESN'T MEAN YOU HAVE TO FORCE IN EXTRA WORK.
IF YOU HAVE EXTRA, WOULDN'T IT BE BEST TO SAVE IT UP?
I'M SURE THEY CAN'T.

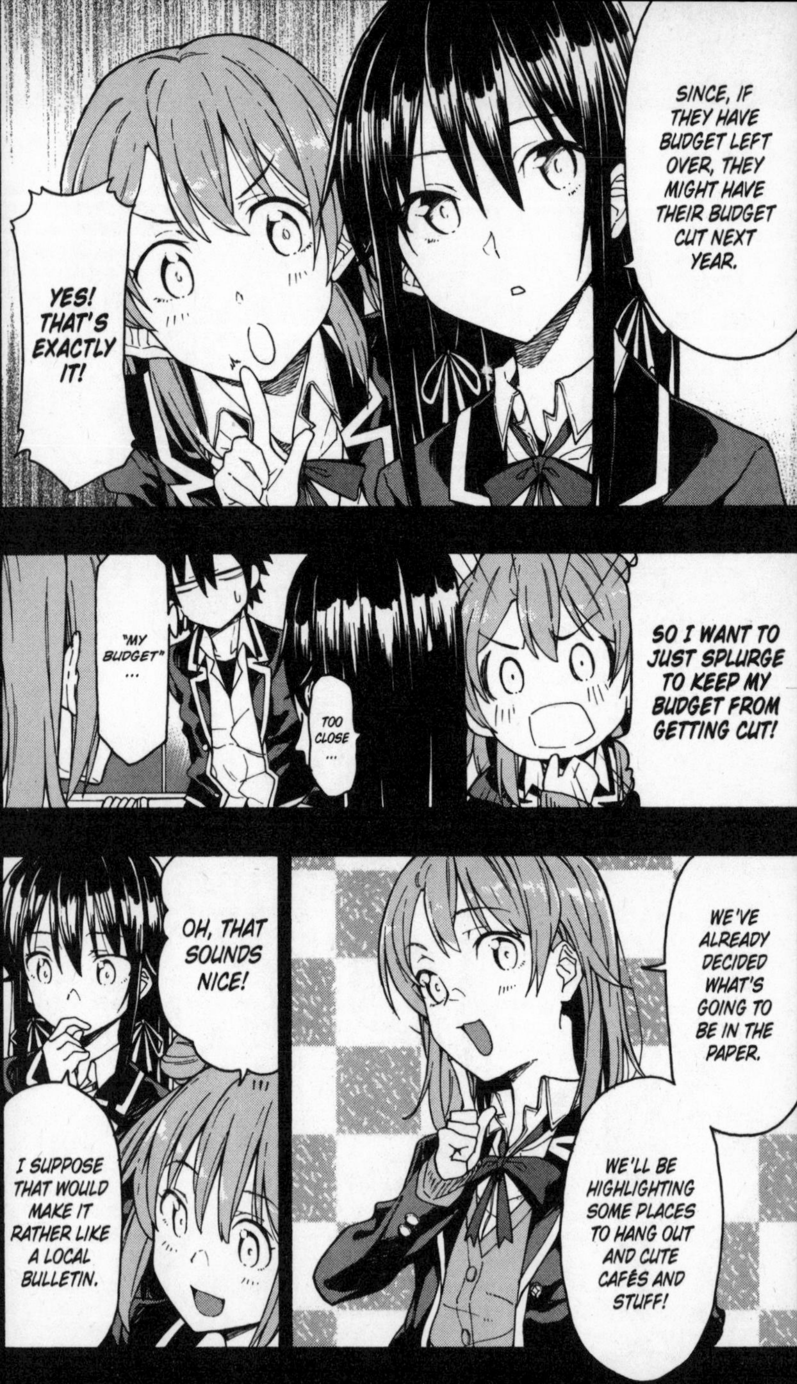
SINCE, IF THEY HAVE BUDGET LEFT OVER, THEY MIGHT HAVE THEIR BUDGET CUT NEXT YEAR.
YES! THAT'S EXACTLY IT!
SO I WANT TO JUST SPLURGE TO KEEP MY BUDGET FROM GETTING CUT!
TOO CLOSE ...
"MY BUDGET" ...
WE'VE ALREADY DECIDED WHAT'S GOING TO BE IN THE PAPER.
WE'LL BE HIGHLIGHTING SOME PLACES TO HANG OUT AND CUTE CAFÉS AND STUFF!
OH, THAT SOUNDS NICE!
I SUPPOSE THAT WOULD MAKE IT RATHER LIKE A LOCAL BULLETIN.

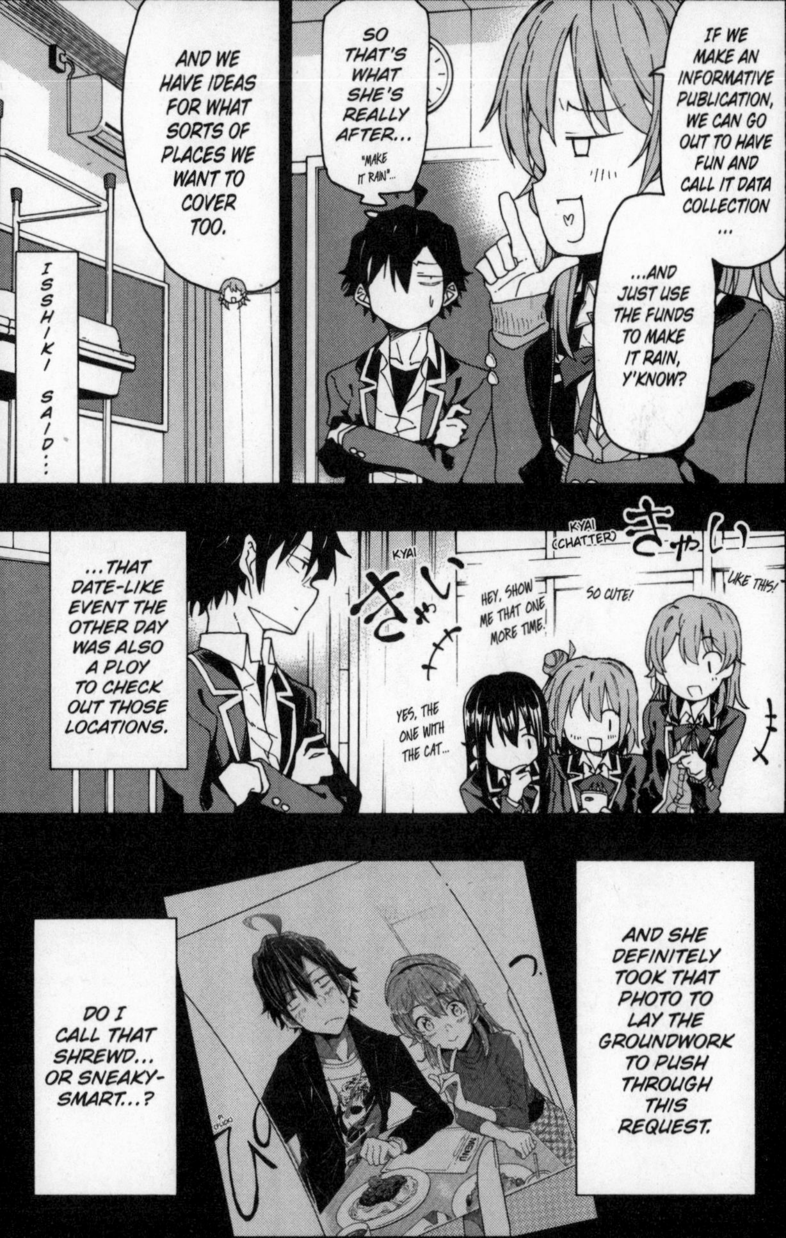

IF WE MAKE AN INFORMATIVE PUBLICATION, WE CAN GO OUT TO HAVE FUN AND CALL IT DATA COLLECTION...
...AND JUST USE THE FUNDS TO MAKE IT RAIN, Y'KNOW?
SO THAT'S WHAT SHE'S REALLY AFTER...
"MAKE IT RAIN"...
AND WE HAVE IDEAS FOR WHAT SORTS OF PLACES WE WANT TO COVER TOO.
ISSHIKI SAID...
KYAI (CHATTER)
LIKE THIS!
SO CUTE!
HEY, SHOW ME THAT ONE MORE TIME!
KYAI
YES, THE ONE WITH THE CAT...
...THAT DATE-LIKE EVENT THE OTHER DAY WAS ALSO A PLOY TO CHECK OUT THOSE LOCATIONS.
AND SHE DEFINITELY TOOK THAT PHOTO TO LAY THE GROUNDWORK TO PUSH THROUGH THIS REQUEST.
DO I CALL THAT SHREWD... OR SNEAKY-SMART...?

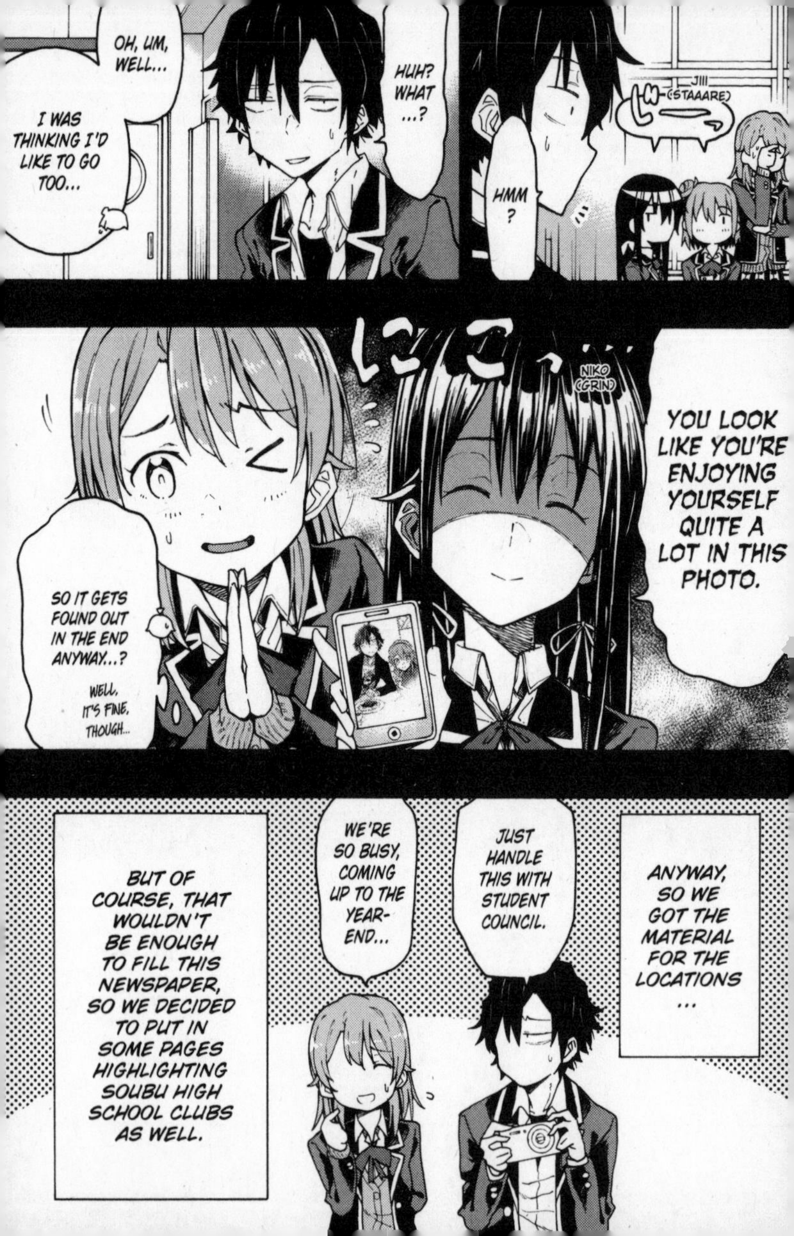
JIII (STAAARE)
HMM ?
HUH? WHAT ...?
OH, UM, WELL...
I WAS THINKING I'D LIKE TO GO TOO...
NIKO (GRIN)
YOU LOOK LIKE YOU'RE ENJOYING YOURSELF QUITE A LOT IN THIS PHOTO.
SO IT GETS FOUND OUT IN THE END ANYWAY...?
WELL, IT'S FINE, THOUGH...
ANYWAY, SO WE GOT THE MATERIAL FOR THE LOCATIONS ...
JUST HANDLE THIS WITH STUDENT COUNCIL.
WE'RE SO BUSY, COMING UP TO THE YEAR-END...
BUT OF COURSE, THAT WOULDN'T BE ENOUGH TO FILL THIS NEWSPAPER, SO WE DECIDED TO PUT IN SOME PAGES HIGHLIGHTING SOUBU HIGH SCHOOL CLUBS AS WELL.

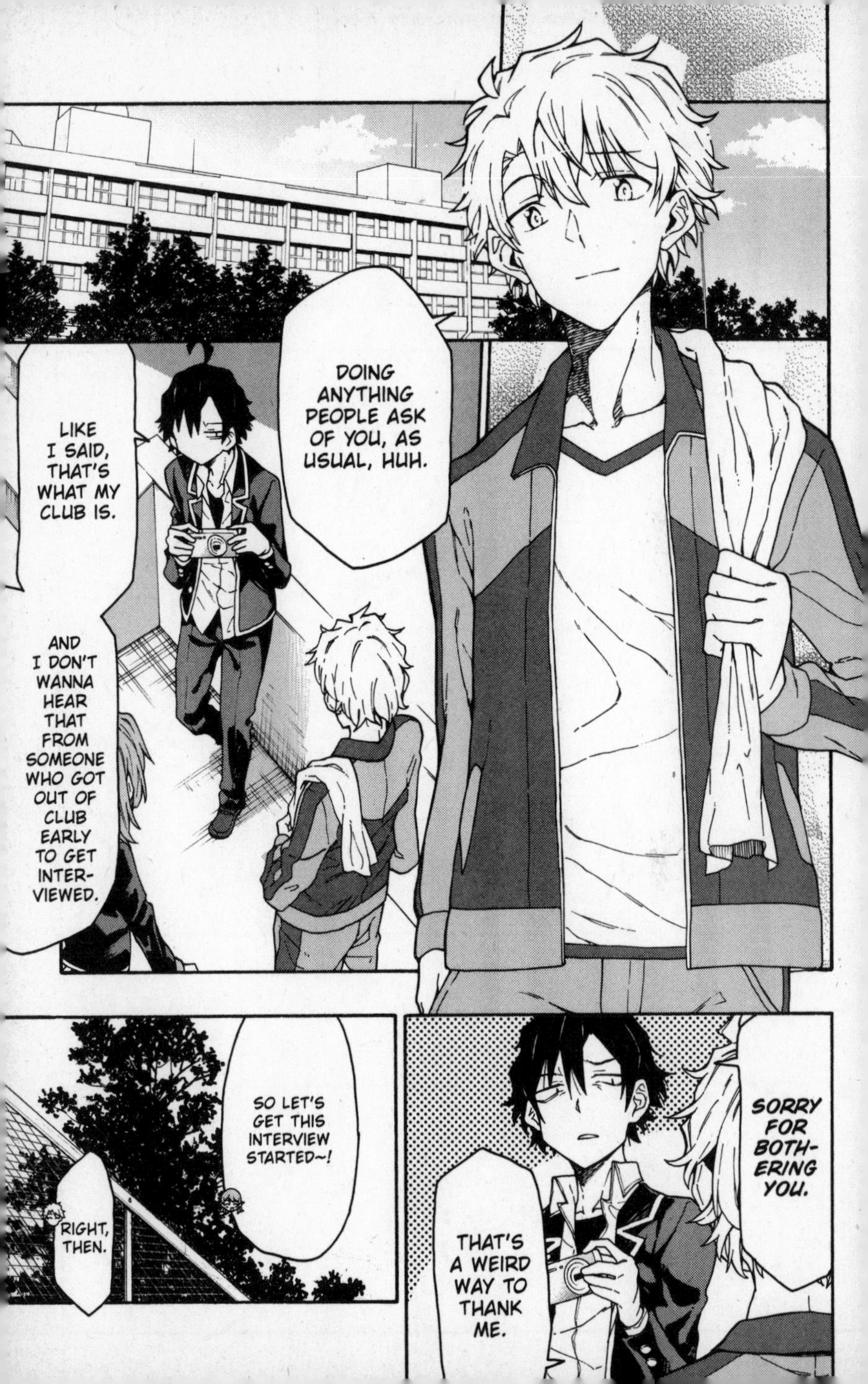
DOING ANYTHING PEOPLE ASK OF YOU, AS USUAL, HUH.
LIKE I SAID, THAT'S WHAT MY CLUB IS.
AND I DON'T WANNA HEAR THAT FROM SOMEONE WHO GOT OUT OF CLUB EARLY TO GET INTER-VIEWED.
SORRY FOR BOTH-ERING YOU.
THAT'S A WEIRD WAY TO THANK ME.
SO LET'S GET THIS INTERVIEW STARTED~!
RIGHT, THEN.

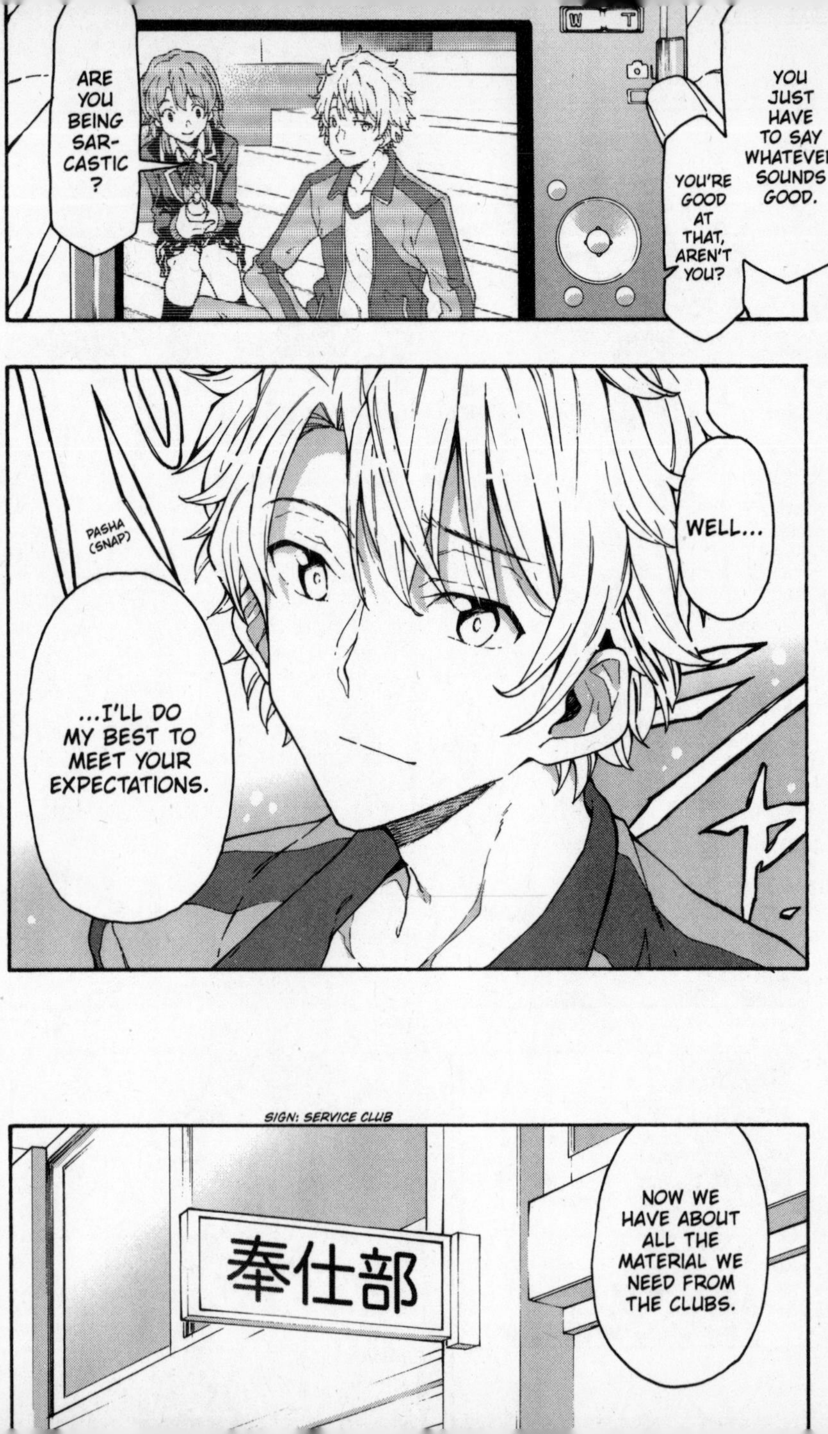
YOU JUST HAVE TO SAY WHATEVER SOUNDS GOOD.
YOU'RE GOOD AT THAT, AREN'T YOU?
ARE YOU BEING SAR-CASTIC?
WELL...
PASHA (SNAP)
...I'LL DO MY BEST TO MEET YOUR EXPECTATIONS.
SIGN: SERVICE CLUB
奉仕部
NOW WE HAVE ABOUT ALL THE MATERIAL WE NEED FROM THE CLUBS.

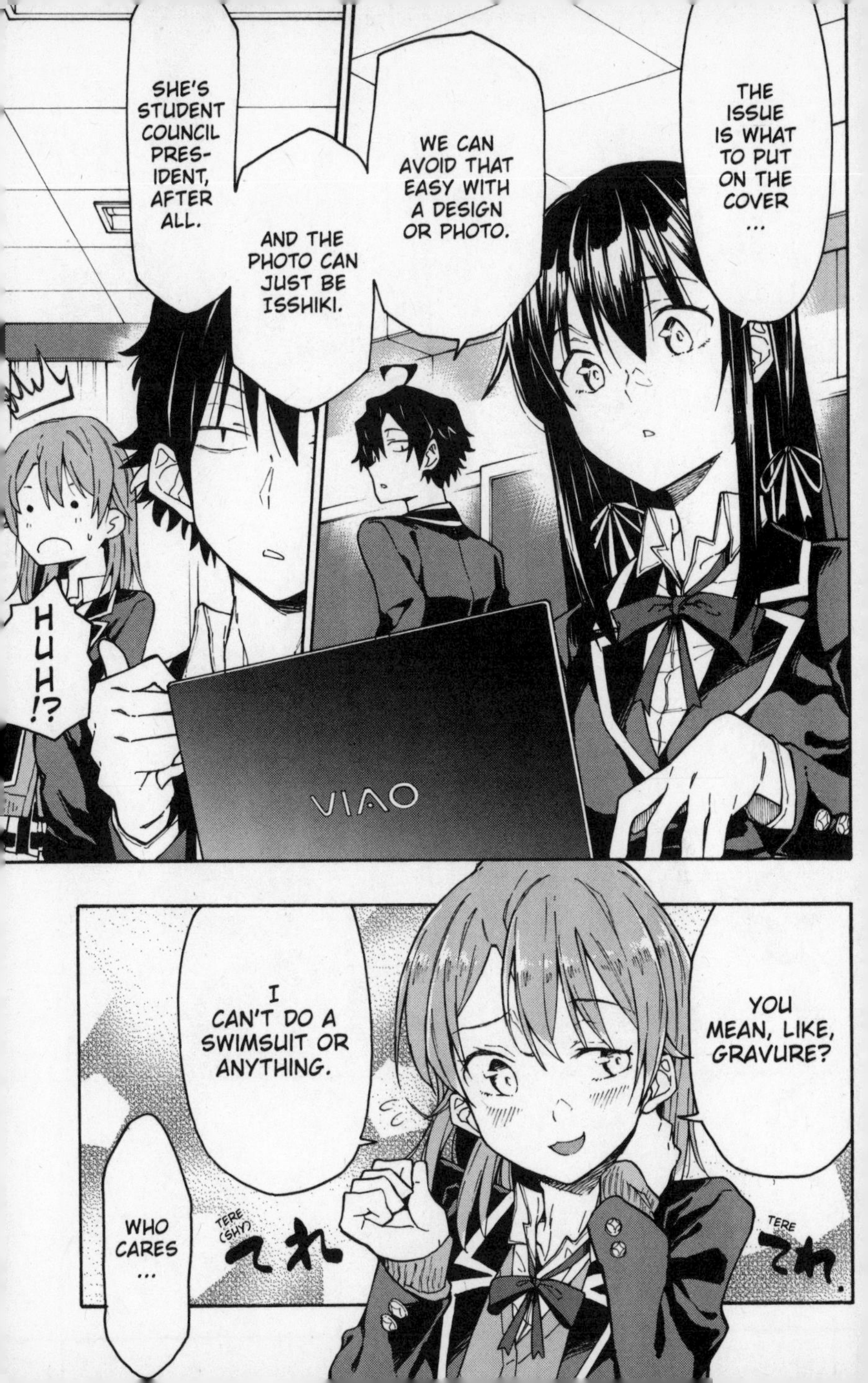
THE ISSUE IS WHAT TO PUT ON THE COVER...
WE CAN AVOID THAT EASY WITH A DESIGN OR PHOTO.
AND THE PHOTO CAN JUST BE ISSHIKI.
SHE'S STUDENT COUNCIL PRESIDENT, AFTER ALL.
HUH!?
VIAO
YOU MEAN, LIKE, GRAVURE?
てれ TERE
I CAN'T DO A SWIMSUIT OR ANYTHING.
てれ TERE (SHY)
WHO CARES...

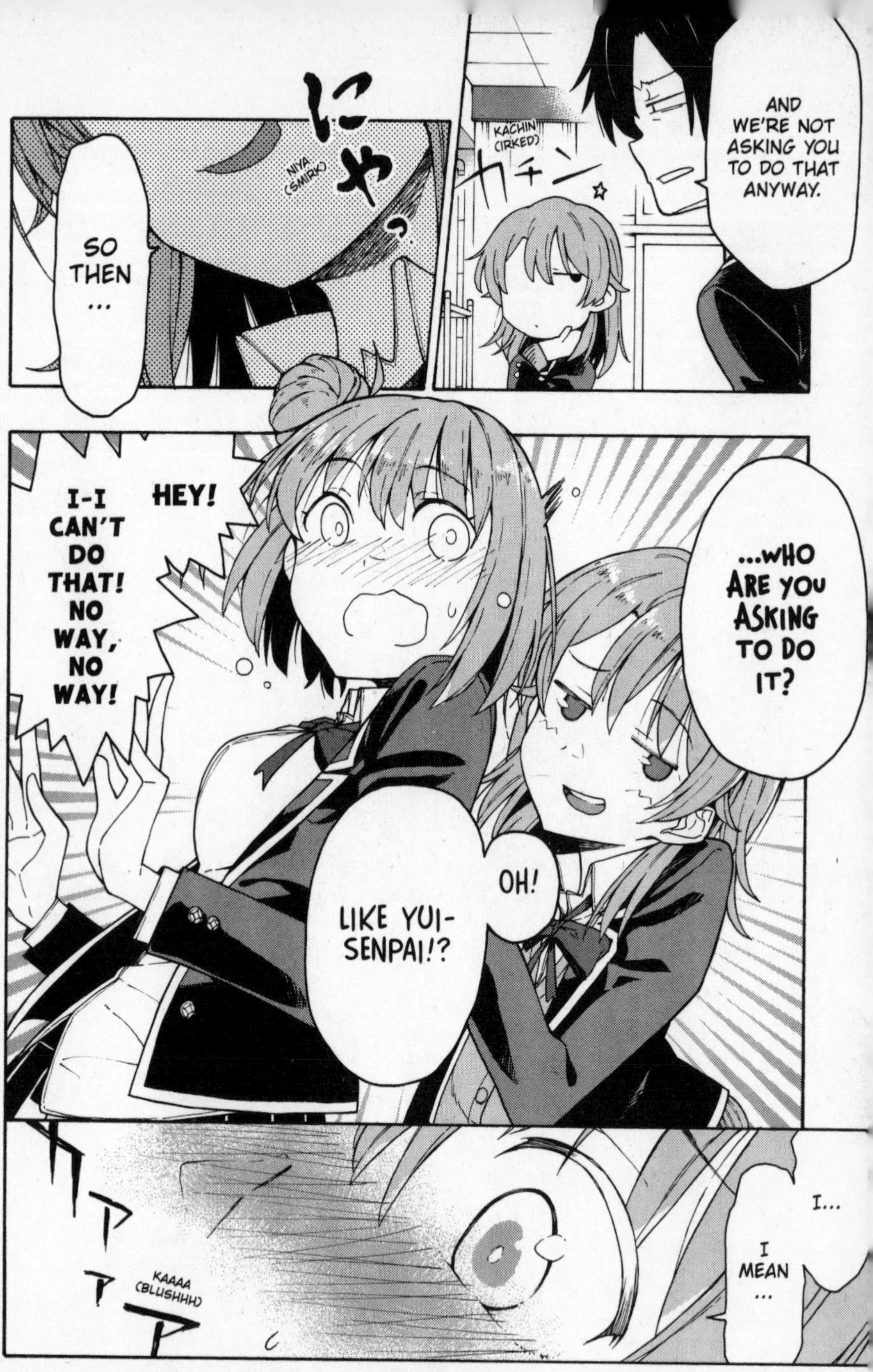
AND WE'RE NOT ASKING YOU TO DO THAT ANYWAY.
KACHIN (IRKED)
にやっ
NIYA (SMIRK)
SO THEN ...
...WHO ARE YOU ASKING TO DO IT?
OH!
LIKE YUI-SENPAI!?
HEY!
I-I CAN'T DO THAT! NO WAY, NO WAY!
I... I MEAN ...
KAAAA (BLUSHHH)

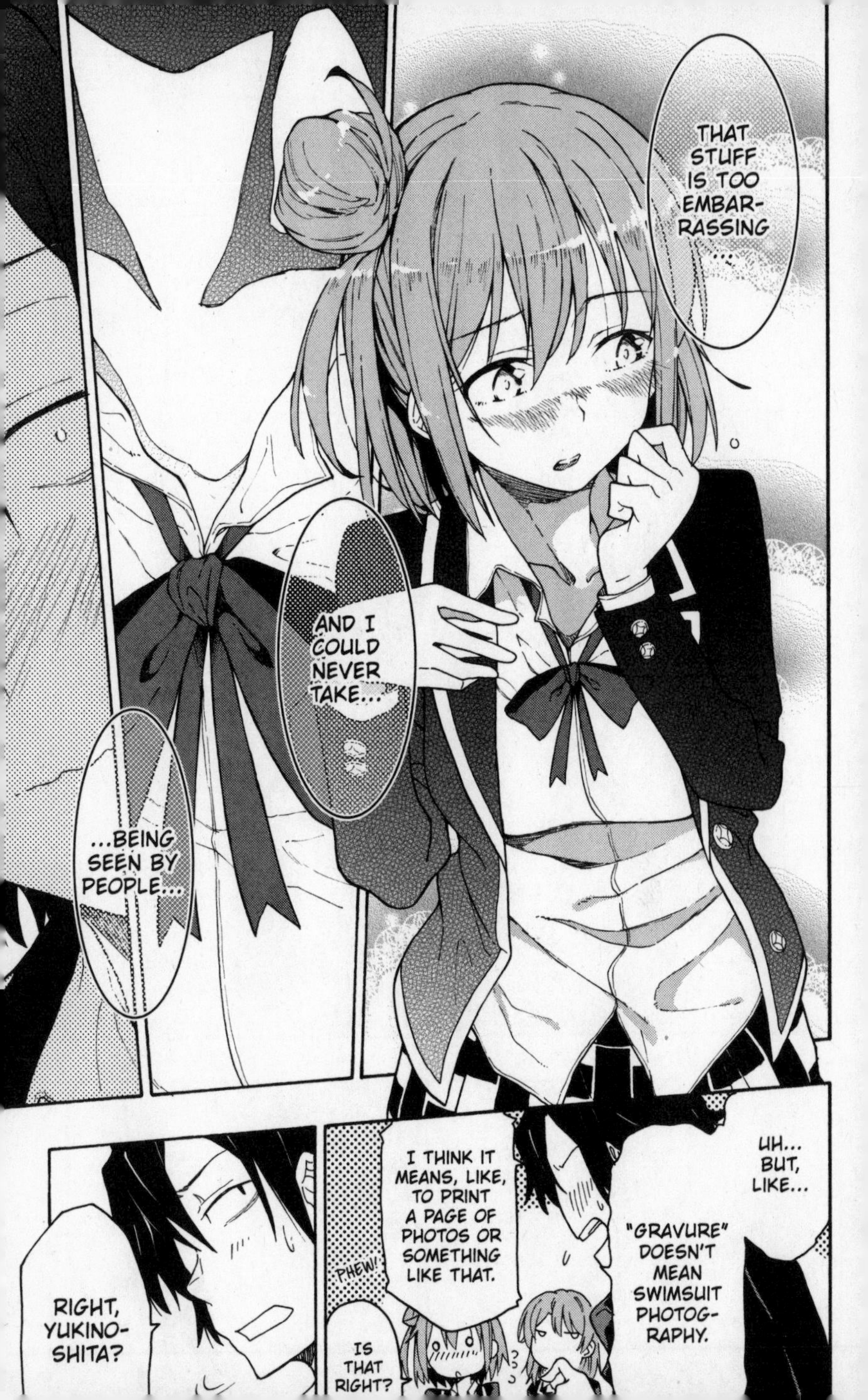
THAT STUFF IS TOO EMBAR-RASSING...
AND I COULD NEVER TAKE...
...BEING SEEN BY PEOPLE...
UH... BUT, LIKE...
"GRAVURE" DOESN'T MEAN SWIMSUIT PHOTOG-RAPHY.
I THINK IT MEANS, LIKE, TO PRINT A PAGE OF PHOTOS OR SOMETHING LIKE THAT.
PHEW!
IS THAT RIGHT?
RIGHT, YUKINO-SHITA?

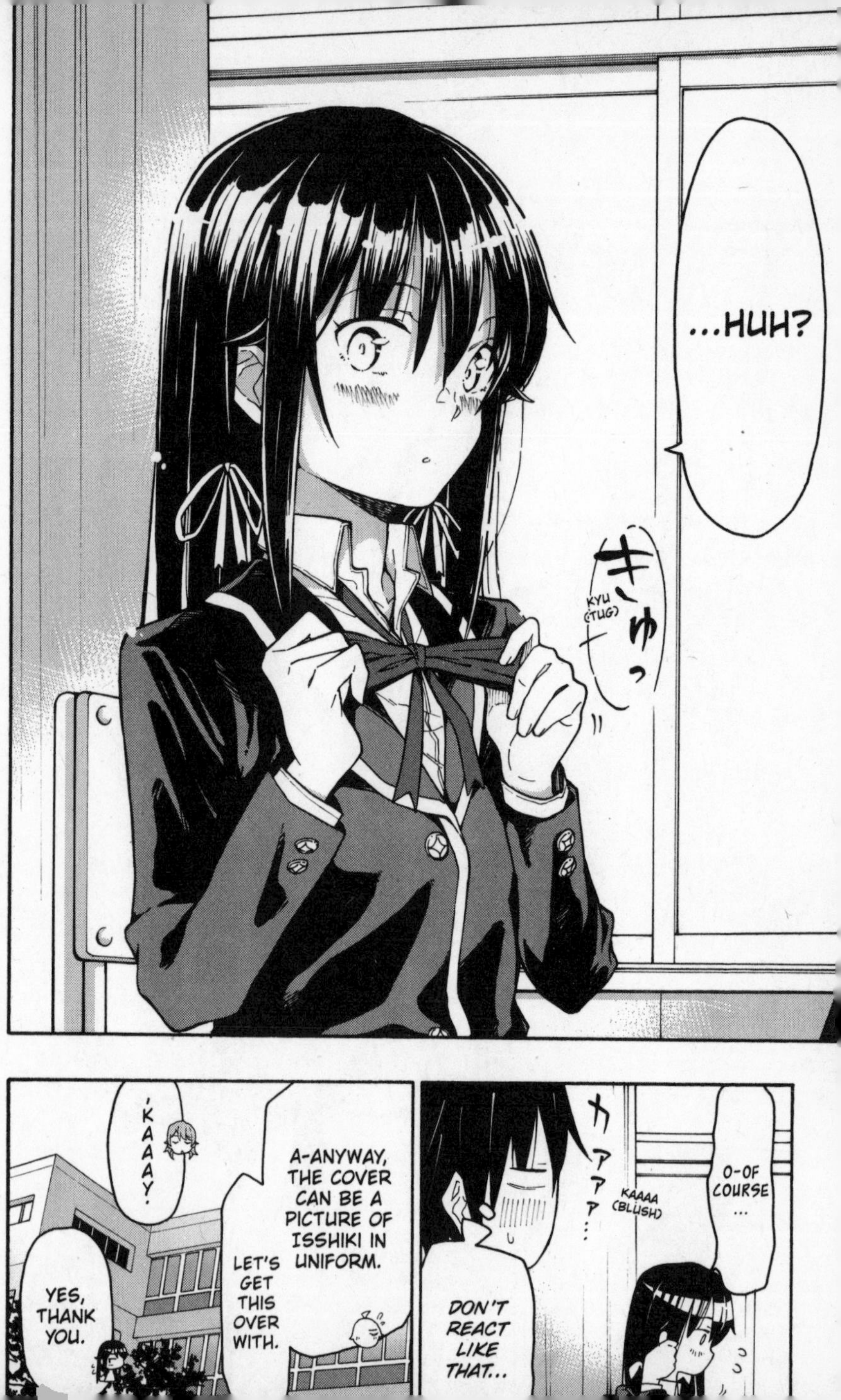
...HUH?
きゅっ
KYU (TUG)
O-OF COURSE...
カァァ…
KAAAA (BLUSH)
DON'T REACT LIKE THAT...
A-ANYWAY, THE COVER CAN BE A PICTURE OF ISSHIKI IN UNIFORM.
LET'S GET THIS OVER WITH.
'KAAAY.
YES, THANK YOU.

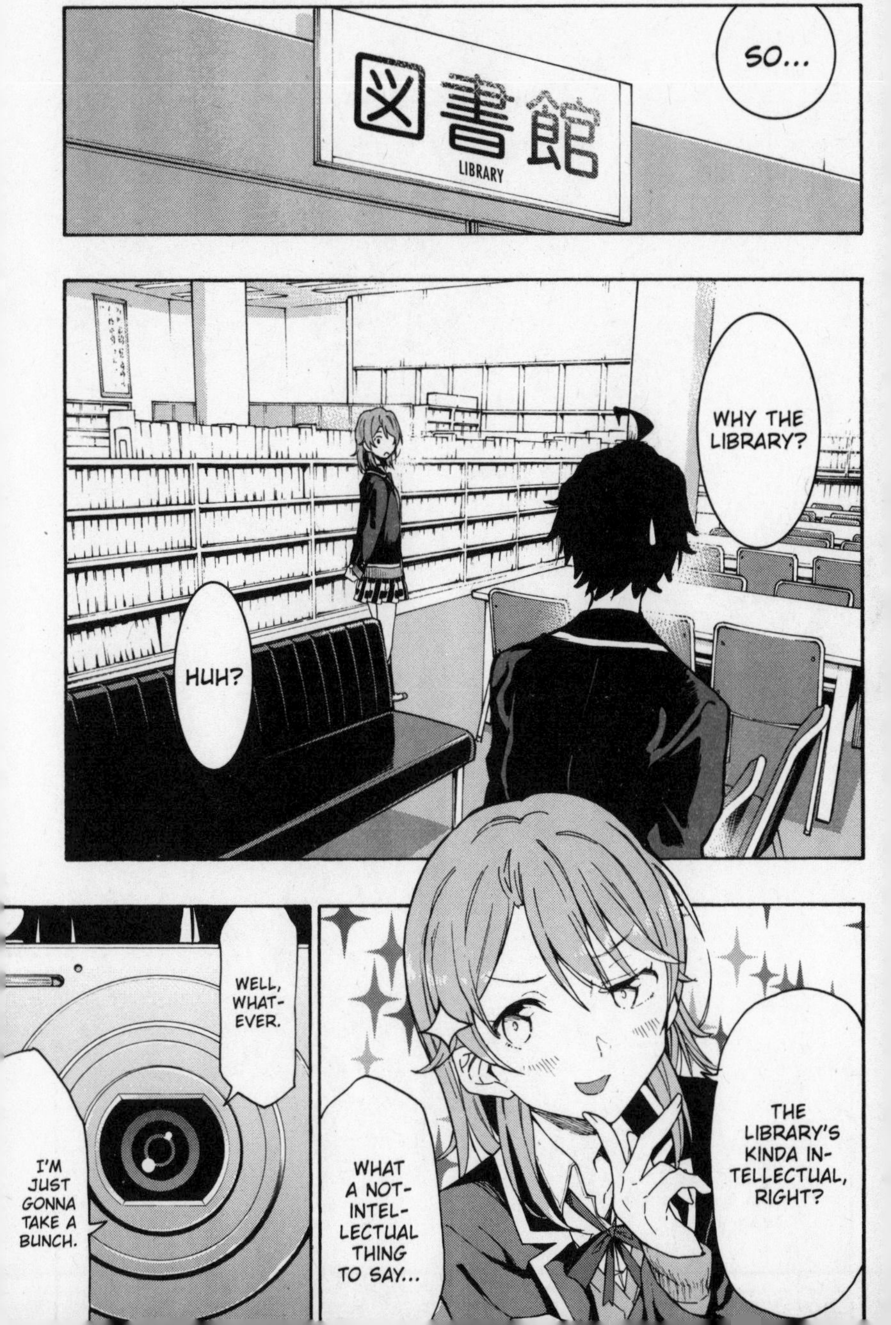
SO...
図書館
LIBRARY
WHY THE LIBRARY?
HUH?
THE LIBRARY'S KINDA INTELLECTUAL, RIGHT?
WHAT A NOT-INTELLECTUAL THING TO SAY...
WELL, WHATEVER.
I'M JUST GONNA TAKE A BUNCH.

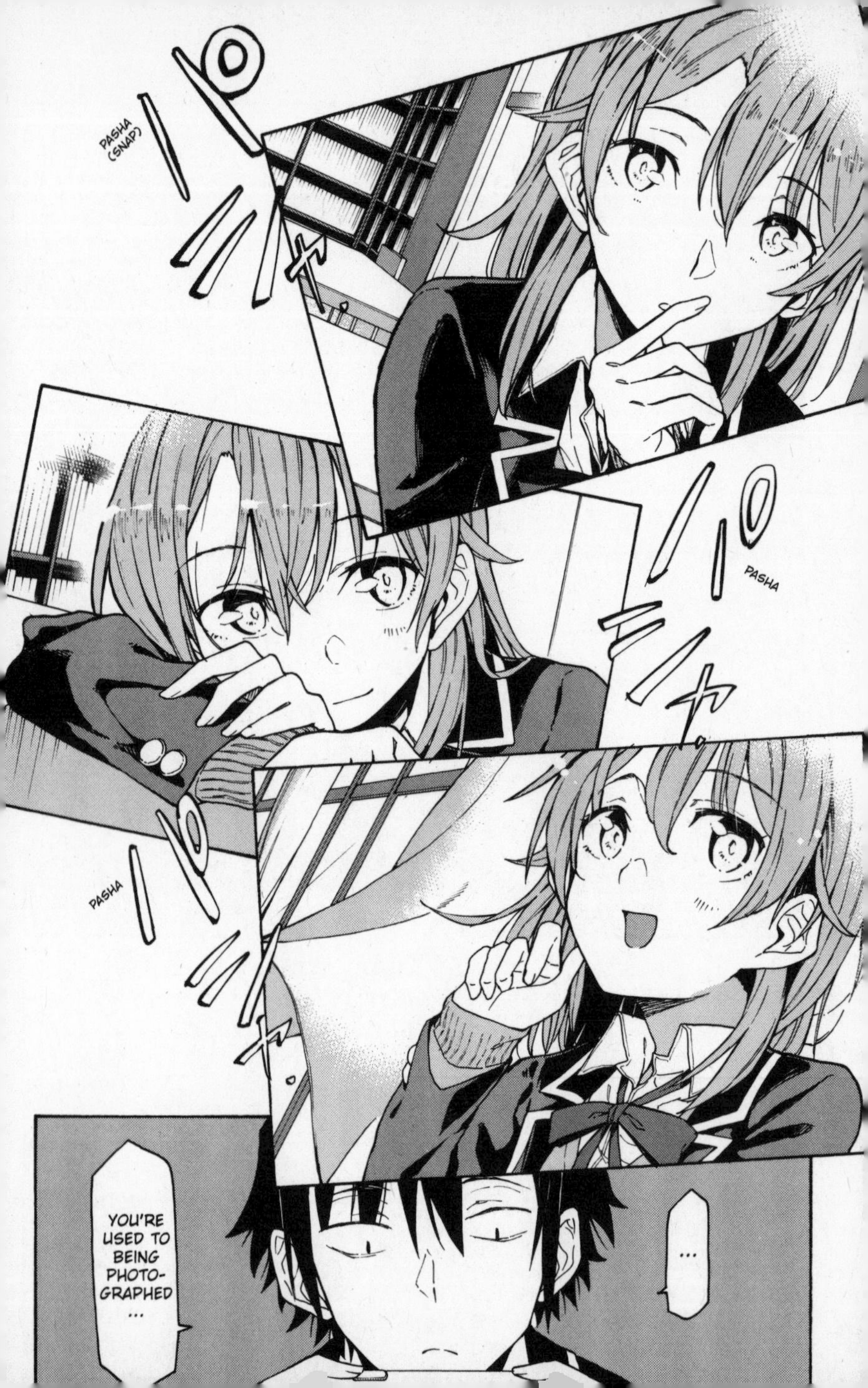
PASHA (SNAP)
PASHA
PASHA
...
YOU'RE USED TO BEING PHOTO-GRAPHED ...

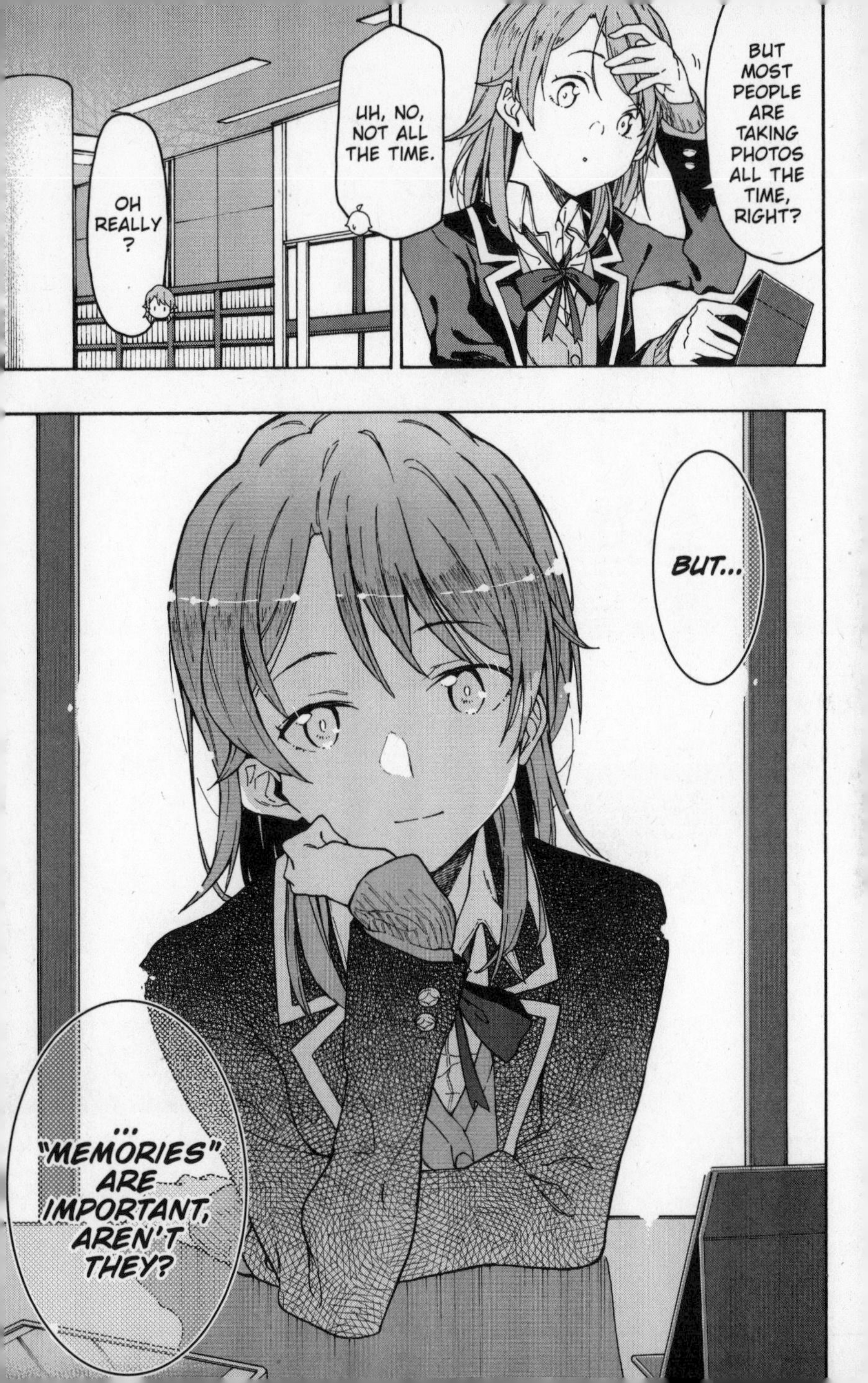
BUT MOST PEOPLE ARE TAKING PHOTOS ALL THE TIME, RIGHT?
UH, NO, NOT ALL THE TIME.
OH REALLY ?
BUT...
... "MEMORIES" ARE IMPORTANT, AREN'T THEY?

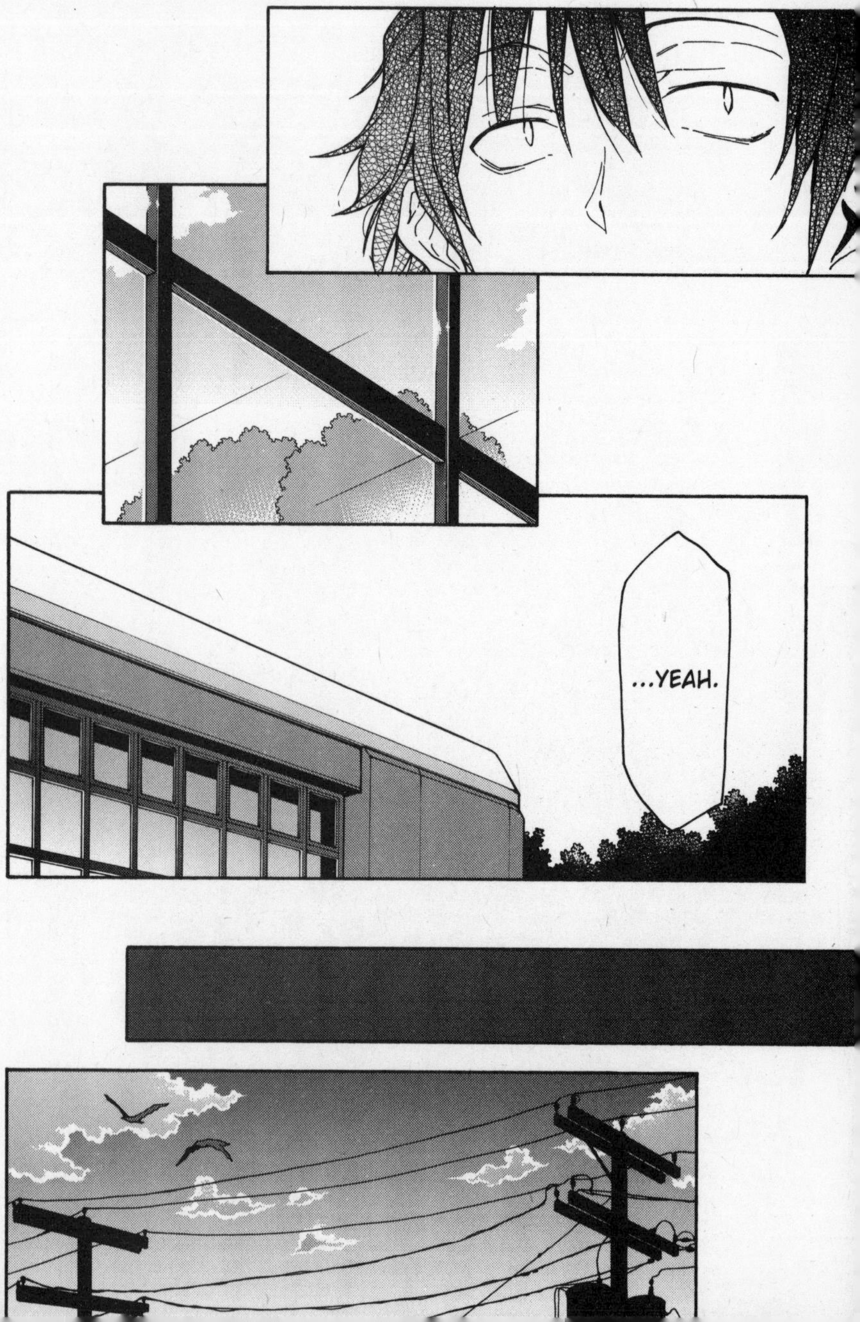
...YEAH.

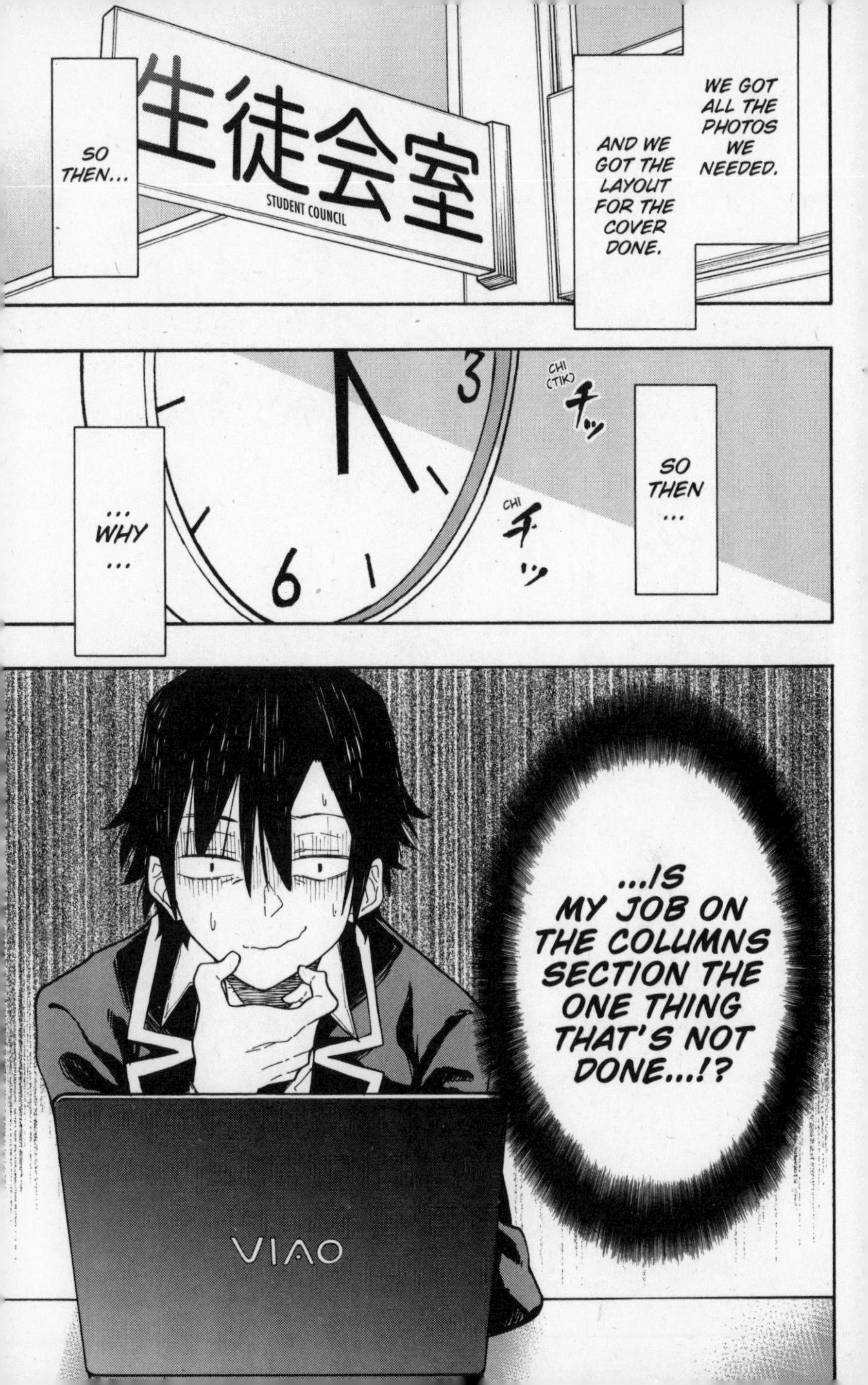
WE GOT ALL THE PHOTOS WE NEEDED.
AND WE GOT THE LAYOUT FOR THE COVER DONE.
生徒会室
STUDENT COUNCIL
SO THEN...
SO THEN ...
CHI (TIK) チッ
CHI チッ
... WHY ...
...IS MY JOB ON THE COLUMNS SECTION THE ONE THING THAT'S NOT DONE...!?
VIAO

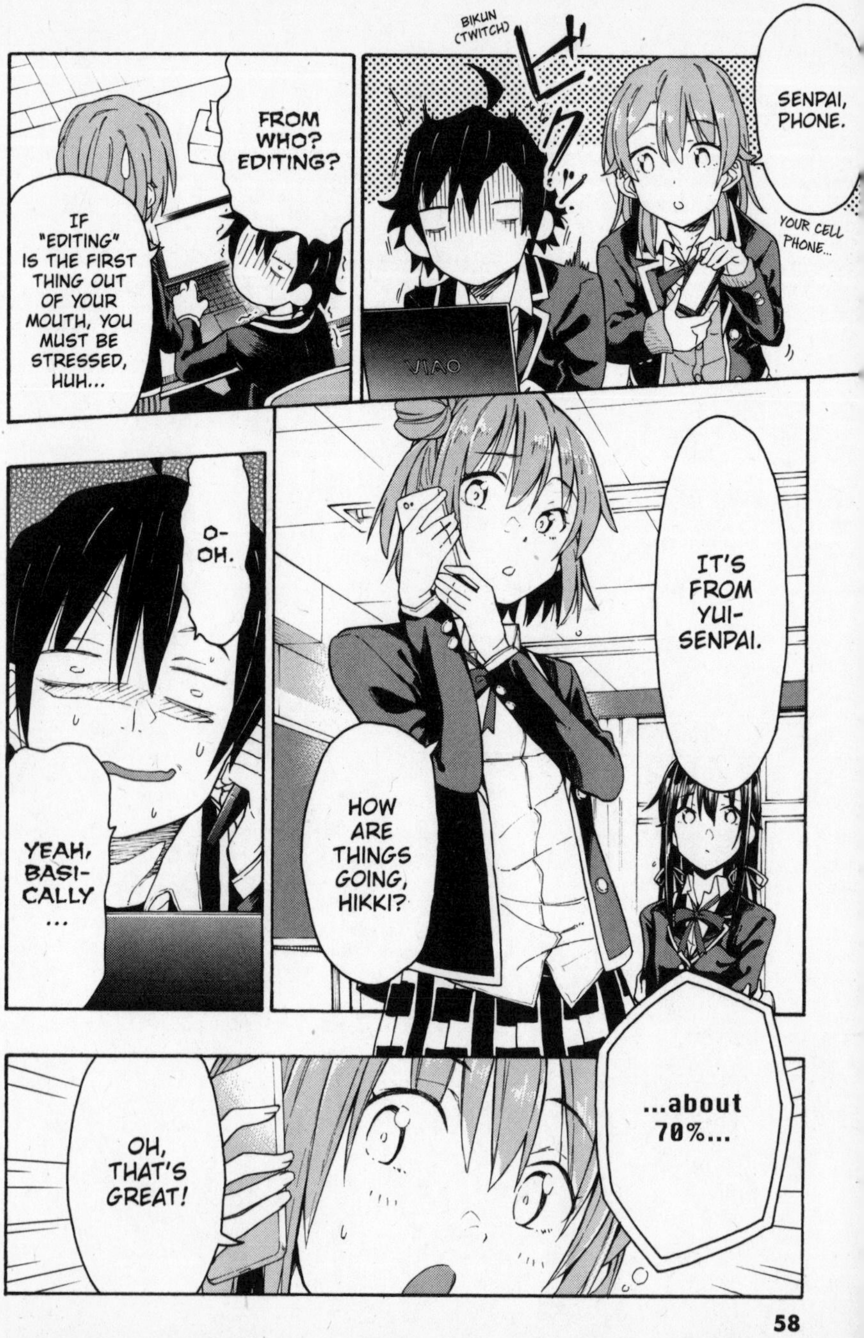

SENPAI, PHONE.
BIKUN (TWITCH)
YOUR CELL PHONE...
FROM WHO? EDITING?
IF "EDITING" IS THE FIRST THING OUT OF YOUR MOUTH, YOU MUST BE STRESSED, HUH...
IT'S FROM YUI-SENPAI.
HOW ARE THINGS GOING, HIKKI?
O-OH.
YEAH, BASI-CALLY ...
...about 70%...
OH, THAT'S GREAT!

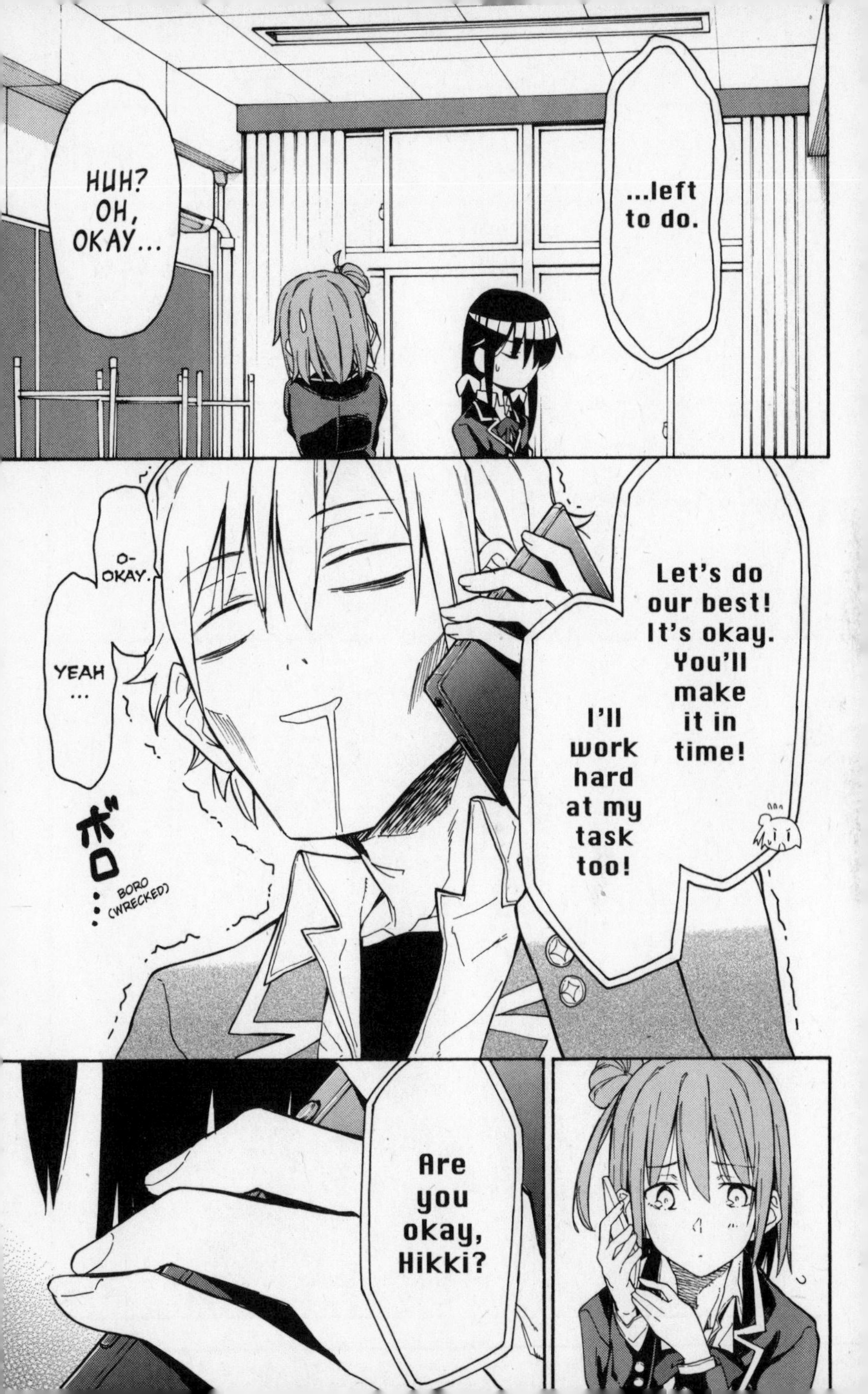
...left to do.
HUH? OH, OKAY...
Let's do our best! It's okay. You'll make it in time! I'll work hard at my task too!
O-OKAY.
YEAH...
ボロ... BORO (WRECKED)
Are you okay, Hikki?

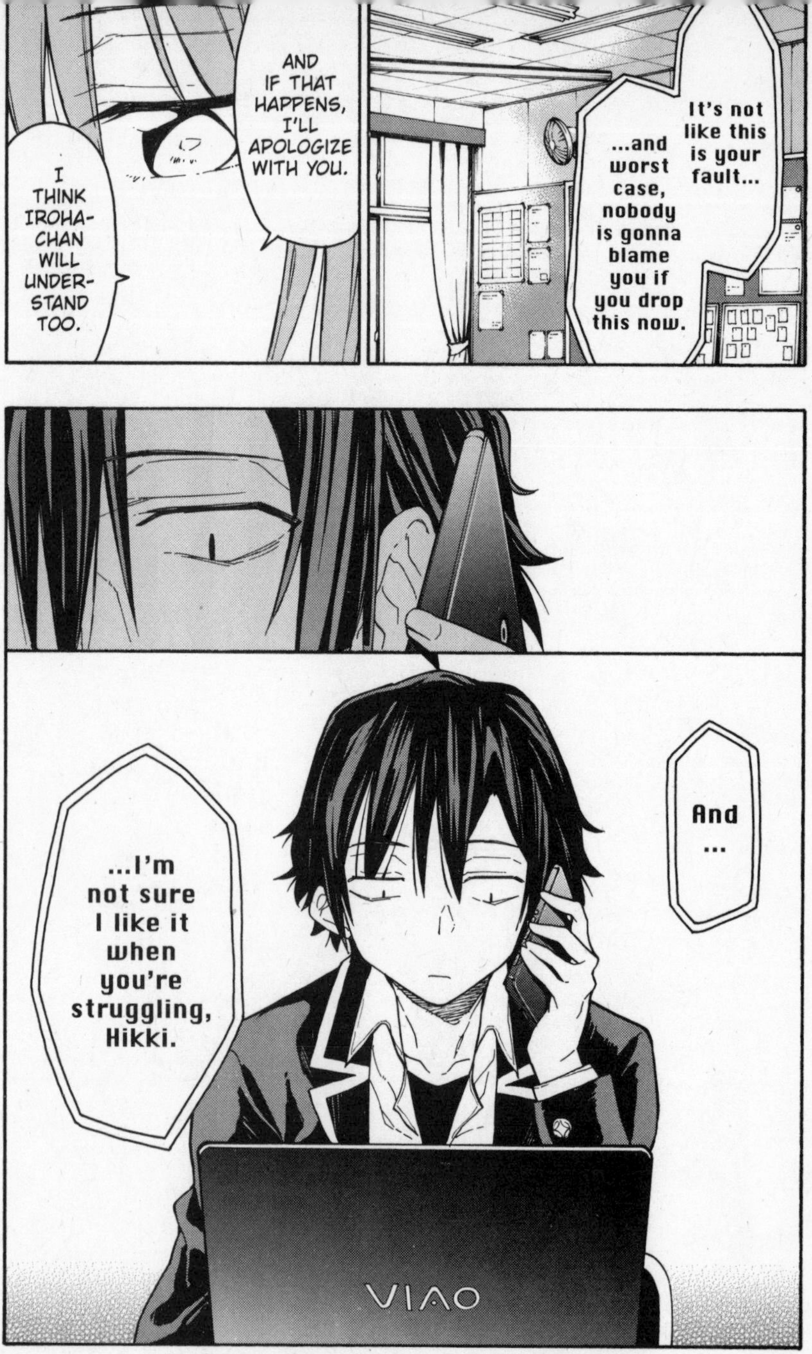
It's not like this is your fault...
...and worst case, nobody is gonna blame you if you drop this now.
AND IF THAT HAPPENS, I'LL APOLOGIZE WITH YOU.
I THINK IROHA-CHAN WILL UNDER-STAND TOO.
And ...
...I'm not sure I like it when you're struggling, Hikki.
VIAO

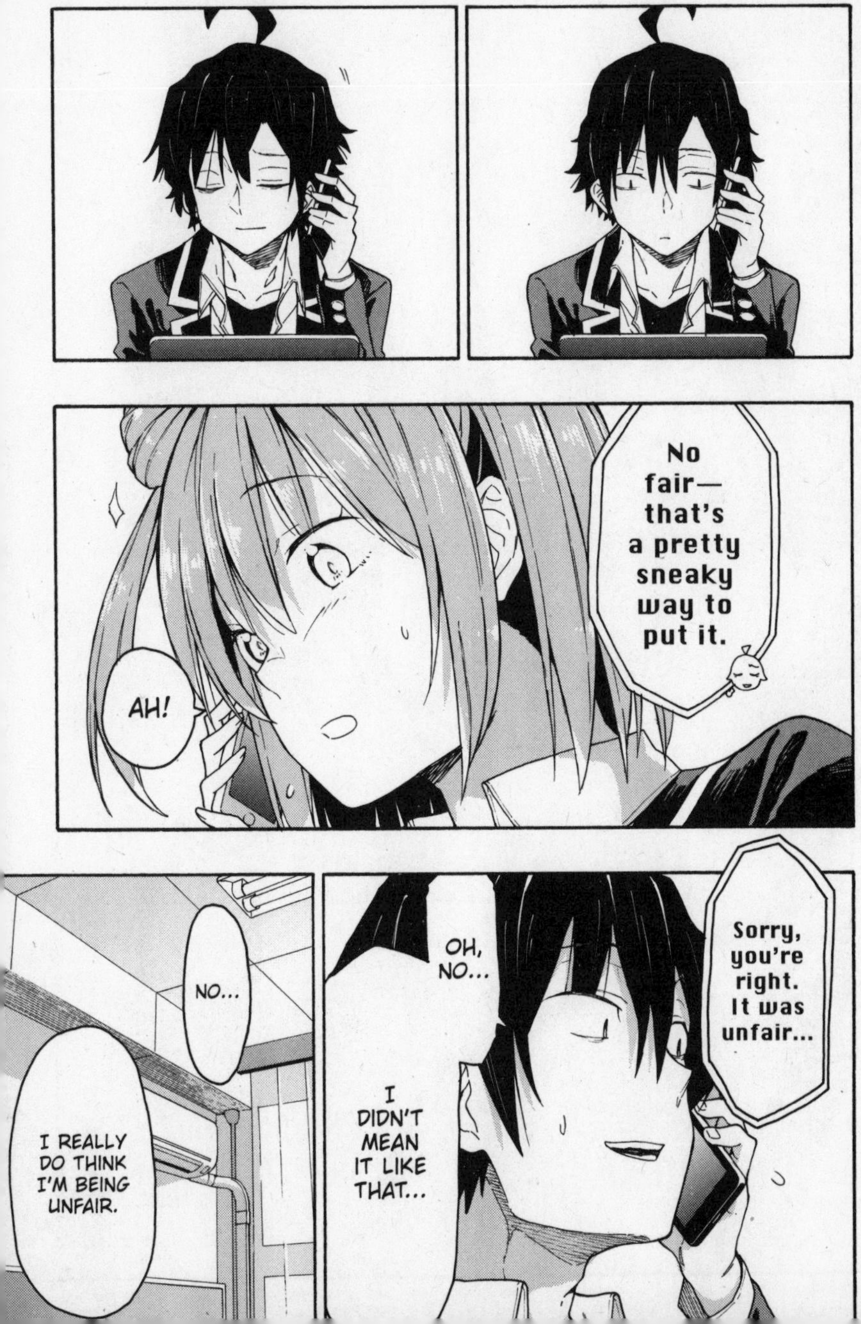
No fair—that's a pretty sneaky way to put it.
AH!
Sorry, you're right. It was unfair...
OH, NO...
I DIDN'T MEAN IT LIKE THAT...
NO...
I REALLY DO THINK I'M BEING UNFAIR.

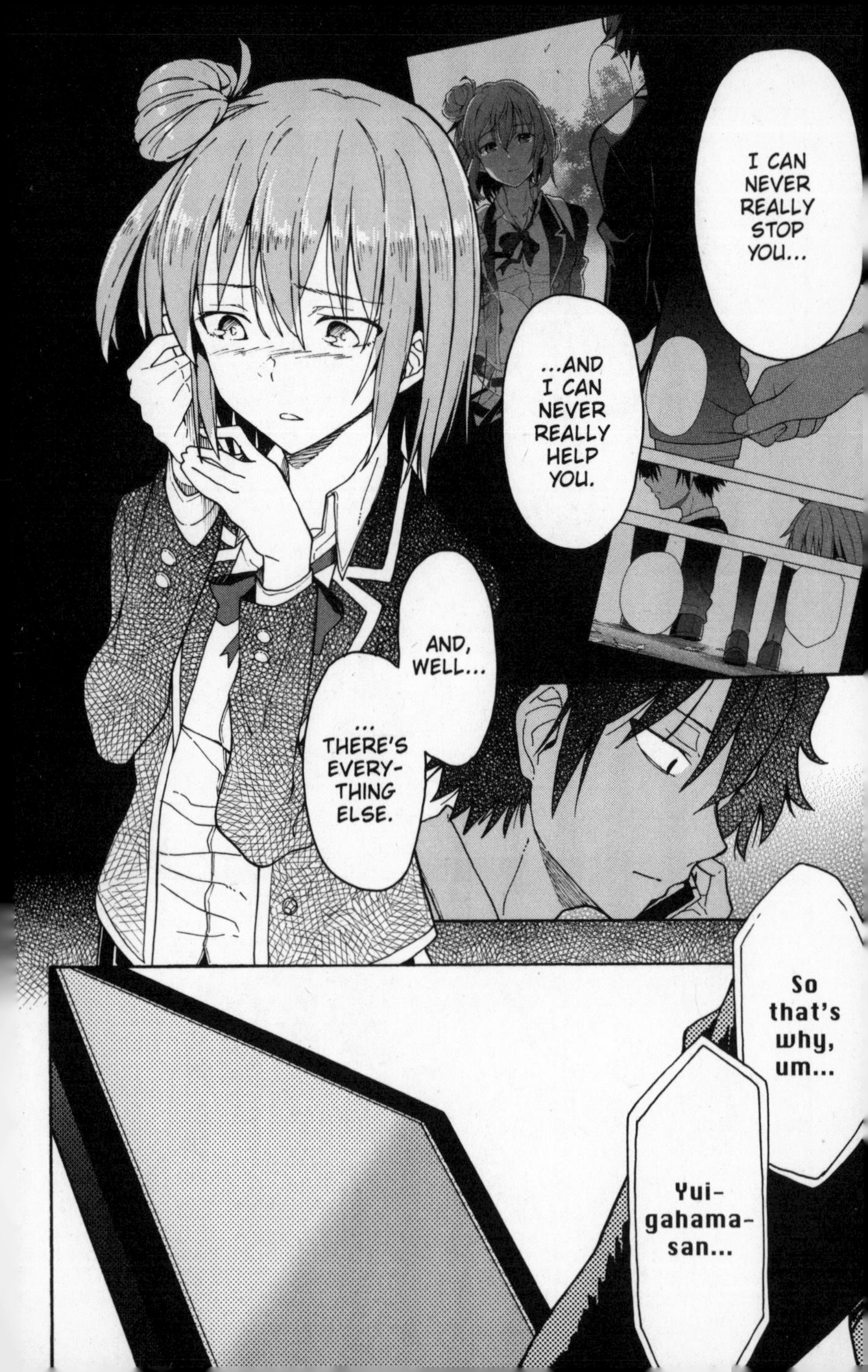
I CAN NEVER REALLY STOP YOU...
...AND I CAN NEVER REALLY HELP YOU.
AND, WELL...
... THERE'S EVERY-THING ELSE.
So that's why, um...
Yui-gahama-san...

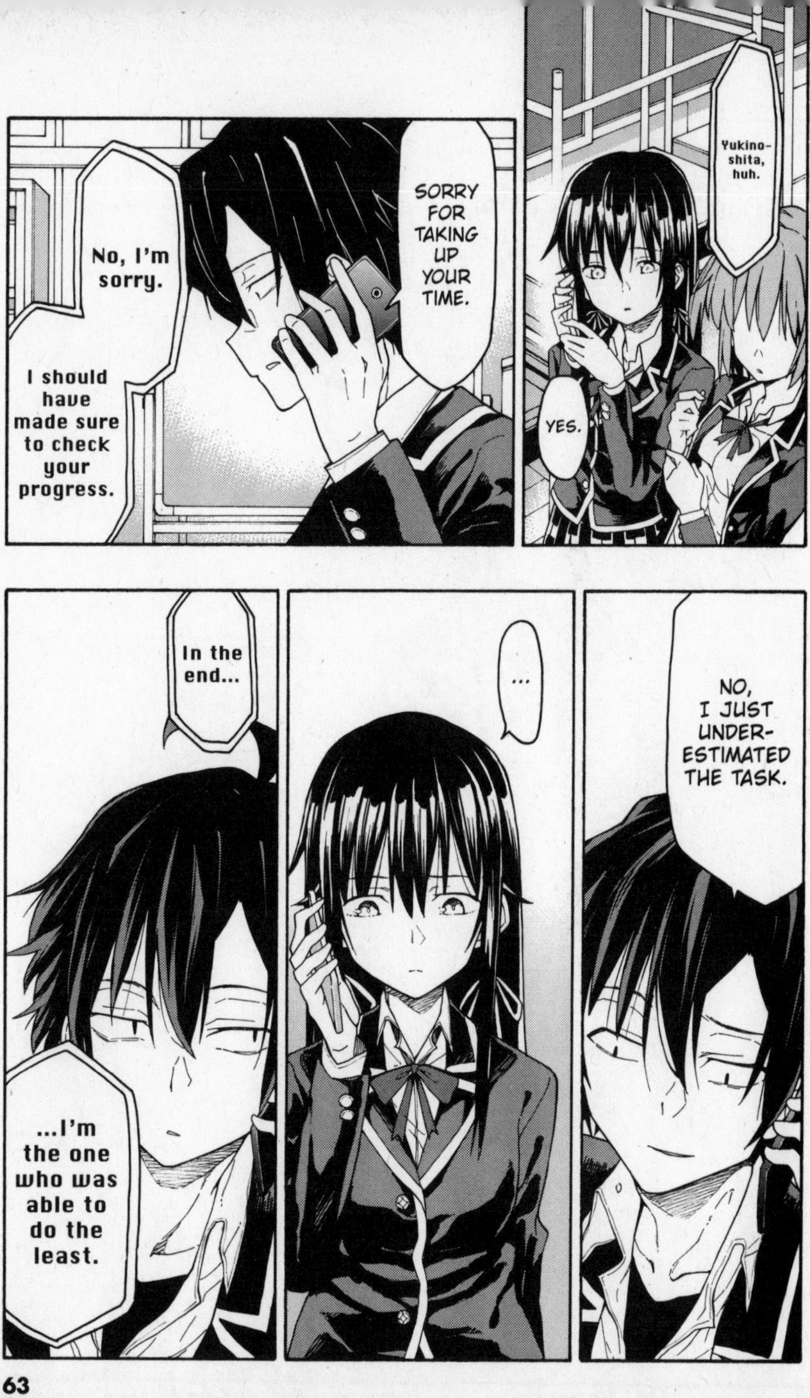
Yukino-shita, huh.
YES.
SORRY FOR TAKING UP YOUR TIME.
No, I'm sorry.
I should have made sure to check your progress.
NO, I JUST UNDER-ESTIMATED THE TASK.
...
In the end...
...I'm the one who was able to do the least.

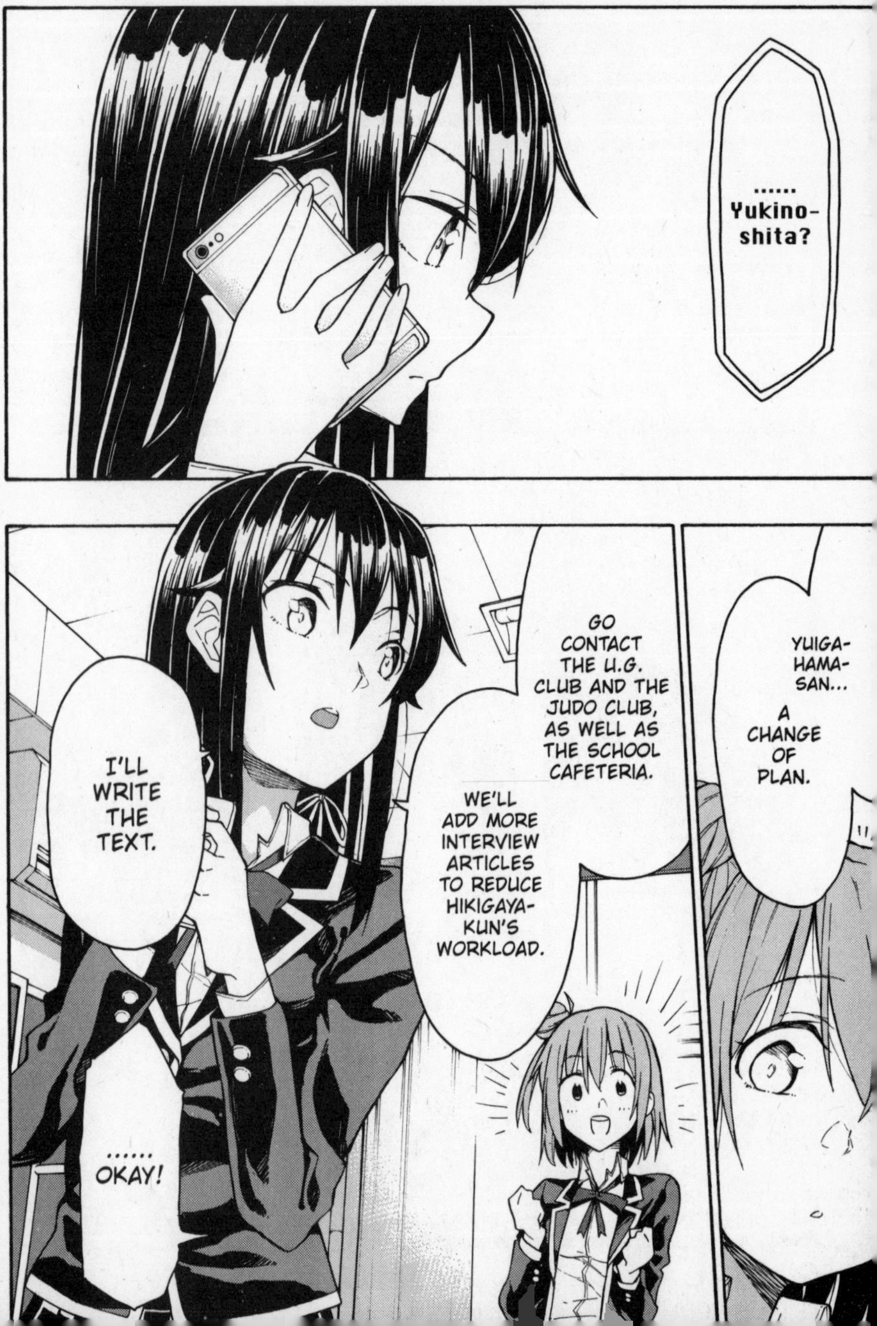
...... Yukino-shita?
YUIGA-HAMA-SAN... A CHANGE OF PLAN.
GO CONTACT THE U.G. CLUB AND THE JUDO CLUB, AS WELL AS THE SCHOOL CAFETERIA.
WE'LL ADD MORE INTERVIEW ARTICLES TO REDUCE HIKIGAYA-KUN'S WORKLOAD.
I'LL WRITE THE TEXT.
...... OKAY!

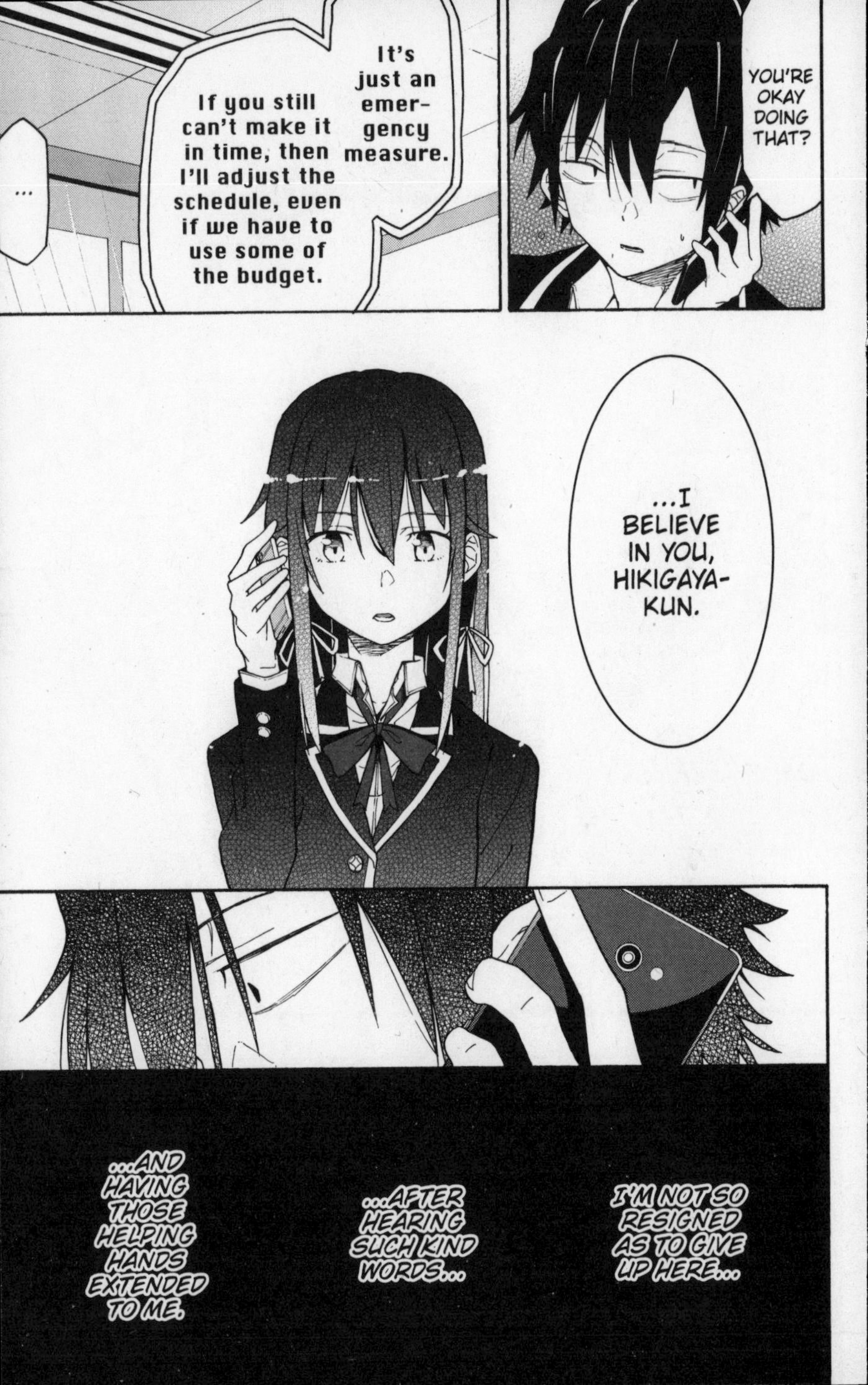
YOU'RE OKAY DOING THAT?
It's just an emergency measure.
If you still can't make it in time, then I'll adjust the schedule, even if we have to use some of the budget.
...
...I BELIEVE IN YOU, HIKIGAYA-KUN.
I'M NOT SO RESIGNED AS TO GIVE UP HERE...
...AFTER HEARING SUCH KIND WORDS...
...AND HAVING THOSE HELPING HANDS EXTENDED TO ME.

GYU
(TUG)

I'LL
FINISH
IT.

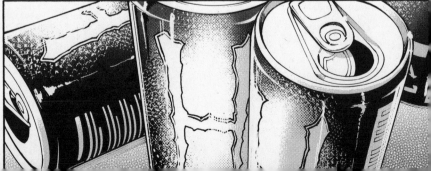

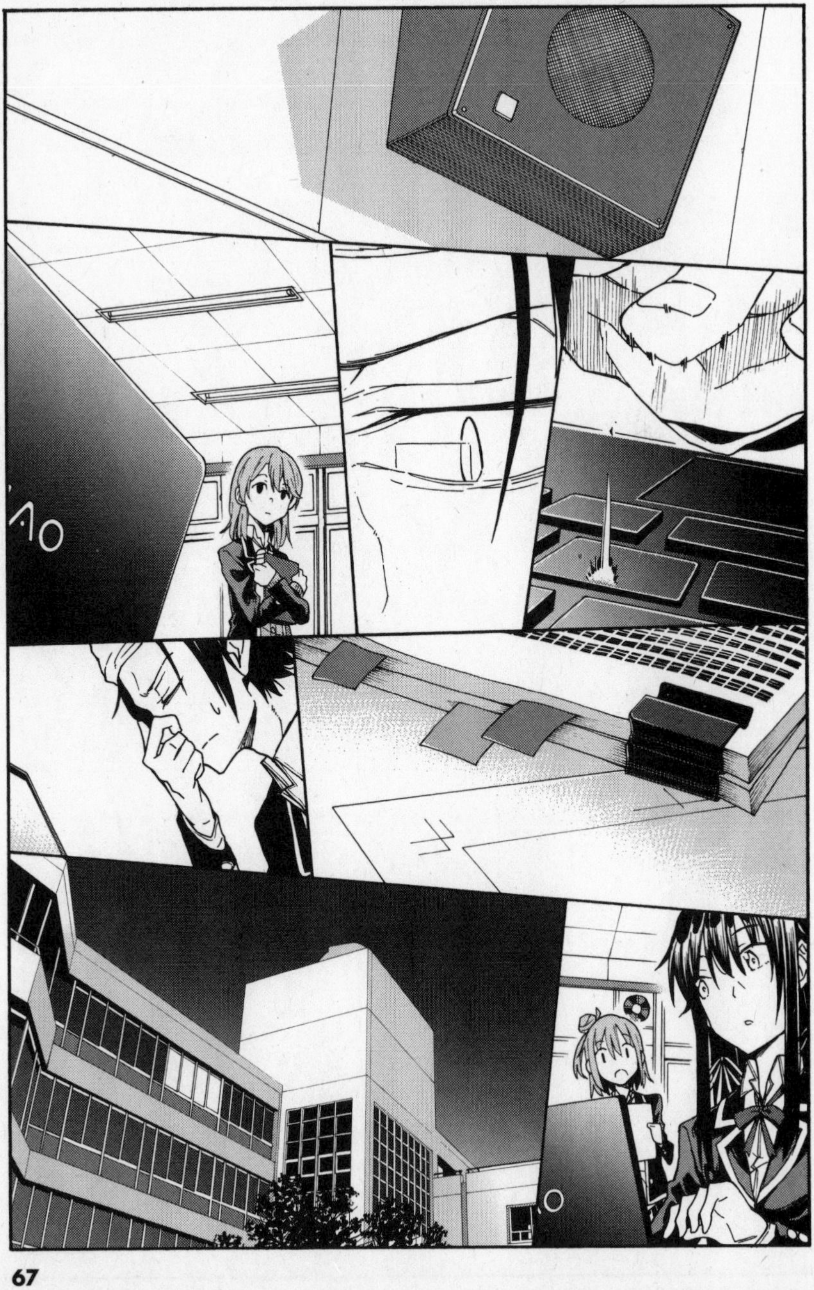

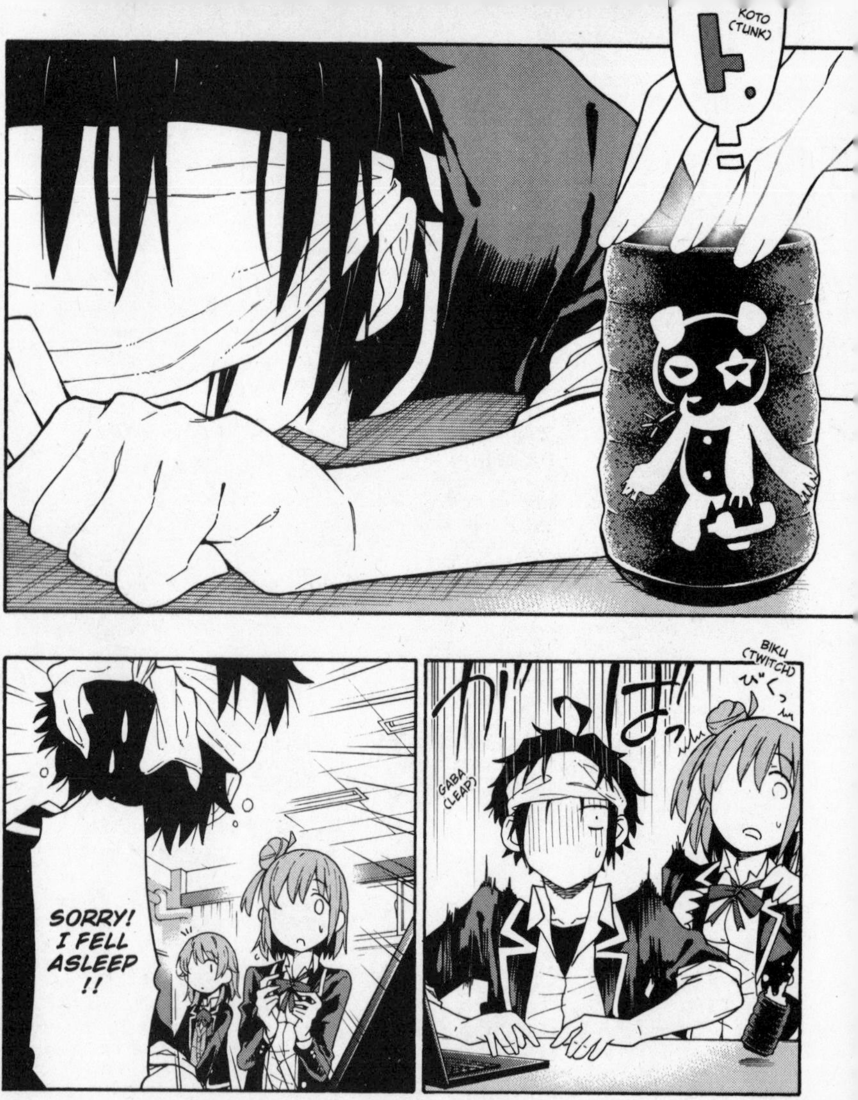
KOTO (TUNK)
BIKU (TWITCH)
びくっ
がばっ
GABA (LEAP)
SORRY! I FELL ASLEEP!!

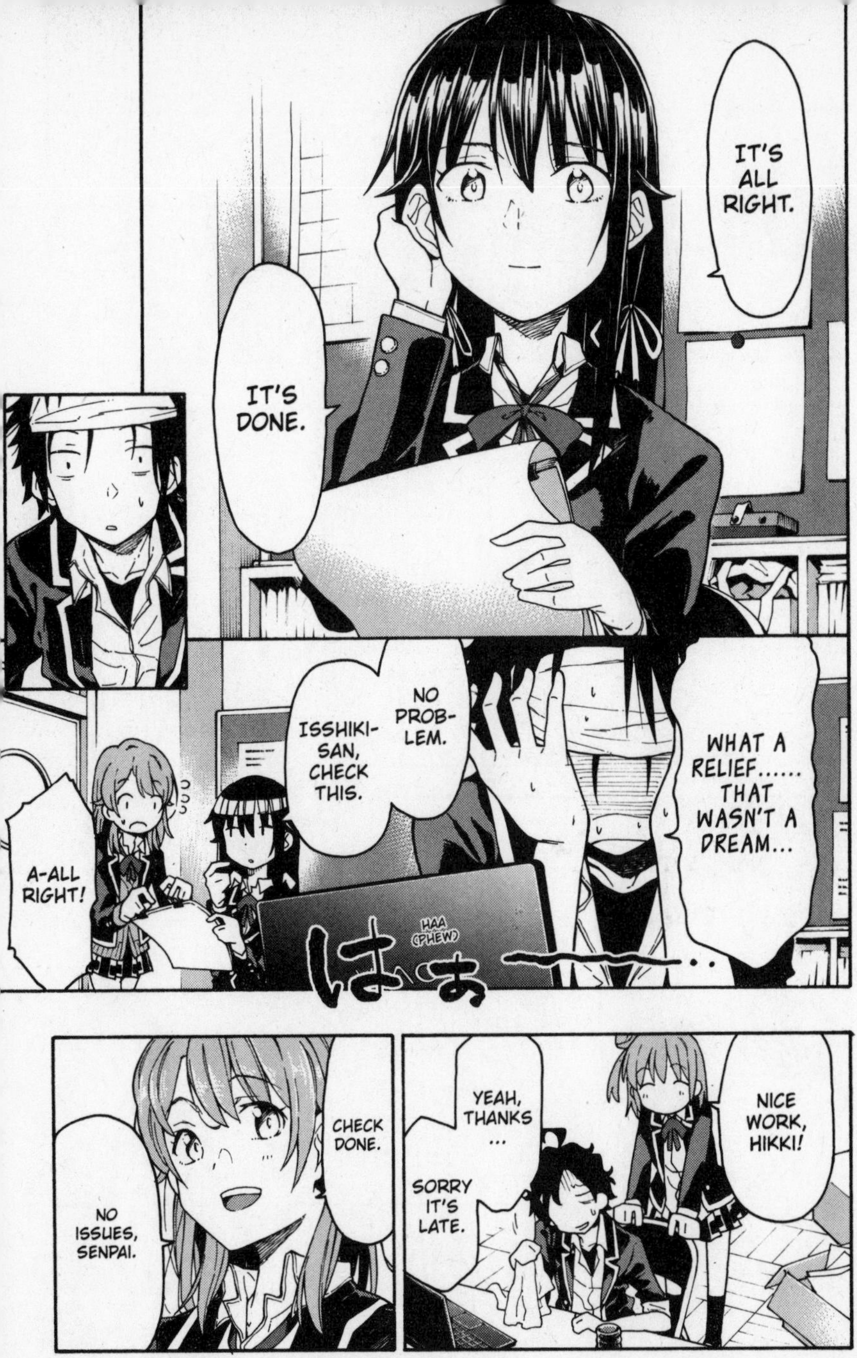
IT'S ALL RIGHT.
IT'S DONE.
WHAT A RELIEF...... THAT WASN'T A DREAM...
NO PROB-LEM.
ISSHIKI-SAN, CHECK THIS.
A-ALL RIGHT!
HAA (PHEW)
はぁ――――‥
NICE WORK, HIKKI!
YEAH, THANKS ...
SORRY IT'S LATE.
CHECK DONE.
NO ISSUES, SENPAI.

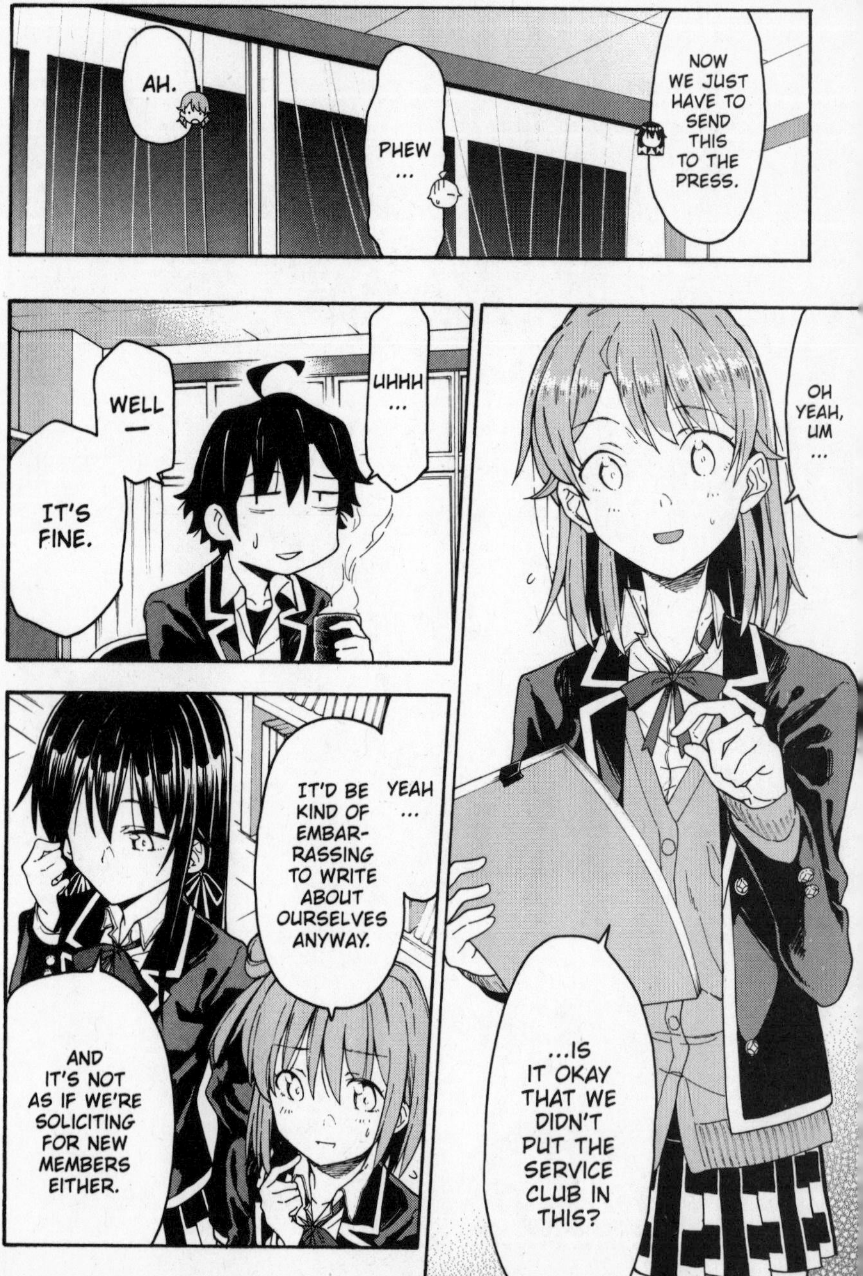
NOW WE JUST HAVE TO SEND THIS TO THE PRESS.
PHEW ...
AH.
OH YEAH, UM ...
...IS IT OKAY THAT WE DIDN'T PUT THE SERVICE CLUB IN THIS?
UHHH ...
WELL —
IT'S FINE.
YEAH ...
IT'D BE KIND OF EMBAR-RASSING TO WRITE ABOUT OURSELVES ANYWAY.
AND IT'S NOT AS IF WE'RE SOLICITING FOR NEW MEMBERS EITHER.

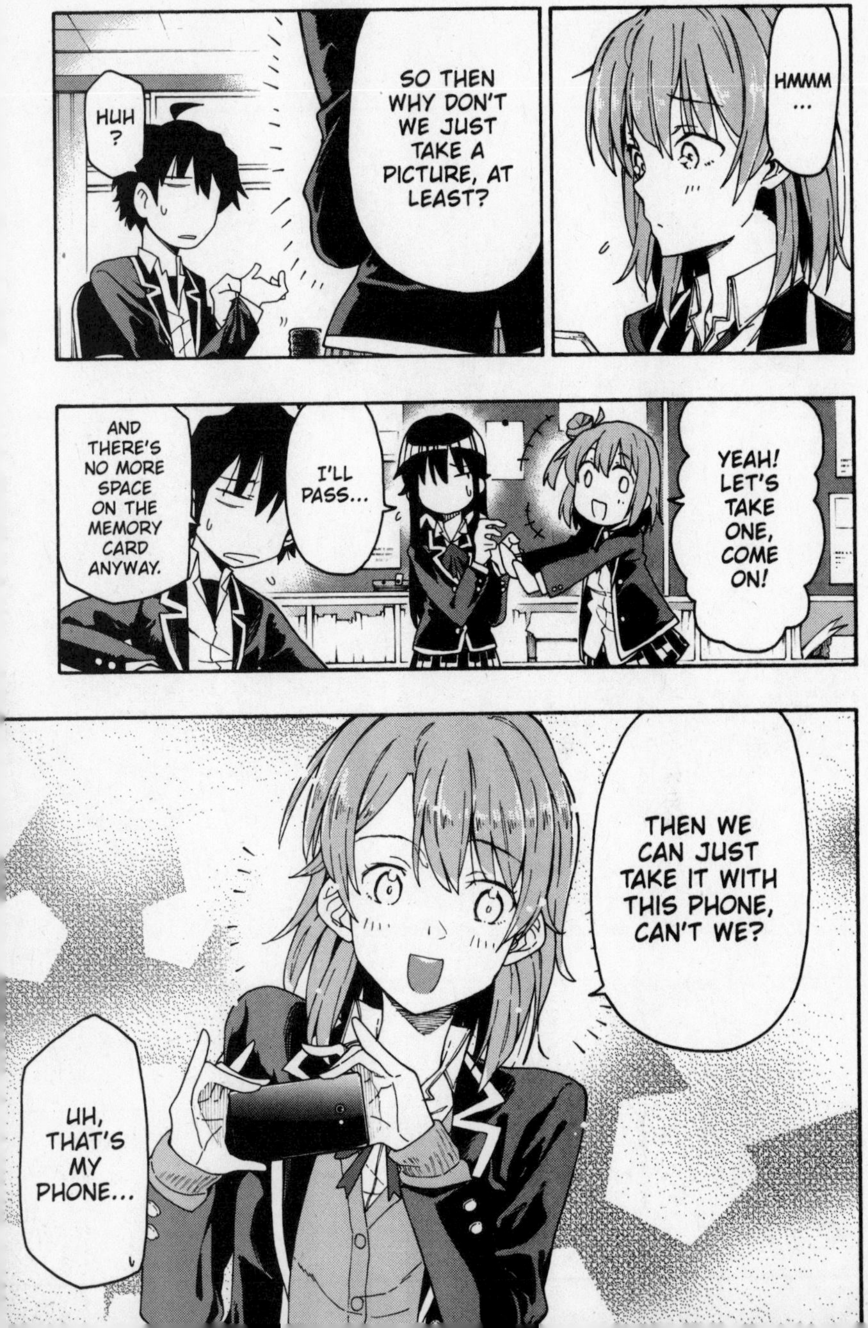
HMMM...
SO THEN WHY DON'T WE JUST TAKE A PICTURE, AT LEAST?
HUH?
YEAH! LET'S TAKE ONE, COME ON!
I'LL PASS...
AND THERE'S NO MORE SPACE ON THE MEMORY CARD ANYWAY.
THEN WE CAN JUST TAKE IT WITH THIS PHONE, CAN'T WE?
UH, THAT'S MY PHONE...

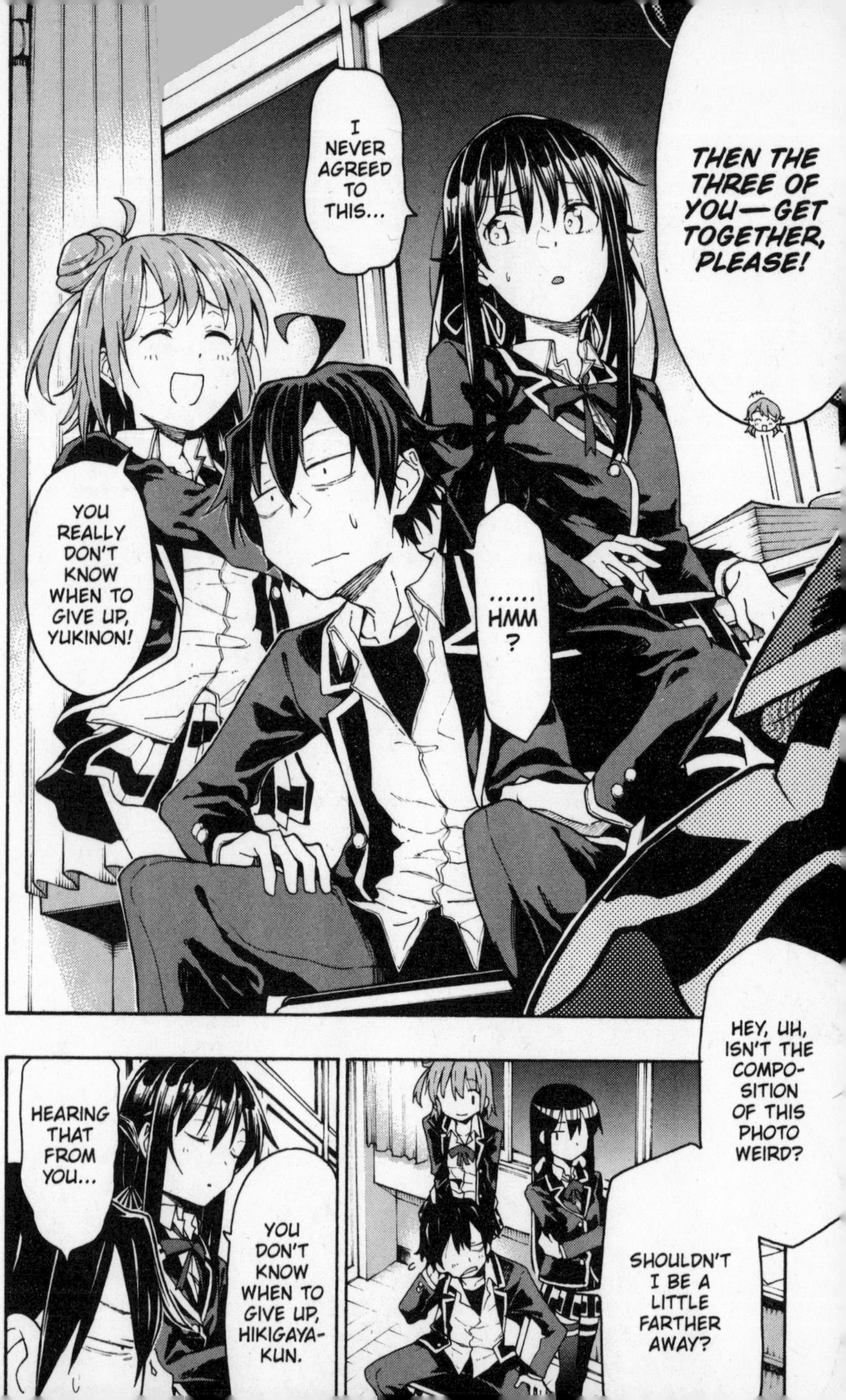
THEN THE THREE OF YOU—GET TOGETHER, PLEASE!
I NEVER AGREED TO THIS...
......HMM?
YOU REALLY DON'T KNOW WHEN TO GIVE UP, YUKINON!
HEY, UH, ISN'T THE COMPOSITION OF THIS PHOTO WEIRD?
SHOULDN'T I BE A LITTLE FARTHER AWAY?
HEARING THAT FROM YOU...
YOU DON'T KNOW WHEN TO GIVE UP, HIKIGAYA-KUN.

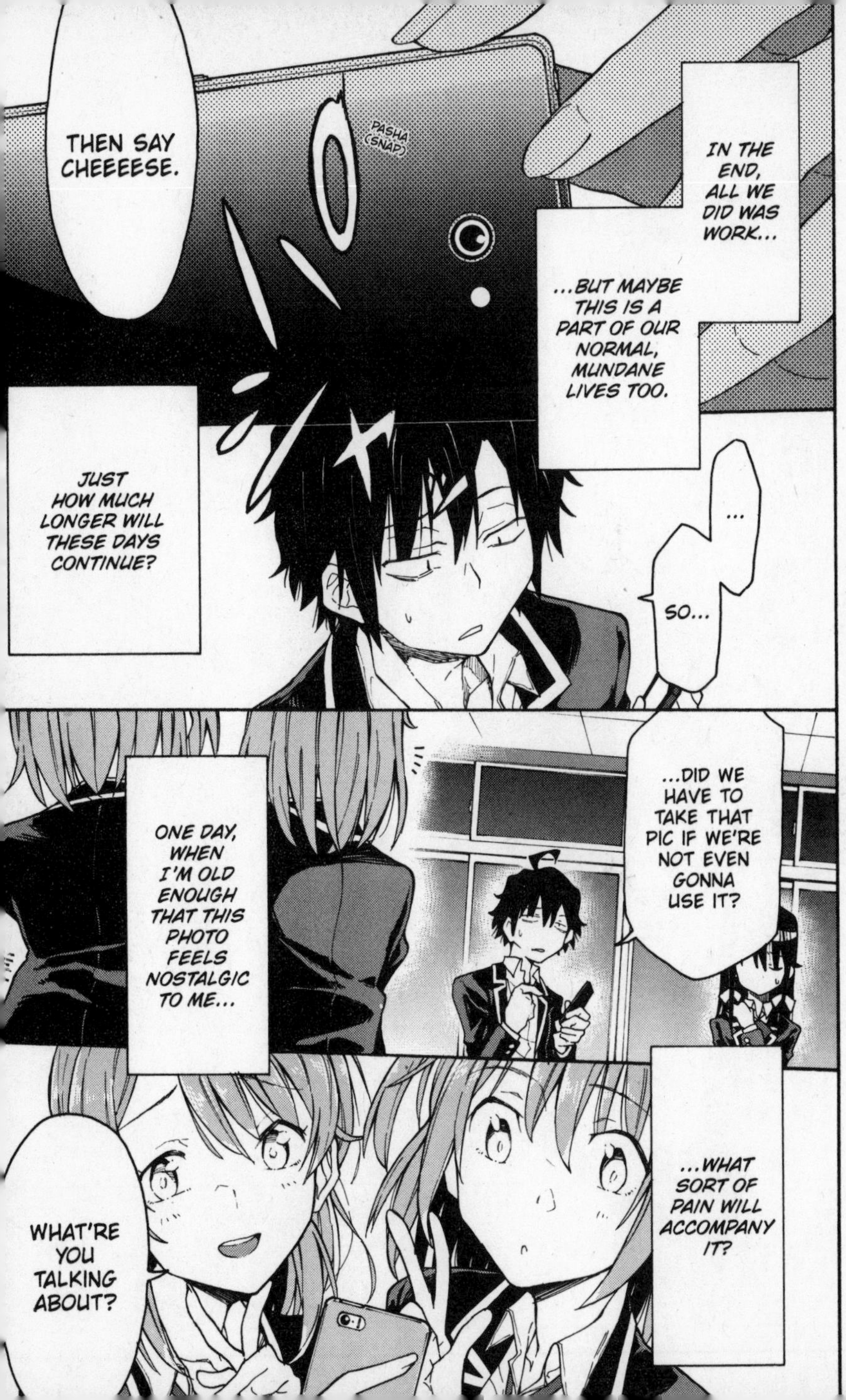
IN THE END, ALL WE DID WAS WORK...
THEN SAY CHEEEESE.
PASHA (SNAP)
...BUT MAYBE THIS IS A PART OF OUR NORMAL, MUNDANE LIVES TOO.
...
SO...
JUST HOW MUCH LONGER WILL THESE DAYS CONTINUE?
...DID WE HAVE TO TAKE THAT PIC IF WE'RE NOT EVEN GONNA USE IT?
ONE DAY, WHEN I'M OLD ENOUGH THAT THIS PHOTO FEELS NOSTALGIC TO ME...
...WHAT SORT OF PAIN WILL ACCOMPANY IT?
WHAT'RE YOU TALKING ABOUT?

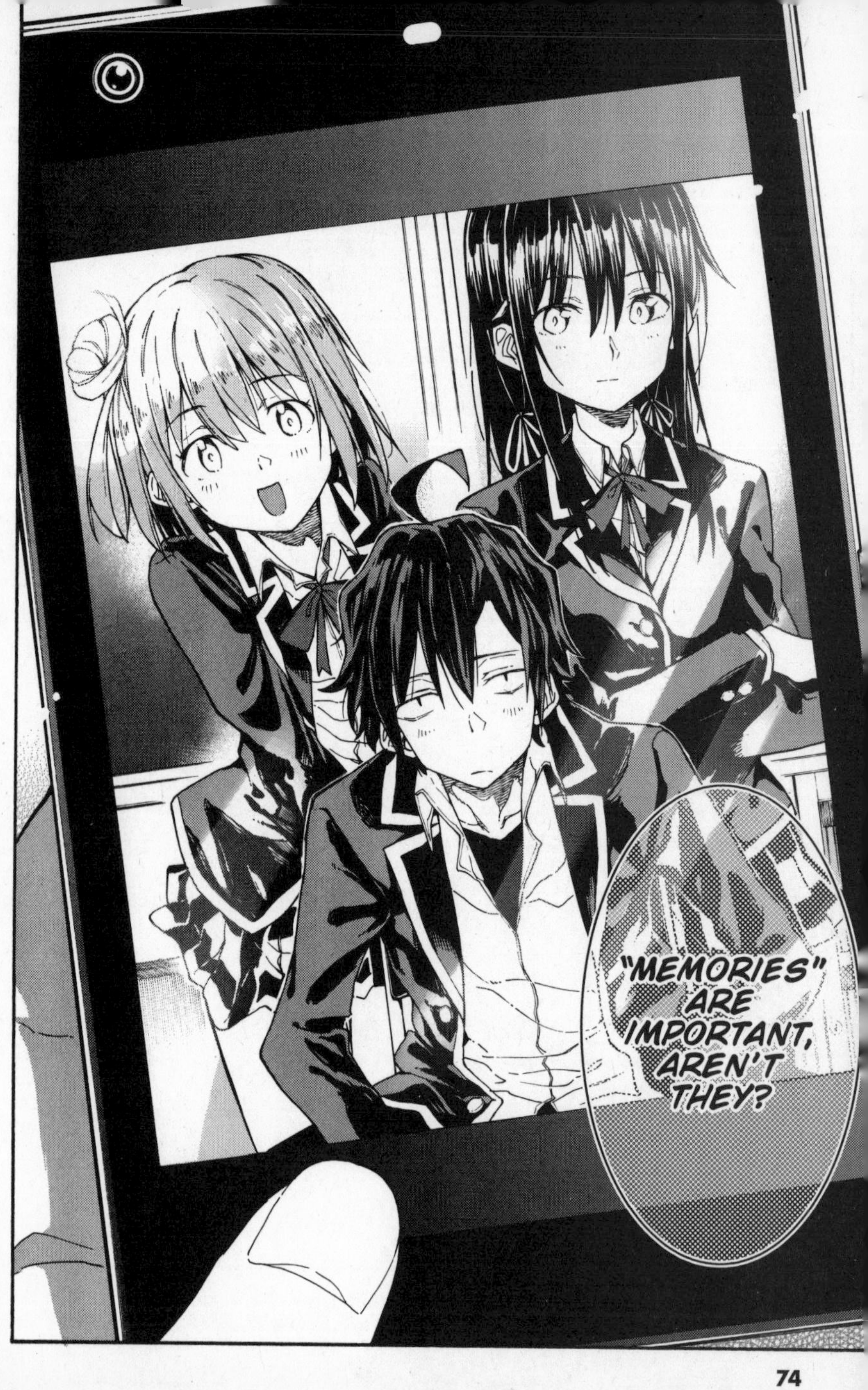
"MEMORIES" ARE IMPORTANT, AREN'T THEY?

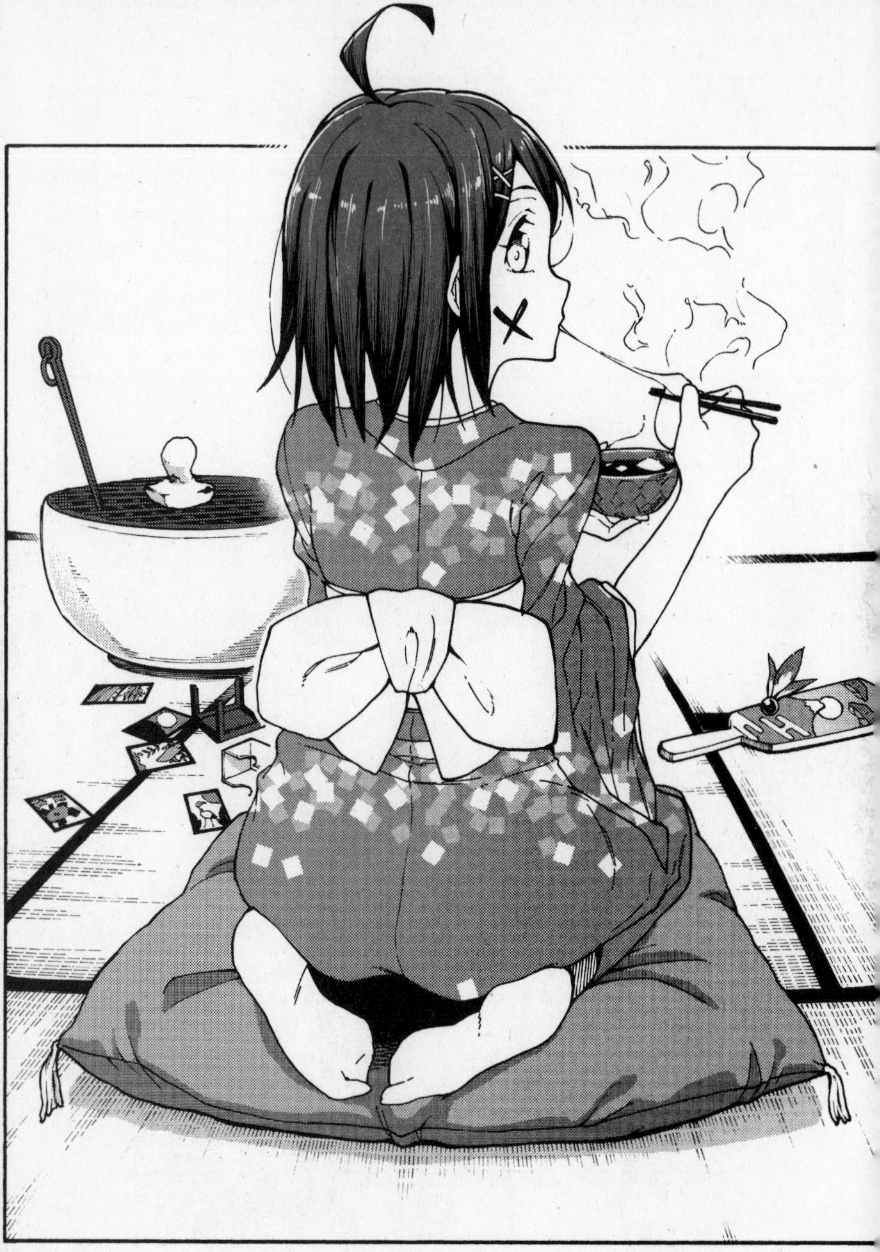

CHAPTER 73 ··· IN THE END, KOMACHI HIKIGAYA LOOKS FOR DIVINE HELP.

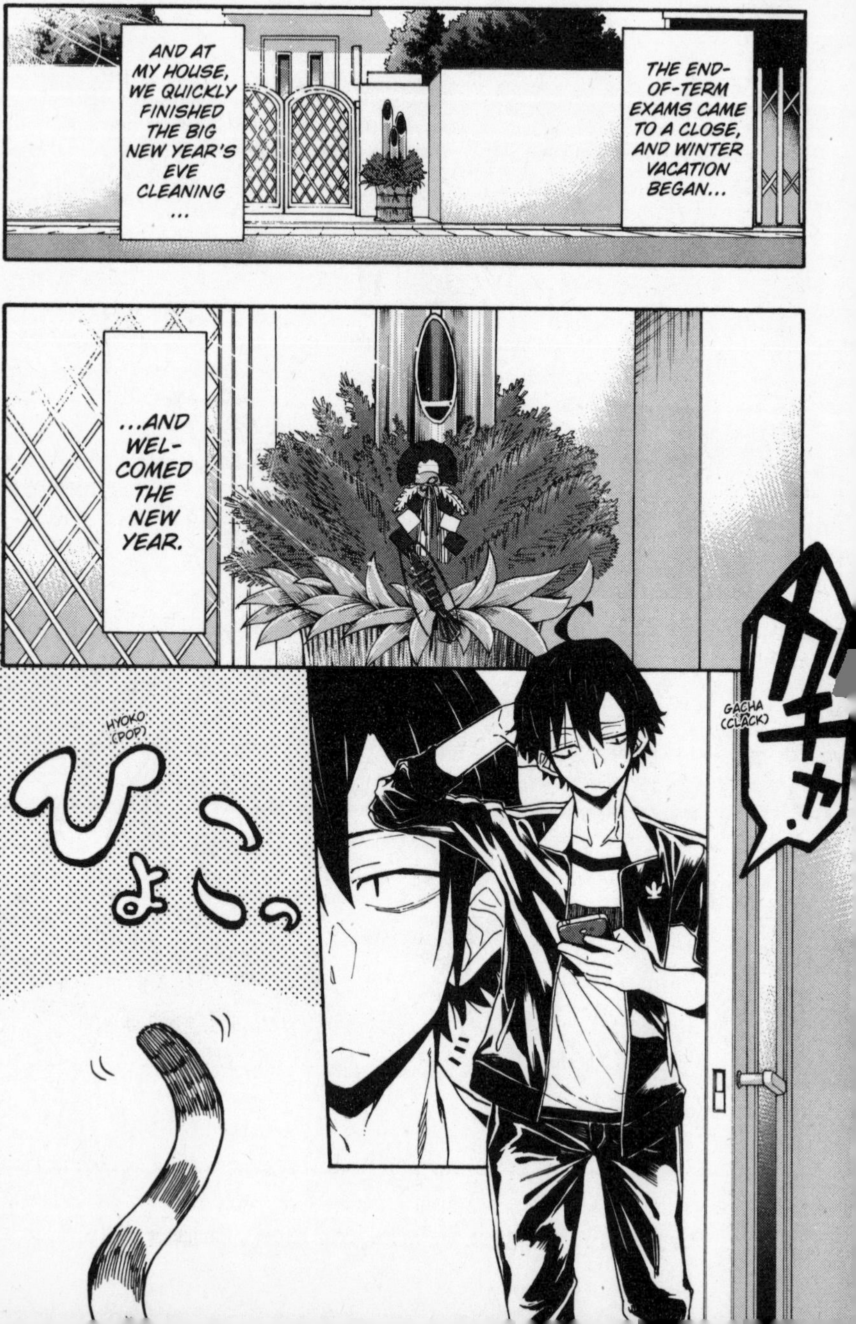
THE END-OF-TERM EXAMS CAME TO A CLOSE, AND WINTER VACATION BEGAN...
AND AT MY HOUSE, WE QUICKLY FINISHED THE BIG NEW YEAR'S EVE CLEANING...
...AND WELCOMED THE NEW YEAR.
GACHA (CLACK)
HYOKO (POP)
ひょこっ

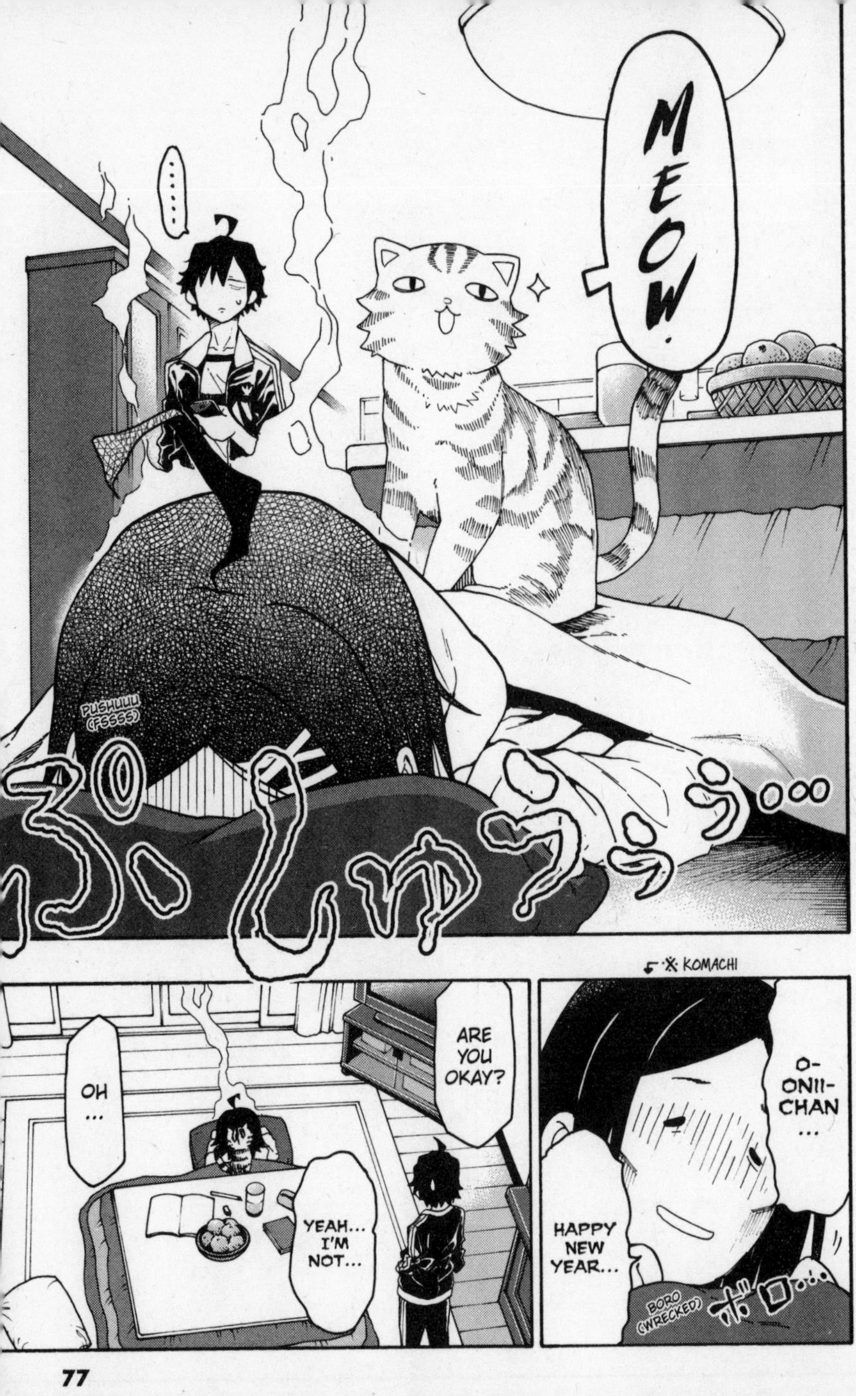
MEOW!
……
PUSHUUU (FSSSS)
ぷしゅぅぅ…
※KOMACHI
O-ONII-CHAN…
HAPPY NEW YEAR…
BORO (WRECKED)
ボロ…
ARE YOU OKAY?
OH…
YEAH… I'M NOT…

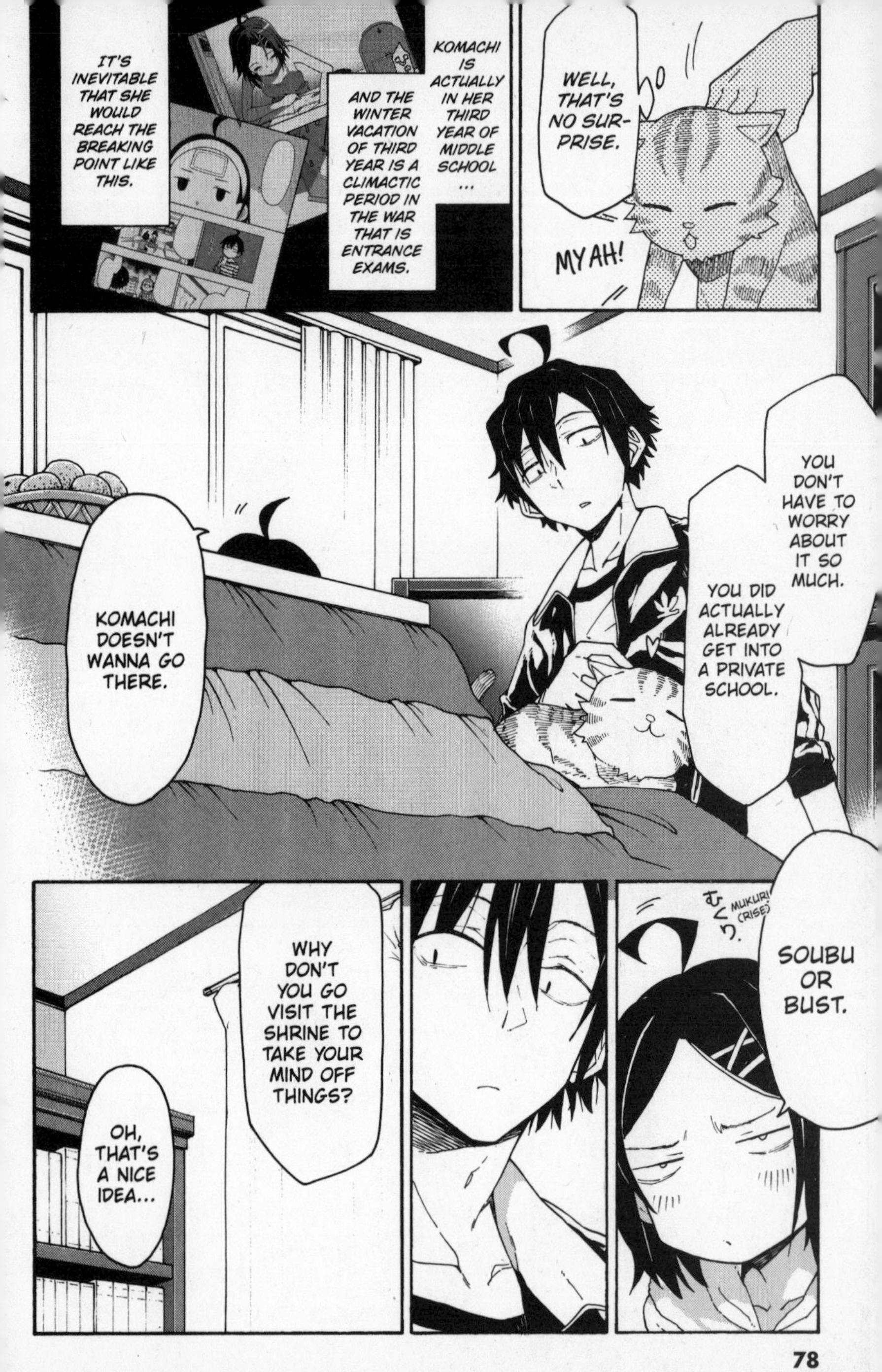
WELL, THAT'S NO SURPRISE.
MYAH!
KOMACHI IS ACTUALLY IN HER THIRD YEAR OF MIDDLE SCHOOL ...
AND THE WINTER VACATION OF THIRD YEAR IS A CLIMACTIC PERIOD IN THE WAR THAT IS ENTRANCE EXAMS.
IT'S INEVITABLE THAT SHE WOULD REACH THE BREAKING POINT LIKE THIS.
YOU DON'T HAVE TO WORRY ABOUT IT SO MUCH.
YOU DID ACTUALLY ALREADY GET INTO A PRIVATE SCHOOL.
KOMACHI DOESN'T WANNA GO THERE.
MUKURI! (RISE)
SOUBU OR BUST.
WHY DON'T YOU GO VISIT THE SHRINE TO TAKE YOUR MIND OFF THINGS?
OH, THAT'S A NICE IDEA...

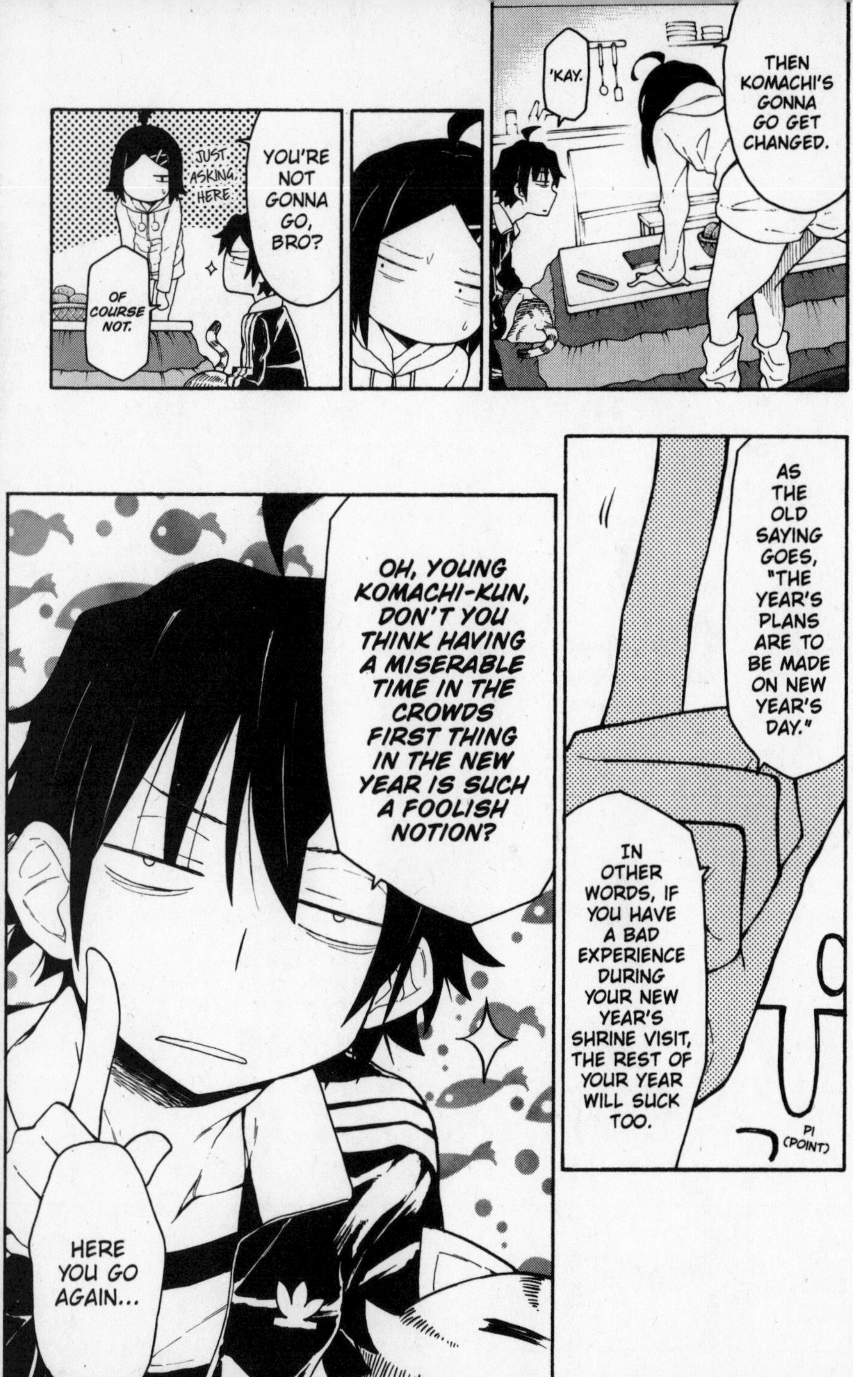
THEN KOMACHI'S GONNA GO GET CHANGED.
'KAY.
YOU'RE NOT GONNA GO, BRO?
JUST ASKING HERE
OF COURSE NOT.
AS THE OLD SAYING GOES, "THE YEAR'S PLANS ARE TO BE MADE ON NEW YEAR'S DAY."
IN OTHER WORDS, IF YOU HAVE A BAD EXPERIENCE DURING YOUR NEW YEAR'S SHRINE VISIT, THE REST OF YOUR YEAR WILL SUCK TOO.
PI (POINT)
OH, YOUNG KOMACHI-KUN, DON'T YOU THINK HAVING A MISERABLE TIME IN THE CROWDS FIRST THING IN THE NEW YEAR IS SUCH A FOOLISH NOTION?
HERE YOU GO AGAIN...

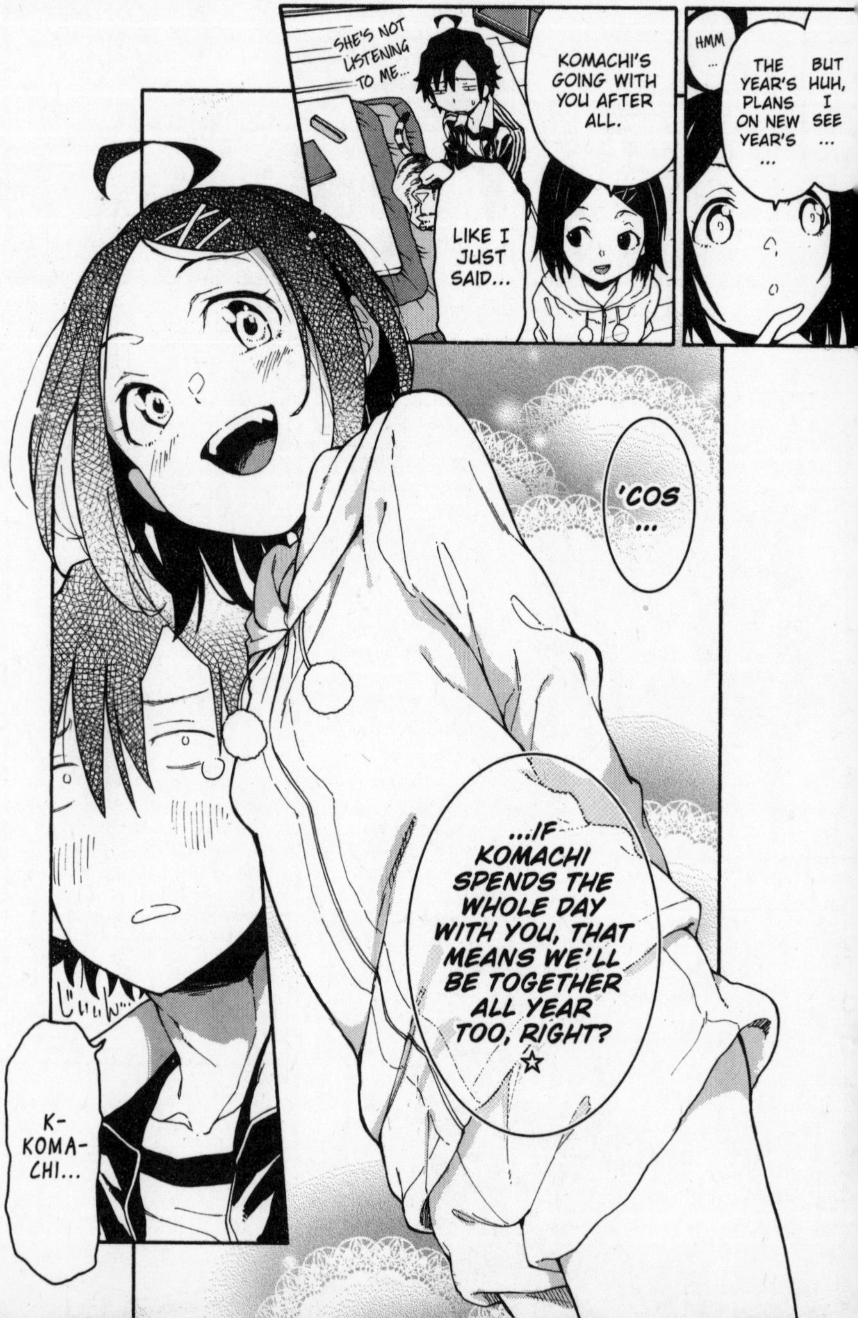
HMM ...
BUT HUH, I SEE ... THE YEAR'S PLANS ON NEW YEAR'S ...
KOMACHI'S GOING WITH YOU AFTER ALL.
SHE'S NOT LISTENING TO ME...
LIKE I JUST SAID...
'COS ...
...IF KOMACHI SPENDS THE WHOLE DAY WITH YOU, THAT MEANS WE'LL BE TOGETHER ALL YEAR TOO, RIGHT? ☆
K-KOMA-CHI...

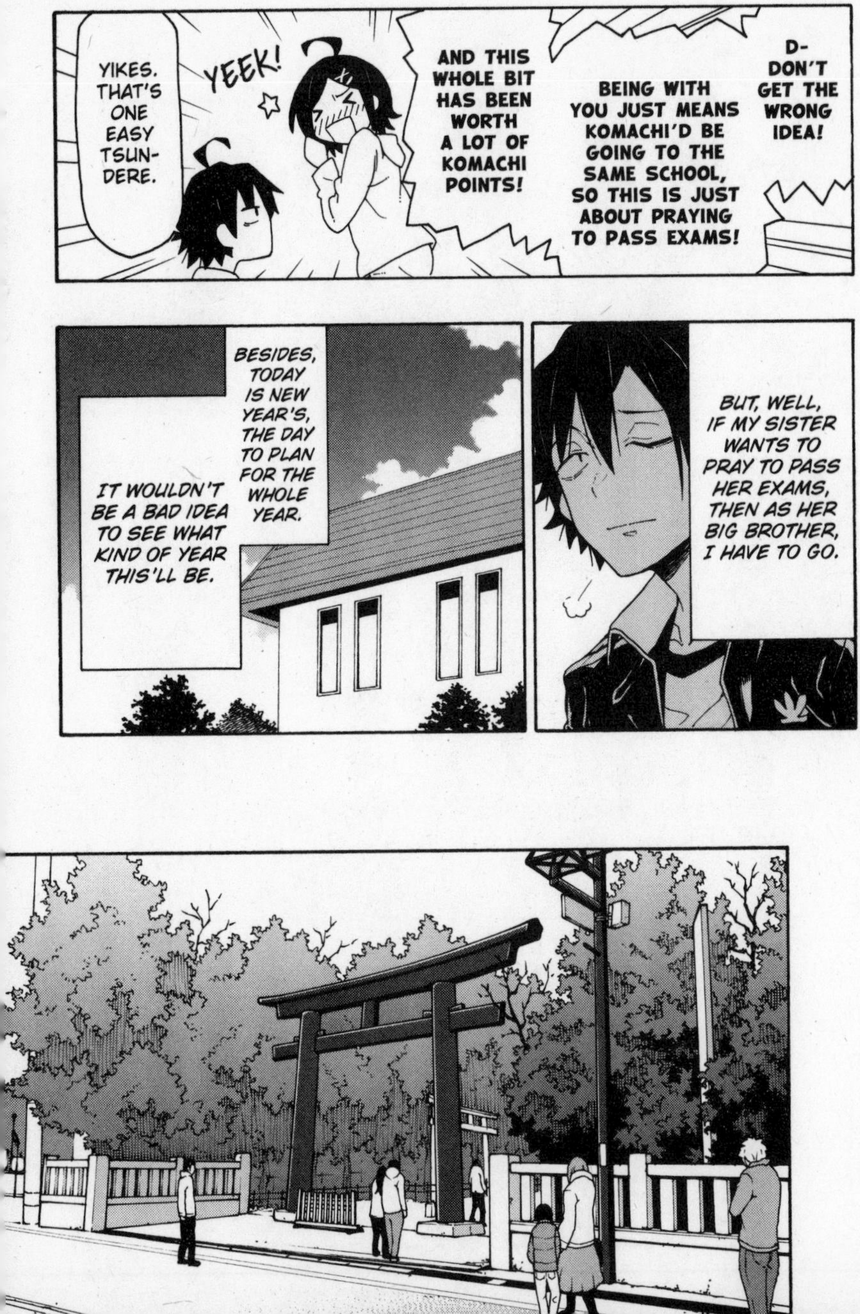
D- DON'T GET THE WRONG IDEA!
BEING WITH YOU JUST MEANS KOMACHI'D BE GOING TO THE SAME SCHOOL, SO THIS IS JUST ABOUT PRAYING TO PASS EXAMS!
AND THIS WHOLE BIT HAS BEEN WORTH A LOT OF KOMACHI POINTS!
YEEK!
YIKES. THAT'S ONE EASY TSUN-DERE.
BUT, WELL, IF MY SISTER WANTS TO PRAY TO PASS HER EXAMS, THEN AS HER BIG BROTHER, I HAVE TO GO.
BESIDES, TODAY IS NEW YEAR'S, THE DAY TO PLAN FOR THE WHOLE YEAR.
IT WOULDN'T BE A BAD IDEA TO SEE WHAT KIND OF YEAR THIS'LL BE.

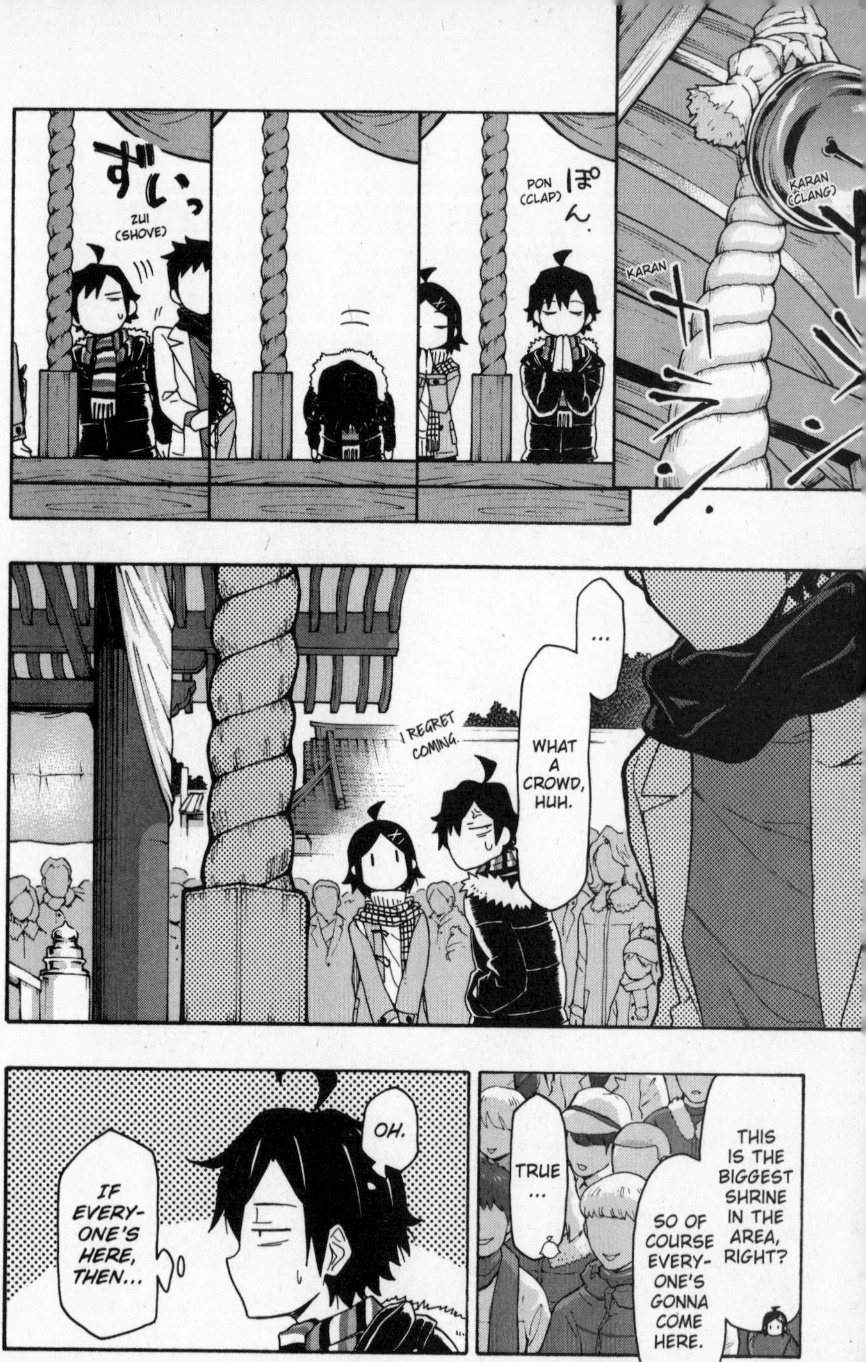
KARAN (CLANG)
KARAN
PON (CLAP)
ぽん。
ずいっ
ZUI (SHOVE)
...
WHAT A CROWD, HUH.
I REGRET COMING.
THIS IS THE BIGGEST SHRINE IN THE AREA, RIGHT?
SO OF COURSE EVERYONE'S GONNA COME HERE.
TRUE...
OH.
IF EVERYONE'S HERE, THEN...

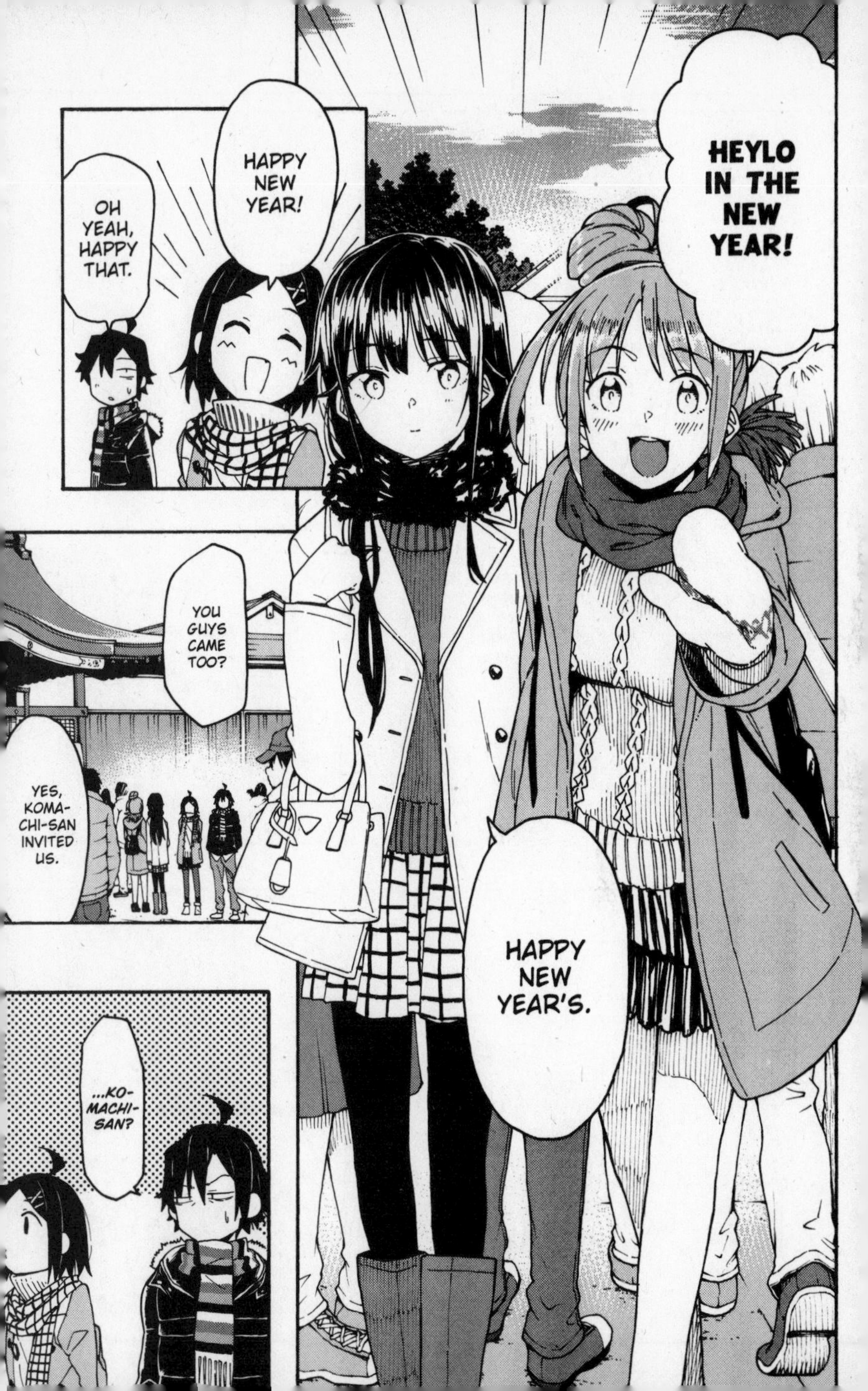
HEYLO IN THE NEW YEAR!
HAPPY NEW YEAR'S.
HAPPY NEW YEAR!
OH YEAH, HAPPY THAT.
YOU GUYS CAME TOO?
YES, KOMA-CHI-SAN INVITED US.
...KO-MACHI-SAN?

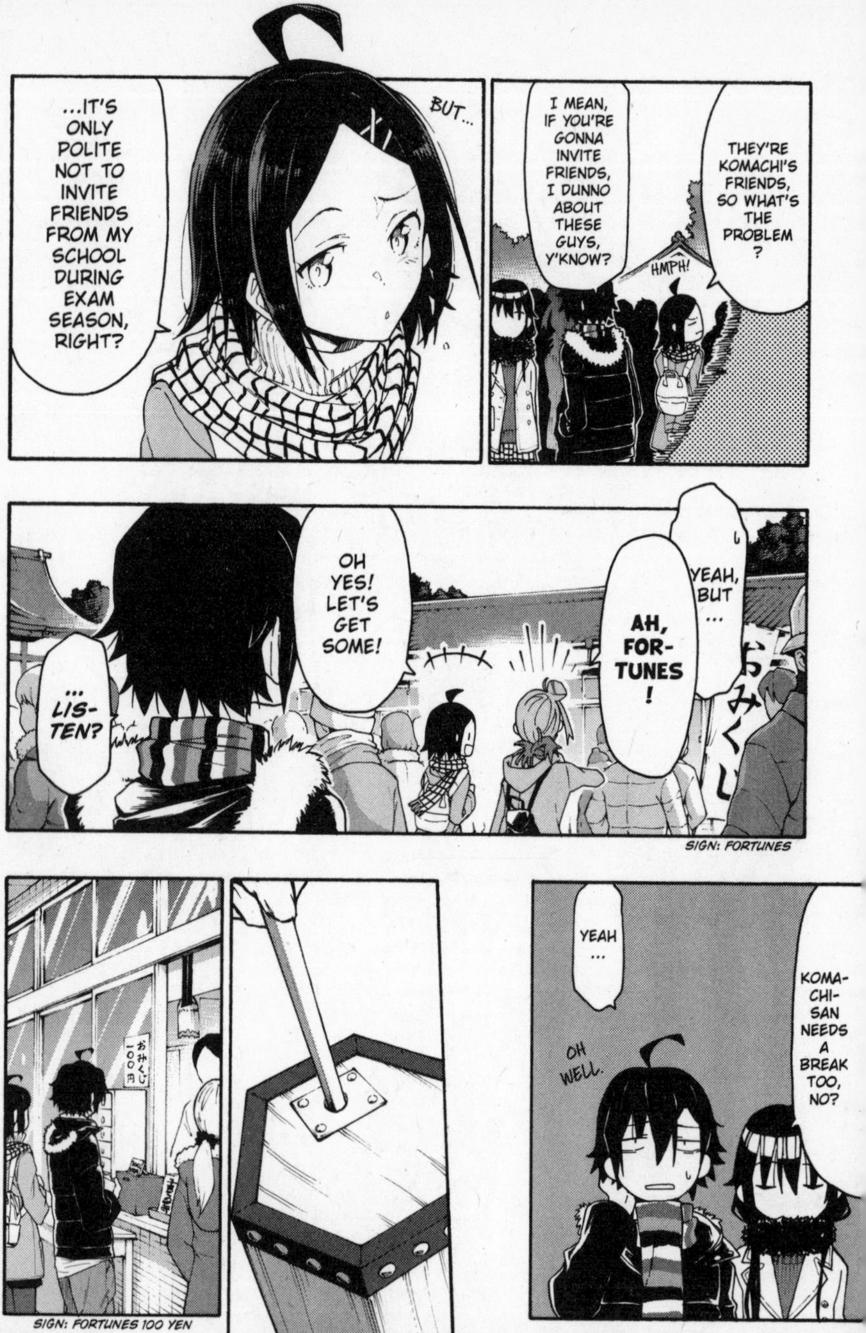
THEY'RE KOMACHI'S FRIENDS, SO WHAT'S THE PROBLEM?
I MEAN, IF YOU'RE GONNA INVITE FRIENDS, I DUNNO ABOUT THESE GUYS, Y'KNOW?
HMPH!
BUT...
...IT'S ONLY POLITE NOT TO INVITE FRIENDS FROM MY SCHOOL DURING EXAM SEASON, RIGHT?
YEAH, BUT ...
AH, FOR-TUNES!
おみくじ
OH YES! LET'S GET SOME!
... LIS-TEN?
SIGN: FORTUNES
KOMA-CHI-SAN NEEDS A BREAK TOO, NO?
YEAH ...
OH WELL.
おみくじ 100円
SIGN: FORTUNES 100 YEN

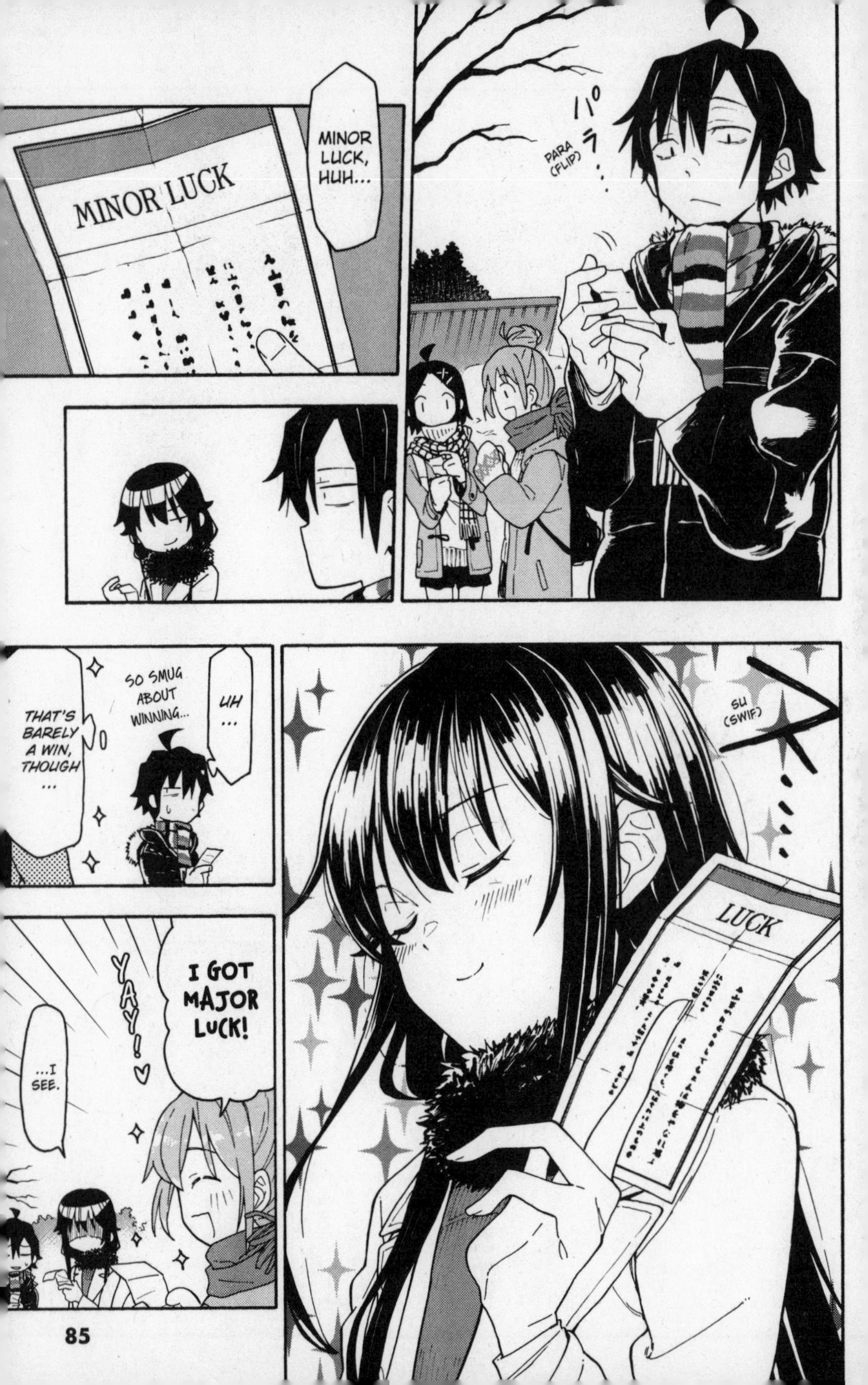
PARA (FLIP)
MINOR LUCK, HUH...
MINOR LUCK
SU (SWIF)
LUCK
UH ...
SO SMUG ABOUT WINNING...
THAT'S BARELY A WIN, THOUGH ...
I GOT MAJOR LUCK!
YAY! ♥
...I SEE.

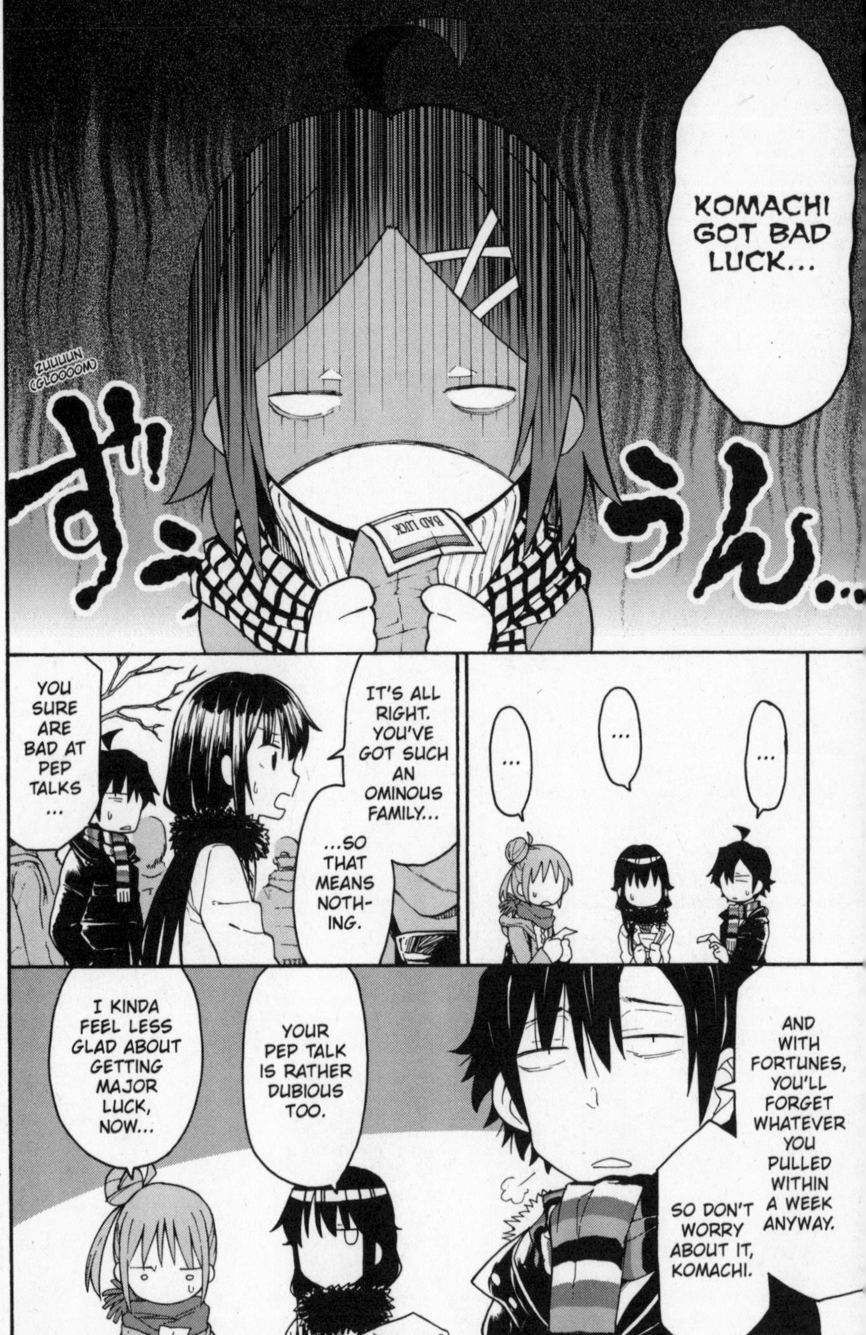
KOMACHI GOT BAD LUCK...
ZUUUUN (GLOOOOM)
ずーうん…
BAD LUCK
...
...
...
IT'S ALL RIGHT. YOU'VE GOT SUCH AN OMINOUS FAMILY...
...SO THAT MEANS NOTHING.
YOU SURE ARE BAD AT PEP TALKS...
AND WITH FORTUNES, YOU'LL FORGET WHATEVER YOU PULLED WITHIN A WEEK ANYWAY.
SO DON'T WORRY ABOUT IT, KOMACHI.
YOUR PEP TALK IS RATHER DUBIOUS TOO.
I KINDA FEEL LESS GLAD ABOUT GETTING MAJOR LUCK, NOW...

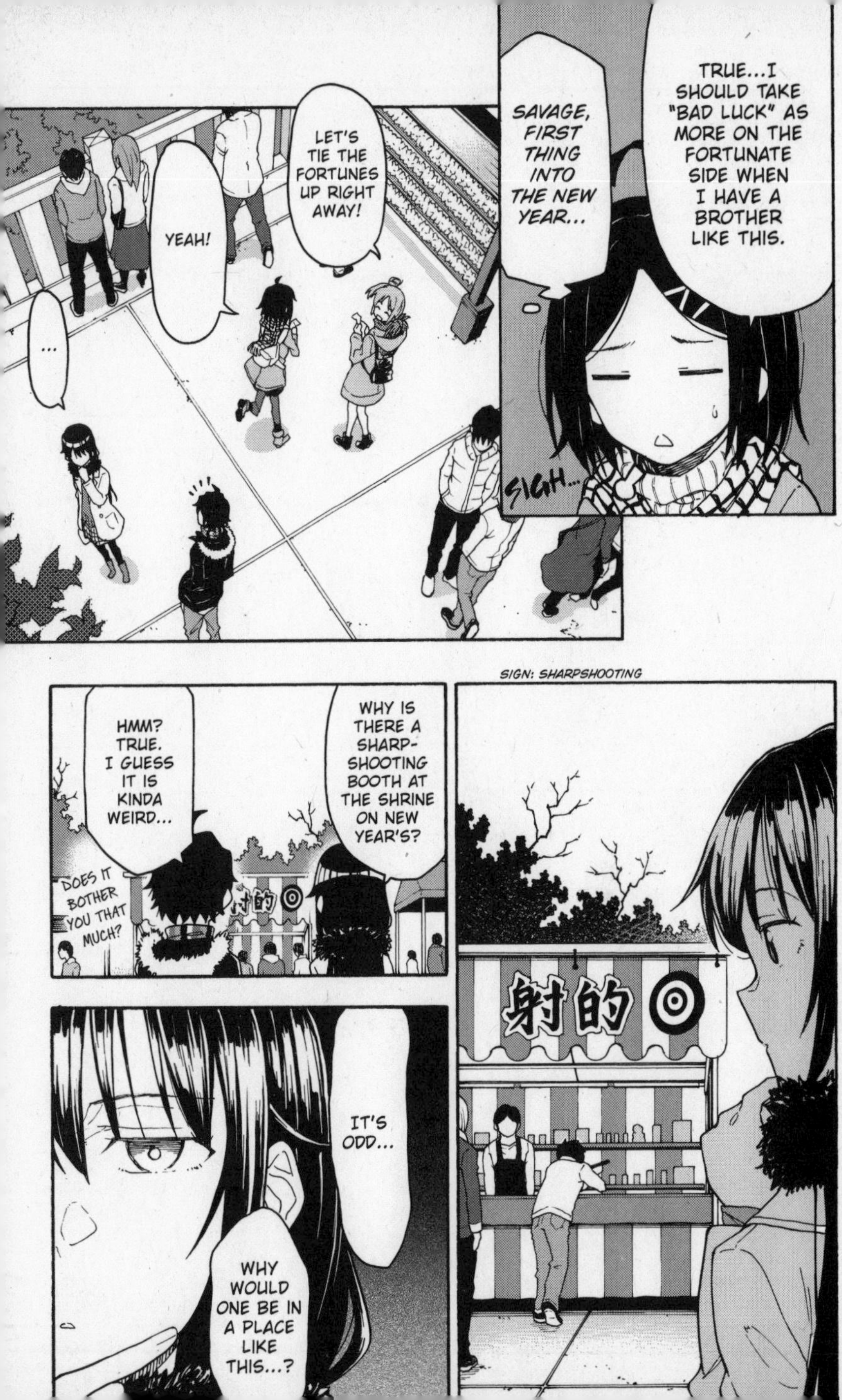
TRUE...I SHOULD TAKE "BAD LUCK" AS MORE ON THE FORTUNATE SIDE WHEN I HAVE A BROTHER LIKE THIS.
SAVAGE, FIRST THING INTO THE NEW YEAR...
SIGH...
LET'S TIE THE FORTUNES UP RIGHT AWAY!
YEAH!
...
SIGN: SHARPSHOOTING
射的
WHY IS THERE A SHARP-SHOOTING BOOTH AT THE SHRINE ON NEW YEAR'S?
HMM? TRUE. I GUESS IT IS KINDA WEIRD...
DOES IT BOTHER YOU THAT MUCH?
IT'S ODD...
WHY WOULD ONE BE IN A PLACE LIKE THIS...?

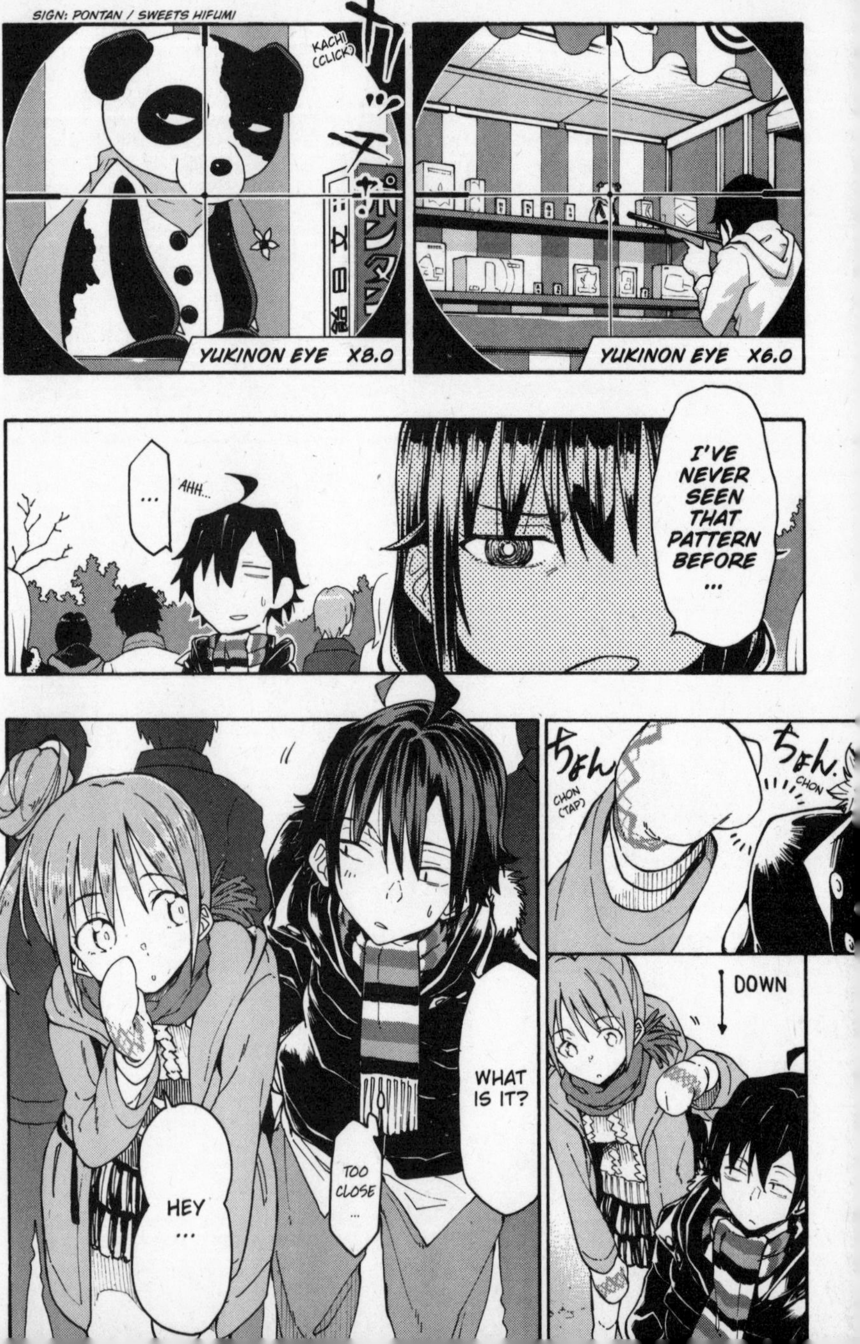

YUKINON EYE X6.0
SIGN: PONTAN / SWEETS HIFUMI
KACHI (CLICK)
YUKINON EYE X8.0
I'VE NEVER SEEN THAT PATTERN BEFORE...
...
AHH...
CHON
CHON (TAP)
DOWN
WHAT IS IT?
TOO CLOSE...
HEY...

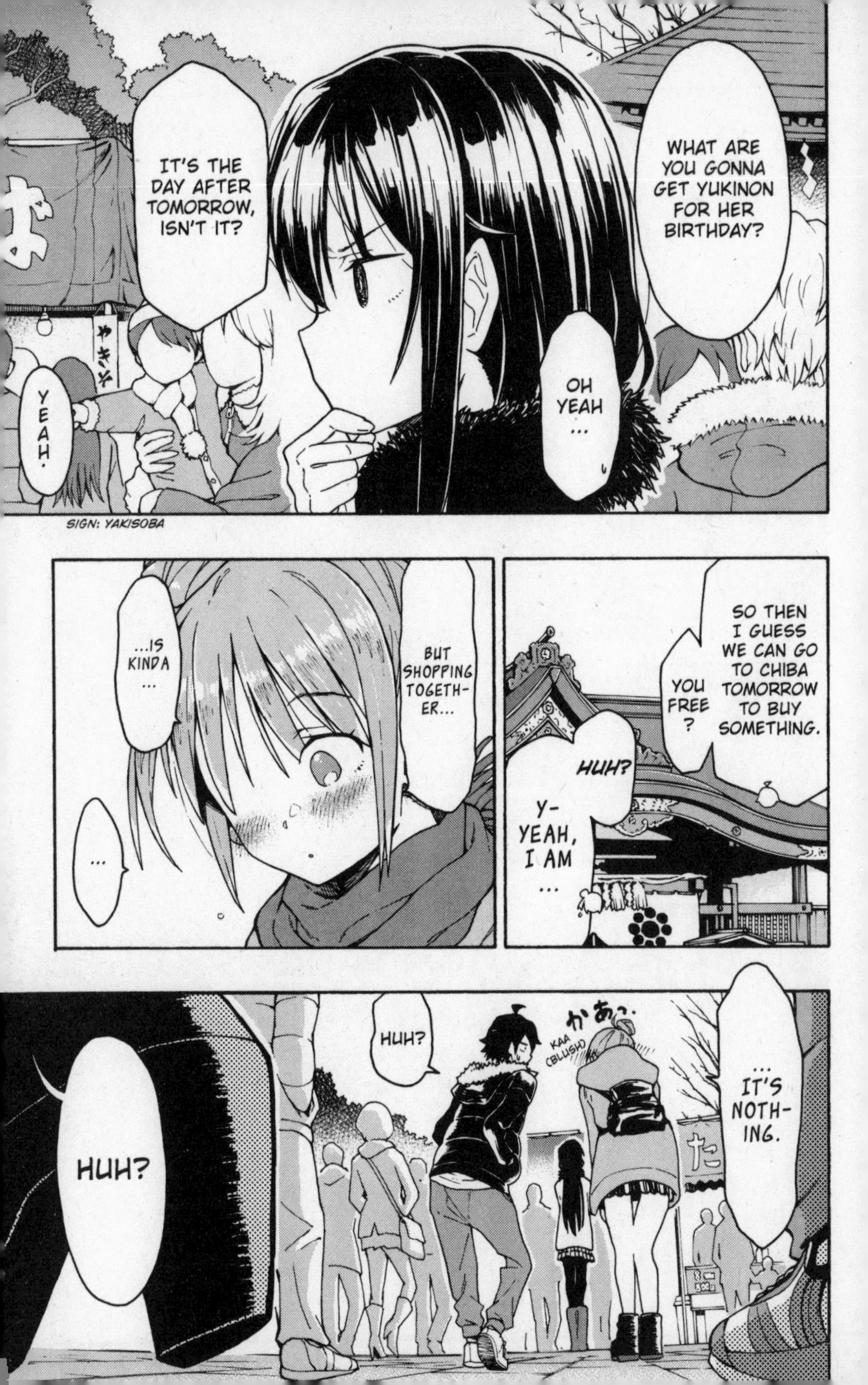
WHAT ARE YOU GONNA GET YUKINON FOR HER BIRTHDAY?
OH YEAH ...
IT'S THE DAY AFTER TOMORROW, ISN'T IT?
YEAH.
SIGN: YAKISOBA
SO THEN I GUESS WE CAN GO TO CHIBA TOMORROW TO BUY SOMETHING.
YOU FREE?
HUH?
Y-YEAH, I AM ...
BUT SHOPPING TOGETHER...
...IS KINDA ...
...
... IT'S NOTHING.
かあっ
KAA (BLUSH)
HUH?
HUH?

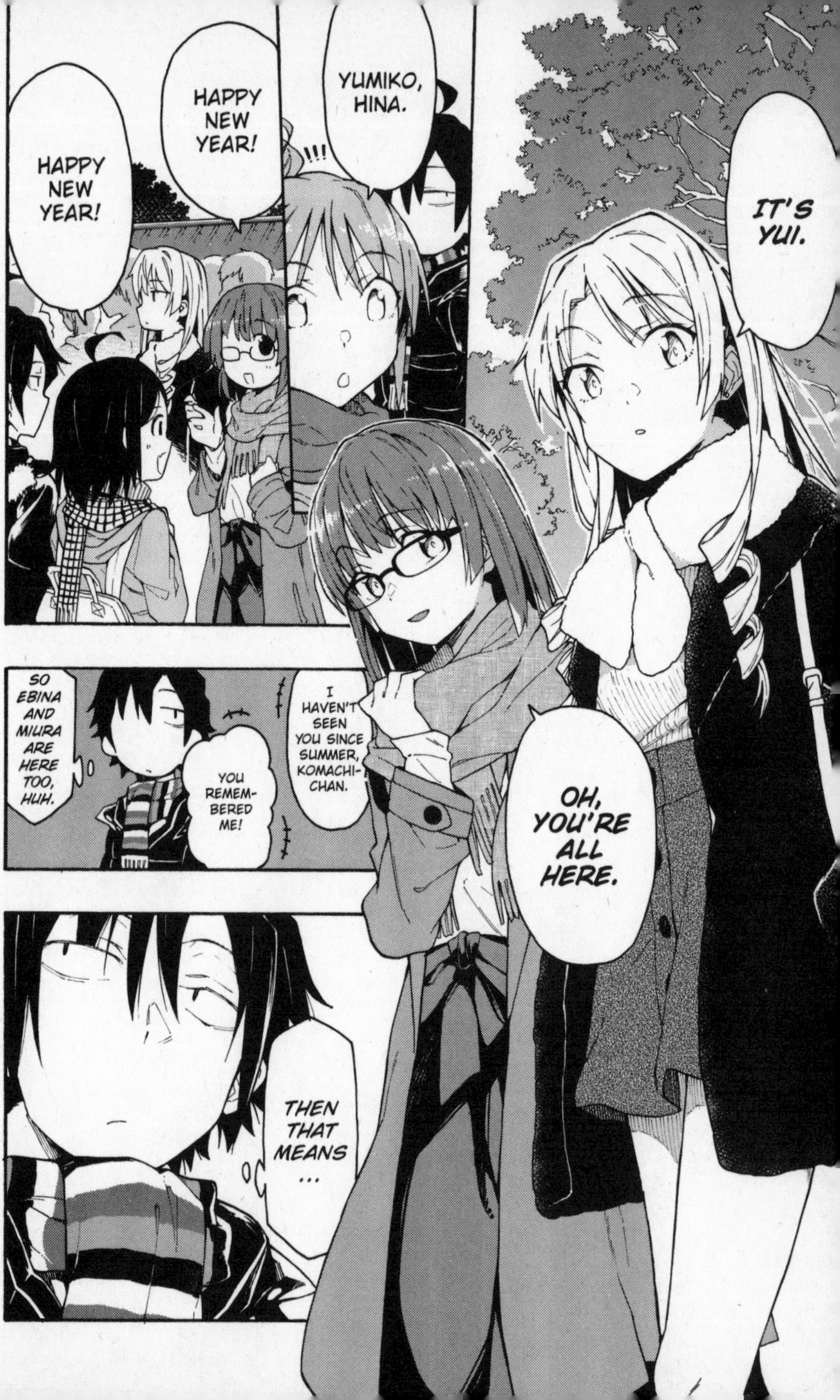
IT'S YUI.
OH, YOU'RE ALL HERE.
YUMIKO, HINA.
!!!
HAPPY NEW YEAR!
HAPPY NEW YEAR!
I HAVEN'T SEEN YOU SINCE SUMMER, KOMACHI-CHAN.
YOU REMEMBERED ME!
SO EBINA AND MIURA ARE HERE TOO, HUH.
THEN THAT MEANS...

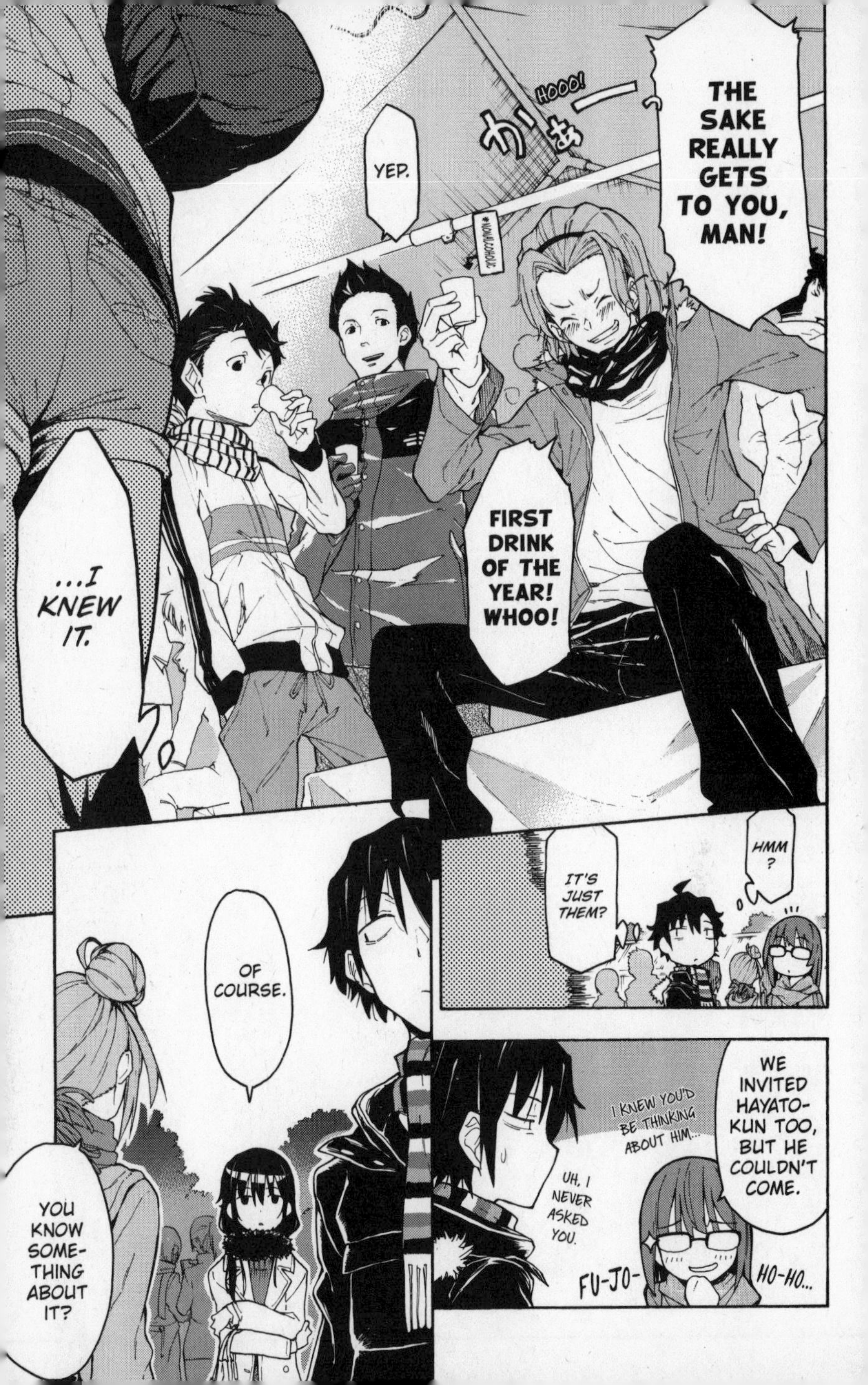
THE SAKE REALLY GETS TO YOU, MAN!
HOOO!
YEP.
FIRST DRINK OF THE YEAR! WHOO!
...I KNEW IT.
HMM?
IT'S JUST THEM?
WE INVITED HAYATO-KUN TOO, BUT HE COULDN'T COME.
I KNEW YOU'D BE THINKING ABOUT HIM...
UH, I NEVER ASKED YOU.
FU-JO-HO-HO...
OF COURSE.
YOU KNOW SOMETHING ABOUT IT?

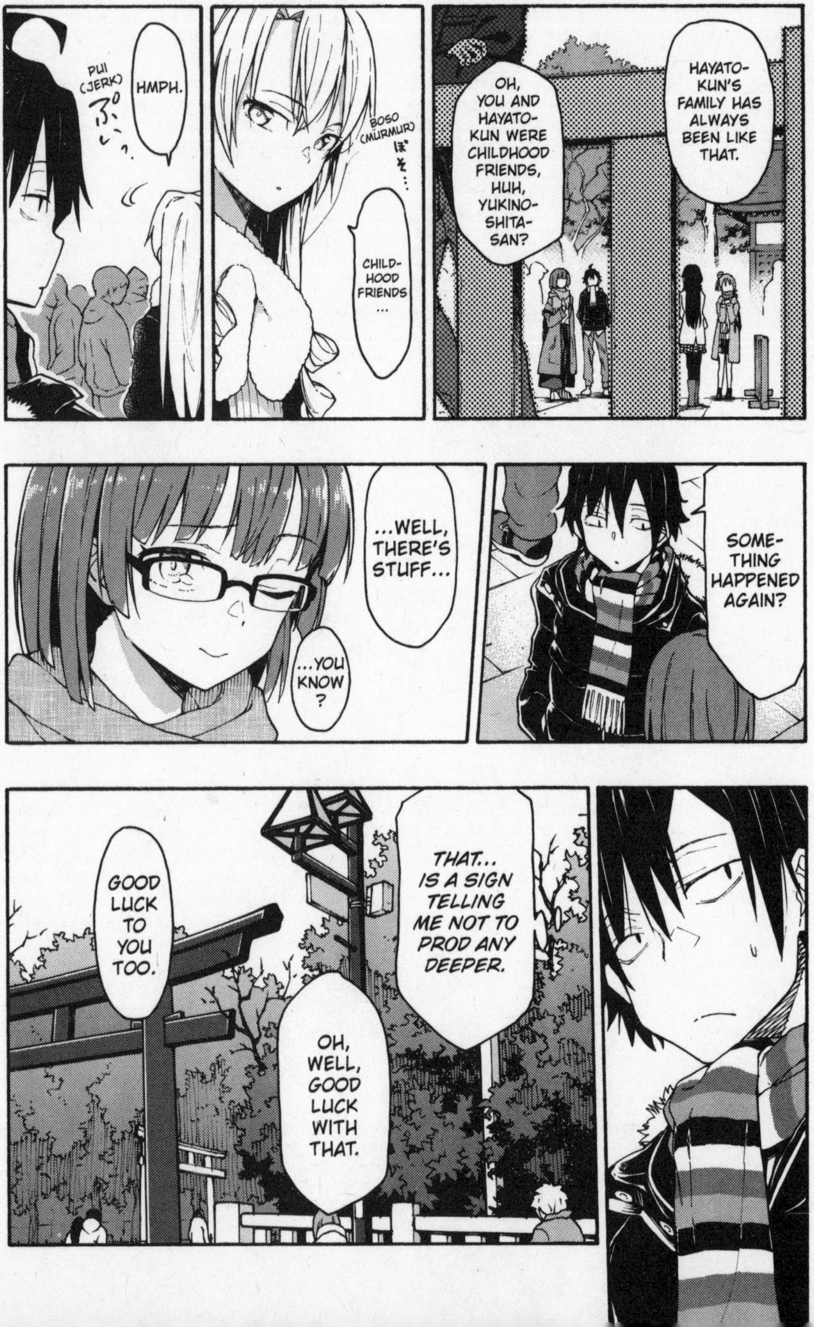
HAYATO-KUN'S FAMILY HAS ALWAYS BEEN LIKE THAT.
OH, YOU AND HAYATO-KUN WERE CHILDHOOD FRIENDS, HUH, YUKINOSHITA-SAN?
BOSO (MÜRMUR) ぼそ…
CHILDHOOD FRIENDS...
HMPH.
PUI (JERK) ぷい
SOMETHING HAPPENED AGAIN?
...WELL, THERE'S STUFF...
...YOU KNOW?
THAT... IS A SIGN TELLING ME NOT TO PROD ANY DEEPER.
OH, WELL, GOOD LUCK WITH THAT.
GOOD LUCK TO YOU TOO.

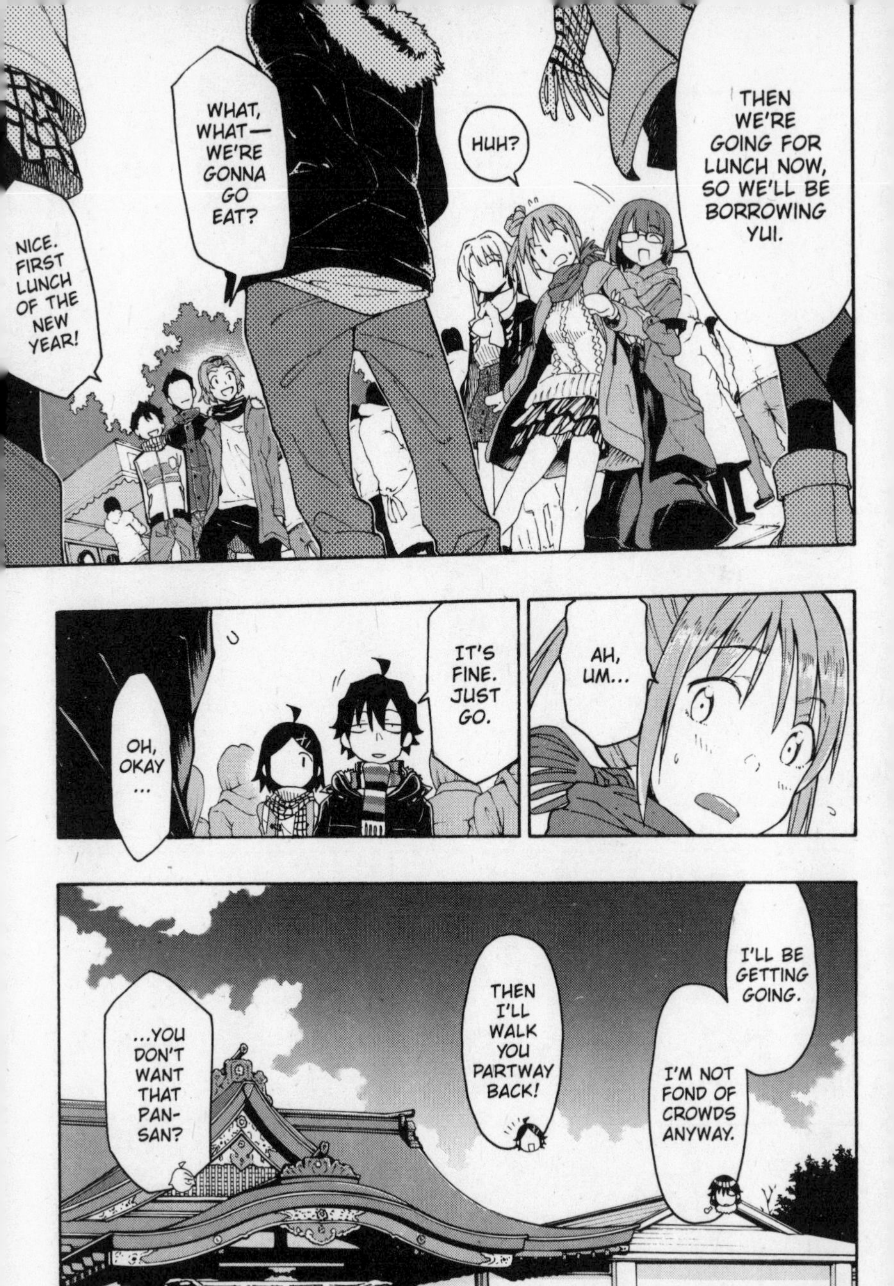
THEN WE'RE GOING FOR LUNCH NOW, SO WE'LL BE BORROWING YUI.
HUH?
WHAT, WHAT— WE'RE GONNA GO EAT?
NICE. FIRST LUNCH OF THE NEW YEAR!
AH, UM...
IT'S FINE. JUST GO.
OH, OKAY ...
I'LL BE GETTING GOING.
I'M NOT FOND OF CROWDS ANYWAY.
THEN I'LL WALK YOU PARTWAY BACK!
...YOU DON'T WANT THAT PAN-SAN?

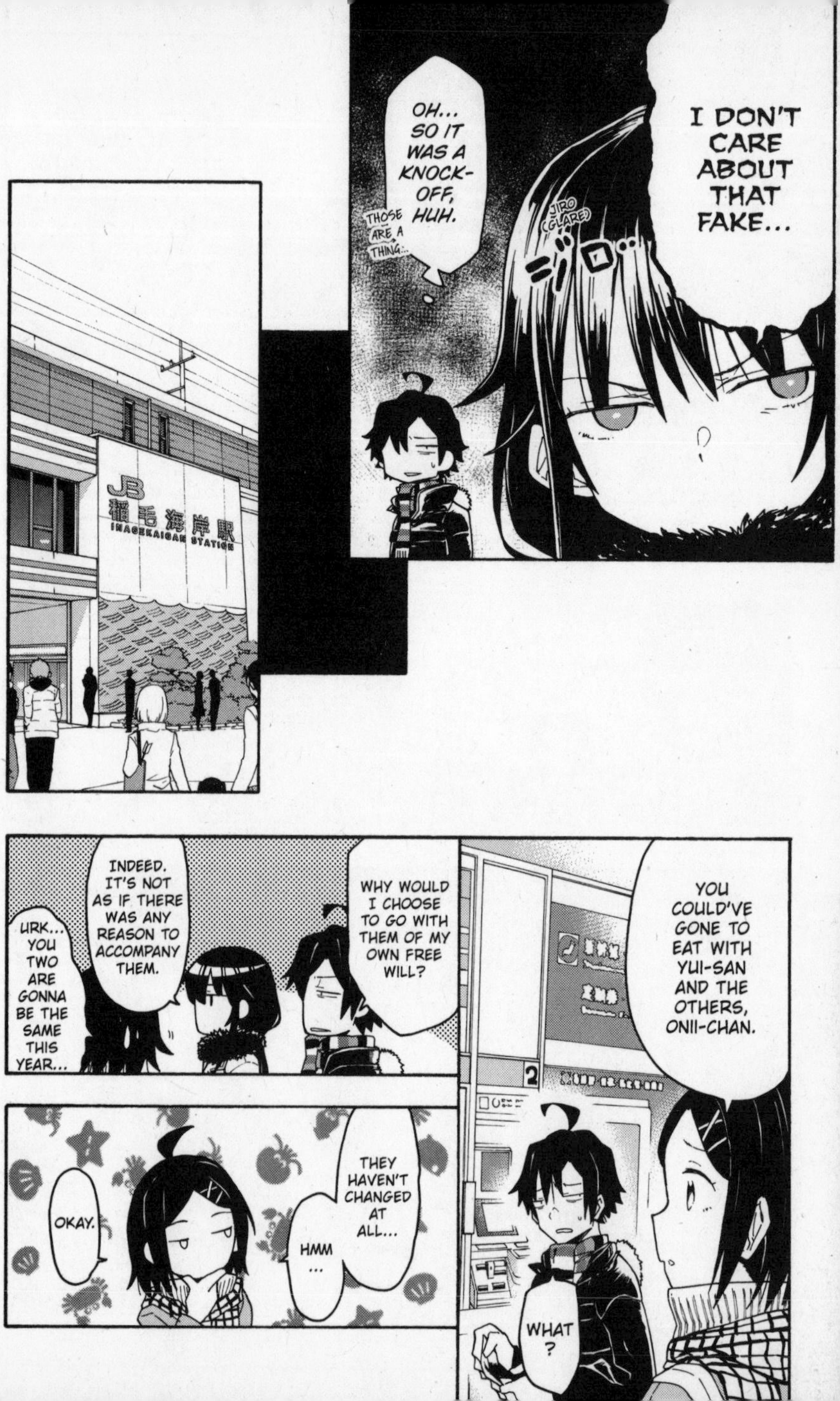
I DON'T CARE ABOUT THAT FAKE...
OH... SO IT WAS A KNOCK-OFF, HUH.
JIRO (GLARE)
THOSE ARE A THING...
JR
稲毛海岸駅
INAGEKAIGAN STATION
YOU COULD'VE GONE TO EAT WITH YUI-SAN AND THE OTHERS, ONII-CHAN.
WHAT?
WHY WOULD I CHOOSE TO GO WITH THEM OF MY OWN FREE WILL?
INDEED. IT'S NOT AS IF THERE WAS ANY REASON TO ACCOMPANY THEM.
URK... YOU TWO ARE GONNA BE THE SAME THIS YEAR...
THEY HAVEN'T CHANGED AT ALL...
HMM...
OKAY.

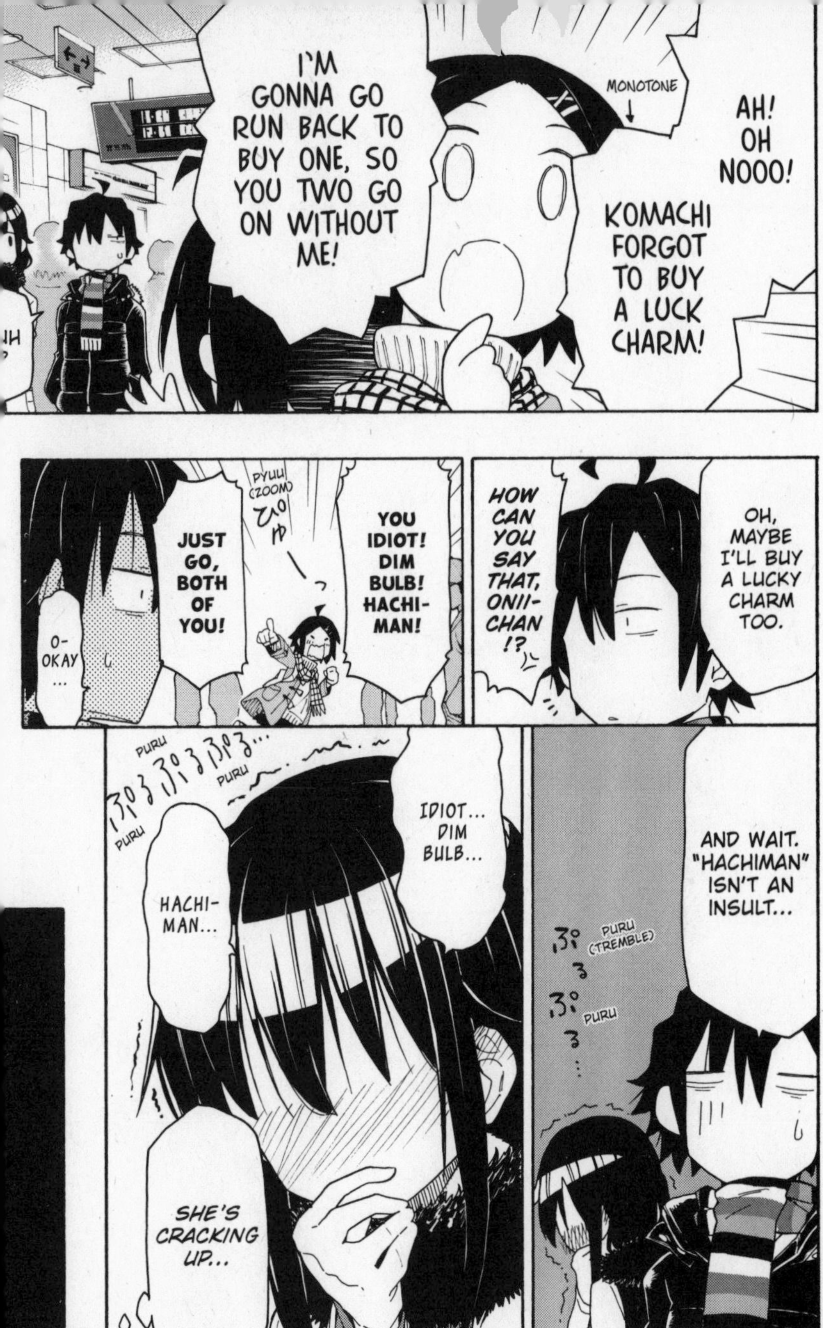
AH! OH NOOO!
MONOTONE
KOMACHI FORGOT TO BUY A LUCK CHARM!
I'M GONNA GO RUN BACK TO BUY ONE, SO YOU TWO GO ON WITHOUT ME!
OH, MAYBE I'LL BUY A LUCKY CHARM TOO.
HOW CAN YOU SAY THAT, ONII-CHAN!?
YOU IDIOT! DIM BULB! HACHI-MAN!
PYUU (ZOOM)
JUST GO, BOTH OF YOU!
O-OKAY...
AND WAIT. "HACHIMAN" ISN'T AN INSULT...
PURU (TREMBLE)
PURU
IDIOT... DIM BULB...
PURU
PURU
PURU
HACHI-MAN...
SHE'S CRACKING UP...

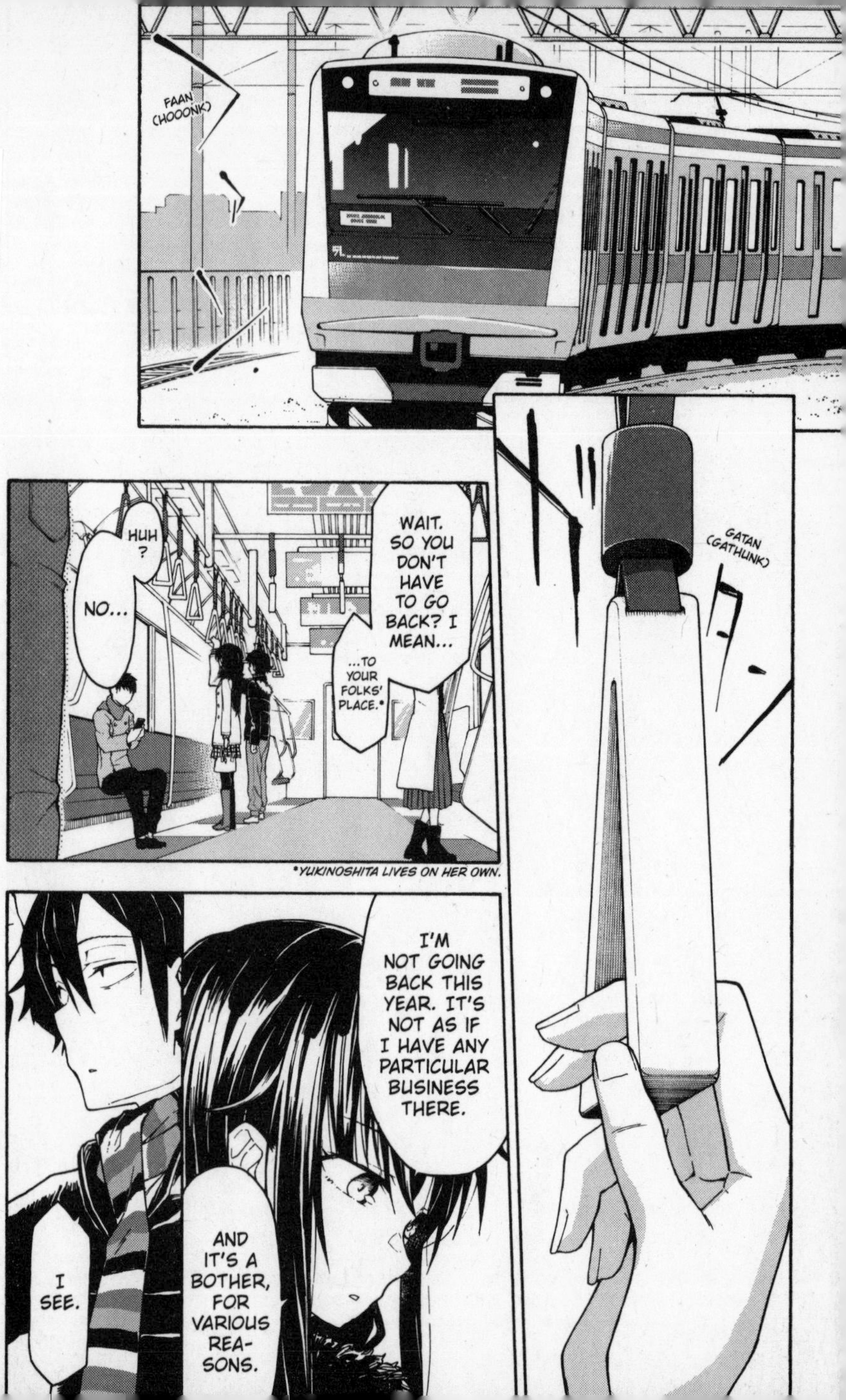
FAAN (HOOONK)
GATAN (GATHUNK)
WAIT. SO YOU DON'T HAVE TO GO BACK? I MEAN...
...TO YOUR FOLKS' PLACE.*
HUH?
NO...
*YUKINOSHITA LIVES ON HER OWN.
I'M NOT GOING BACK THIS YEAR. IT'S NOT AS IF I HAVE ANY PARTICULAR BUSINESS THERE.
AND IT'S A BOTHER, FOR VARIOUS REA-SONS.
I SEE.

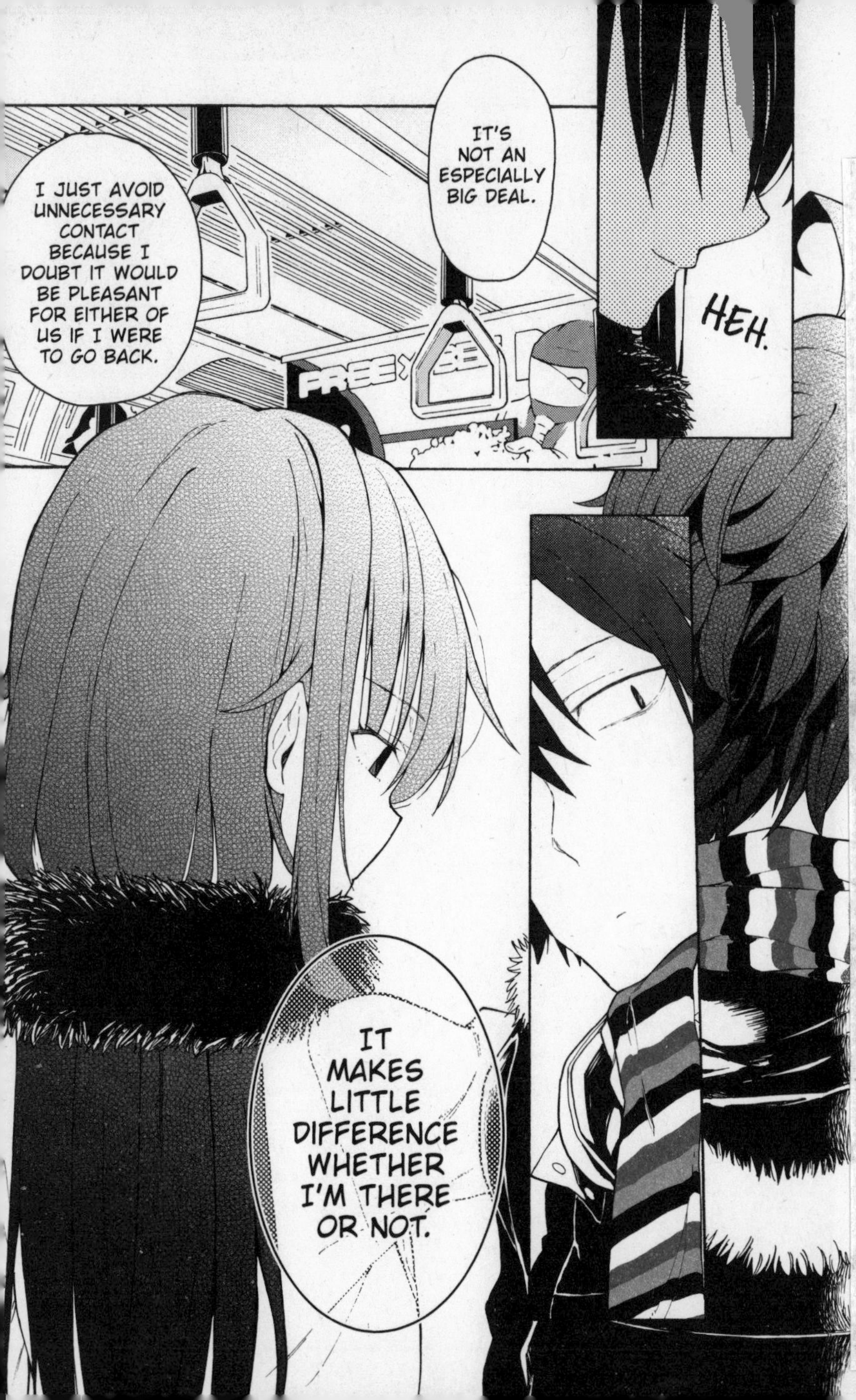
HEH.
IT'S NOT AN ESPECIALLY BIG DEAL.
I JUST AVOID UNNECESSARY CONTACT BECAUSE I DOUBT IT WOULD BE PLEASANT FOR EITHER OF US IF I WERE TO GO BACK.
IT MAKES LITTLE DIFFERENCE WHETHER I'M THERE OR NOT.

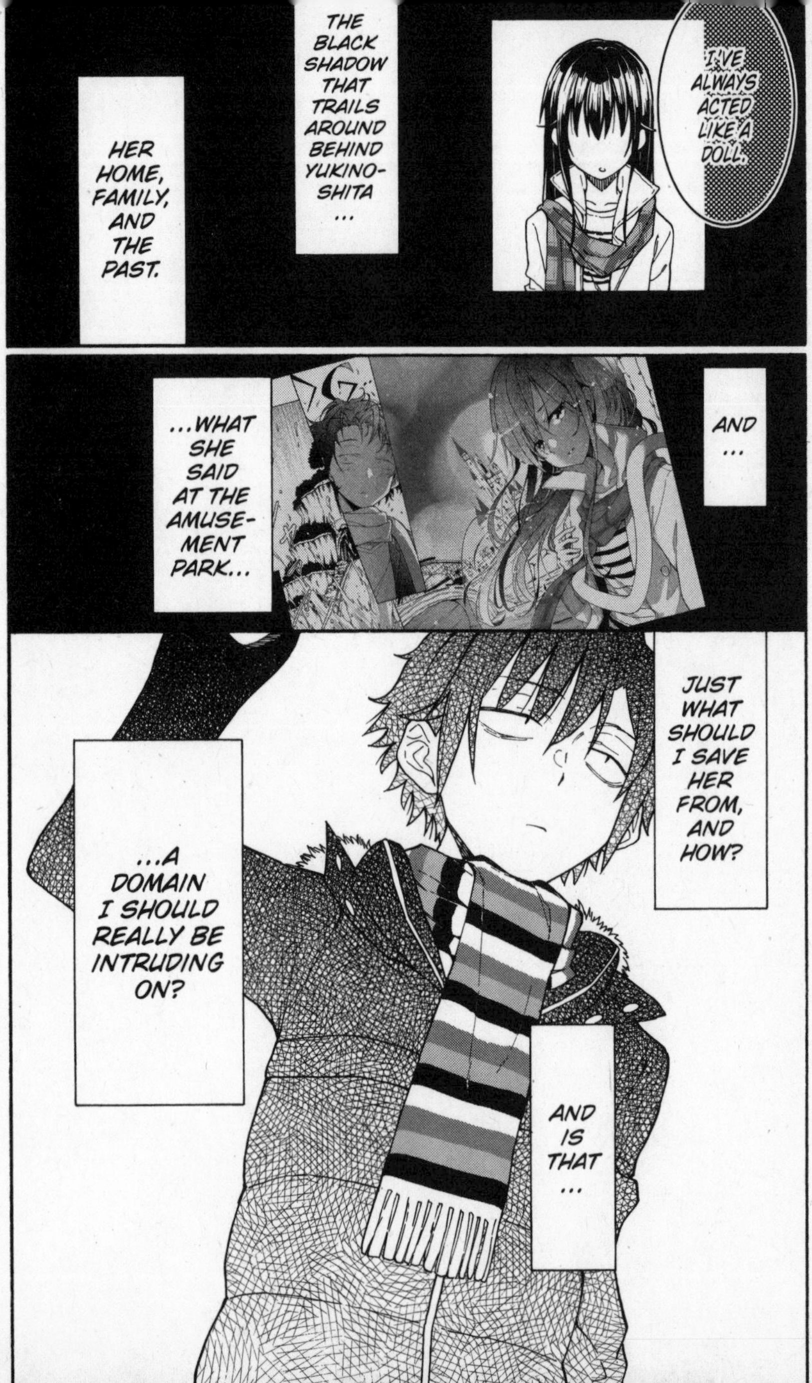
I'VE ALWAYS ACTED LIKE A DOLL.
THE BLACK SHADOW THAT TRAILS AROUND BEHIND YUKINO-SHITA ...
HER HOME, FAMILY, AND THE PAST.
AND ...
...WHAT SHE SAID AT THE AMUSEMENT PARK...
JUST WHAT SHOULD I SAVE HER FROM, AND HOW?
AND IS THAT ...
...A DOMAIN I SHOULD REALLY BE INTRUDING ON?

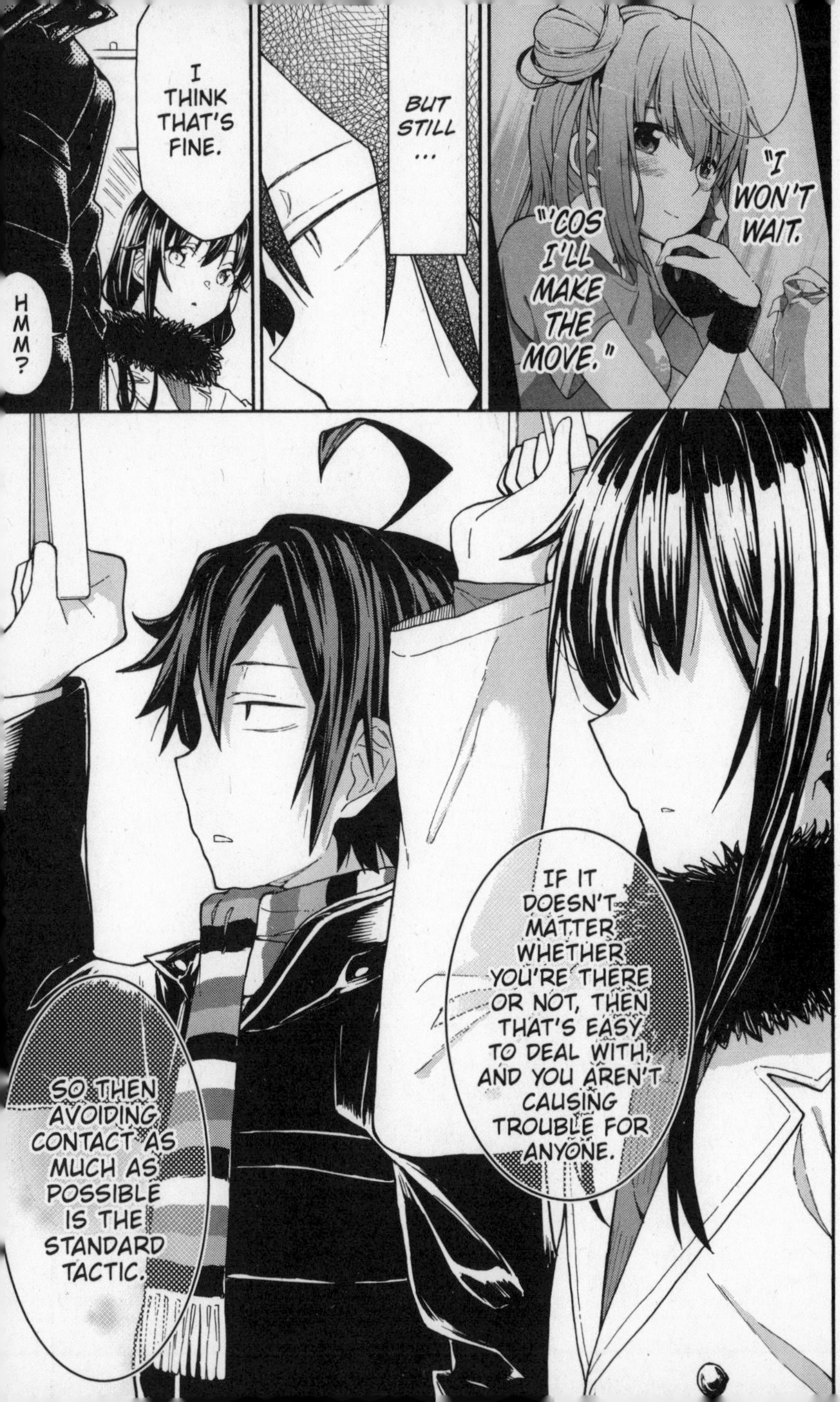
"I WON'T WAIT.
"'COS I'LL MAKE THE MOVE."
BUT STILL ...
I THINK THAT'S FINE.
HMM?
IF IT DOESN'T MATTER WHETHER YOU'RE THERE OR NOT, THEN THAT'S EASY TO DEAL WITH, AND YOU AREN'T CAUSING TROUBLE FOR ANYONE.
SO THEN AVOIDING CONTACT AS MUCH AS POSSIBLE IS THE STANDARD TACTIC.

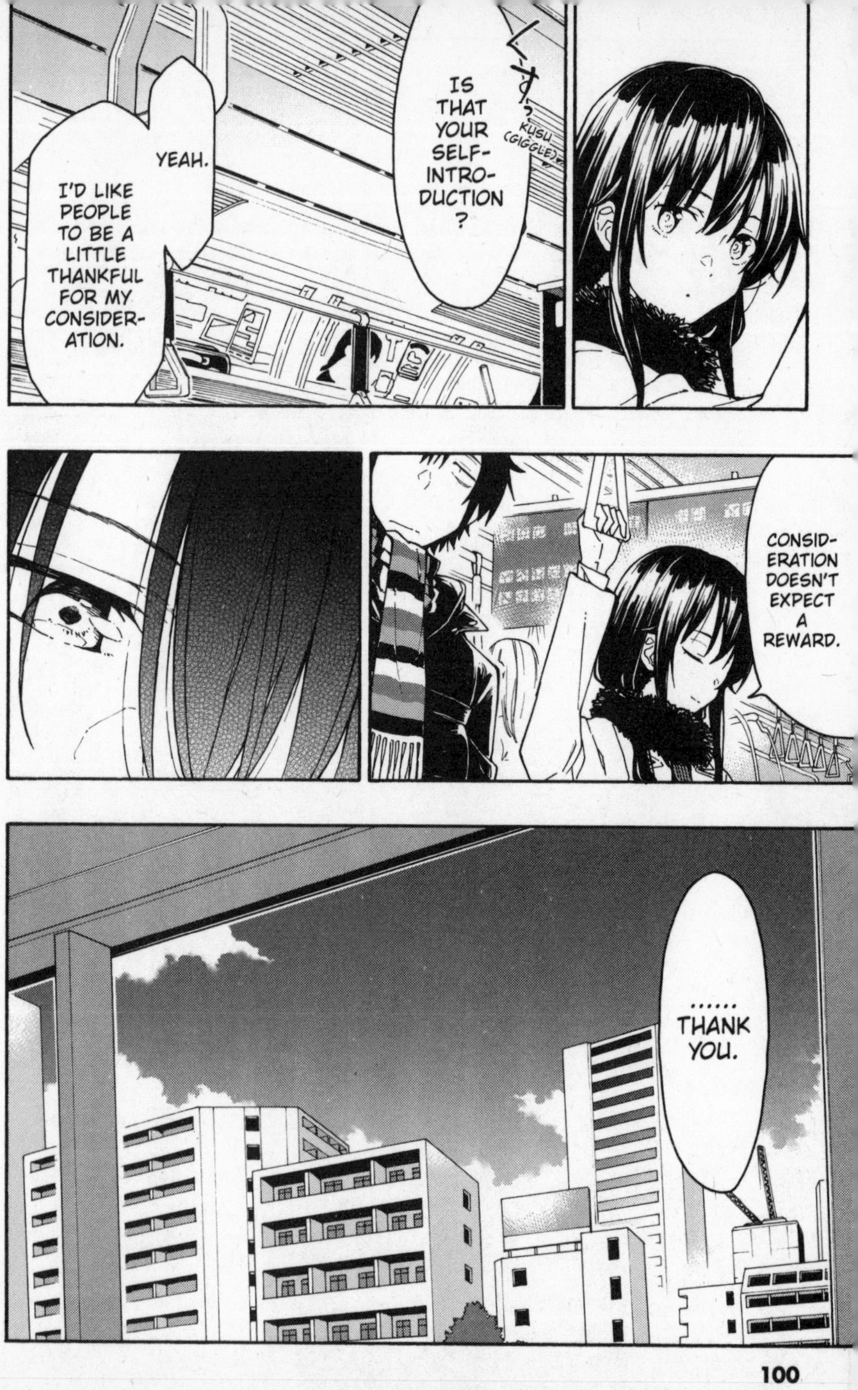
くすっ
KUSU (GIGGLE)
IS THAT YOUR SELF-INTRODUCTION?
YEAH.
I'D LIKE PEOPLE TO BE A LITTLE THANKFUL FOR MY CONSIDERATION.
CONSIDERATION DOESN'T EXPECT A REWARD.
......THANK YOU.

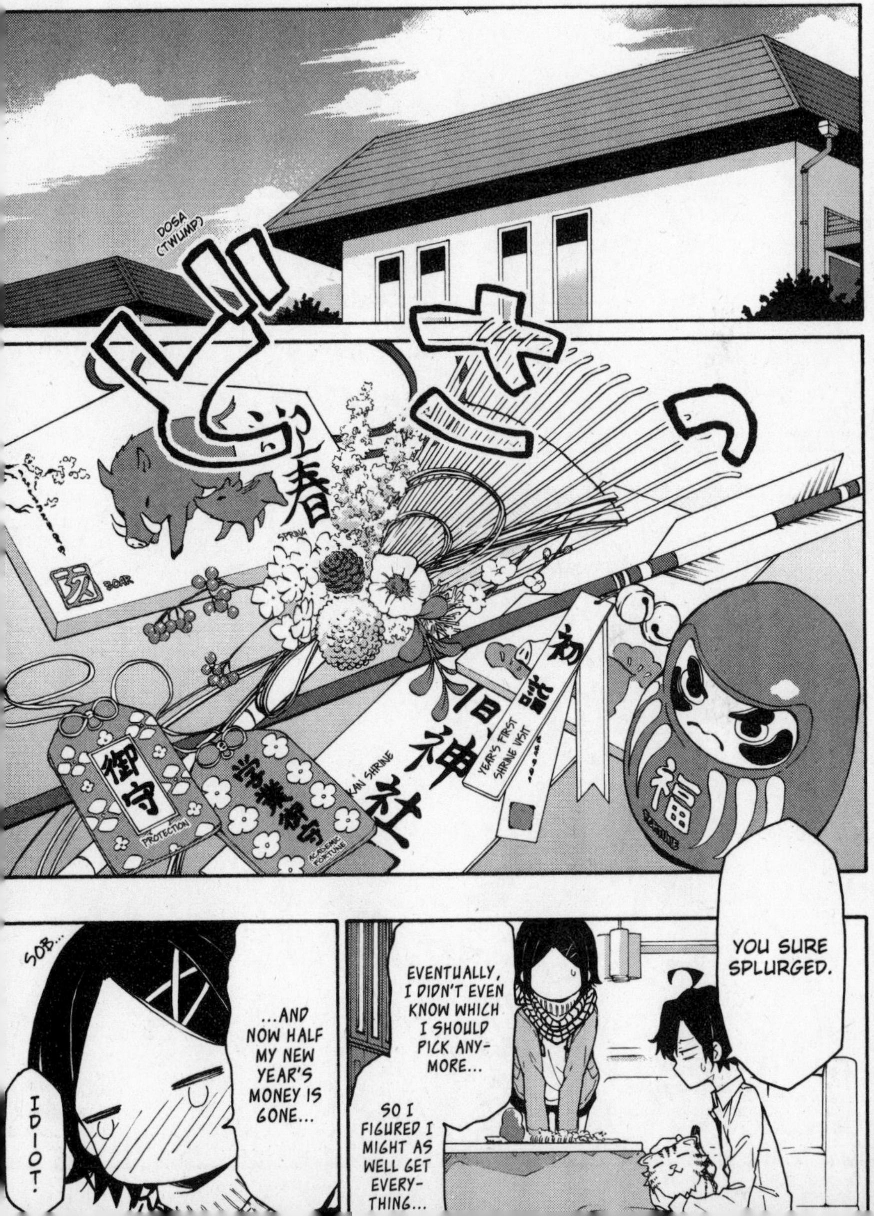
DOSA (TWUMP)
春
SPRING
BOAR
初詣
YEAR'S FIRST SHRINE VISIT
KAN SHRINE
福
御守
PROTECTION
ACADEMIC FORTUNE
YOU SURE SPLURGED.
EVENTUALLY, I DIDN'T EVEN KNOW WHICH I SHOULD PICK ANY-MORE...
SO I FIGURED I MIGHT AS WELL GET EVERY-THING...
...AND NOW HALF MY NEW YEAR'S MONEY IS GONE...
IDIOT!
SOB...

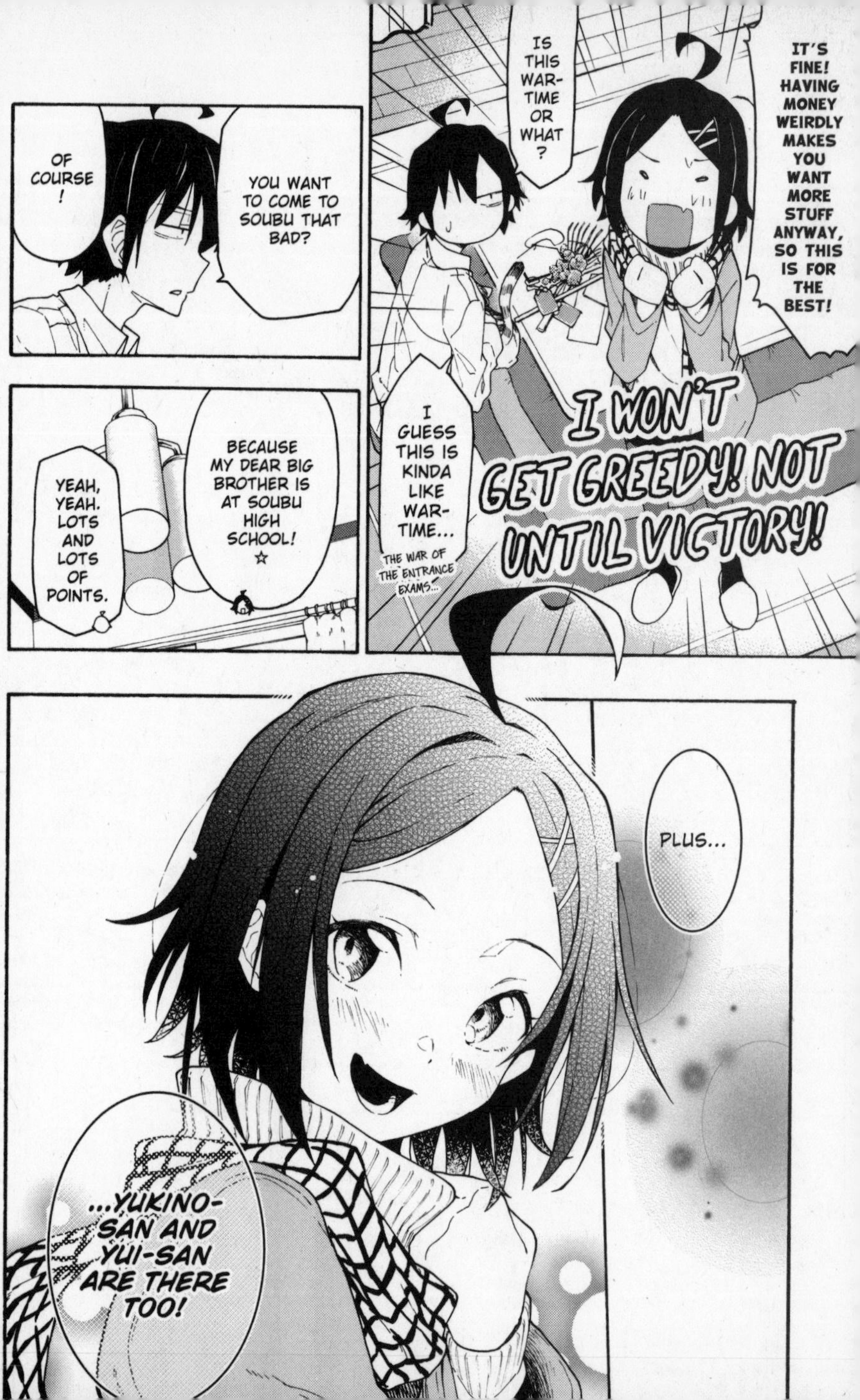
IT'S FINE! HAVING MONEY WEIRDLY MAKES YOU WANT MORE STUFF ANYWAY, SO THIS IS FOR THE BEST!
IS THIS WAR-TIME OR WHAT?
I WON'T GET GREEDY! NOT UNTIL VICTORY!
I GUESS THIS IS KINDA LIKE WAR-TIME...
THE WAR OF THE ENTRANCE EXAMS...
YOU WANT TO COME TO SOUBU THAT BAD?
OF COURSE!
BECAUSE MY DEAR BIG BROTHER IS AT SOUBU HIGH SCHOOL! ☆
YEAH, YEAH. LOTS AND LOTS OF POINTS.
PLUS...
...YUKINO-SAN AND YUI-SAN ARE THERE TOO!

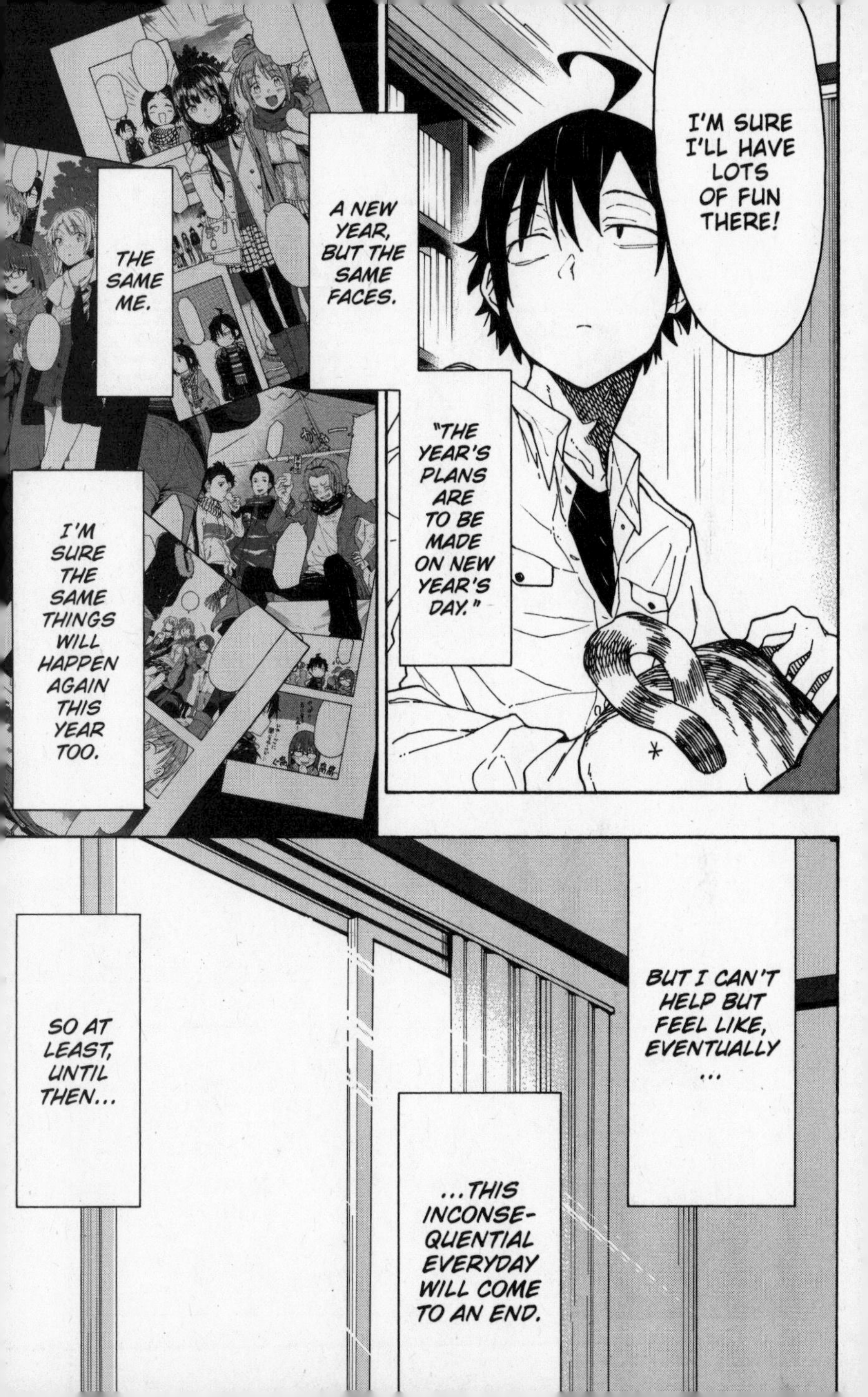
I'M SURE I'LL HAVE LOTS OF FUN THERE!
"THE YEAR'S PLANS ARE TO BE MADE ON NEW YEAR'S DAY."
A NEW YEAR, BUT THE SAME FACES.
THE SAME ME.
I'M SURE THE SAME THINGS WILL HAPPEN AGAIN THIS YEAR TOO.
BUT I CAN'T HELP BUT FEEL LIKE, EVENTUALLY...
...THIS INCONSE-QUENTIAL EVERYDAY WILL COME TO AN END.
SO AT LEAST, UNTIL THEN...

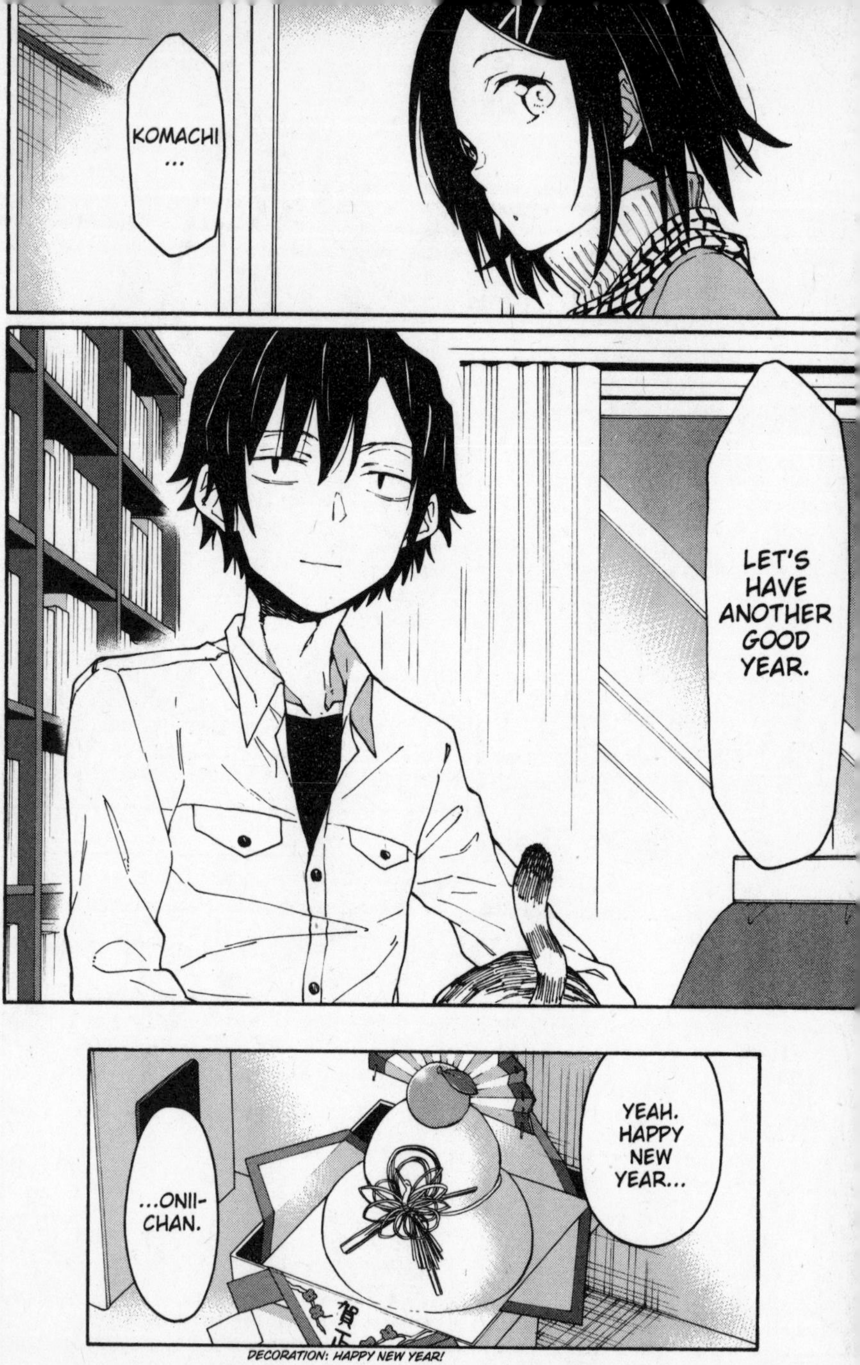
KOMACHI ...
LET'S HAVE ANOTHER GOOD YEAR.
YEAH. HAPPY NEW YEAR...
...ONII-CHAN.

DECORATION: HAPPY NEW YEAR!

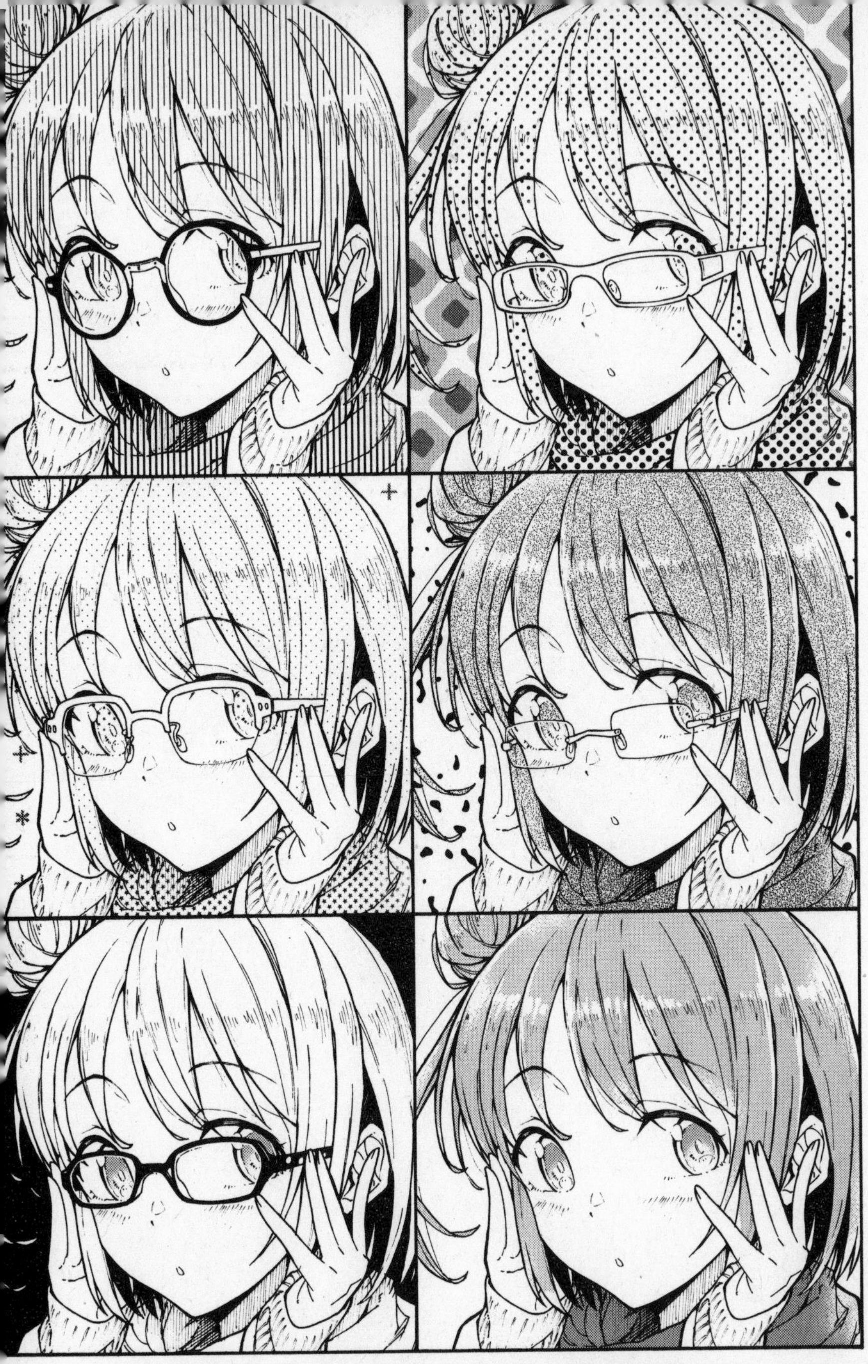

CHAPTER 74 ... AS USUAL, HARUNO YUKINOSHITA STIRS THINGS UP.

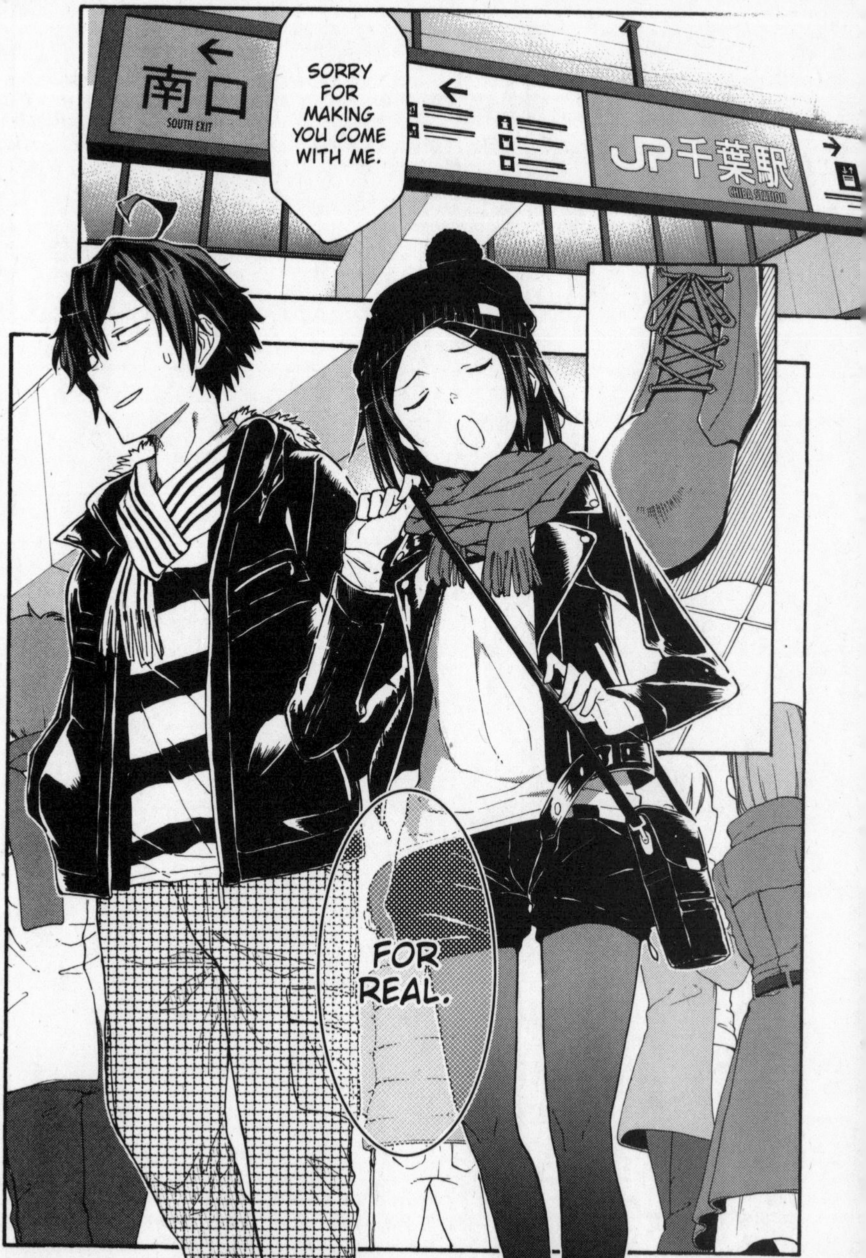

南口
SOUTH EXIT
SORRY FOR MAKING YOU COME WITH ME.
JR 千葉駅
CHIBA STATION
FOR REAL.

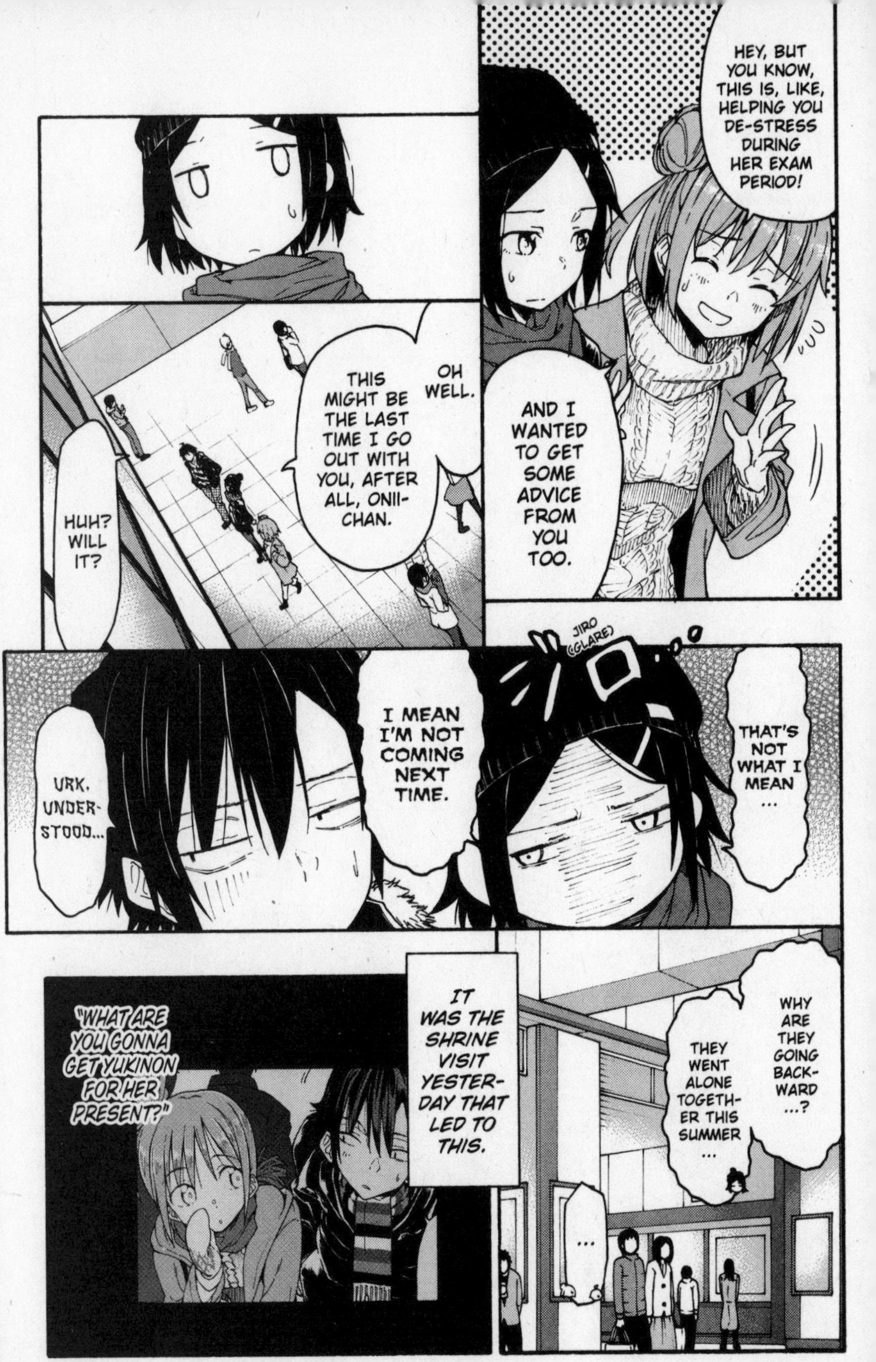
HEY, BUT YOU KNOW, THIS IS, LIKE, HELPING YOU DE-STRESS DURING HER EXAM PERIOD!
AND I WANTED TO GET SOME ADVICE FROM YOU TOO.
OH WELL.
THIS MIGHT BE THE LAST TIME I GO OUT WITH YOU, AFTER ALL, ONII-CHAN.
HUH? WILL IT?
JIRO (GLARE)
THAT'S NOT WHAT I MEAN...
I MEAN I'M NOT COMING NEXT TIME.
URK. UNDER-STOOD...
WHY ARE THEY GOING BACK-WARD...?
THEY WENT ALONE TOGETH-ER THIS SUMMER...
...
IT WAS THE SHRINE VISIT YESTER-DAY THAT LED TO THIS.
"WHAT ARE YOU GONNA GET YUKINON FOR HER PRESENT?"

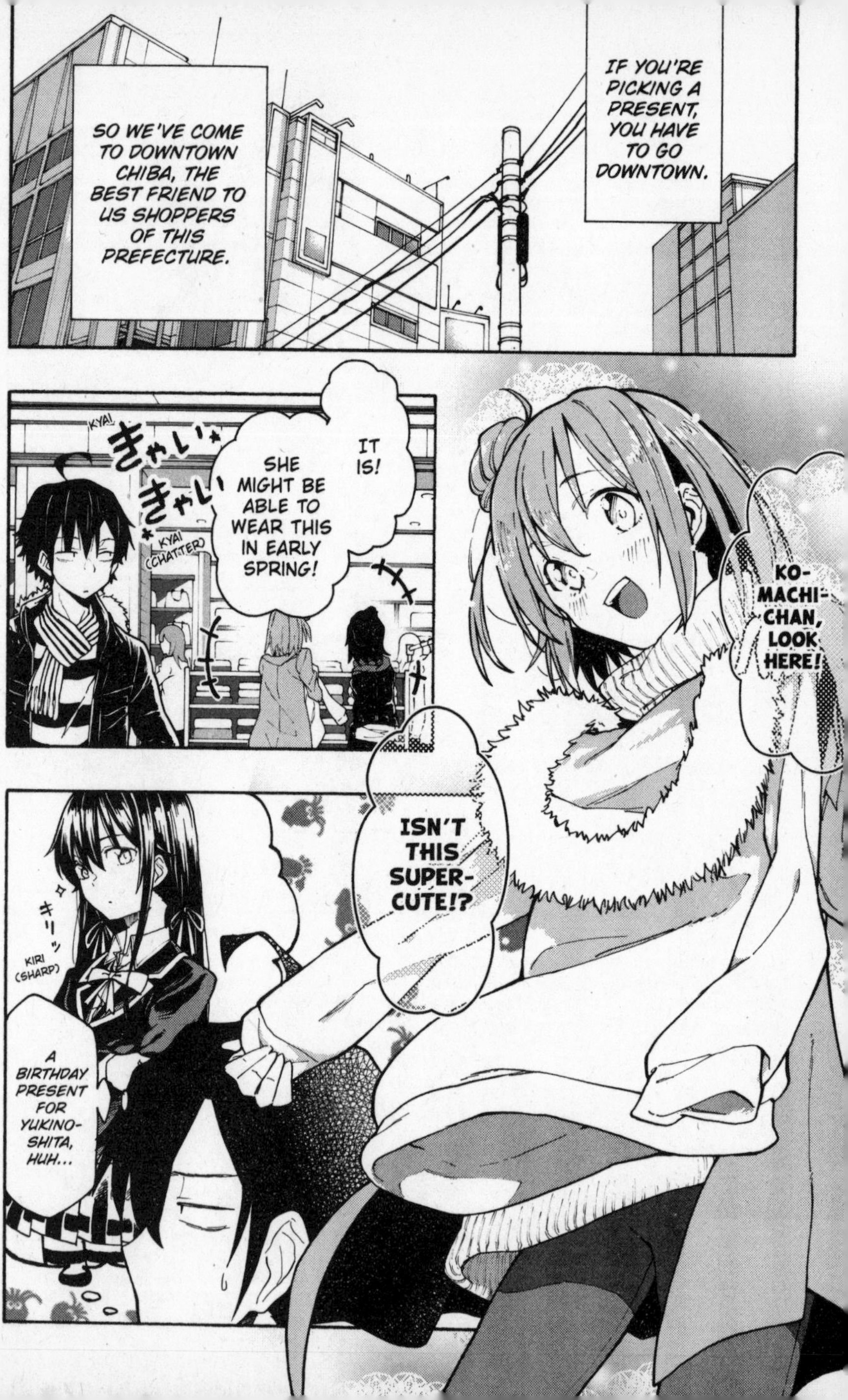
IF YOU'RE PICKING A PRESENT, YOU HAVE TO GO DOWNTOWN.
SO WE'VE COME TO DOWNTOWN CHIBA, THE BEST FRIEND TO US SHOPPERS OF THIS PREFECTURE.
KO-MACHI-CHAN, LOOK HERE!
ISN'T THIS SUPER-CUTE!?
IT IS!
SHE MIGHT BE ABLE TO WEAR THIS IN EARLY SPRING!
きゃいきゃい
KYAI KYAI (CHATTER)
キリッ
KIRI (SHARP)
A BIRTHDAY PRESENT FOR YUKINO-SHITA, HUH...

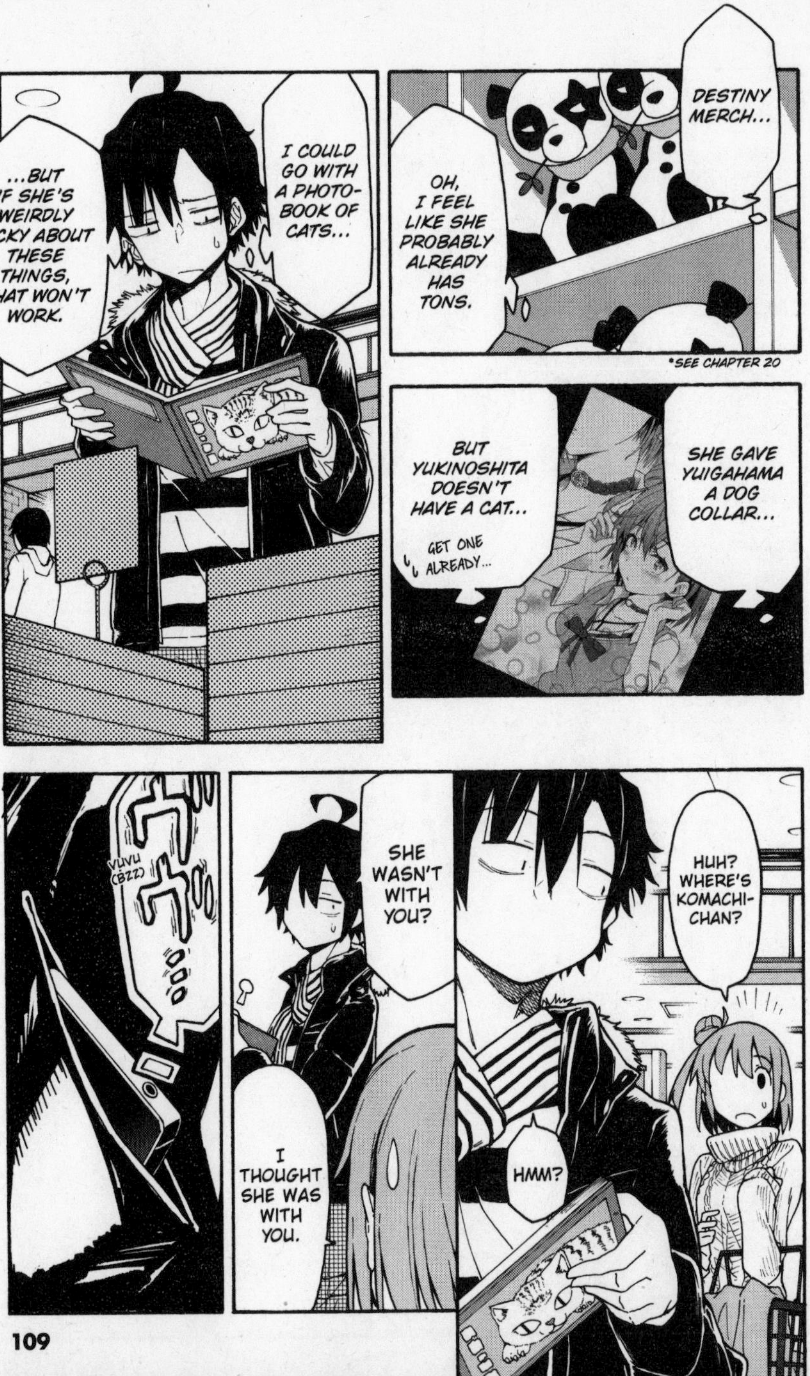
DESTINY MERCH...
OH, I FEEL LIKE SHE PROBABLY ALREADY HAS TONS.
*SEE CHAPTER 20
SHE GAVE YUIGAHAMA A DOG COLLAR...
BUT YUKINOSHITA DOESN'T HAVE A CAT...
GET ONE ALREADY...
I COULD GO WITH A PHOTO-BOOK OF CATS...
...BUT IF SHE'S WEIRDLY PICKY ABOUT THESE THINGS, THAT WON'T WORK.
HUH? WHERE'S KOMACHI-CHAN?
HMM?
SHE WASN'T WITH YOU?
I THOUGHT SHE WAS WITH YOU.
VUVU (BZZ)

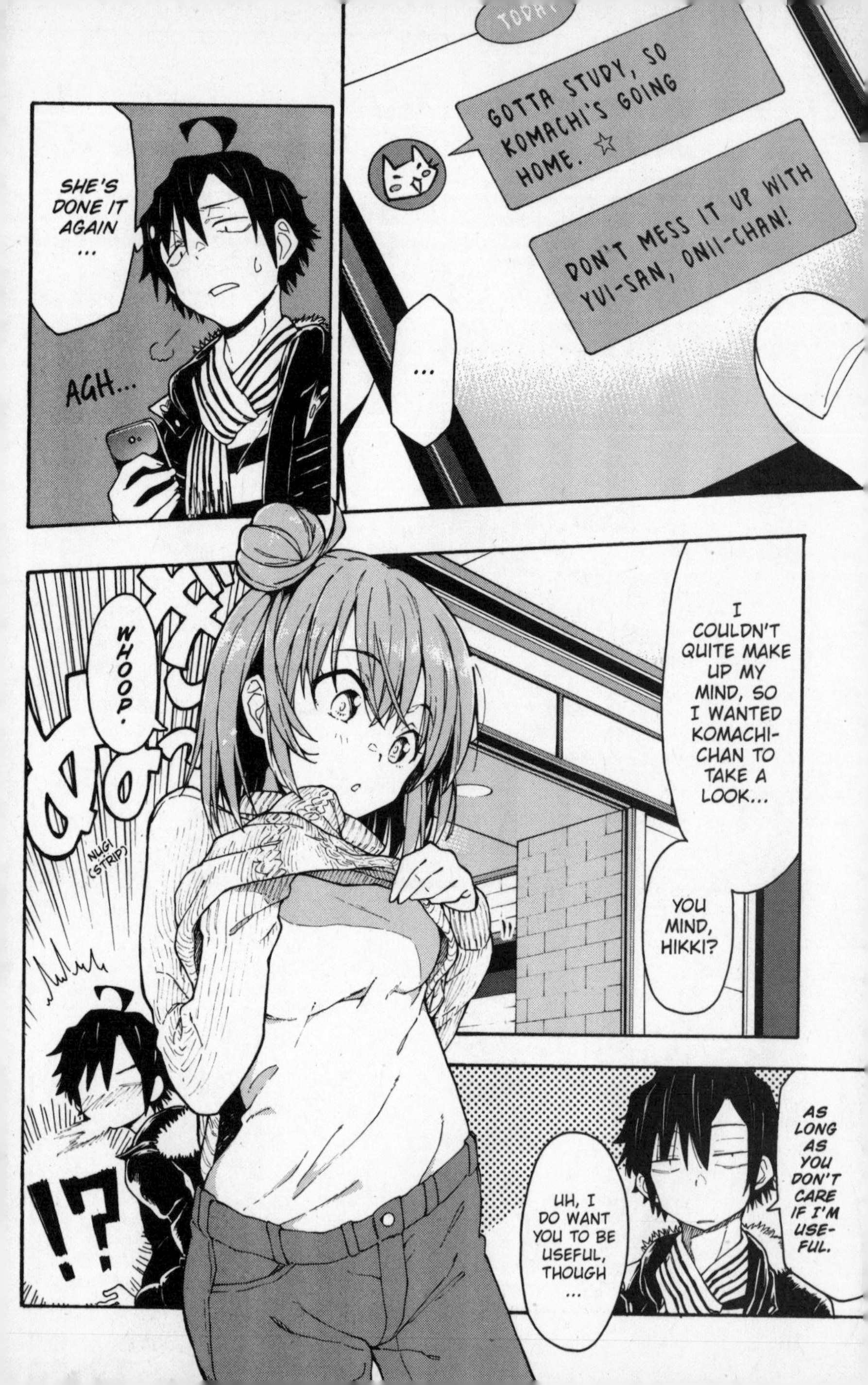
GOTTA STUDY, SO KOMACHI'S GOING HOME. ☆
DON'T MESS IT UP WITH YUI-SAN, ONII-CHAN!
...
SHE'S DONE IT AGAIN ...
AGH...
I COULDN'T QUITE MAKE UP MY MIND, SO I WANTED KOMACHI-CHAN TO TAKE A LOOK...
YOU MIND, HIKKI?
AS LONG AS YOU DON'T CARE IF I'M USE-FUL.
UH, I DO WANT YOU TO BE USEFUL, THOUGH ...
WHOOP.
NUGI (STRIP)
!?

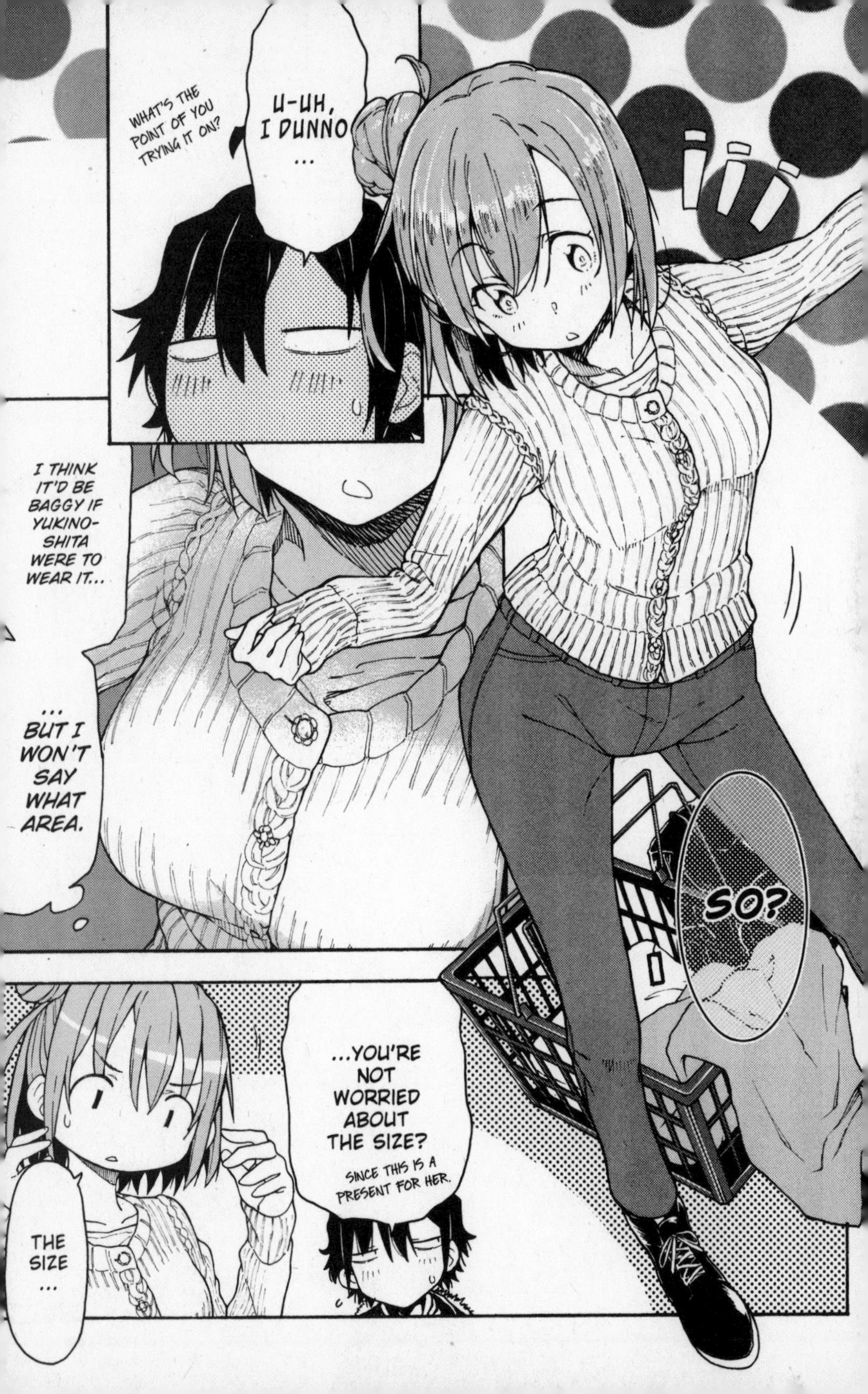

WHAT'S THE POINT OF YOU TRYING IT ON?
U-UH, I DUNNO ...
I THINK IT'D BE BAGGY IF YUKINO-SHITA WERE TO WEAR IT...
... BUT I WON'T SAY WHAT AREA.
SO?
...YOU'RE NOT WORRIED ABOUT THE SIZE?
SINCE THIS IS A PRESENT FOR HER.
THE SIZE ...

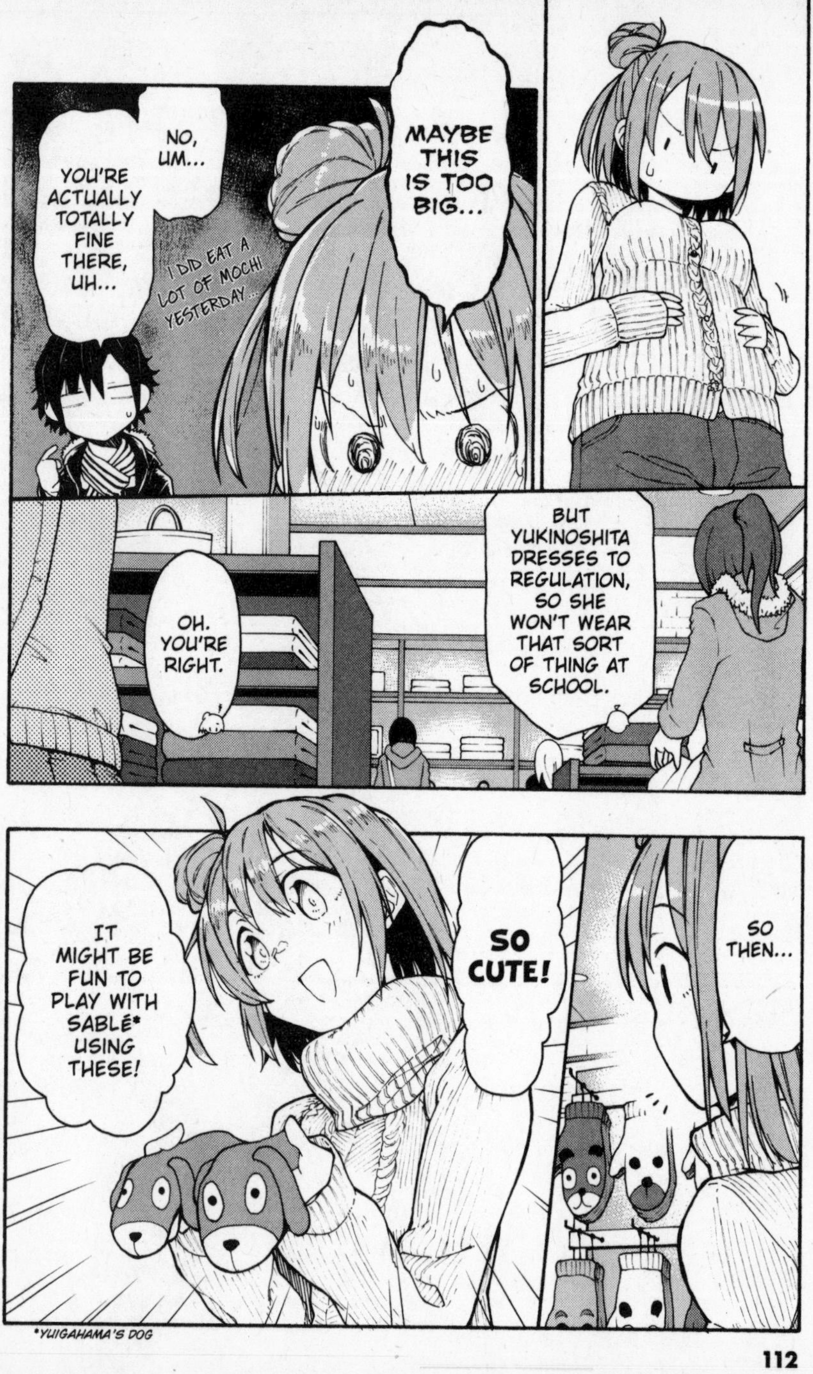
MAYBE THIS IS TOO BIG...
I DID EAT A LOT OF MOCHI YESTERDAY...
NO, UM...
YOU'RE ACTUALLY TOTALLY FINE THERE, UH...
BUT YUKINOSHITA DRESSES TO REGULATION, SO SHE WON'T WEAR THAT SORT OF THING AT SCHOOL.
OH. YOU'RE RIGHT.
SO THEN...
SO CUTE!
IT MIGHT BE FUN TO PLAY WITH SABLÉ* USING THESE!

*YUIGAHAMA'S DOG

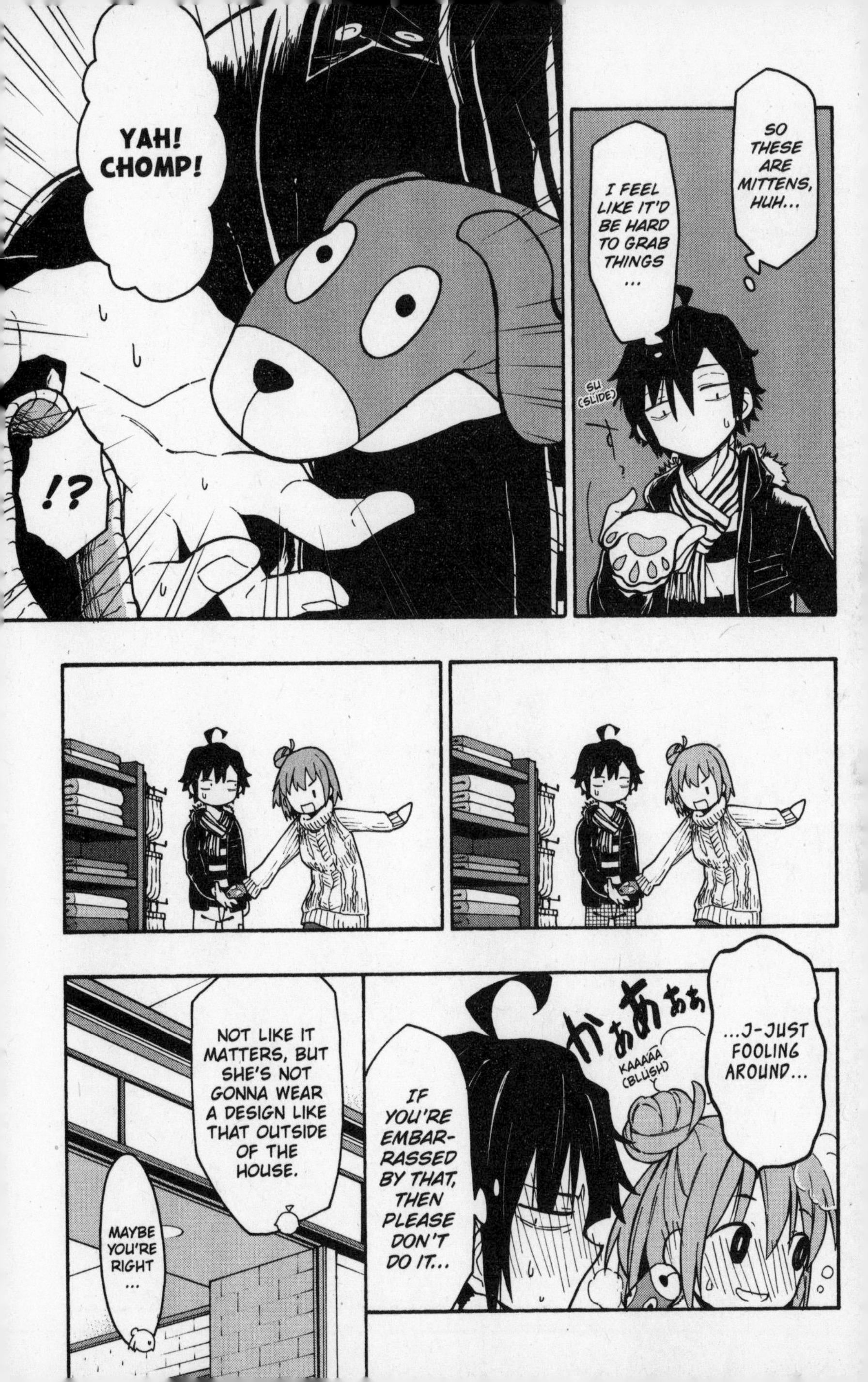
SO THESE ARE MITTENS, HUH...
I FEEL LIKE IT'D BE HARD TO GRAB THINGS ...
SU (SLIDE)
YAH! CHOMP!
!?
...J-JUST FOOLING AROUND...
かぁあぁぁ
KAAAAA (BLUSH)
IF YOU'RE EMBAR-RASSED BY THAT, THEN PLEASE DON'T DO IT...
NOT LIKE IT MATTERS, BUT SHE'S NOT GONNA WEAR A DESIGN LIKE THAT OUTSIDE OF THE HOUSE.
MAYBE YOU'RE RIGHT ...

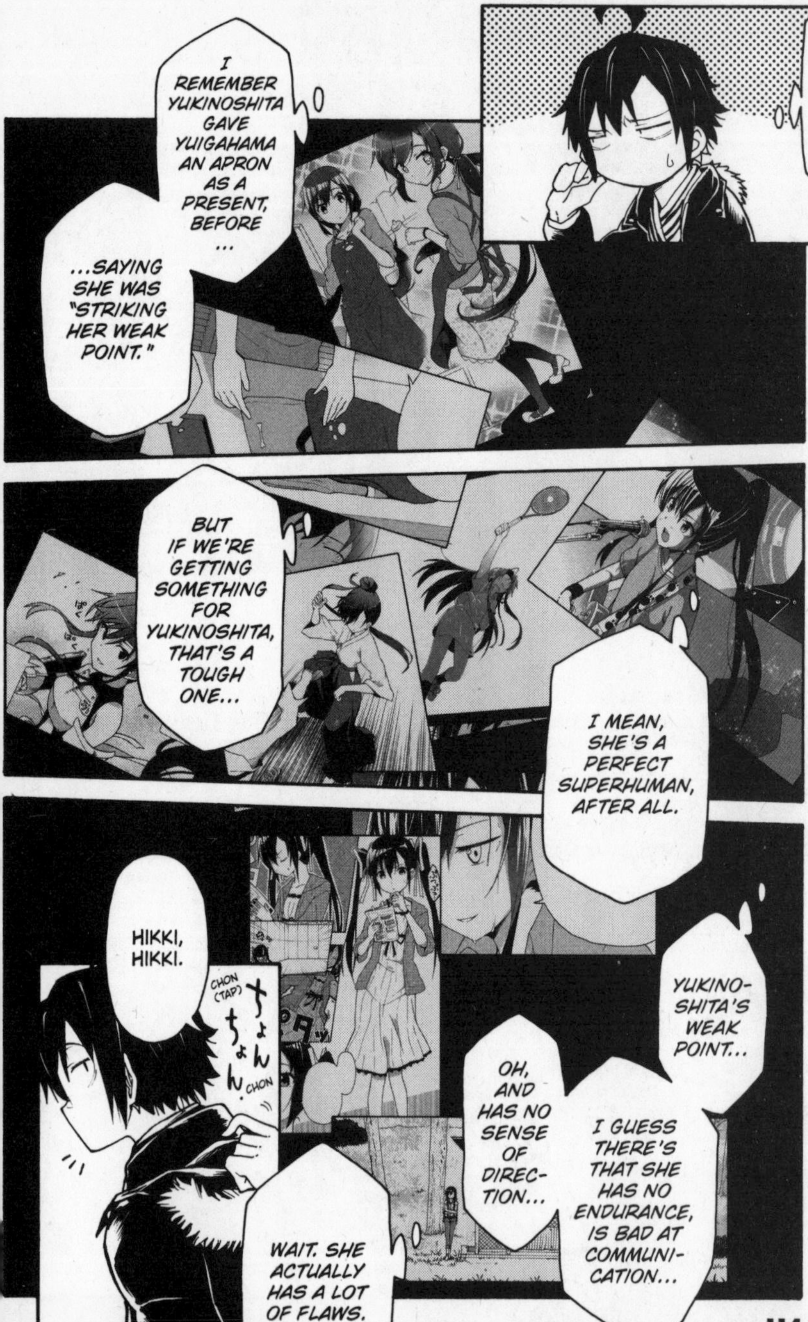
I CAN'T QUITE DECIDE ON ANYTHING.
I REMEMBER YUKINOSHITA GAVE YUIGAHAMA AN APRON AS A PRESENT, BEFORE ...
...SAYING SHE WAS "STRIKING HER WEAK POINT."
BUT IF WE'RE GETTING SOMETHING FOR YUKINOSHITA, THAT'S A TOUGH ONE...
I MEAN, SHE'S A PERFECT SUPERHUMAN, AFTER ALL.
YUKINOSHITA'S WEAK POINT...
I GUESS THERE'S THAT SHE HAS NO ENDURANCE, IS BAD AT COMMUNICATION...
OH, AND HAS NO SENSE OF DIRECTION...
WAIT. SHE ACTUALLY HAS A LOT OF FLAWS.
SHE'S NOT PERFECT.
HIKKI, HIKKI.
CHON (TAP) ちょん CHON ちょん.

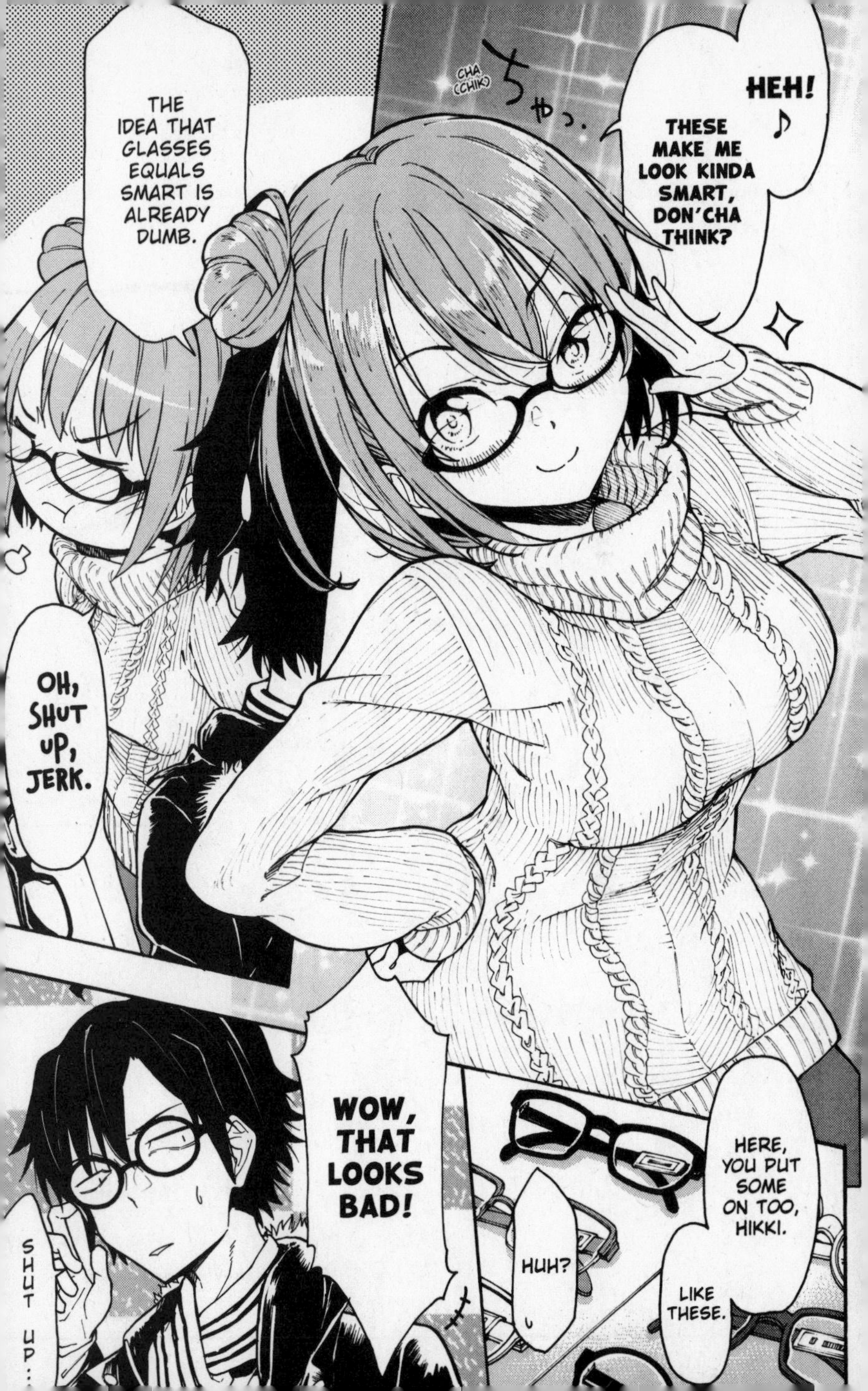
HEH! ♪
THESE MAKE ME LOOK KINDA SMART, DON'CHA THINK?
CHA (CHIK)
THE IDEA THAT GLASSES EQUALS SMART IS ALREADY DUMB.
OH, SHUT UP, JERK.
HERE, YOU PUT SOME ON TOO, HIKKI.
LIKE THESE.
HUH?
WOW, THAT LOOKS BAD!
SHUT UP...

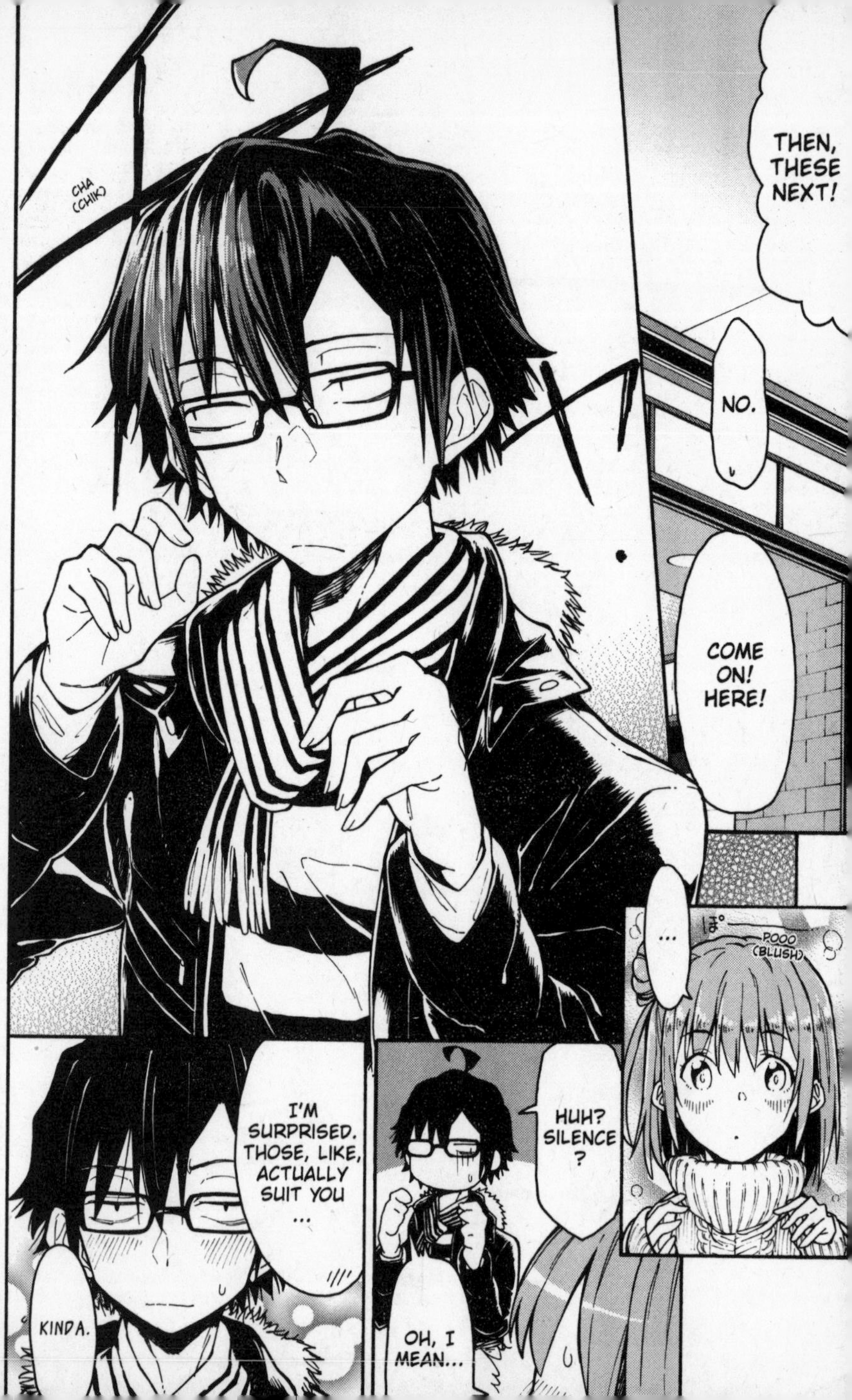
THEN, THESE NEXT!
NO.
COME ON! HERE!
CHA (CHIK)
...
ぽ
POOO (BLUSH)
HUH? SILENCE?
OH, I MEAN...
I'M SURPRISED. THOSE, LIKE, ACTUALLY SUIT YOU...
KINDA.

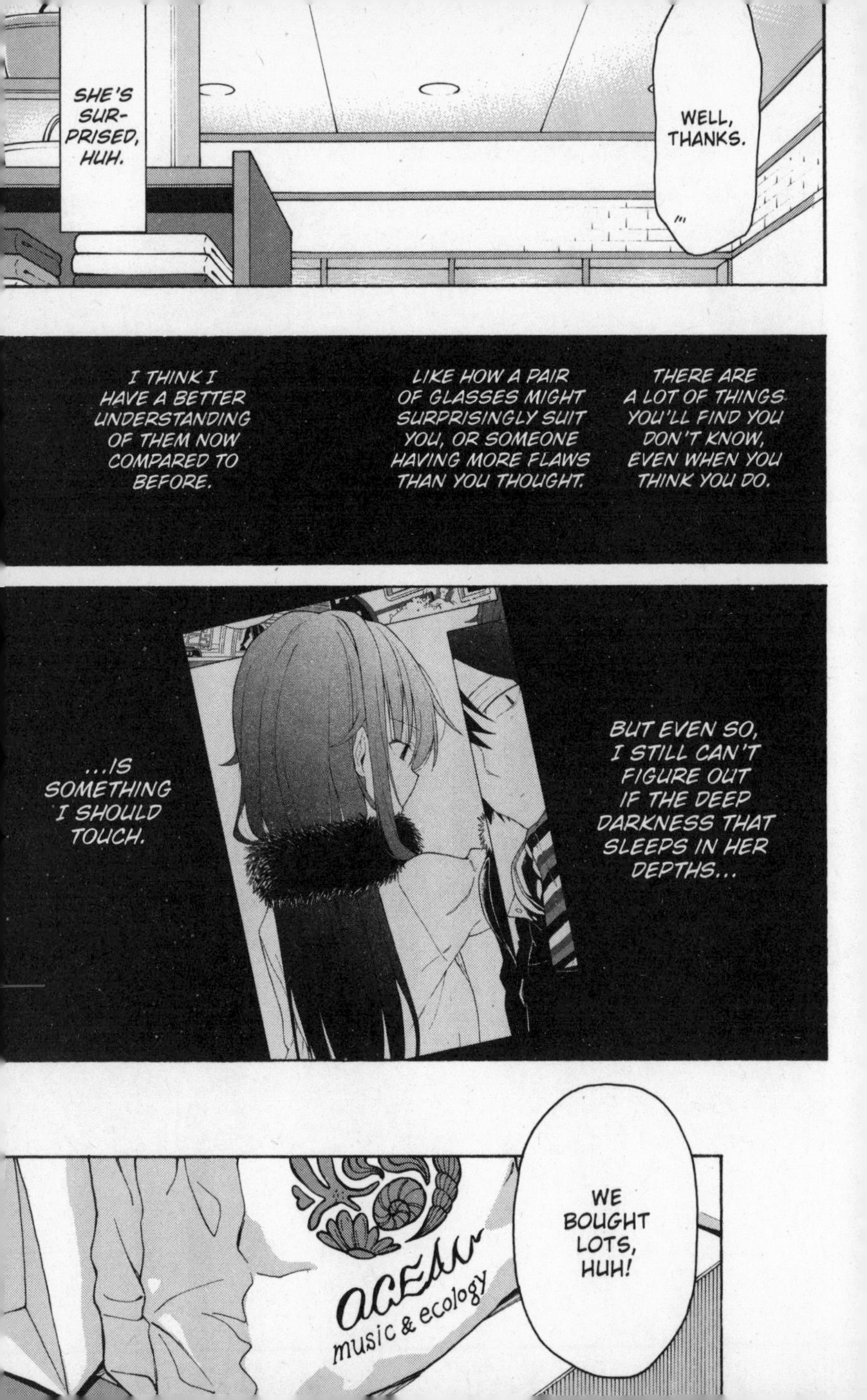
WELL, THANKS.
SHE'S SUR-PRISED, HUH.
THERE ARE A LOT OF THINGS YOU'LL FIND YOU DON'T KNOW, EVEN WHEN YOU THINK YOU DO.
LIKE HOW A PAIR OF GLASSES MIGHT SURPRISINGLY SUIT YOU, OR SOMEONE HAVING MORE FLAWS THAN YOU THOUGHT.
I THINK I HAVE A BETTER UNDERSTANDING OF THEM NOW COMPARED TO BEFORE.
BUT EVEN SO, I STILL CAN'T FIGURE OUT IF THE DEEP DARKNESS THAT SLEEPS IN HER DEPTHS...
...IS SOMETHING I SHOULD TOUCH.
WE BOUGHT LOTS, HUH!
music & ecology

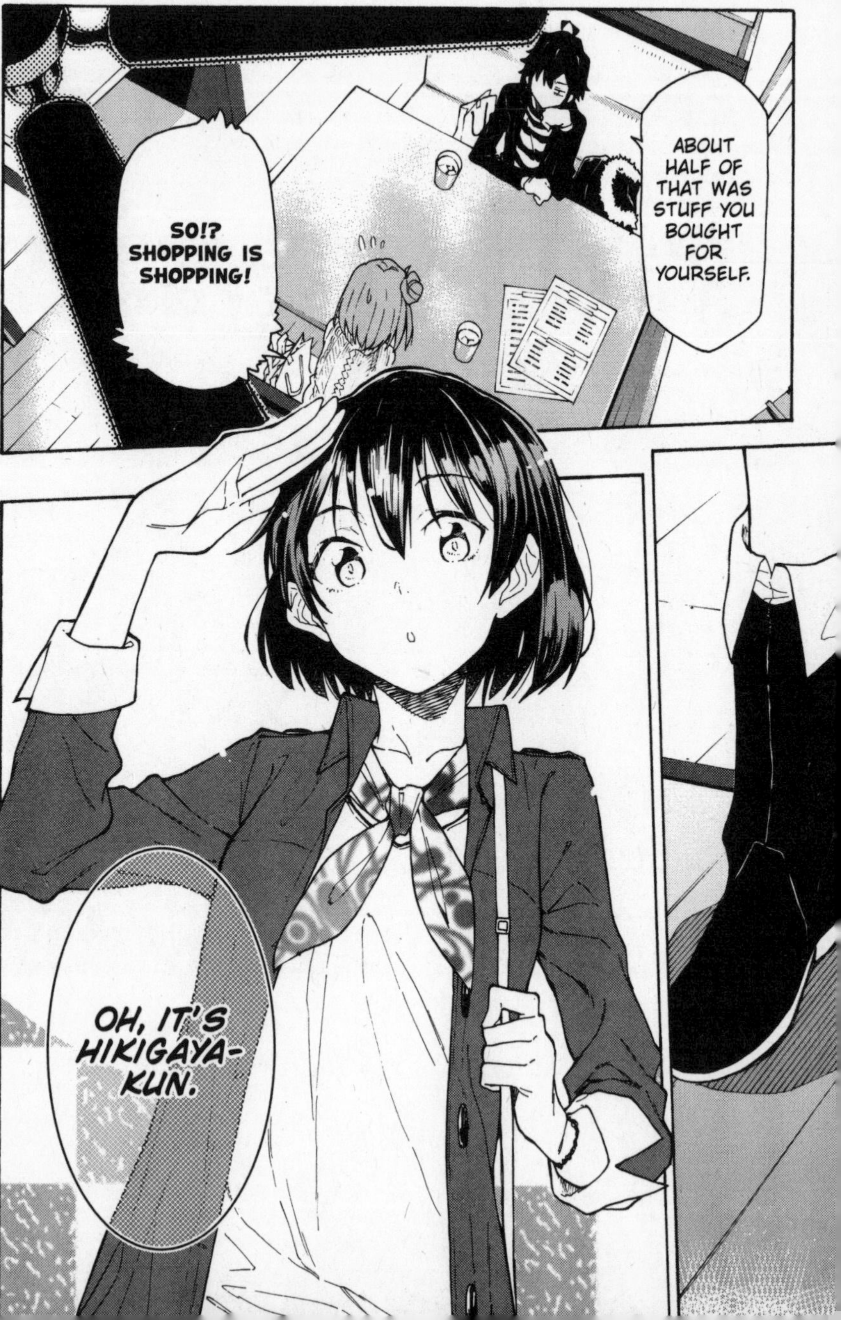
ABOUT HALF OF THAT WAS STUFF YOU BOUGHT FOR YOURSELF.
SO!? SHOPPING IS SHOPPING!
OH, IT'S HIKIGAYA-KUN.

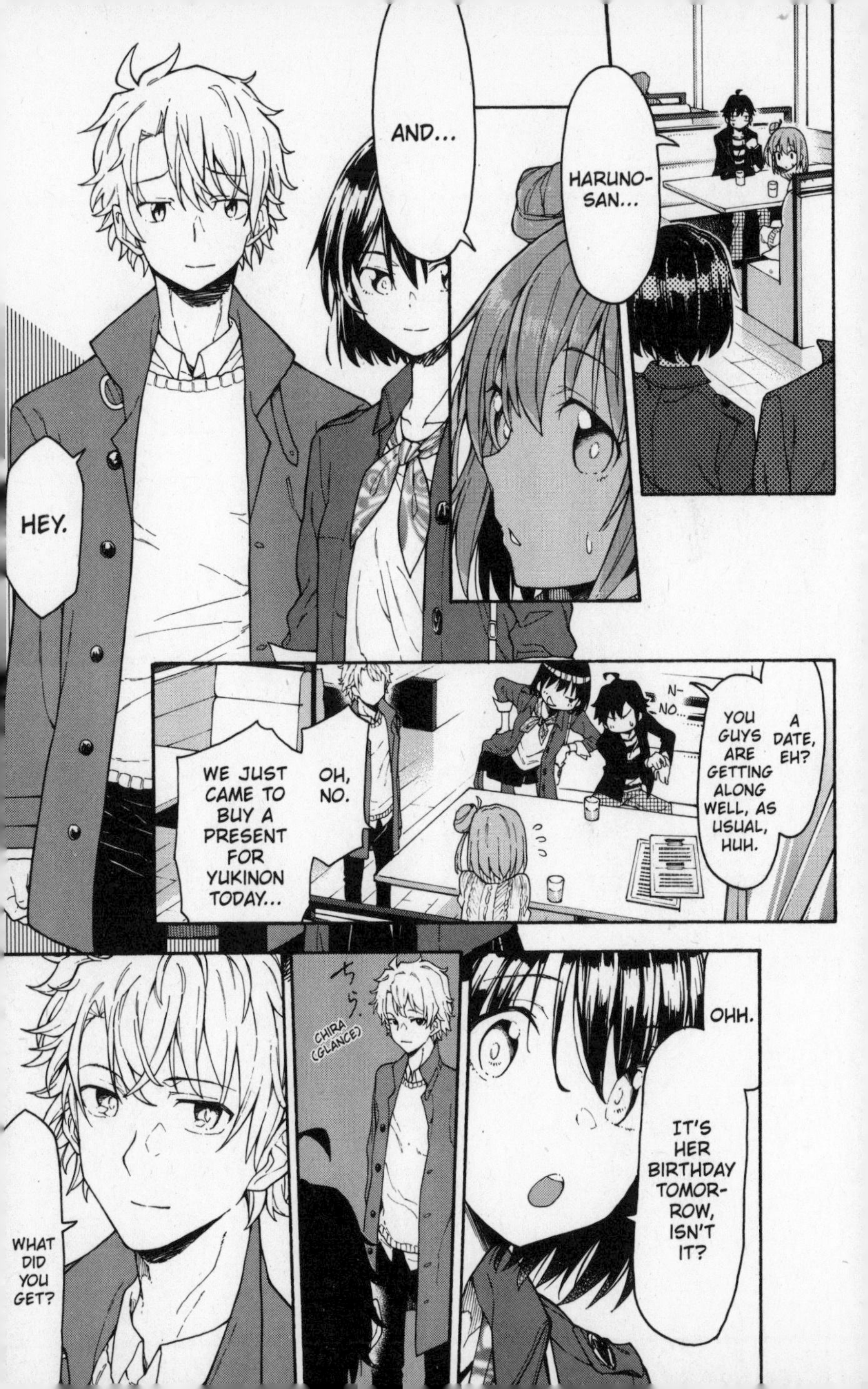

HARUNO-SAN...
AND...
A DATE, EH?
YOU GUYS ARE GETTING ALONG WELL, AS USUAL, HUH.
N-NO...
OH, NO.
WE JUST CAME TO BUY A PRESENT FOR YUKINON TODAY...
HEY.
OHH.
IT'S HER BIRTHDAY TOMORROW, ISN'T IT?
ちら
CHIRA (GLANCE)
WHAT DID YOU GET?

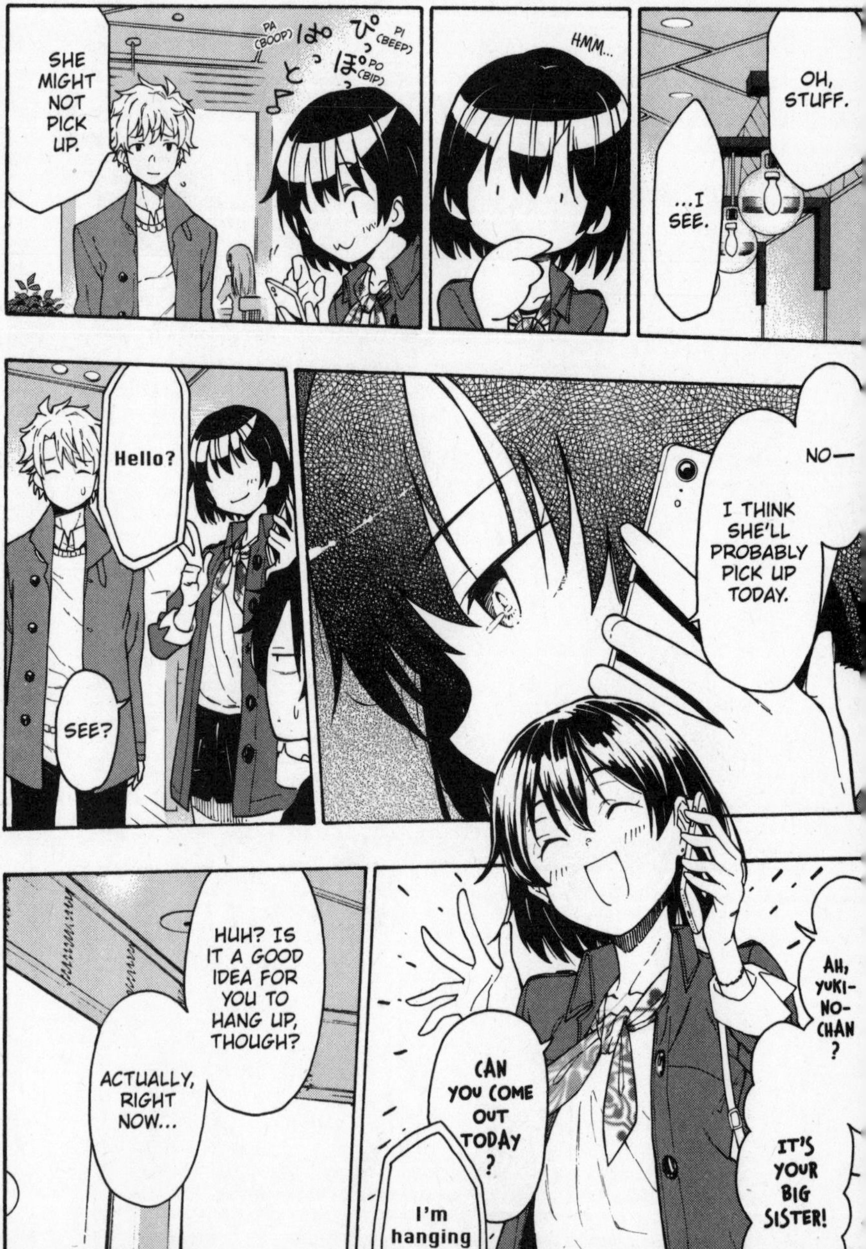
OH, STUFF.
...I SEE.
HMM...
PI (BEEP)
PO (BIP)
PA (BOOP)
ぴっぽっぱっと♪
SHE MIGHT NOT PICK UP.
NO—
I THINK SHE'LL PROBABLY PICK UP TODAY.
Hello?
SEE?
AH, YUKI-NO-CHAN?
IT'S YOUR BIG SISTER!
CAN YOU COME OUT TODAY?
I'm hanging up.
HUH? IS IT A GOOD IDEA FOR YOU TO HANG UP, THOUGH?
ACTUALLY, RIGHT NOW...

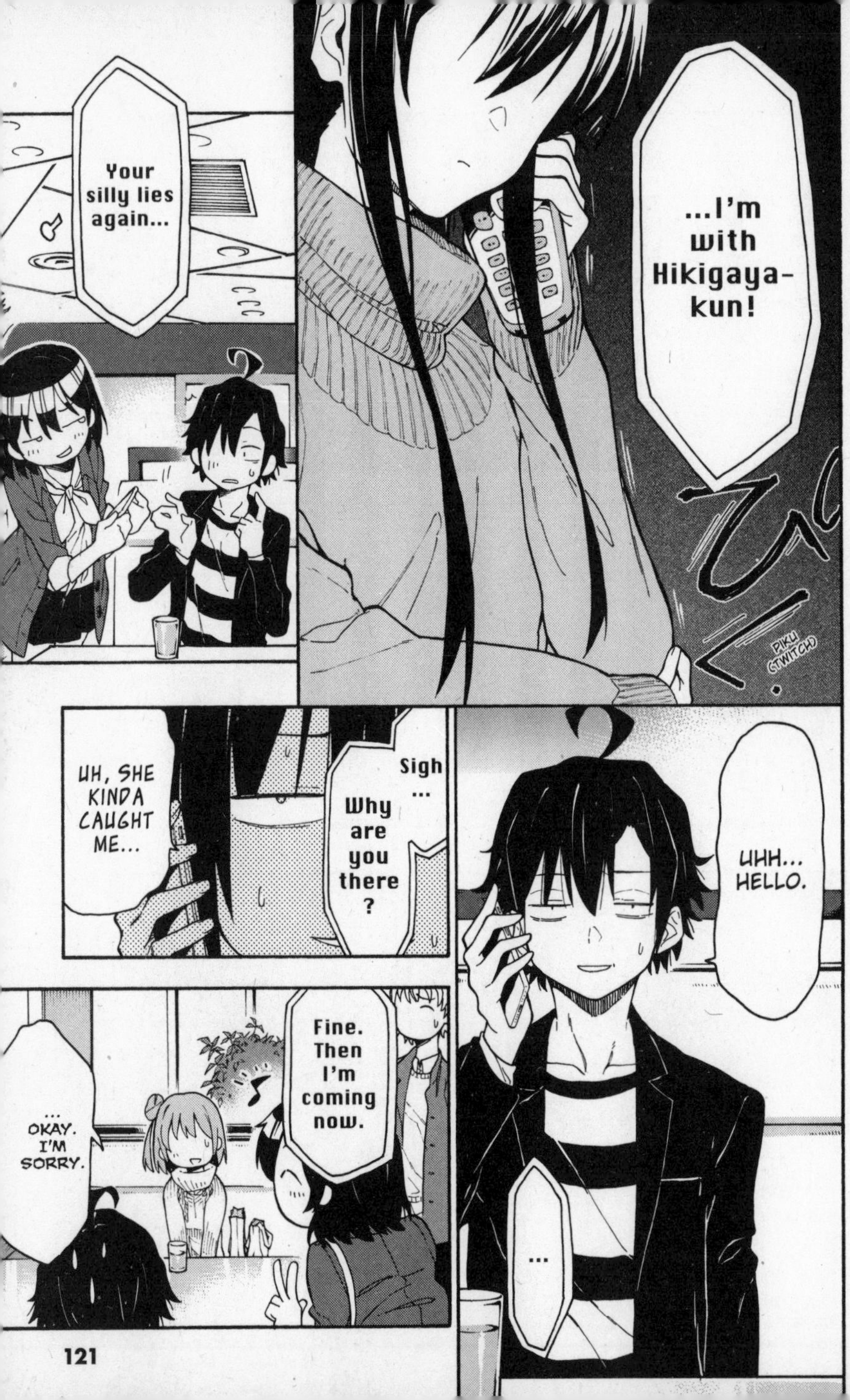
...I'm with Hikigaya-kun!
PIKU (TWITCH)
Your silly lies again...
UHH... HELLO.
...
Sigh... Why are you there?
UH, SHE KINDA CAUGHT ME...
Fine. Then I'm coming now.
...OKAY. I'M SORRY.

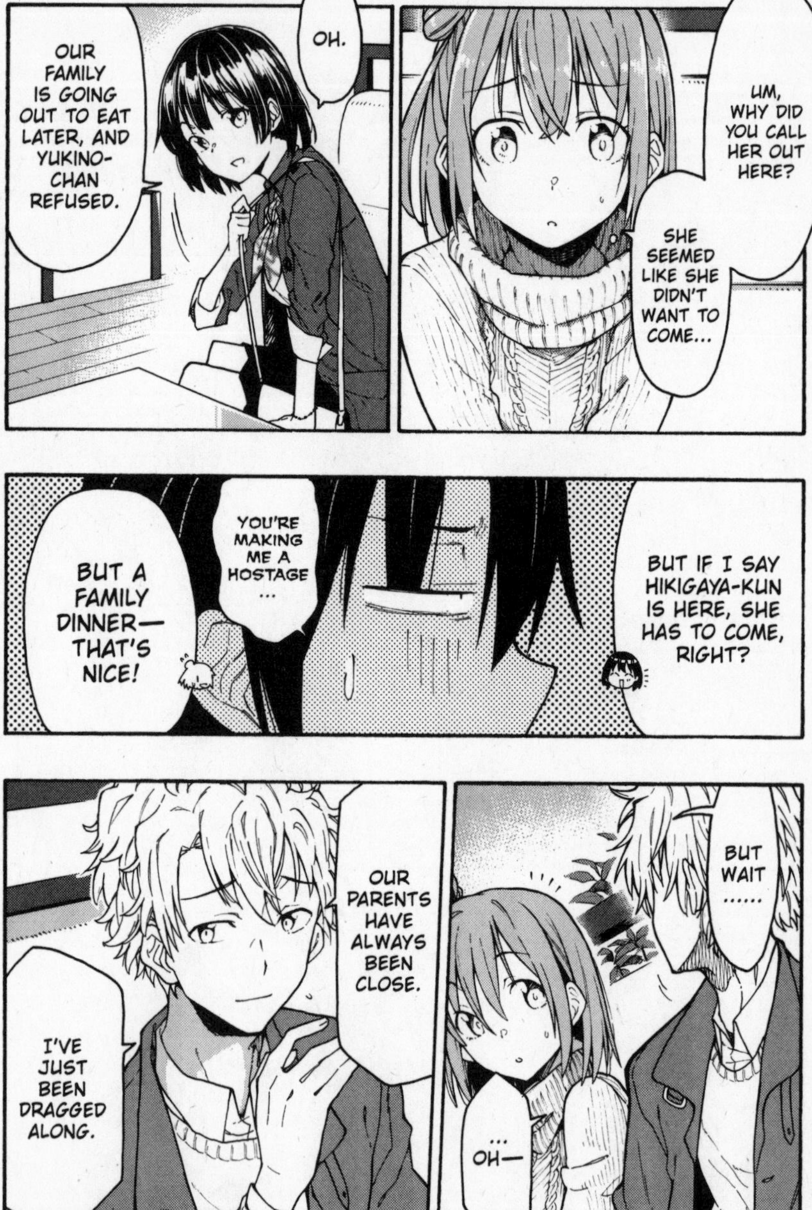
UM, WHY DID YOU CALL HER OUT HERE?
SHE SEEMED LIKE SHE DIDN'T WANT TO COME...
OH.
OUR FAMILY IS GOING OUT TO EAT LATER, AND YUKINO-CHAN REFUSED.
BUT IF I SAY HIKIGAYA-KUN IS HERE, SHE HAS TO COME, RIGHT?
YOU'RE MAKING ME A HOSTAGE...
BUT A FAMILY DINNER—THAT'S NICE!
BUT WAIT......
...OH—
OUR PARENTS HAVE ALWAYS BEEN CLOSE.
I'VE JUST BEEN DRAGGED ALONG.

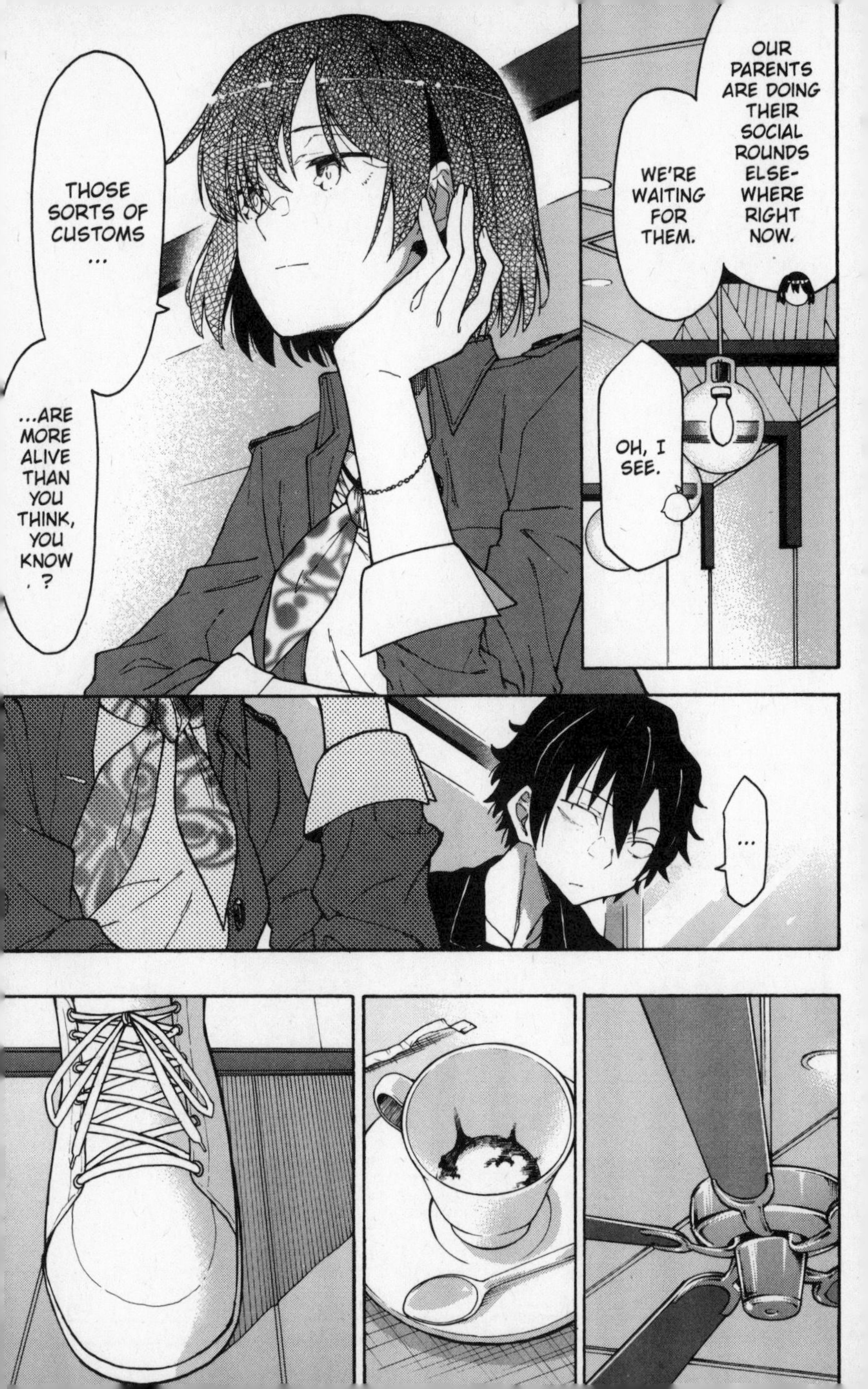
OUR PARENTS ARE DOING THEIR SOCIAL ROUNDS ELSE-WHERE RIGHT NOW.
WE'RE WAITING FOR THEM.
OH, I SEE.
THOSE SORTS OF CUSTOMS...
...ARE MORE ALIVE THAN YOU THINK, YOU KNOW...?
...

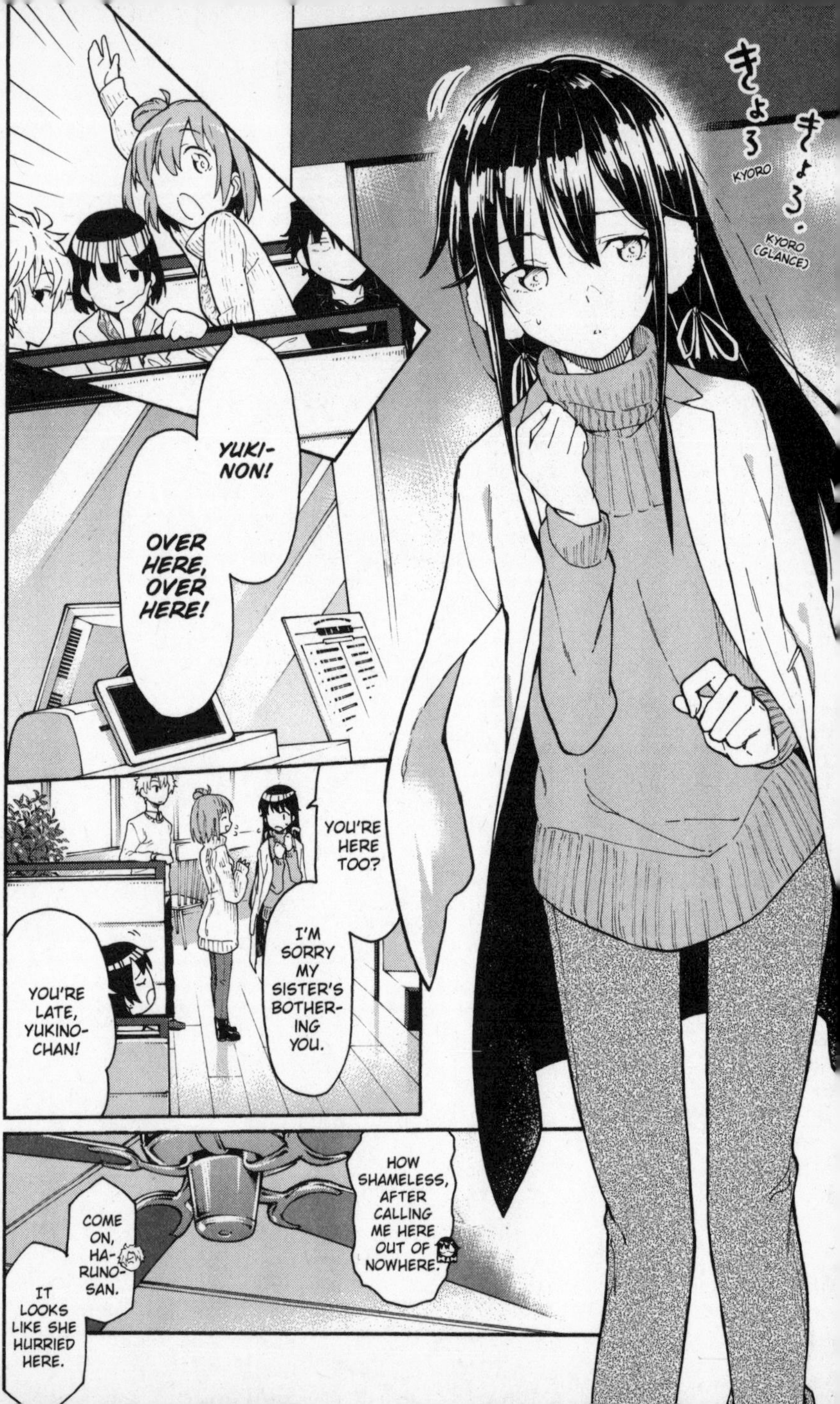
きょろ
KYORO
きょろ。
KYORO (GLANCE)
YUKI-NON!
OVER HERE, OVER HERE!
YOU'RE HERE TOO?
I'M SORRY MY SISTER'S BOTHER-ING YOU.
YOU'RE LATE, YUKINO-CHAN!
HOW SHAMELESS, AFTER CALLING ME HERE OUT OF NOWHERE.
COME ON, HA-RUNO-SAN.
IT LOOKS LIKE SHE HURRIED HERE.

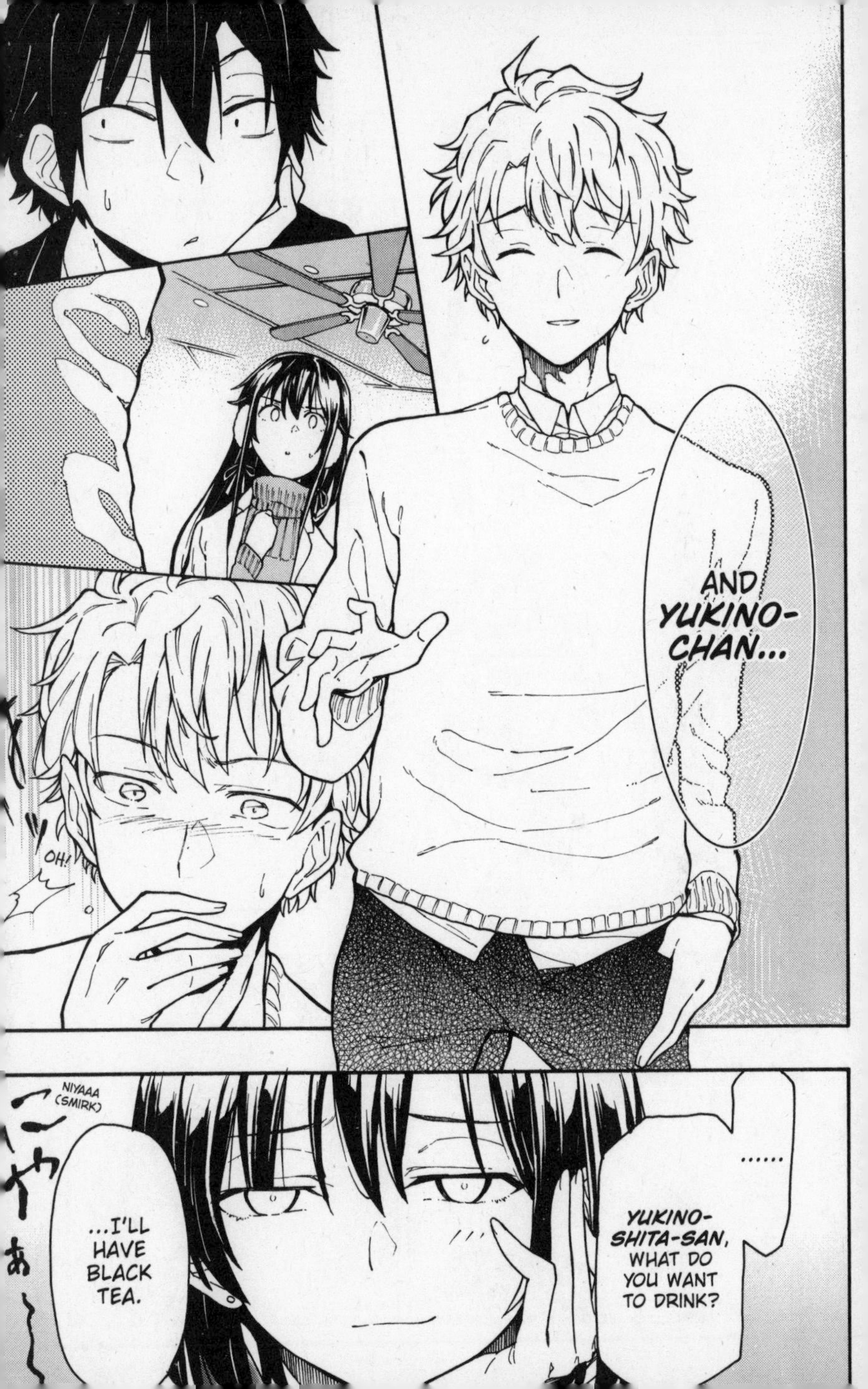
AND YUKINO-CHAN...
OH!
......
YUKINO-SHITA-SAN, WHAT DO YOU WANT TO DRINK?
NIYAAA (SMIRK)
...I'LL HAVE BLACK TEA.

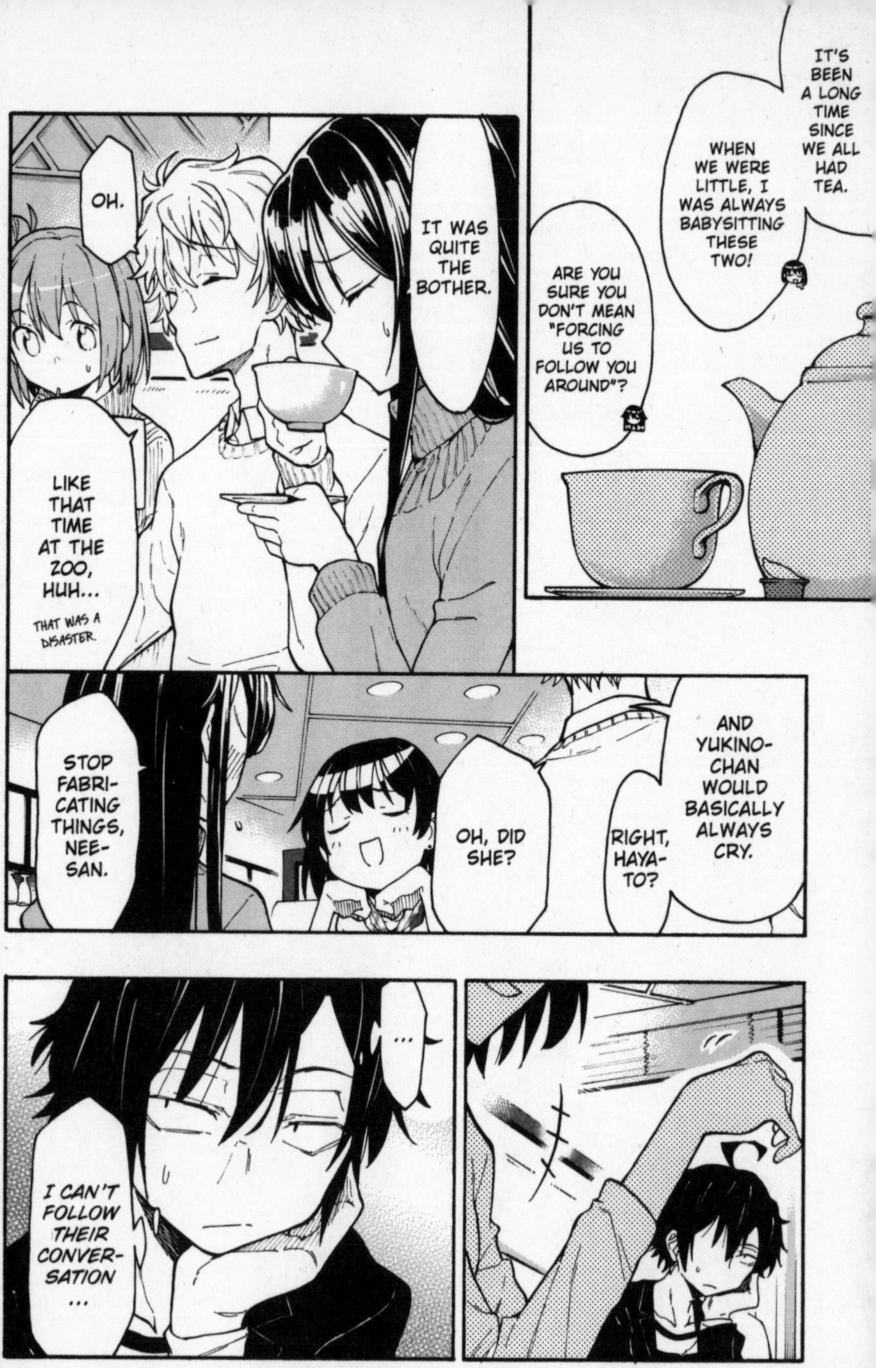
IT'S BEEN A LONG TIME SINCE WE ALL HAD TEA.
WHEN WE WERE LITTLE, I WAS ALWAYS BABYSITTING THESE TWO!
ARE YOU SURE YOU DON'T MEAN "FORCING US TO FOLLOW YOU AROUND"?
IT WAS QUITE THE BOTHER.
OH.
LIKE THAT TIME AT THE ZOO, HUH...
THAT WAS A DISASTER.
AND YUKINO-CHAN WOULD BASICALLY ALWAYS CRY.
RIGHT, HAYA-TO?
OH, DID SHE?
STOP FABRICATING THINGS, NEE-SAN.
...
I CAN'T FOLLOW THEIR CONVER-SATION...

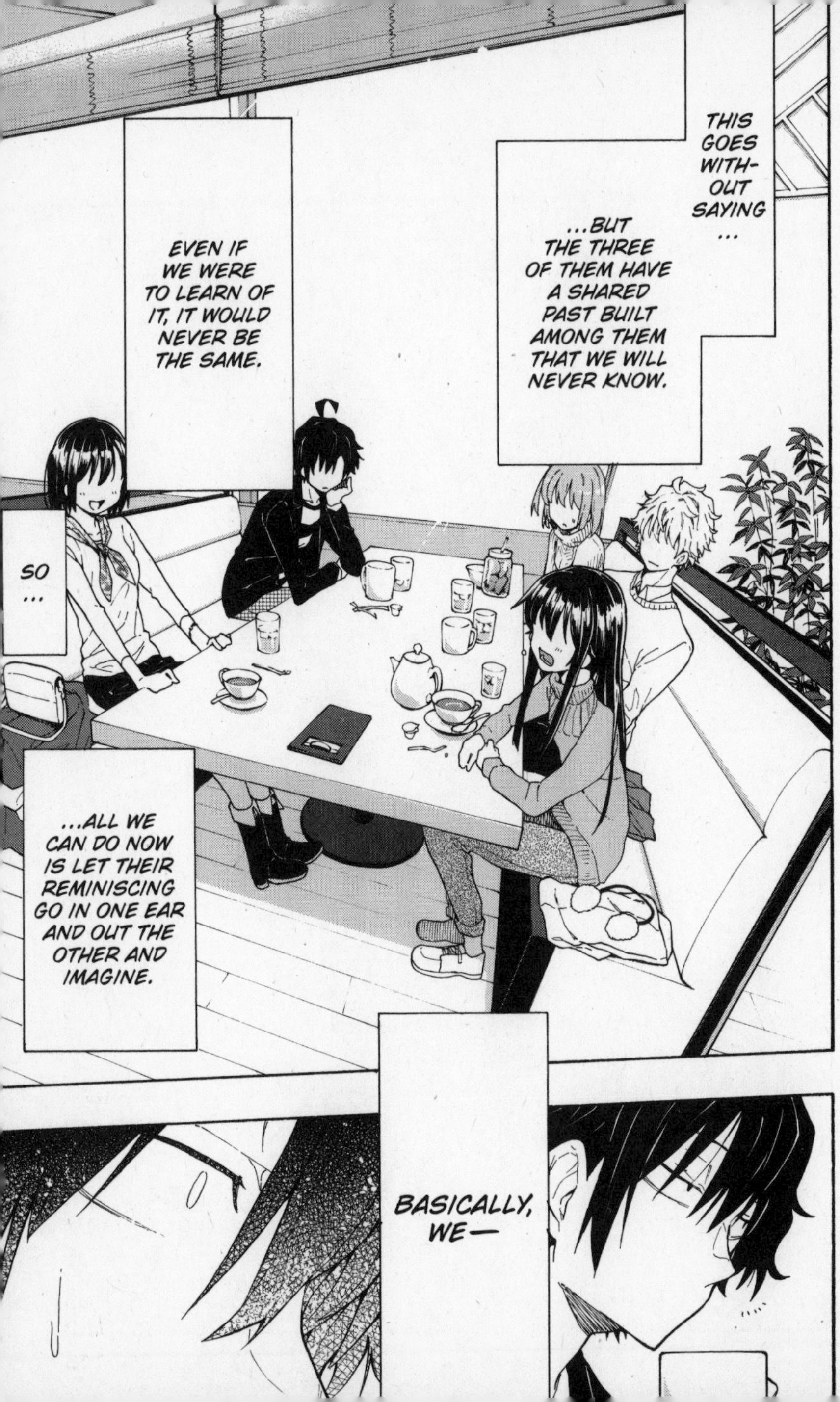
THIS GOES WITH-OUT SAYING...
...BUT THE THREE OF THEM HAVE A SHARED PAST BUILT AMONG THEM THAT WE WILL NEVER KNOW.
EVEN IF WE WERE TO LEARN OF IT, IT WOULD NEVER BE THE SAME.
SO...
...ALL WE CAN DO NOW IS LET THEIR REMINISCING GO IN ONE EAR AND OUT THE OTHER AND IMAGINE.
BASICALLY, WE—

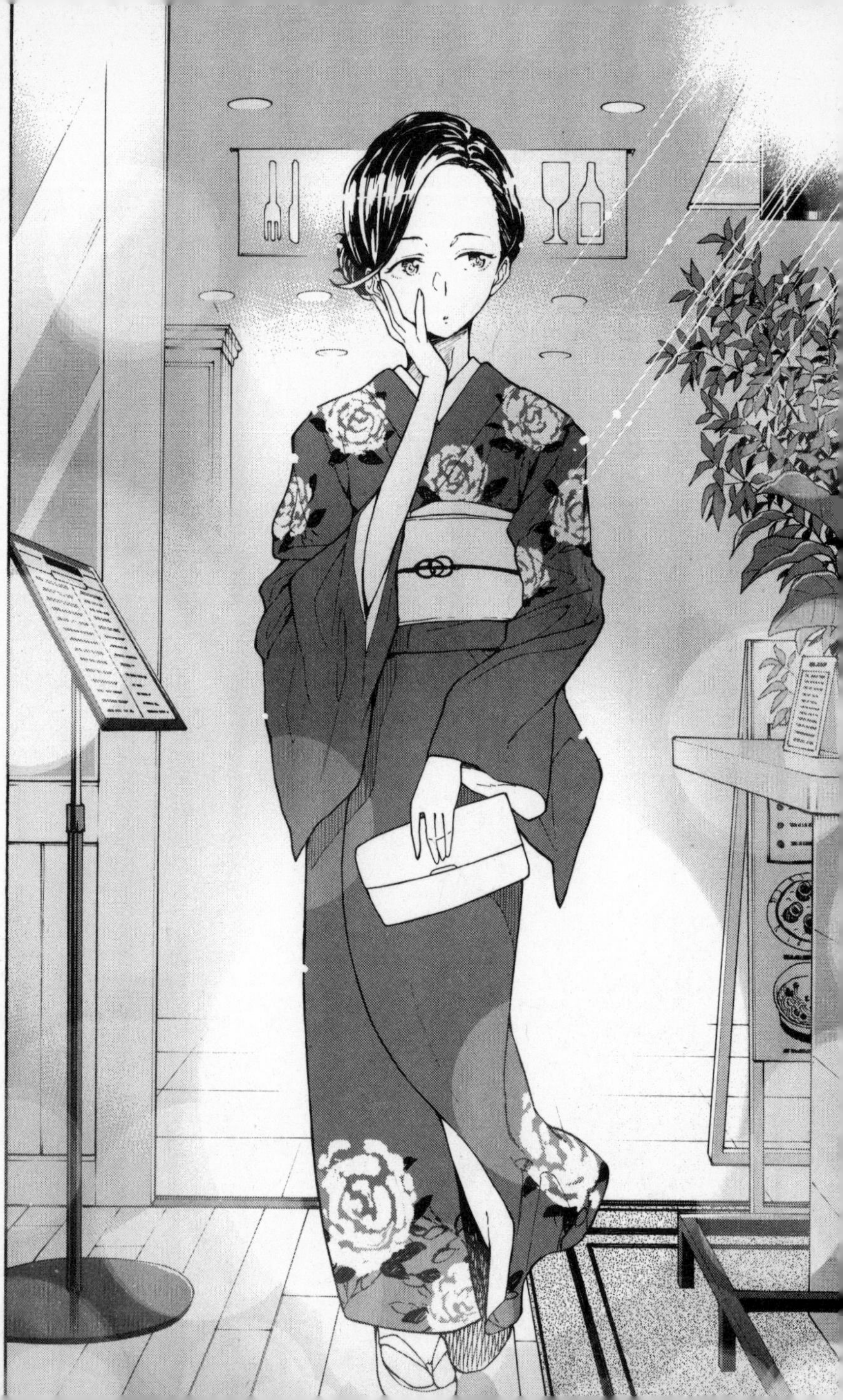

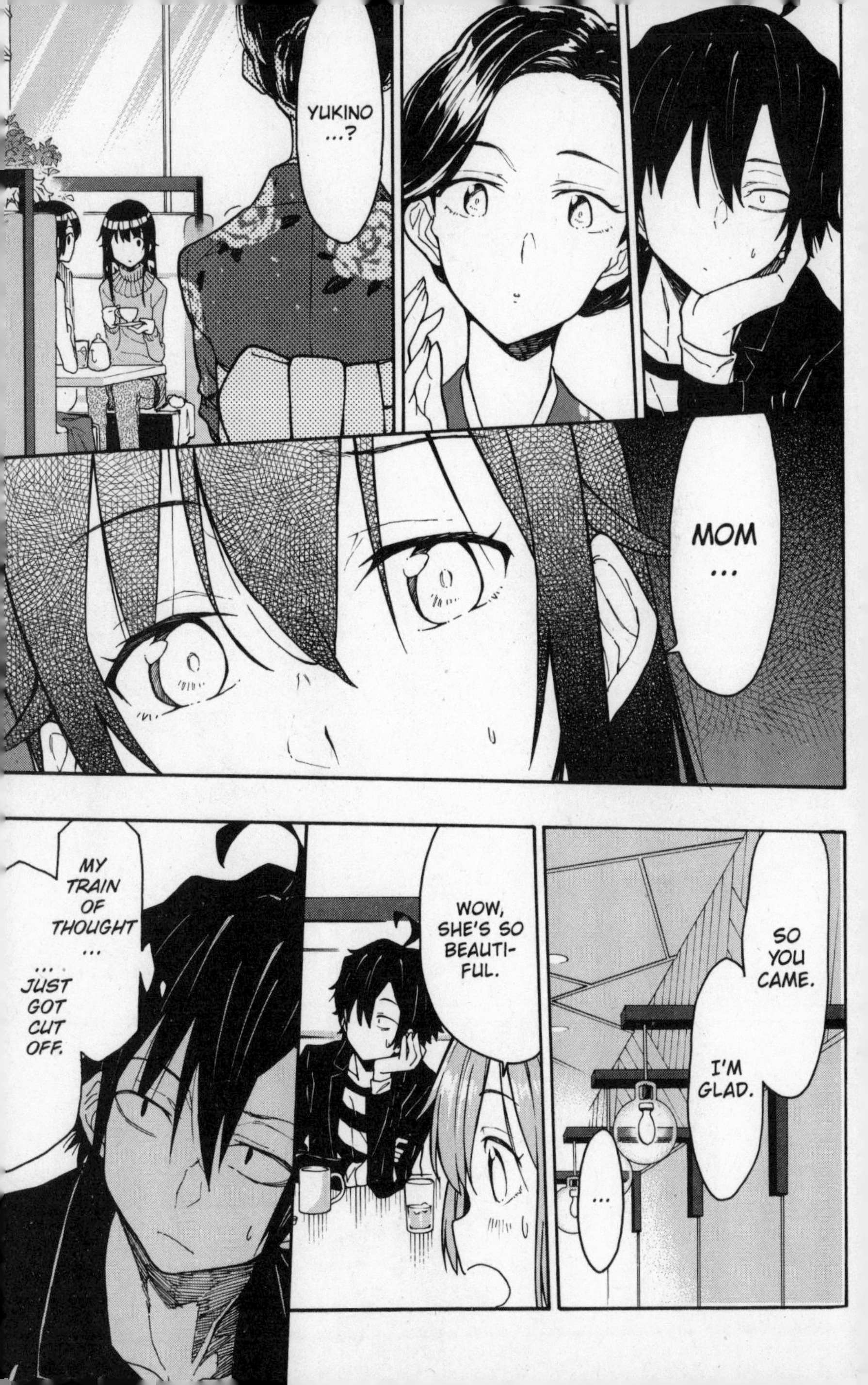
YUKINO ...?
MOM ...
SO YOU CAME.
I'M GLAD.
...
WOW, SHE'S SO BEAUTI-FUL.
MY TRAIN OF THOUGHT ...
... JUST GOT CUT OFF.

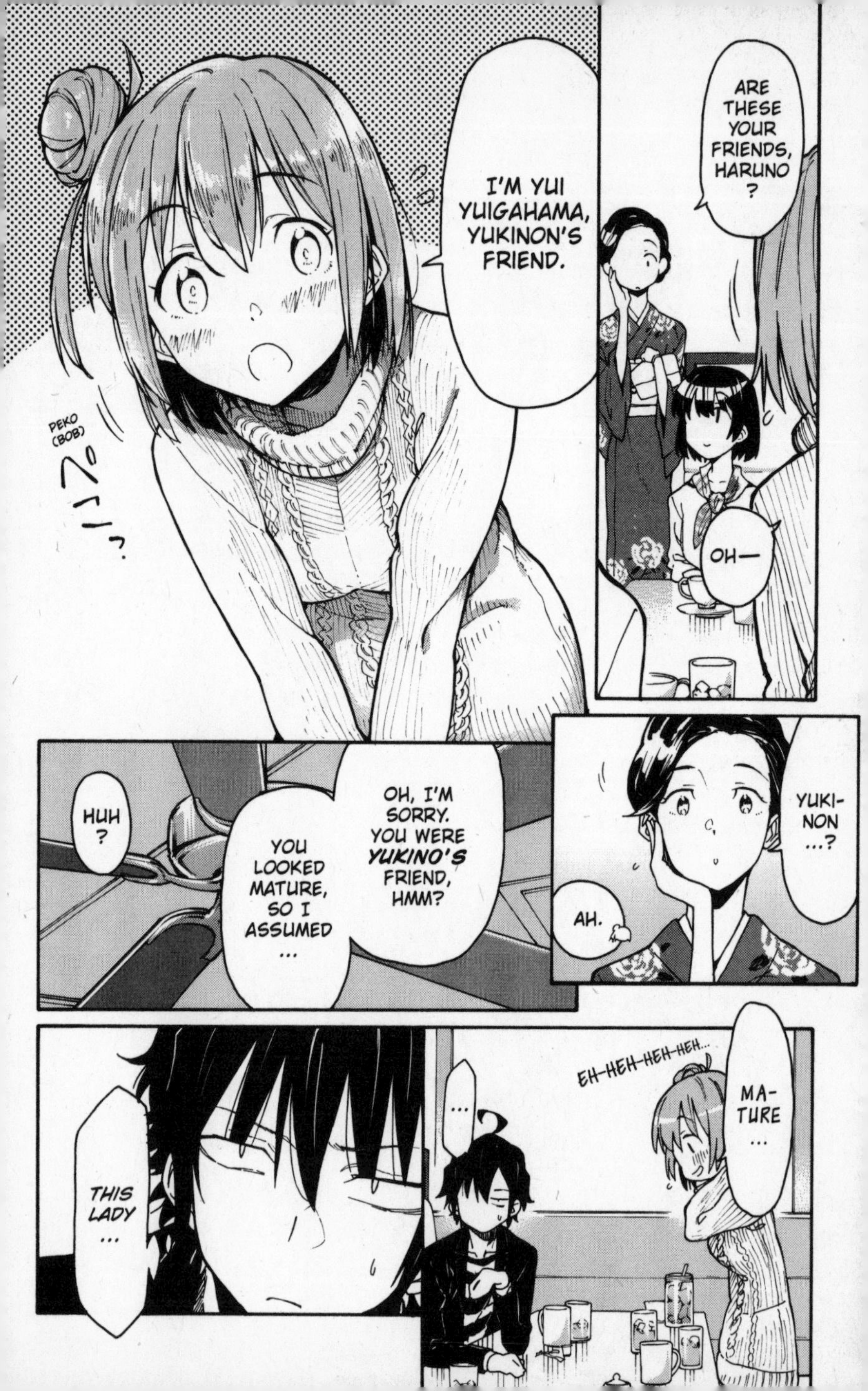
ARE THESE YOUR FRIENDS, HARUNO?
OH—
I'M YUI YUIGAHAMA, YUKINON'S FRIEND.
PEKO (BOB)
YUKI-NON...?
AH.
OH, I'M SORRY. YOU WERE *YUKINO'S* FRIEND, HMM?
YOU LOOKED MATURE, SO I ASSUMED...
HUH?
MA-TURE...
EH-HEH-HEH-HEH...
...
THIS LADY...

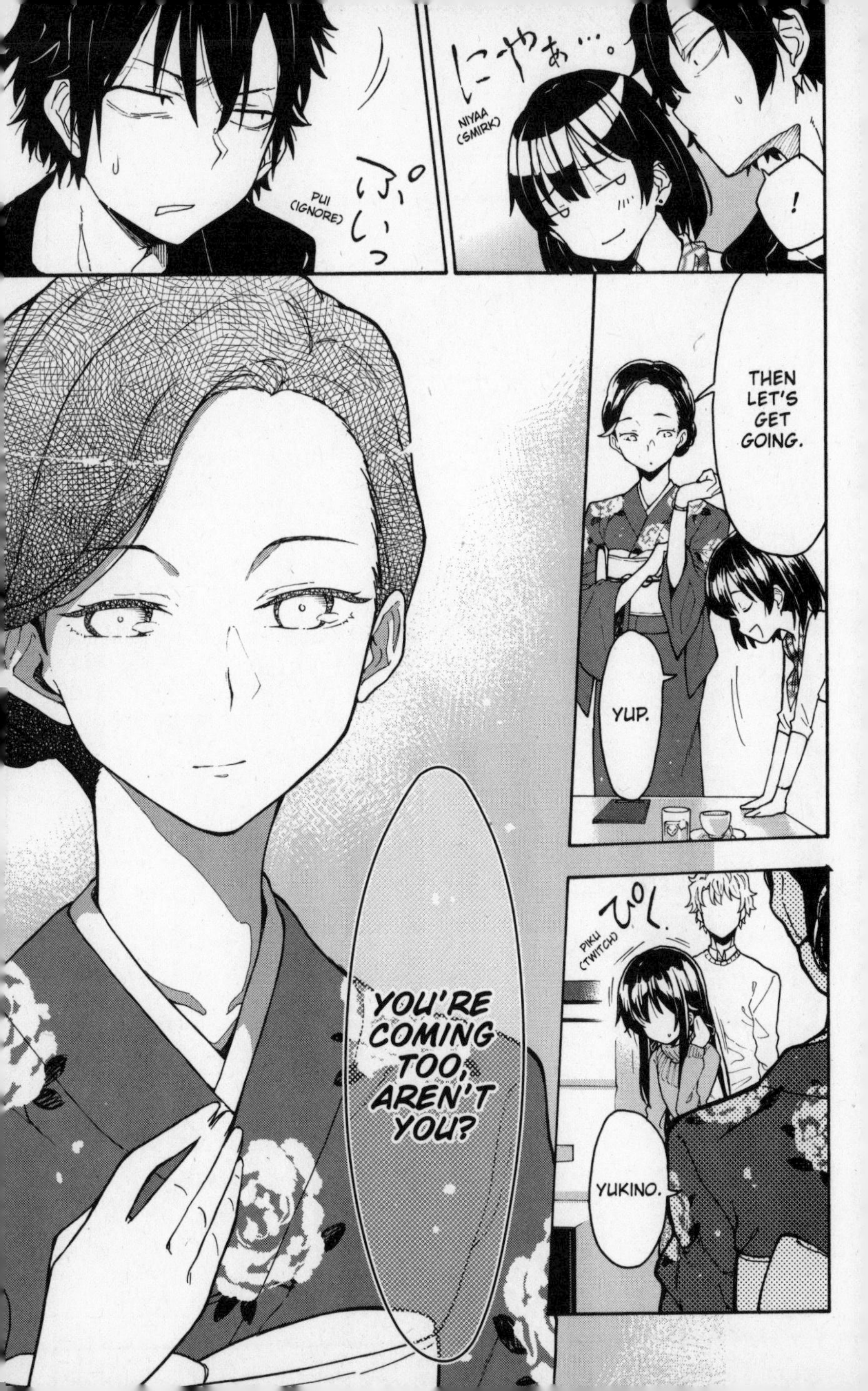

にやぁ…。
NIYAA (SMIRK)
!
ぷいっ
PUI (IGNORE)
THEN LET'S GET GOING.
YUP.
ぴく.
PIKU (TWITCH)
YUKINO.
YOU'RE COMING TOO, AREN'T YOU?

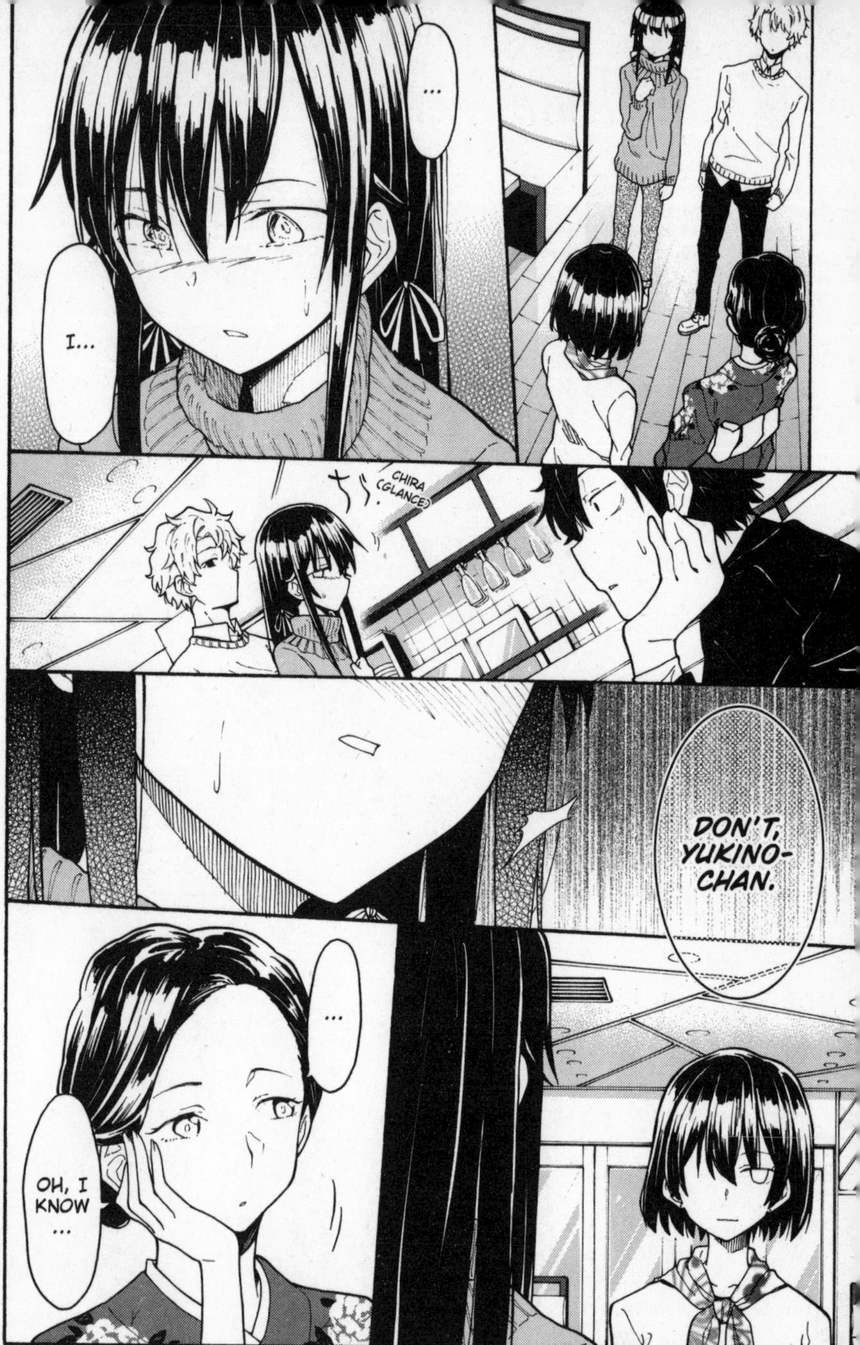
...
I...
CHIRA (GLANCE)
DON'T, YUKINO-CHAN.
...
OH, I KNOW ...

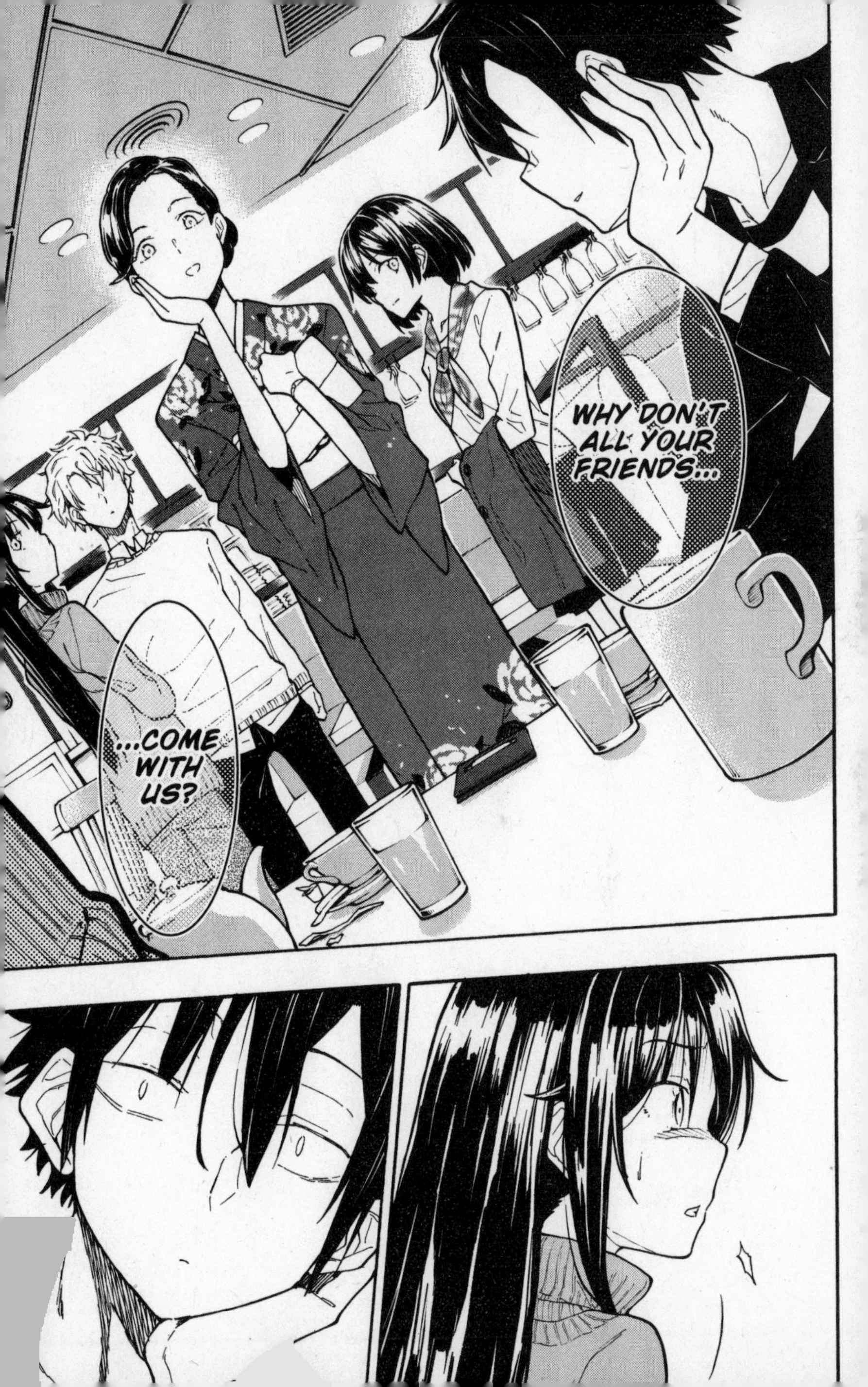
WHY DON'T ALL YOUR FRIENDS...
...COME WITH US?

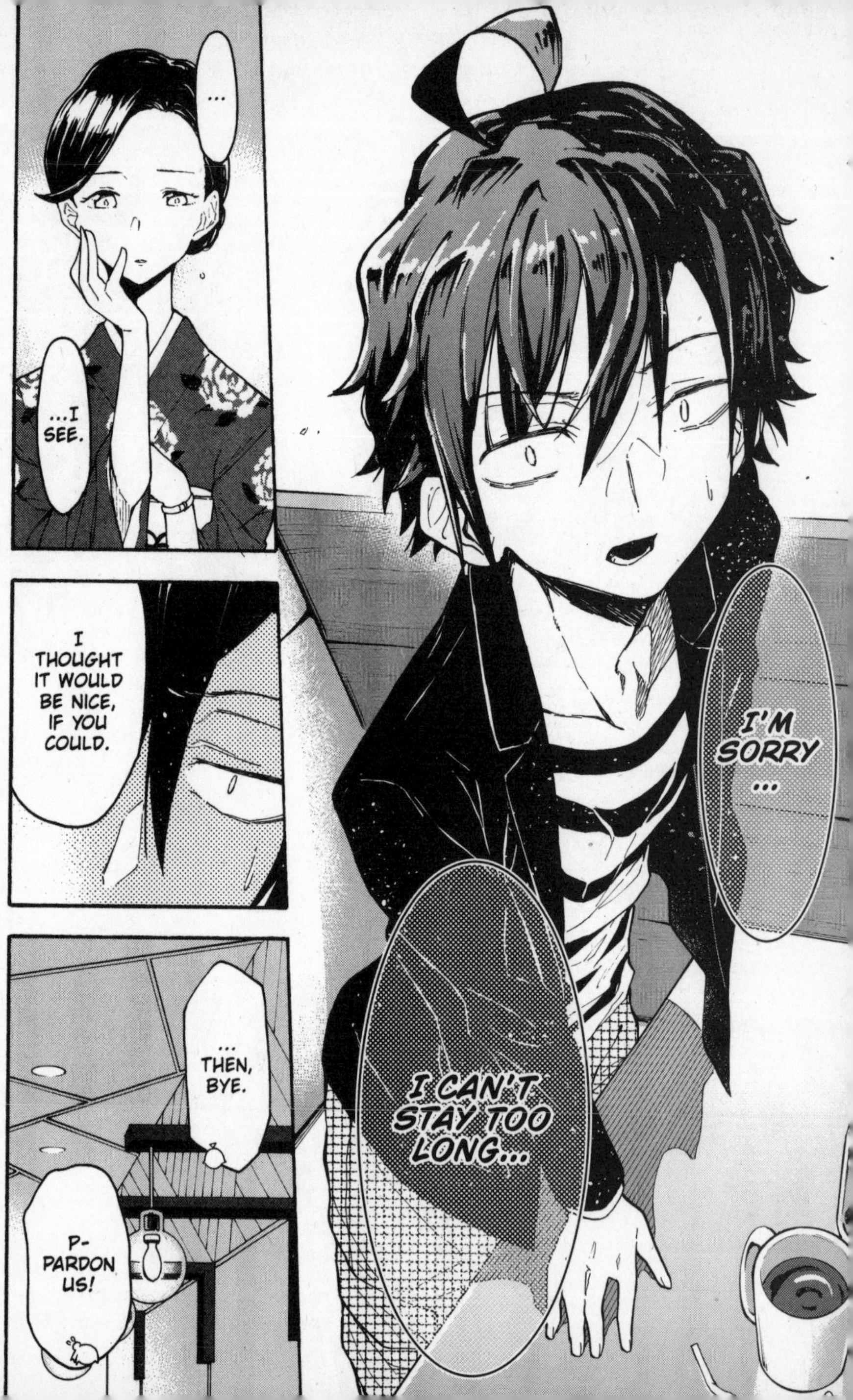
I'M SORRY...
I CAN'T STAY TOO LONG...
...
...I SEE.
I THOUGHT IT WOULD BE NICE, IF YOU COULD.
...THEN, BYE.
P-PARDON US!

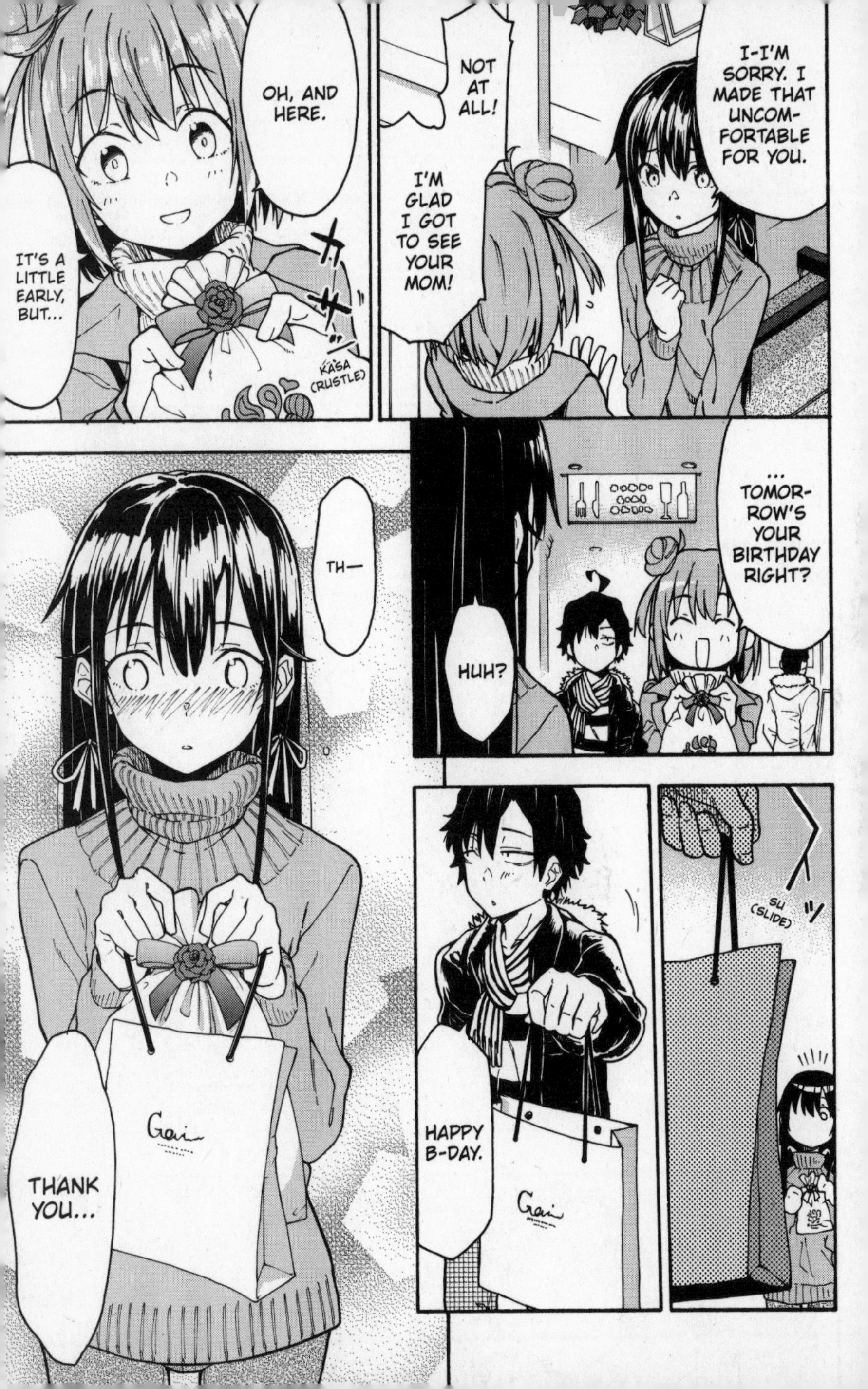
I-I'M SORRY. I MADE THAT UNCOM-FORTABLE FOR YOU.
NOT AT ALL!
I'M GLAD I GOT TO SEE YOUR MOM!
OH, AND HERE.
IT'S A LITTLE EARLY, BUT...
KASA (RUSTLE)
... TOMOR-ROW'S YOUR BIRTHDAY RIGHT?
HUH?
SU (SLIDE)
HAPPY B-DAY.
TH—
THANK YOU...

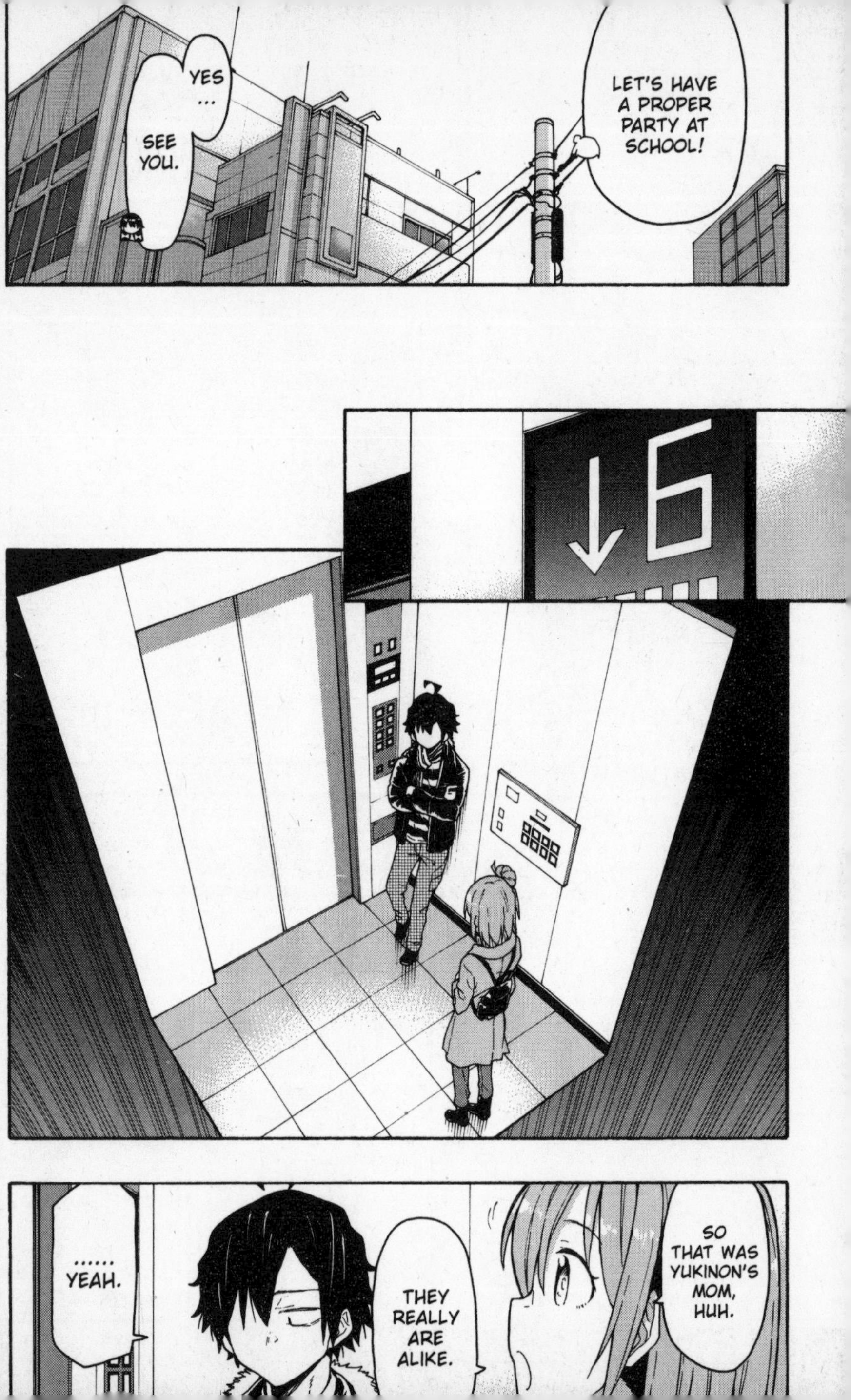
LET'S HAVE A PROPER PARTY AT SCHOOL!
YES ... SEE YOU.
SO THAT WAS YUKINON'S MOM, HUH.
THEY REALLY ARE ALIKE.
...... YEAH.

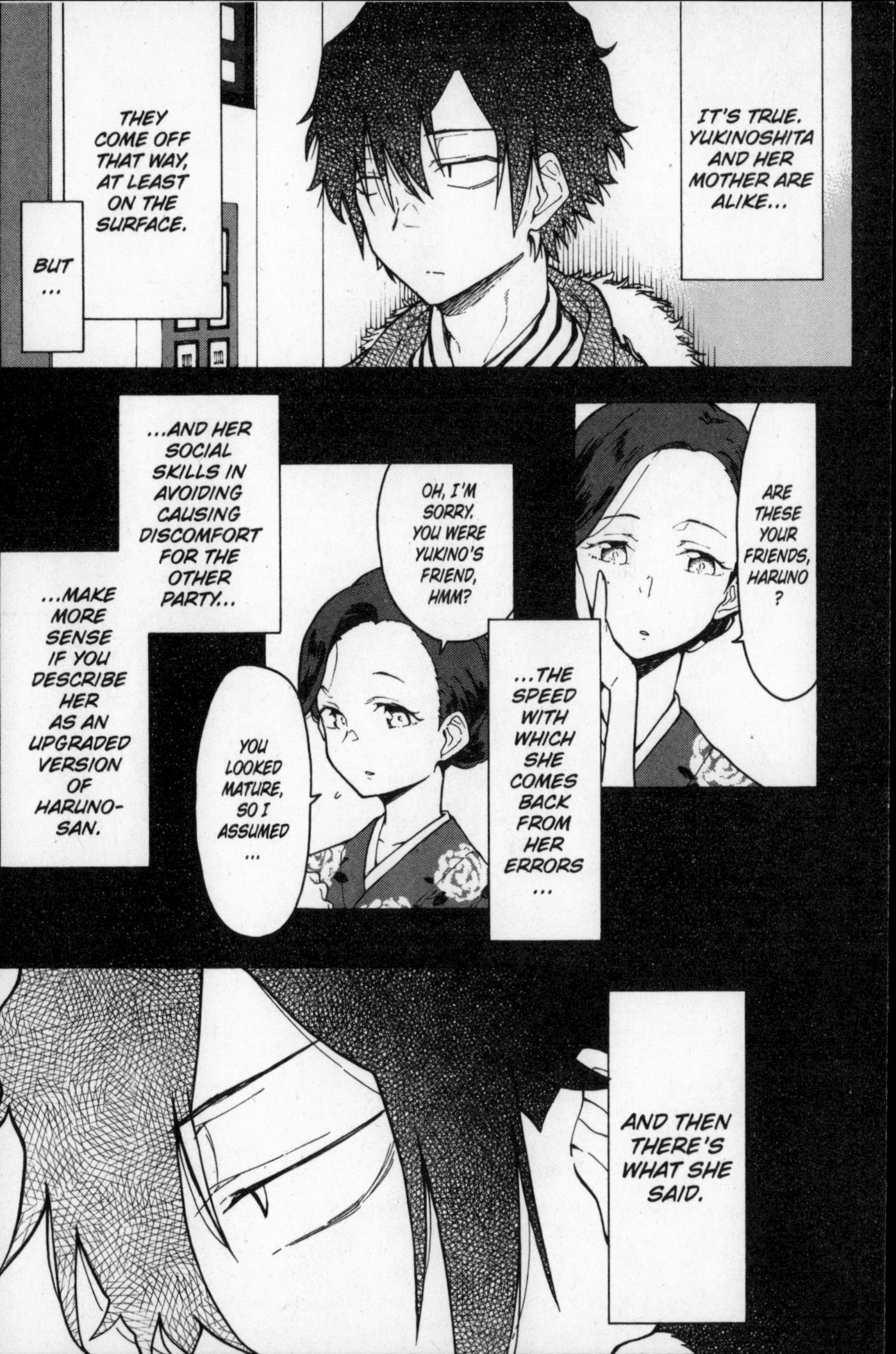
IT'S TRUE. YUKINOSHITA AND HER MOTHER ARE ALIKE...
THEY COME OFF THAT WAY, AT LEAST ON THE SURFACE.
BUT ...
ARE THESE YOUR FRIENDS, HARUNO?
...THE SPEED WITH WHICH SHE COMES BACK FROM HER ERRORS ...
OH, I'M SORRY. YOU WERE YUKINO'S FRIEND, HMM?
YOU LOOKED MATURE, SO I ASSUMED ...
...AND HER SOCIAL SKILLS IN AVOIDING CAUSING DISCOMFORT FOR THE OTHER PARTY...
...MAKE MORE SENSE IF YOU DESCRIBE HER AS AN UPGRADED VERSION OF HARUNO-SAN.
AND THEN THERE'S WHAT SHE SAID.

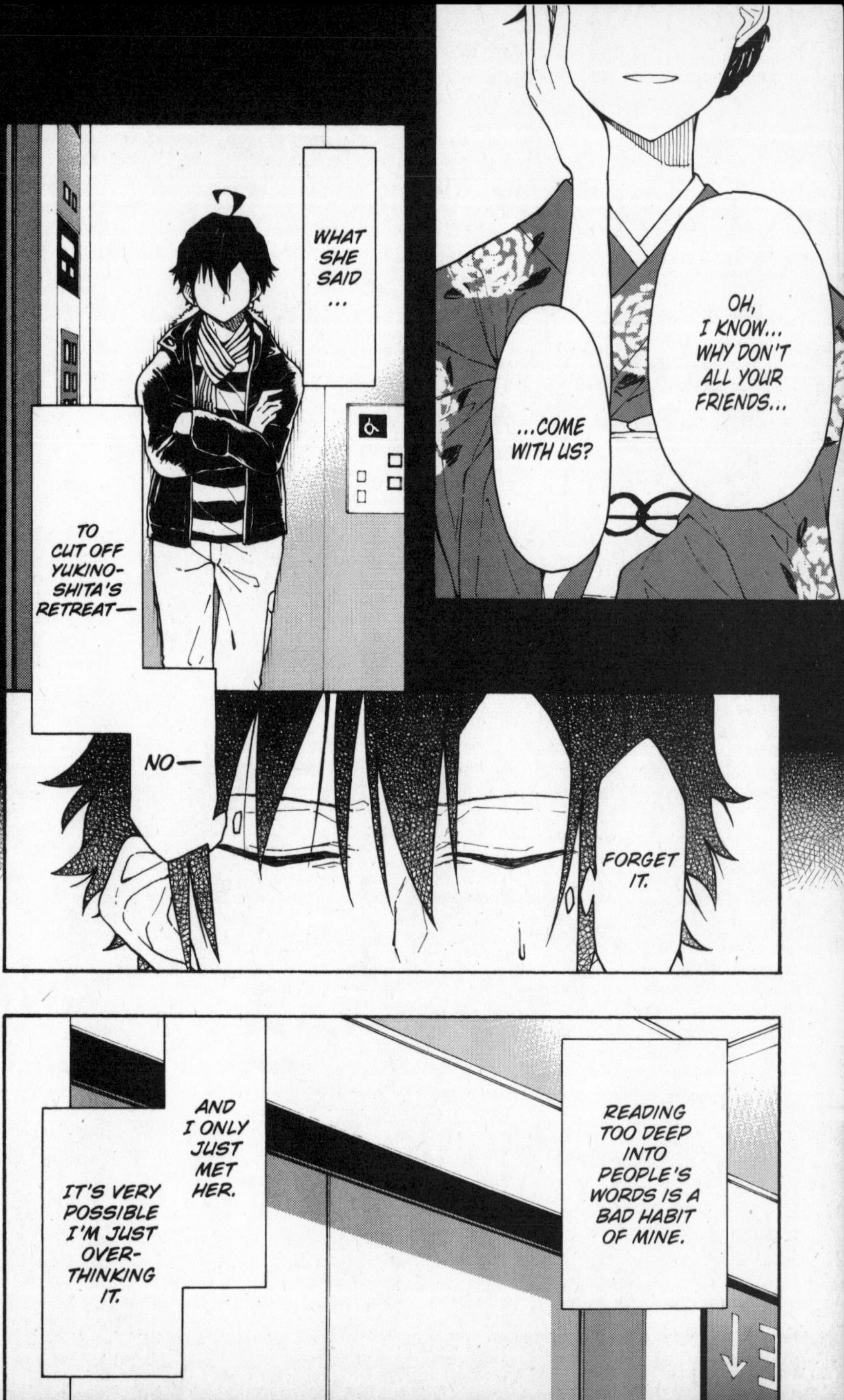
OH, I KNOW... WHY DON'T ALL YOUR FRIENDS...
...COME WITH US?
WHAT SHE SAID ...
TO CUT OFF YUKINOSHITA'S RETREAT—
NO—
FORGET IT.
READING TOO DEEP INTO PEOPLE'S WORDS IS A BAD HABIT OF MINE.
AND I ONLY JUST MET HER.
IT'S VERY POSSIBLE I'M JUST OVER-THINKING IT.

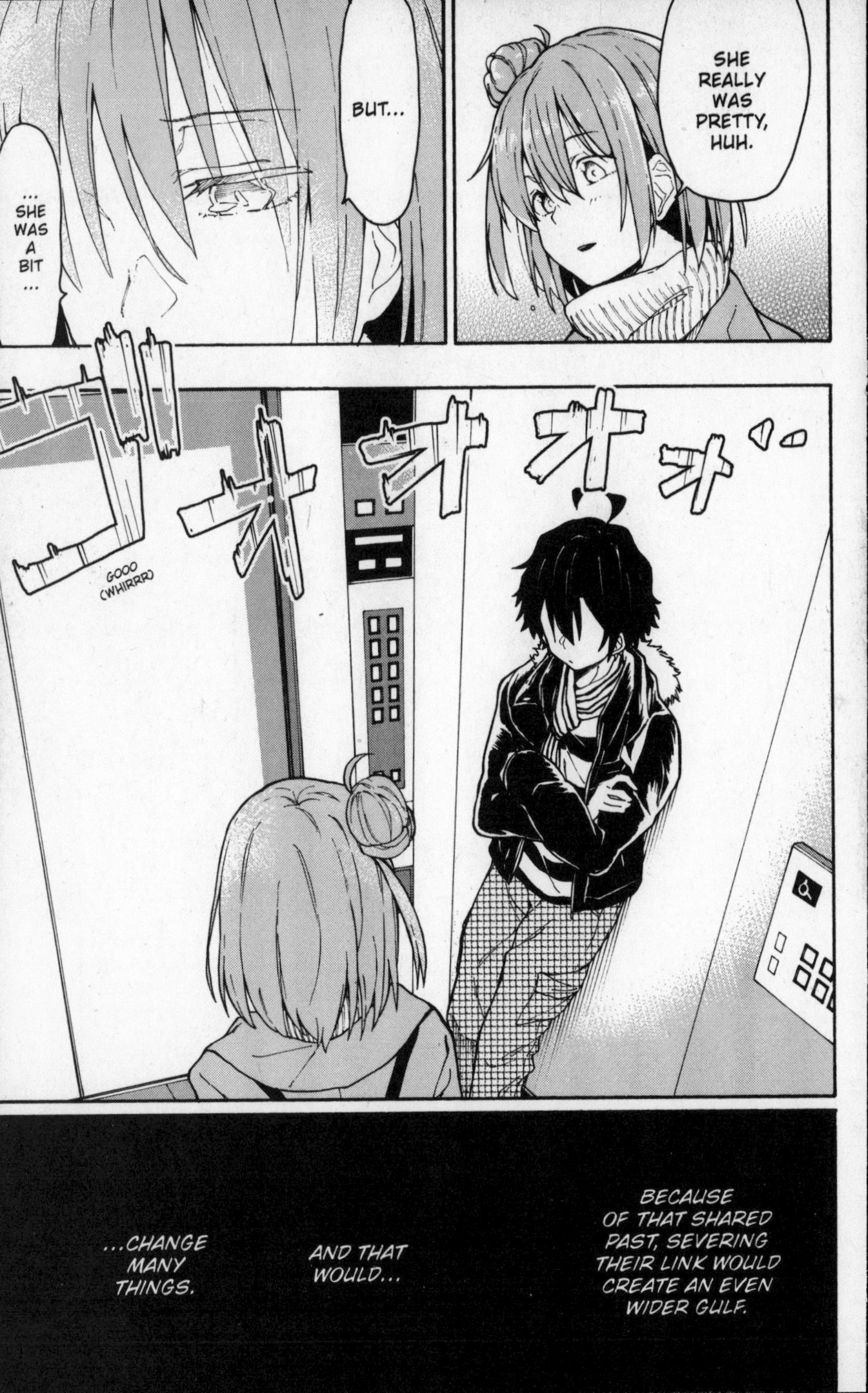
SHE REALLY WAS PRETTY, HUH.
BUT...
...SHE WAS A BIT...
GOOO (WHIRRR)
BECAUSE OF THAT SHARED PAST, SEVERING THEIR LINK WOULD CREATE AN EVEN WIDER GULF.
AND THAT WOULD...
...CHANGE MANY THINGS.

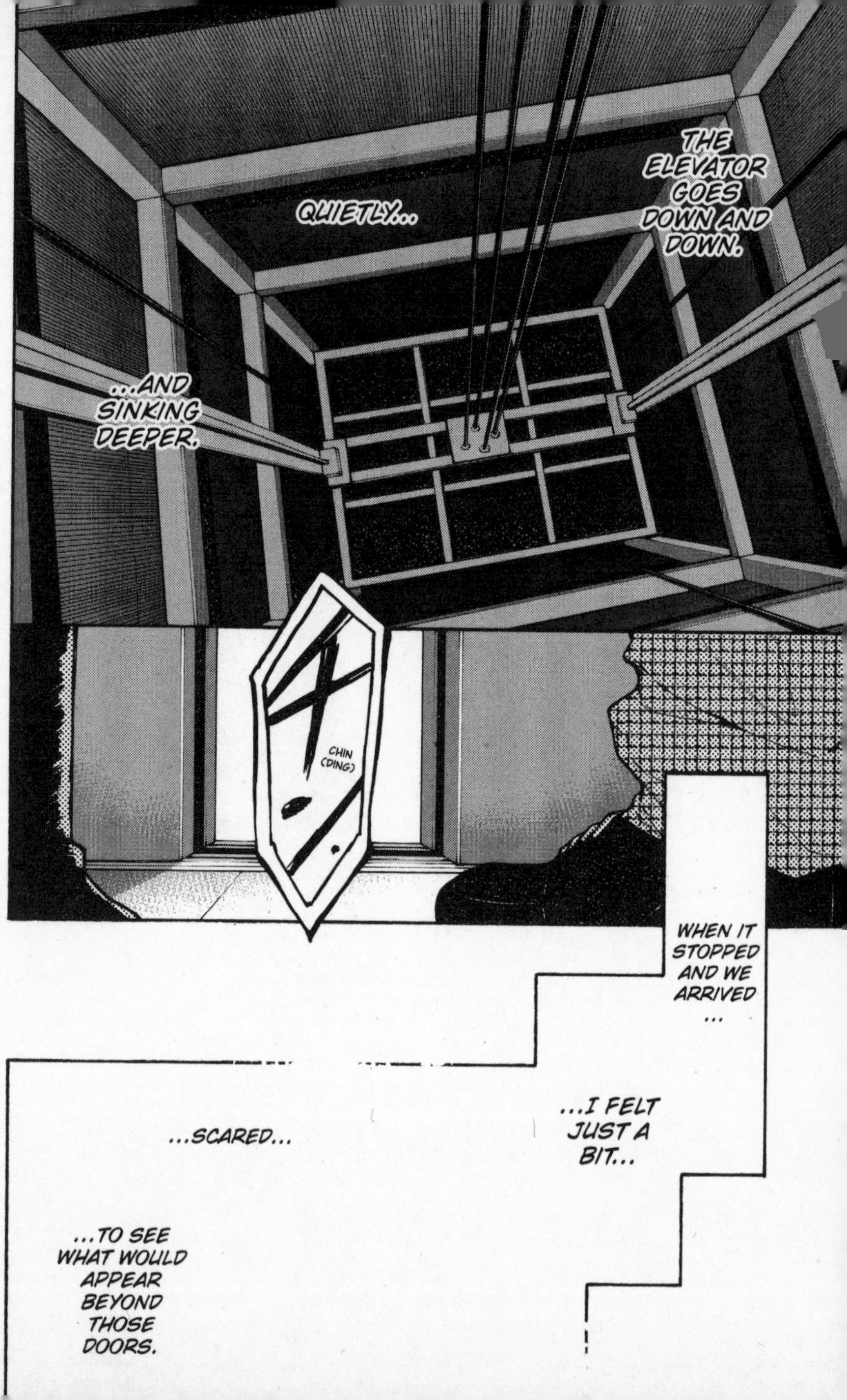
THE ELEVATOR GOES DOWN AND DOWN.
QUIETLY...
...AND SINKING DEEPER.
CHIN (DING)
WHEN IT STOPPED AND WE ARRIVED...
...I FELT JUST A BIT...
...SCARED...
...TO SEE WHAT WOULD APPEAR BEYOND THOSE DOORS.

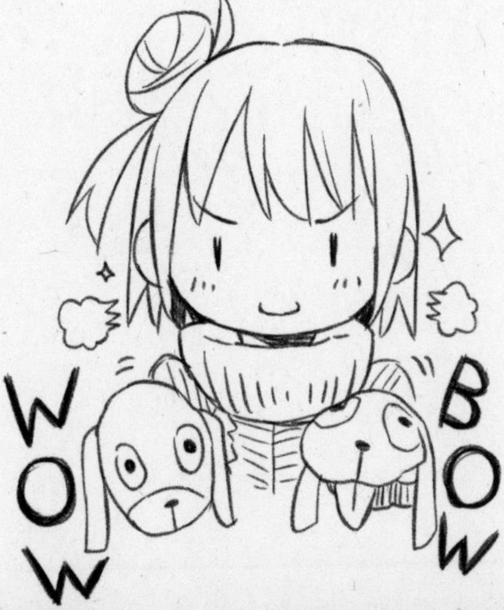
BOW
WOW

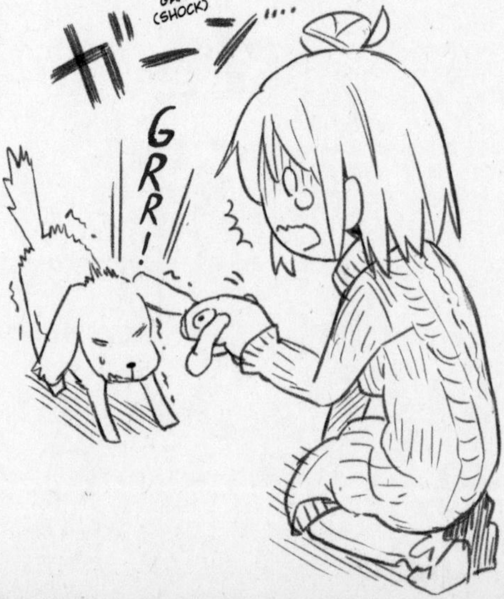
GAAN
(SHOCK)
ガーン…
GRR!

CHAPTER 75 ··· AT SOME POINT, IROHA ISSHIKI STARTED HANGING AROUND.

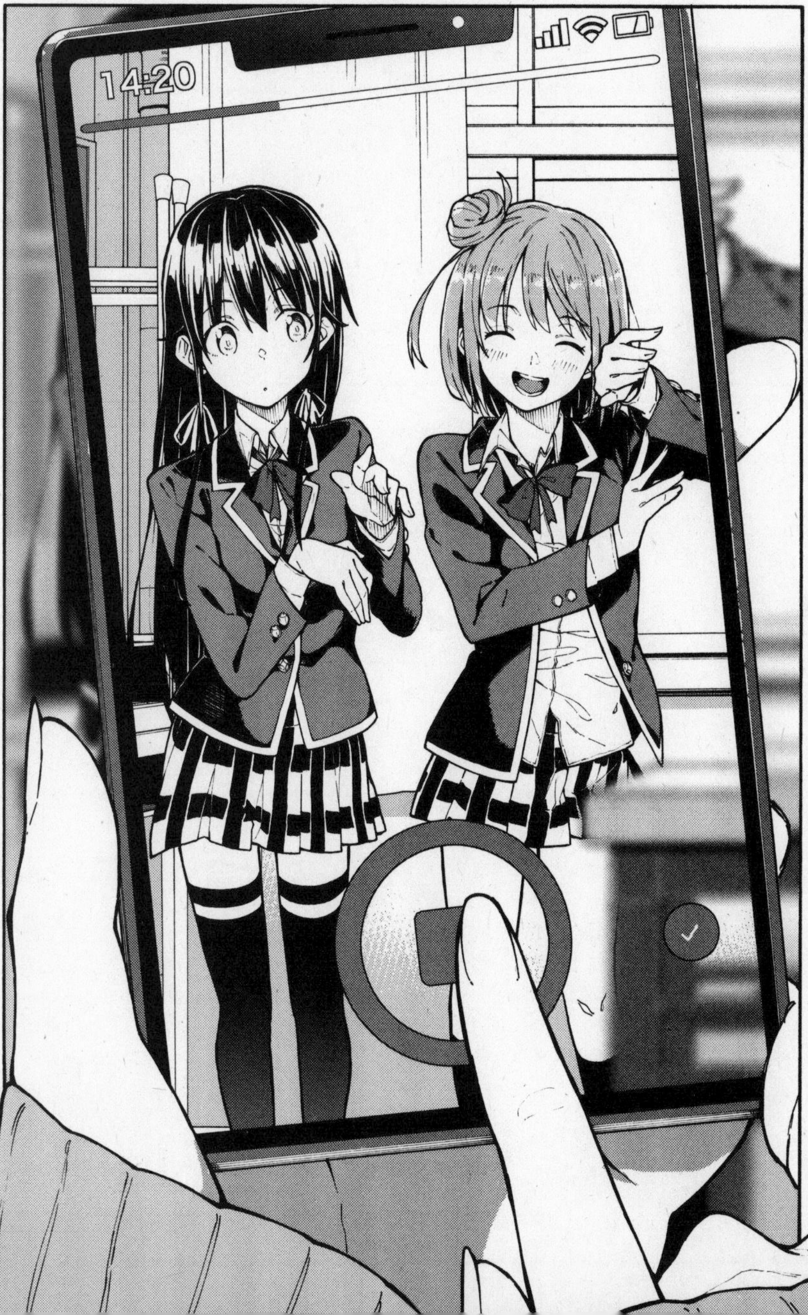
14:20

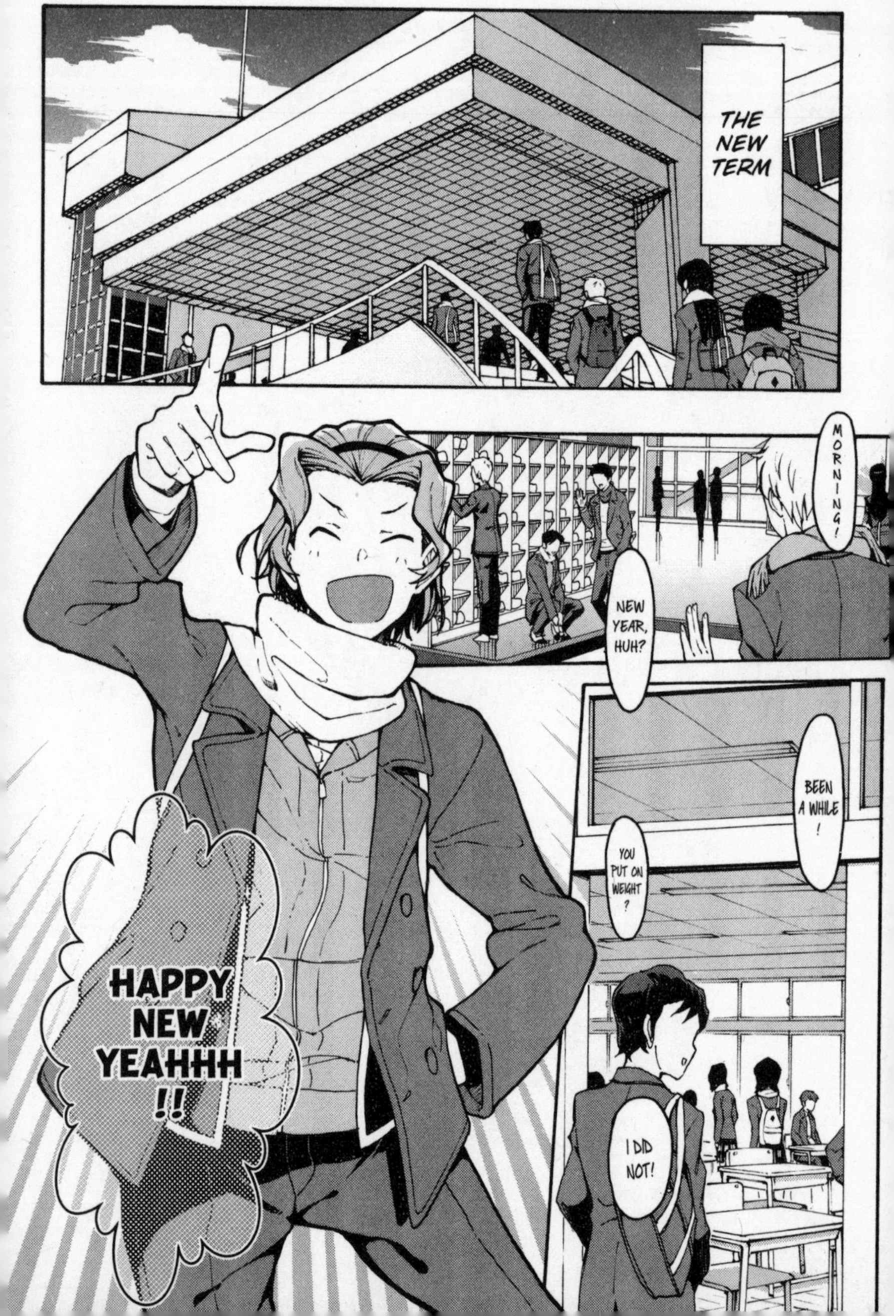
THE NEW TERM
MORNING!
NEW YEAR, HUH?
BEEN A WHILE!
YOU PUT ON WEIGHT?
I DID NOT!
HAPPY NEW YEAHHH!!

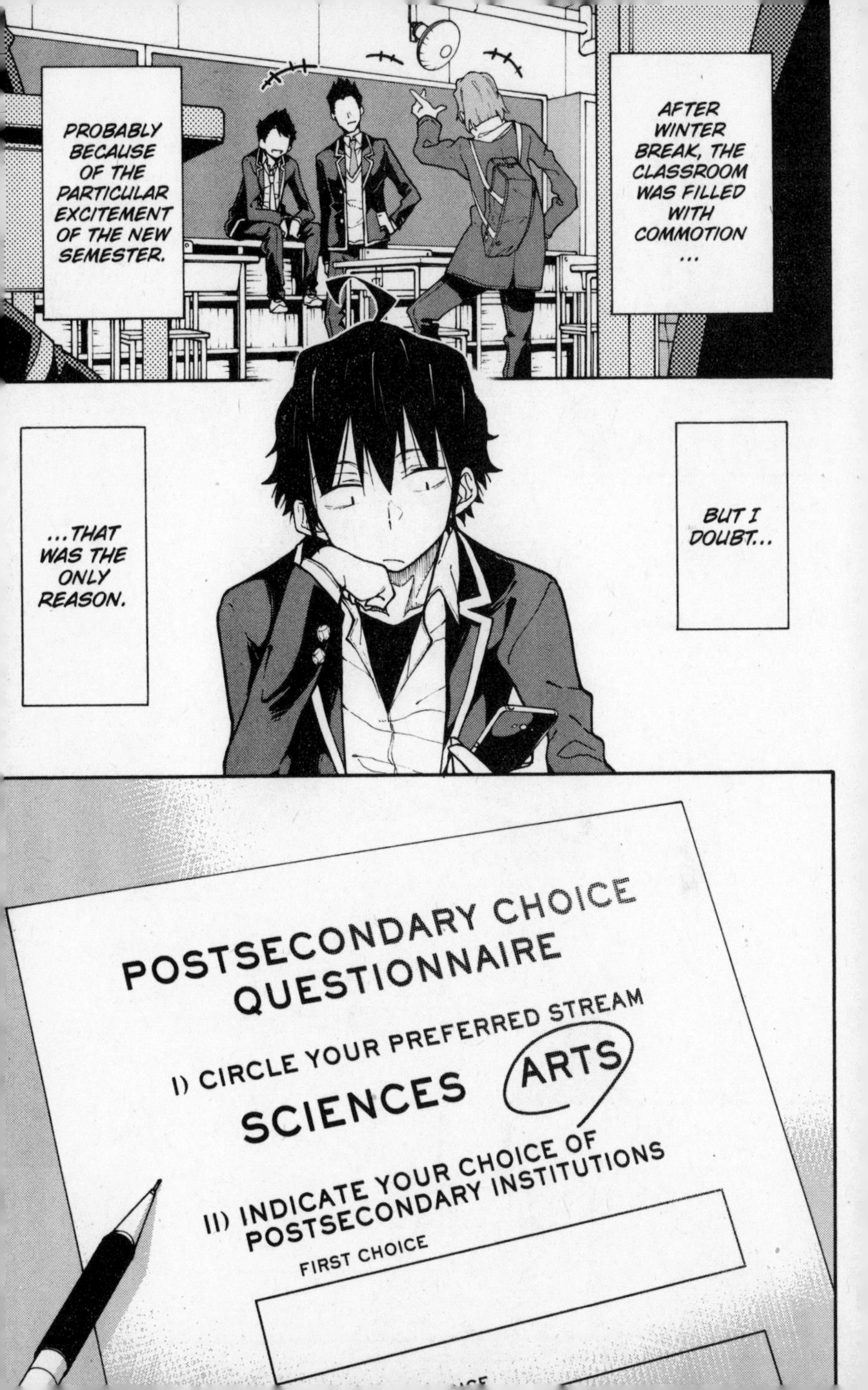
AFTER WINTER BREAK, THE CLASSROOM WAS FILLED WITH COMMOTION...
PROBABLY BECAUSE OF THE PARTICULAR EXCITEMENT OF THE NEW SEMESTER.
BUT I DOUBT...
...THAT WAS THE ONLY REASON.
POSTSECONDARY CHOICE QUESTIONNAIRE
I) CIRCLE YOUR PREFERRED STREAM
SCIENCES ARTS
II) INDICATE YOUR CHOICE OF POSTSECONDARY INSTITUTIONS
FIRST CHOICE

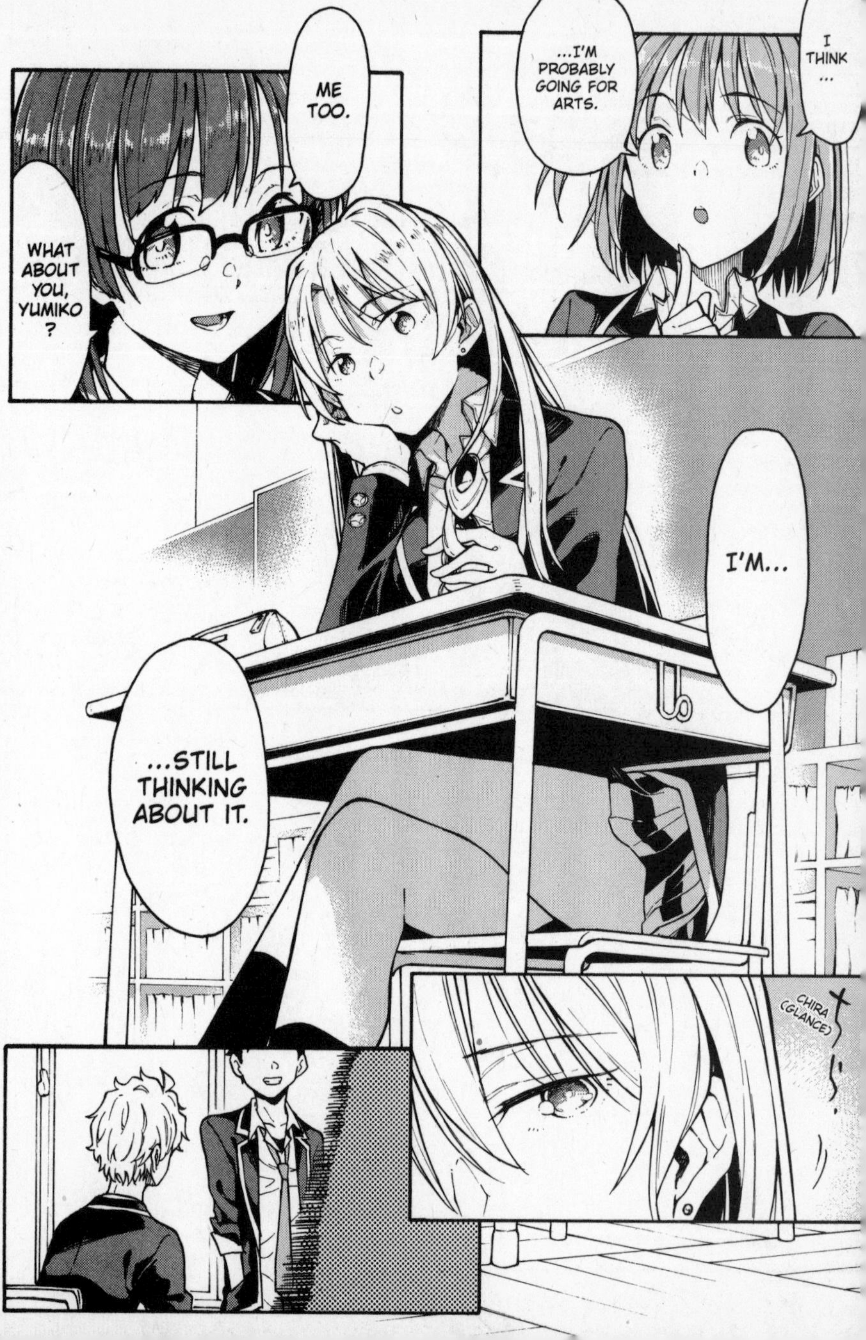
I THINK...
...I'M PROBABLY GOING FOR ARTS.
ME TOO.
WHAT ABOUT YOU, YUMIKO?
I'M...
...STILL THINKING ABOUT IT.
CHIRA (GLANCE)

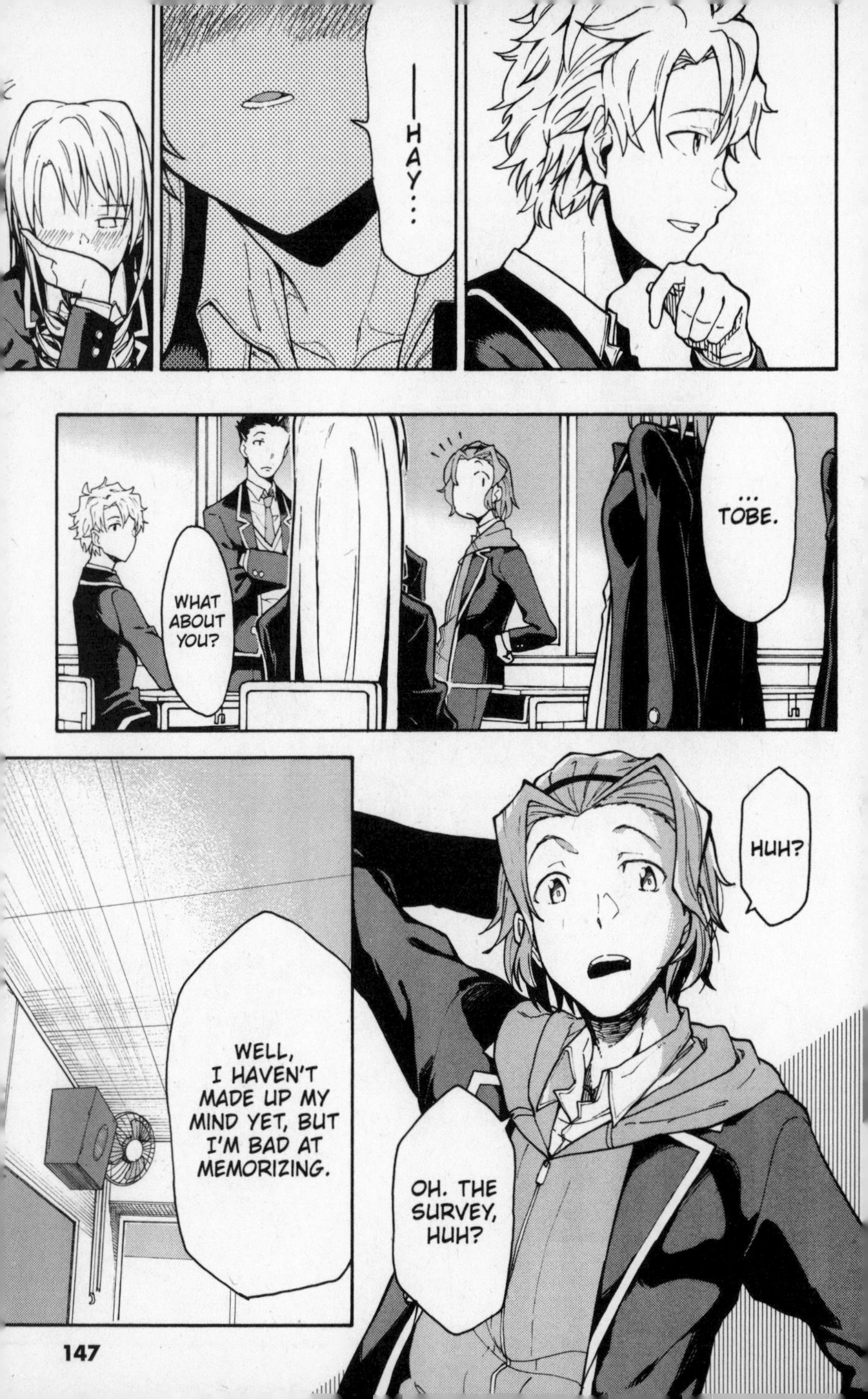
—HAY...
...TOBE.
WHAT ABOUT YOU?
HUH?
OH. THE SURVEY, HUH?
WELL, I HAVEN'T MADE UP MY MIND YET, BUT I'M BAD AT MEMORIZING.

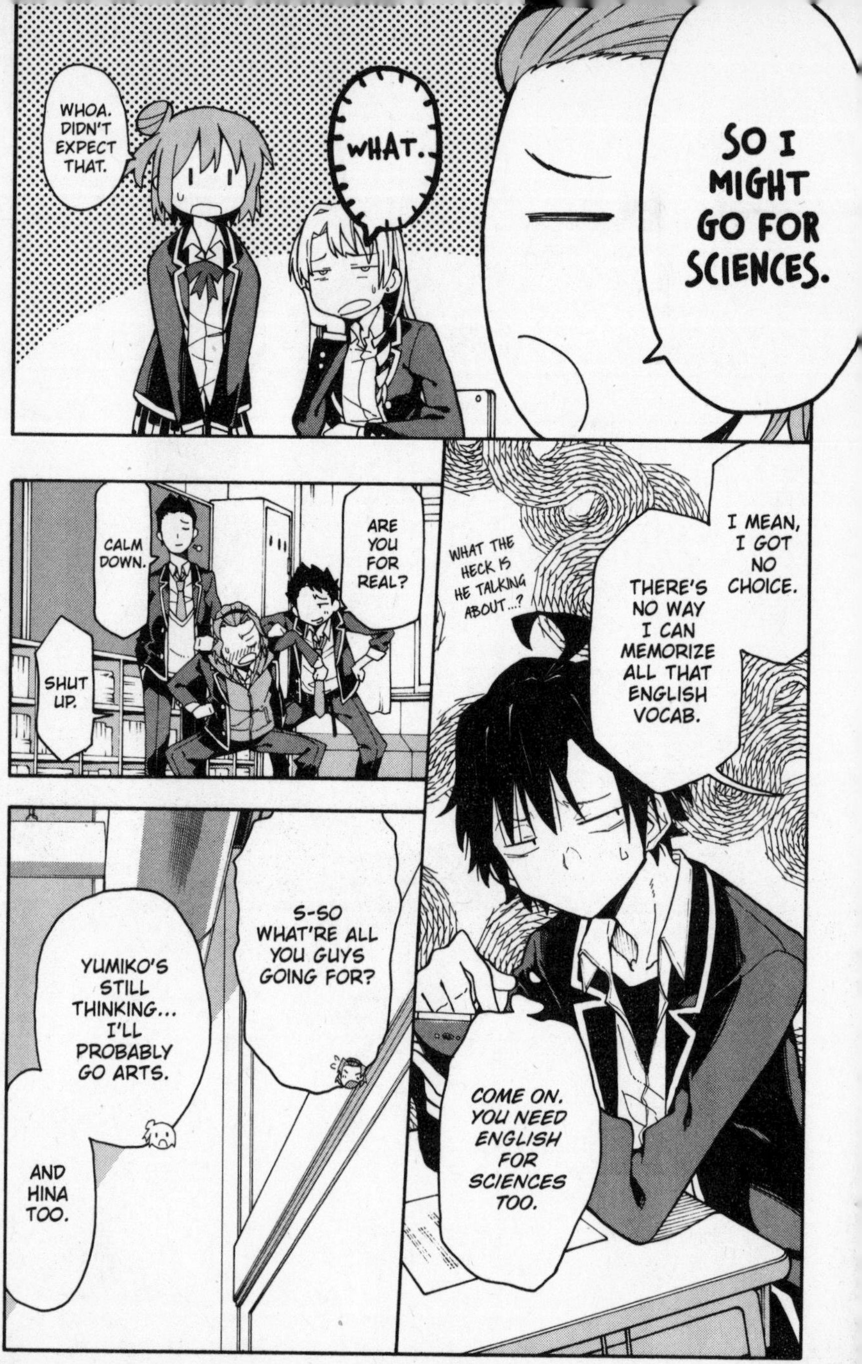
SO I MIGHT GO FOR SCIENCES.
WHAT.
WHOA. DIDN'T EXPECT THAT.
I MEAN, I GOT NO CHOICE.
THERE'S NO WAY I CAN MEMORIZE ALL THAT ENGLISH VOCAB.
WHAT THE HECK IS HE TALKING ABOUT...?
COME ON. YOU NEED ENGLISH FOR SCIENCES TOO.
ARE YOU FOR REAL?
CALM DOWN.
SHUT UP.
S-SO WHAT'RE ALL YOU GUYS GOING FOR?
YUMIKO'S STILL THINKING... I'LL PROBABLY GO ARTS.
AND HINA TOO.

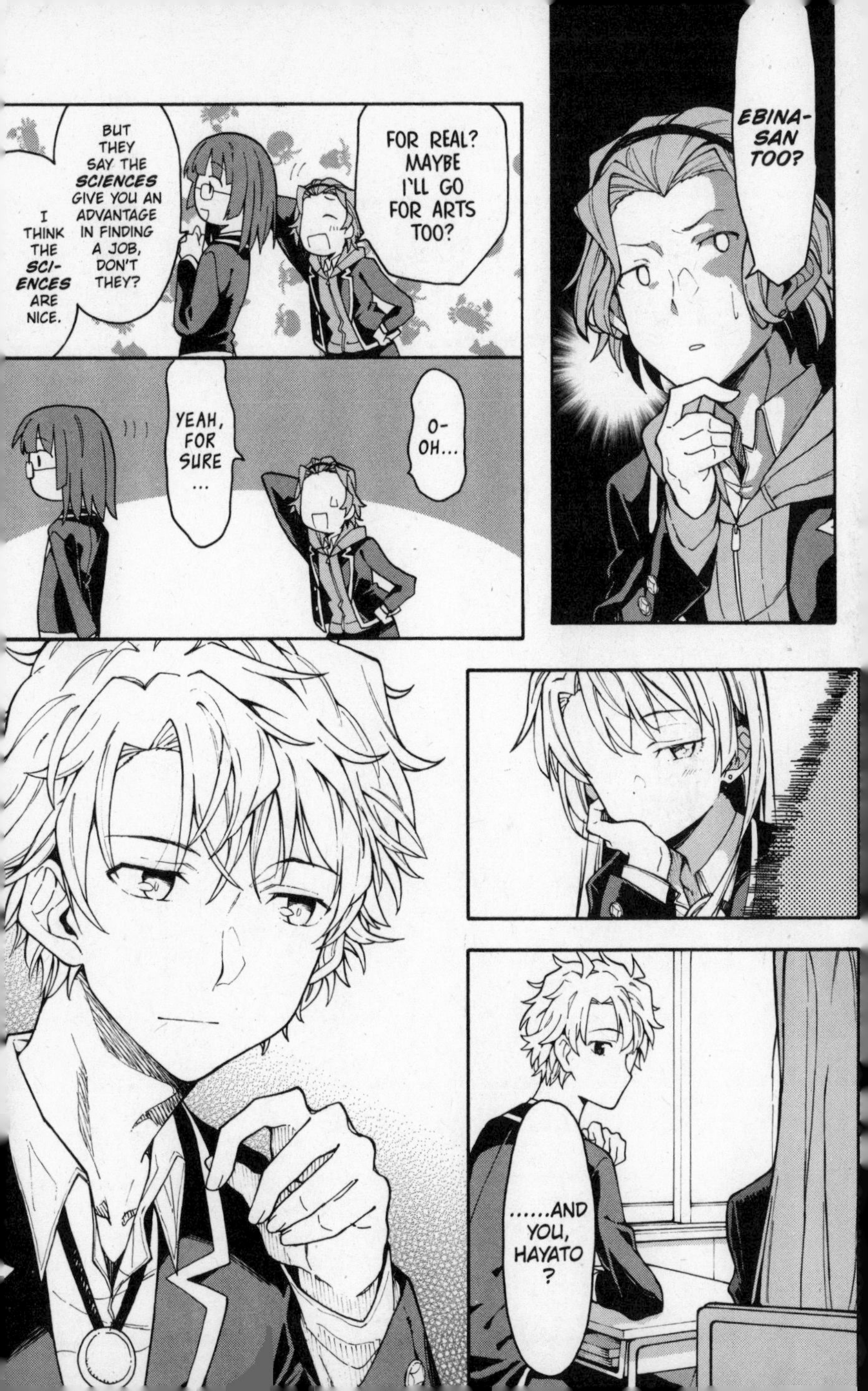
EBINA-SAN TOO?
FOR REAL? MAYBE I'LL GO FOR ARTS TOO?
BUT THEY SAY THE ***SCIENCES*** GIVE YOU AN ADVANTAGE IN FINDING A JOB, DON'T THEY?
I THINK THE ***SCI-ENCES*** ARE NICE.
O-OH...
YEAH, FOR SURE...
......AND YOU, HAYATO?

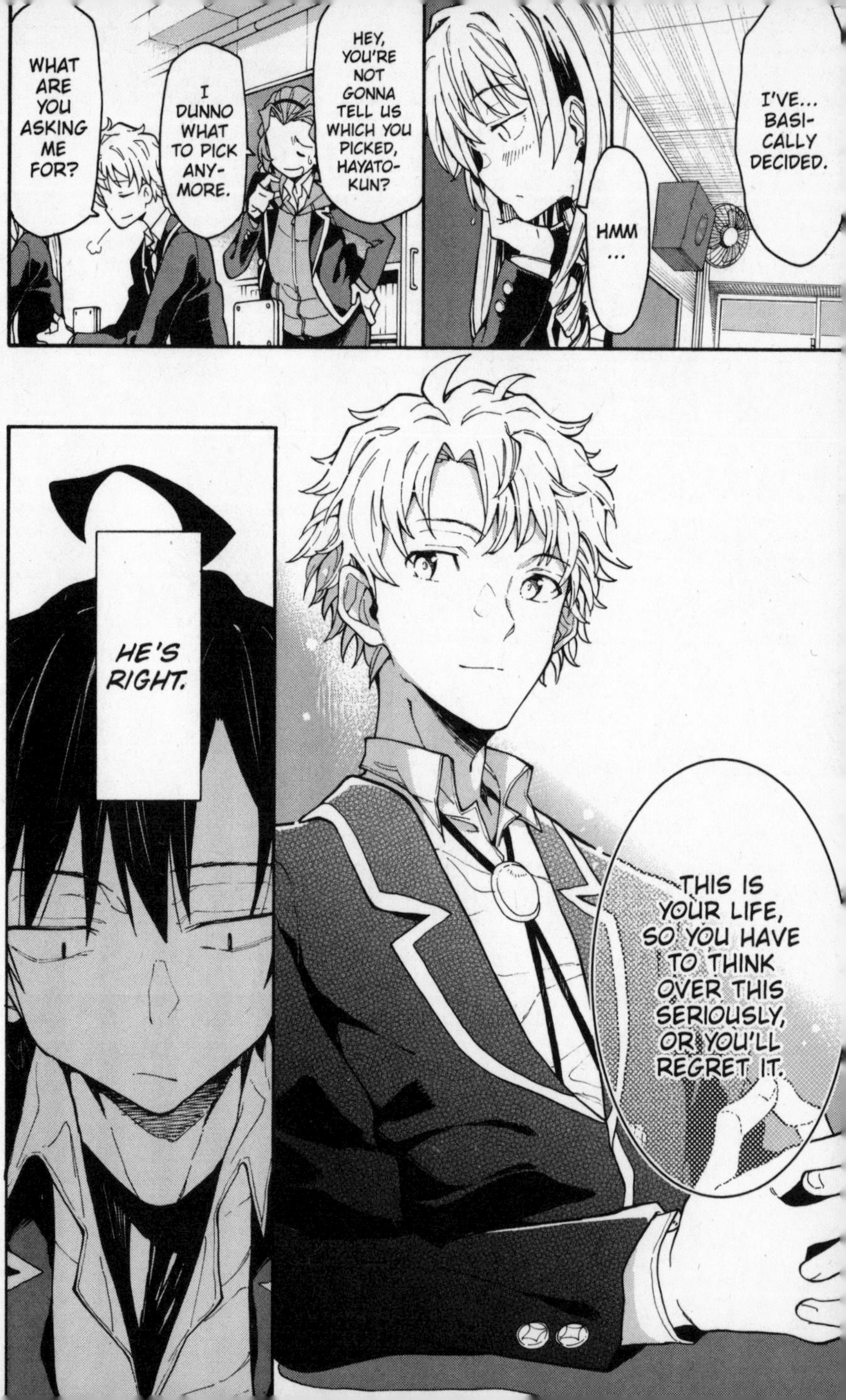
I'VE... BASICALLY DECIDED.
HMM...
HEY, YOU'RE NOT GONNA TELL US WHICH YOU PICKED, HAYATO-KUN?
I DUNNO WHAT TO PICK ANYMORE.
WHAT ARE YOU ASKING ME FOR?
THIS IS YOUR LIFE, SO YOU HAVE TO THINK OVER THIS SERIOUSLY, OR YOU'LL REGRET IT.
HE'S RIGHT.

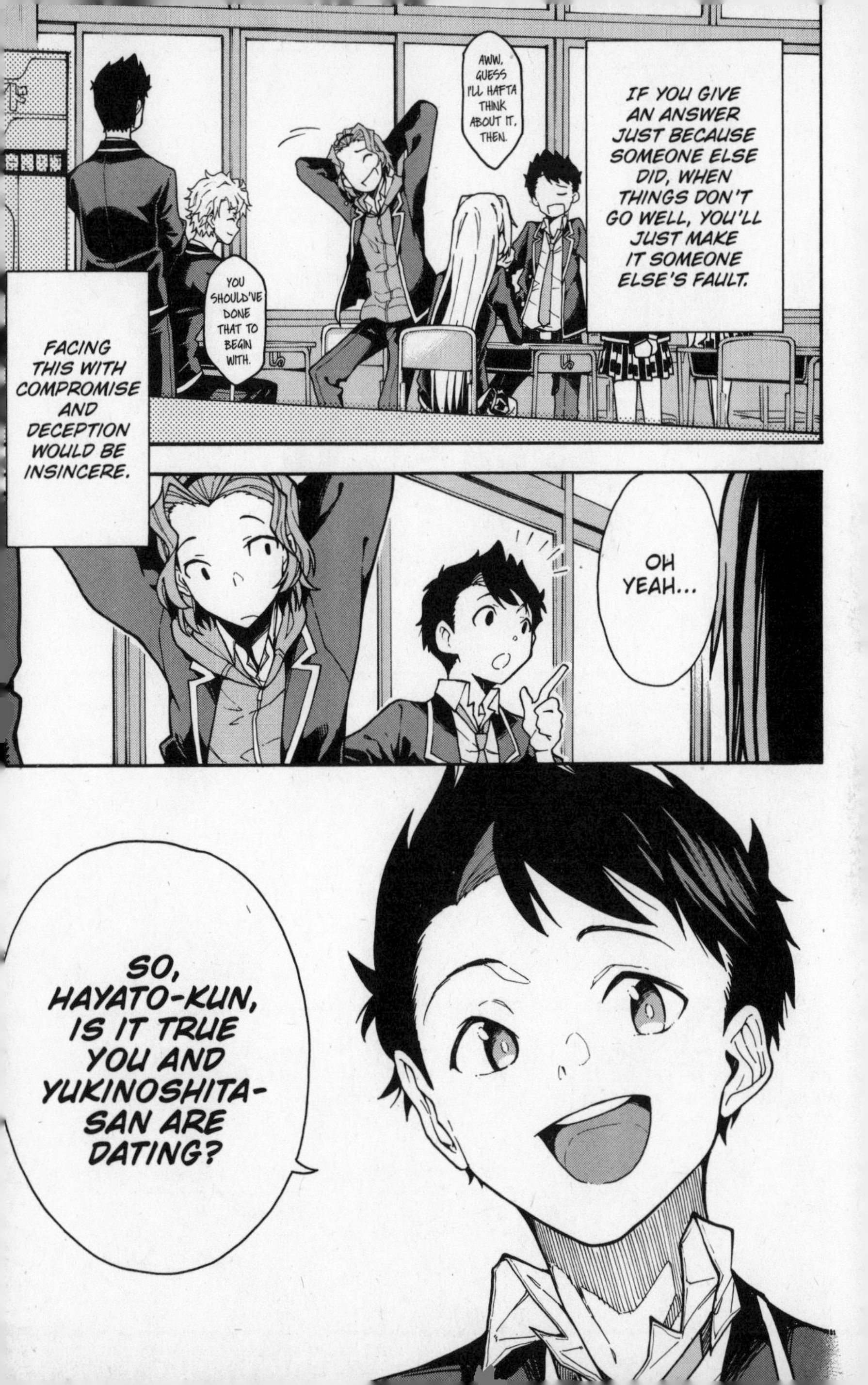
IF YOU GIVE AN ANSWER JUST BECAUSE SOMEONE ELSE DID, WHEN THINGS DON'T GO WELL, YOU'LL JUST MAKE IT SOMEONE ELSE'S FAULT.
AWW, GUESS I'LL HAFTA THINK ABOUT IT, THEN.
YOU SHOULD'VE DONE THAT TO BEGIN WITH.
FACING THIS WITH COMPROMISE AND DECEPTION WOULD BE INSINCERE.
OH YEAH...
SO, HAYATO-KUN, IS IT TRUE YOU AND YUKINOSHITA-SAN ARE DATING?

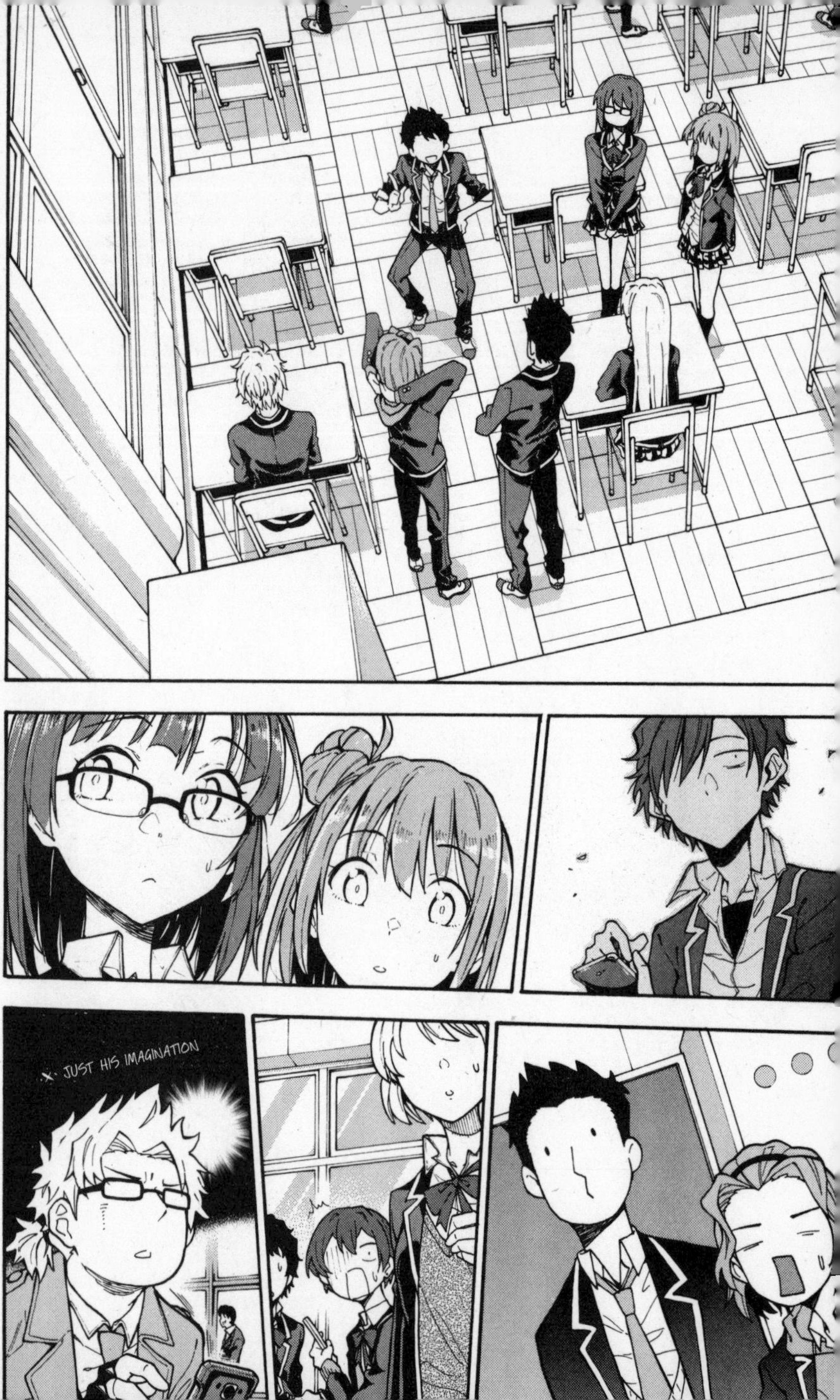
※ JUST HIS IMAGINATION

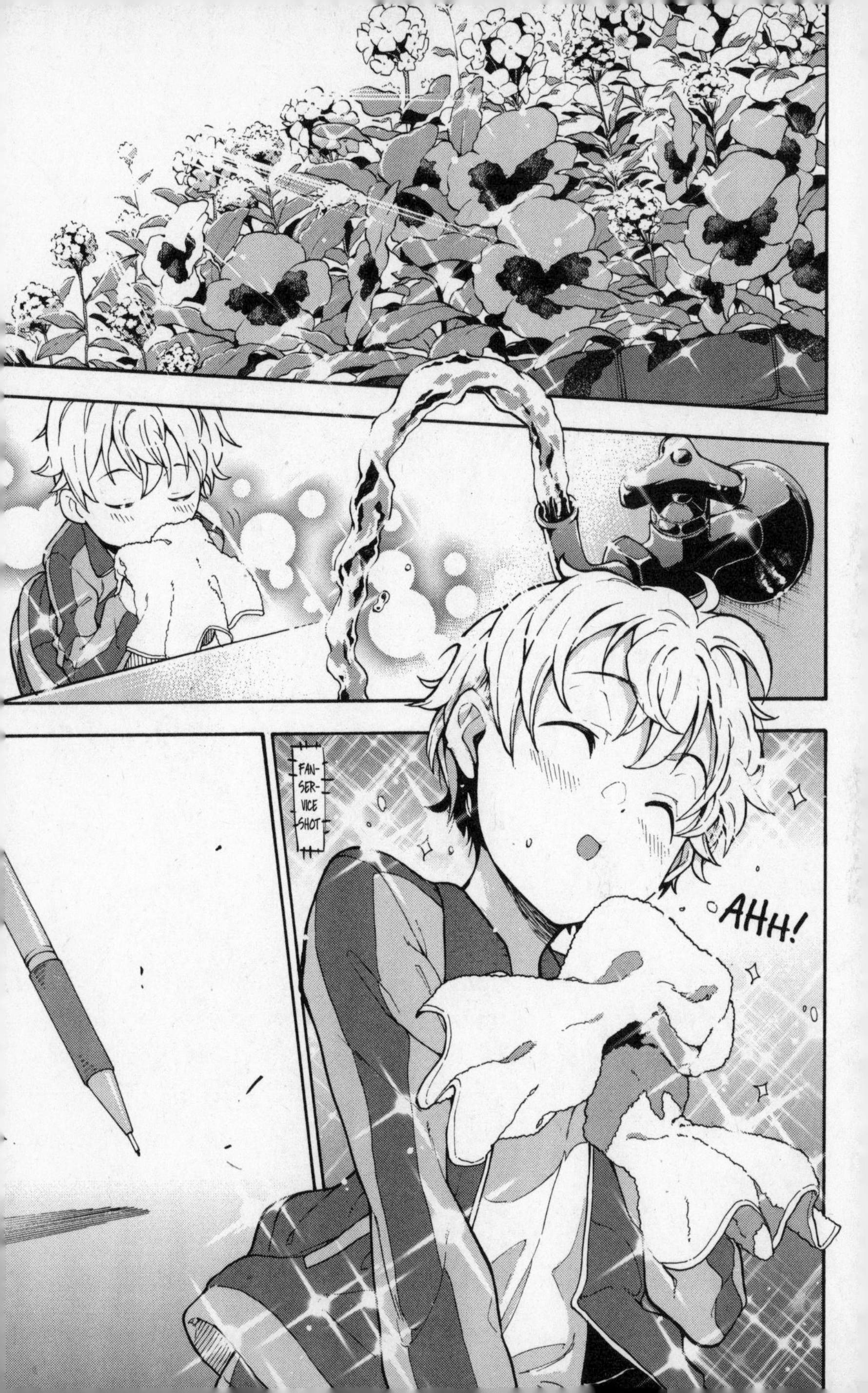
AHH!
FAN-
SER-
VICE
SHOT

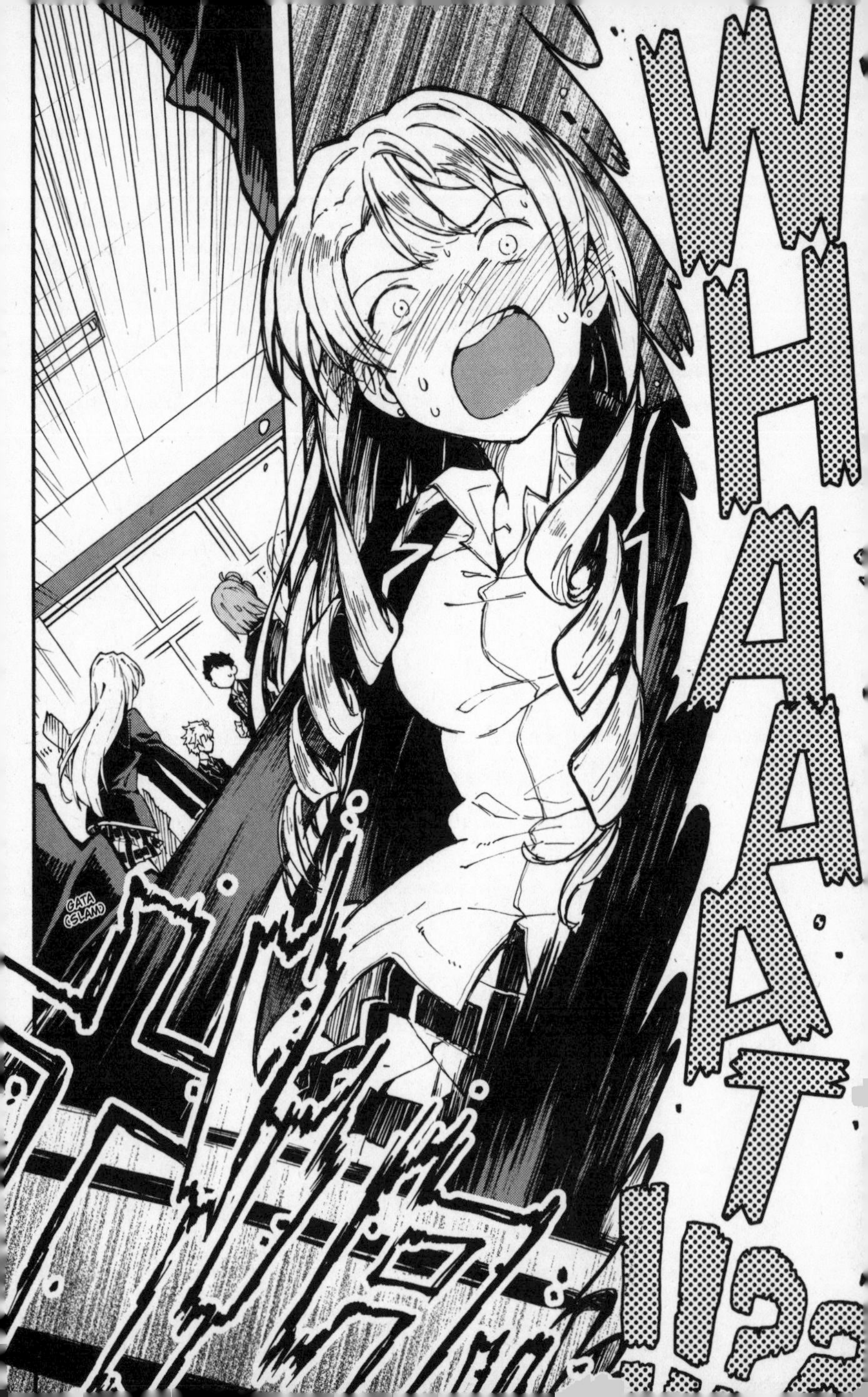
WHAAAT!!??
GATA
(SLAM)

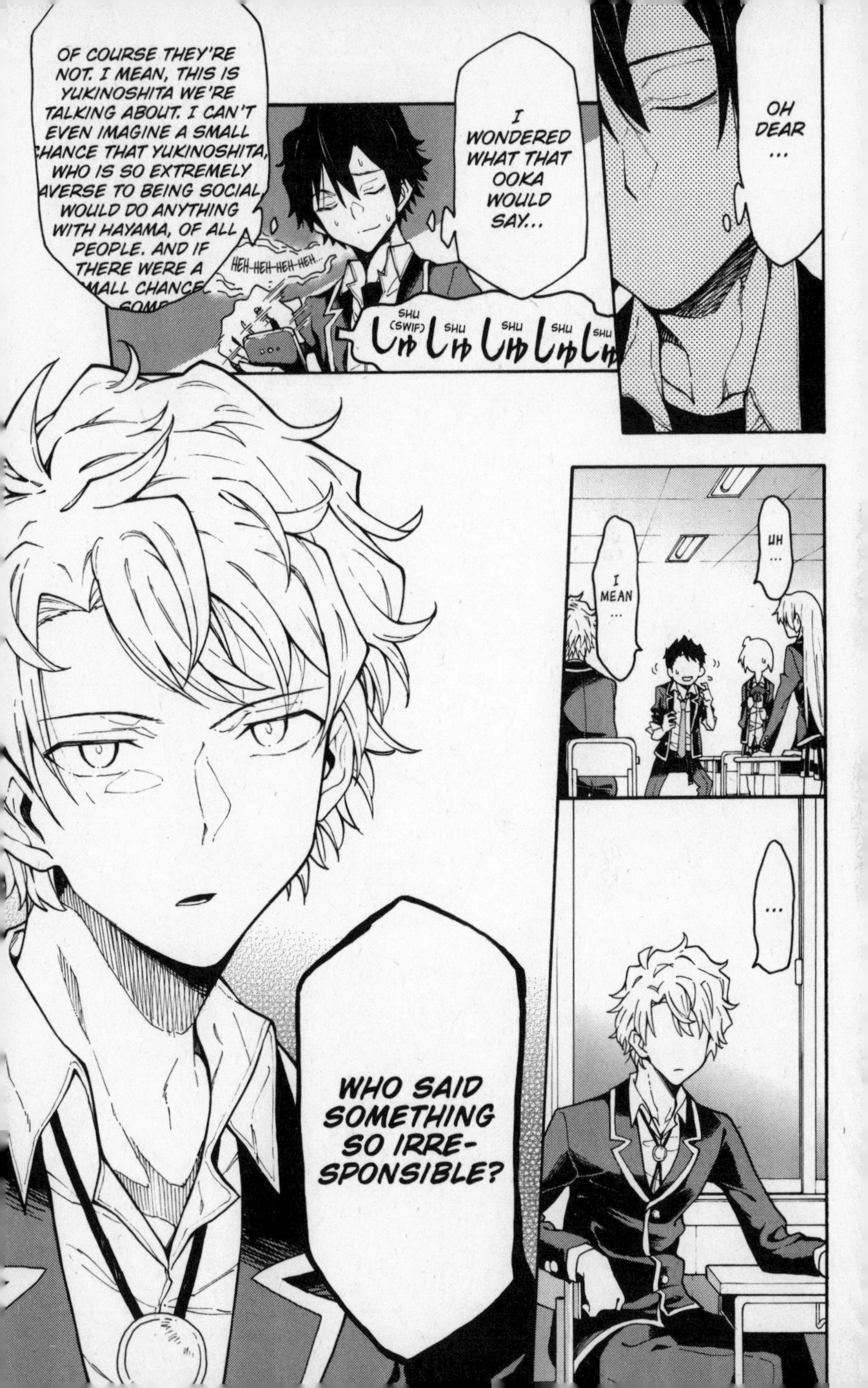
OH DEAR ...
I WONDERED WHAT THAT OOKA WOULD SAY...
OF COURSE THEY'RE NOT. I MEAN, THIS IS YUKINOSHITA WE'RE TALKING ABOUT. I CAN'T EVEN IMAGINE A SMALL CHANCE THAT YUKINOSHITA, WHO IS SO EXTREMELY AVERSE TO BEING SOCIAL, WOULD DO ANYTHING WITH HAYAMA, OF ALL PEOPLE. AND IF THERE WERE A SMALL CHANCE
HEH HEH HEH HEH...
SHU (SWIF) しゅ SHU しゅ SHU しゅ SHU しゅ SHU しゅ
UH ...
I MEAN ...
...
WHO SAID SOMETHING SO IRRE-SPONSIBLE?

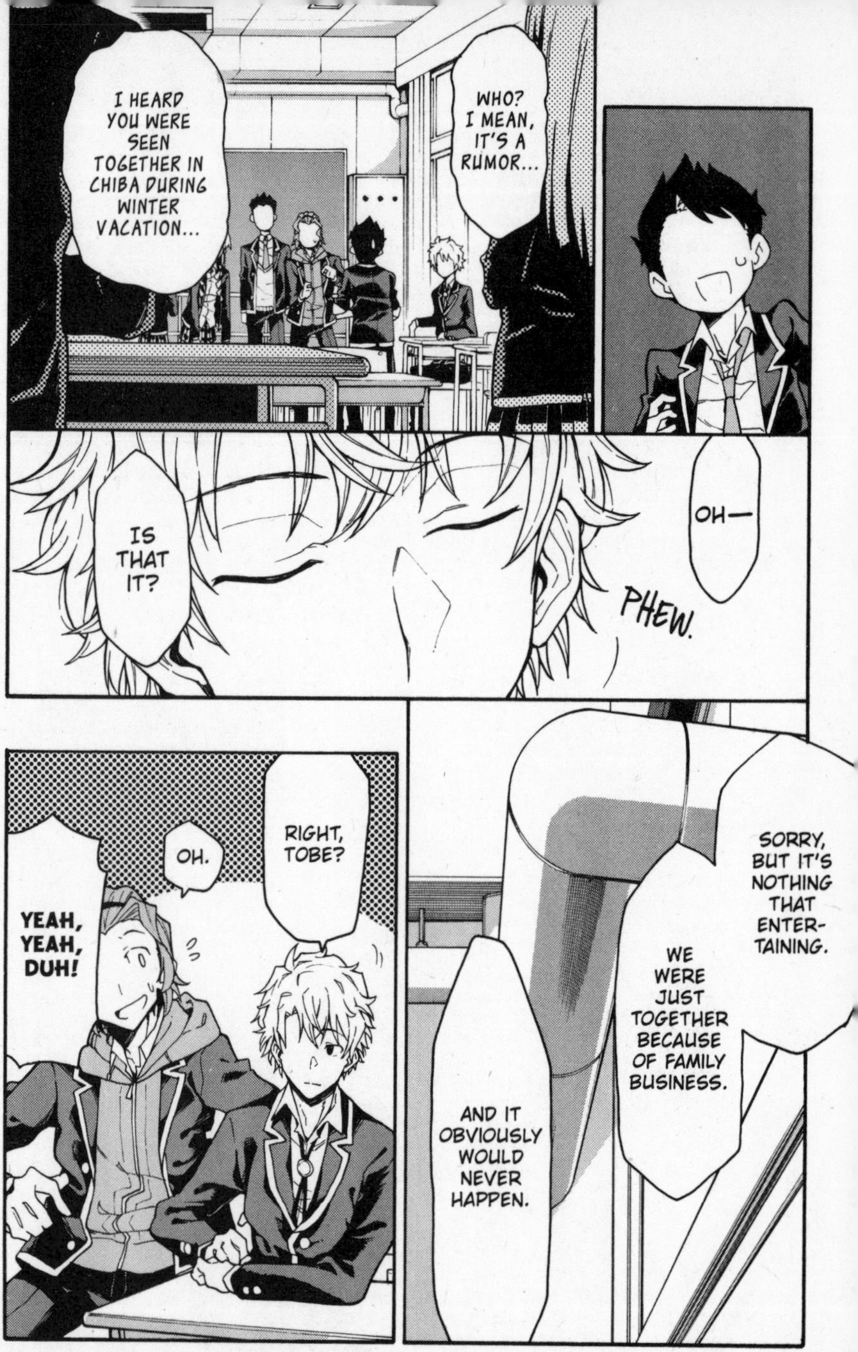
WHO? I MEAN, IT'S A RUMOR...
I HEARD YOU WERE SEEN TOGETHER IN CHIBA DURING WINTER VACATION...
OH—
PHEW.
IS THAT IT?
SORRY, BUT IT'S NOTHING THAT ENTER-TAINING.
WE WERE JUST TOGETHER BECAUSE OF FAMILY BUSINESS.
AND IT OBVIOUSLY WOULD NEVER HAPPEN.
RIGHT, TOBE?
OH.
YEAH, YEAH, DUH!

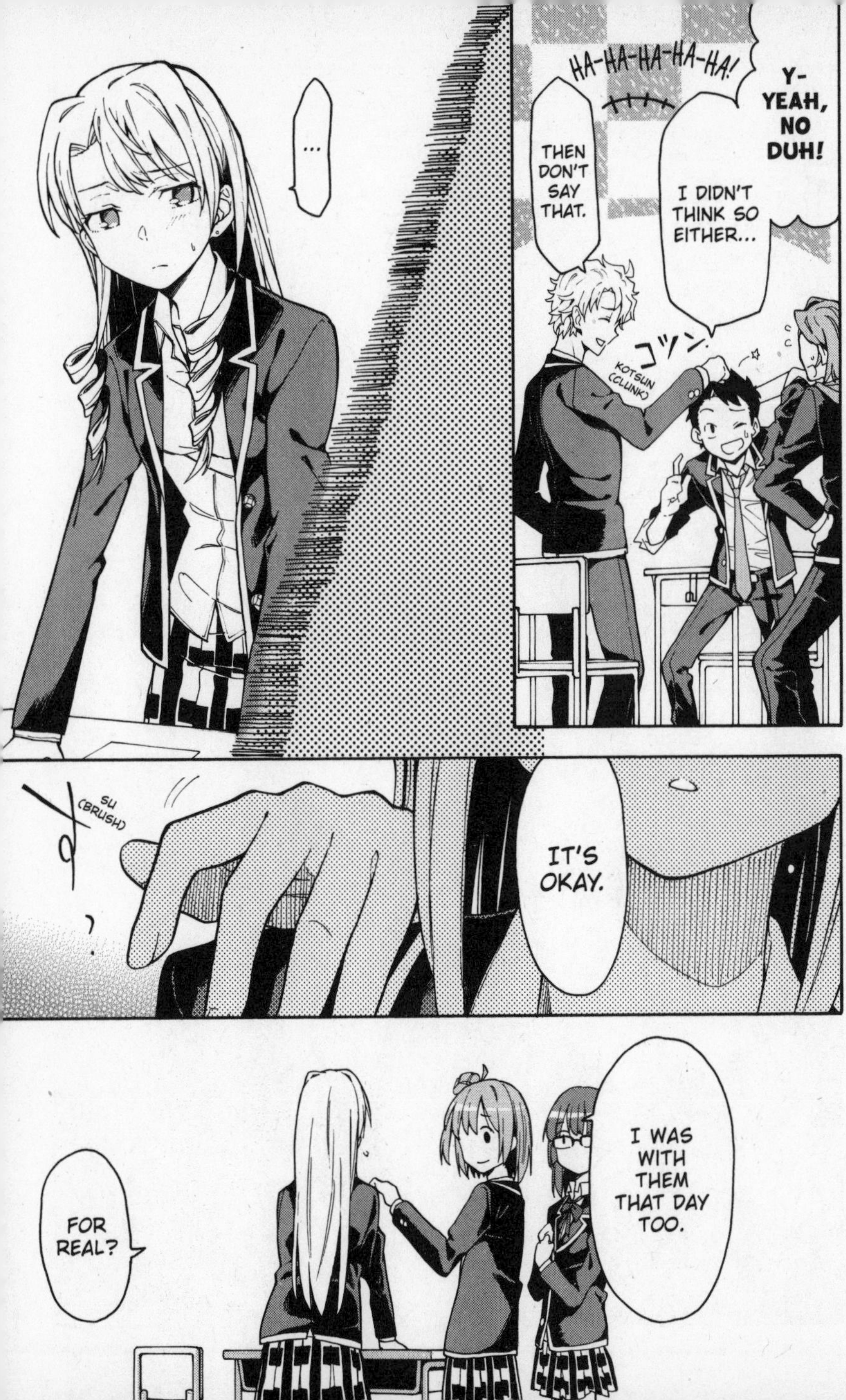
Y-YEAH, NO DUH!
HA-HA-HA-HA-HA!
I DIDN'T THINK SO EITHER...
THEN DON'T SAY THAT.
ゴツン
KOTSUN (CLUNK)
...
IT'S OKAY.
SU (BRUSH)
I WAS WITH THEM THAT DAY TOO.
FOR REAL?

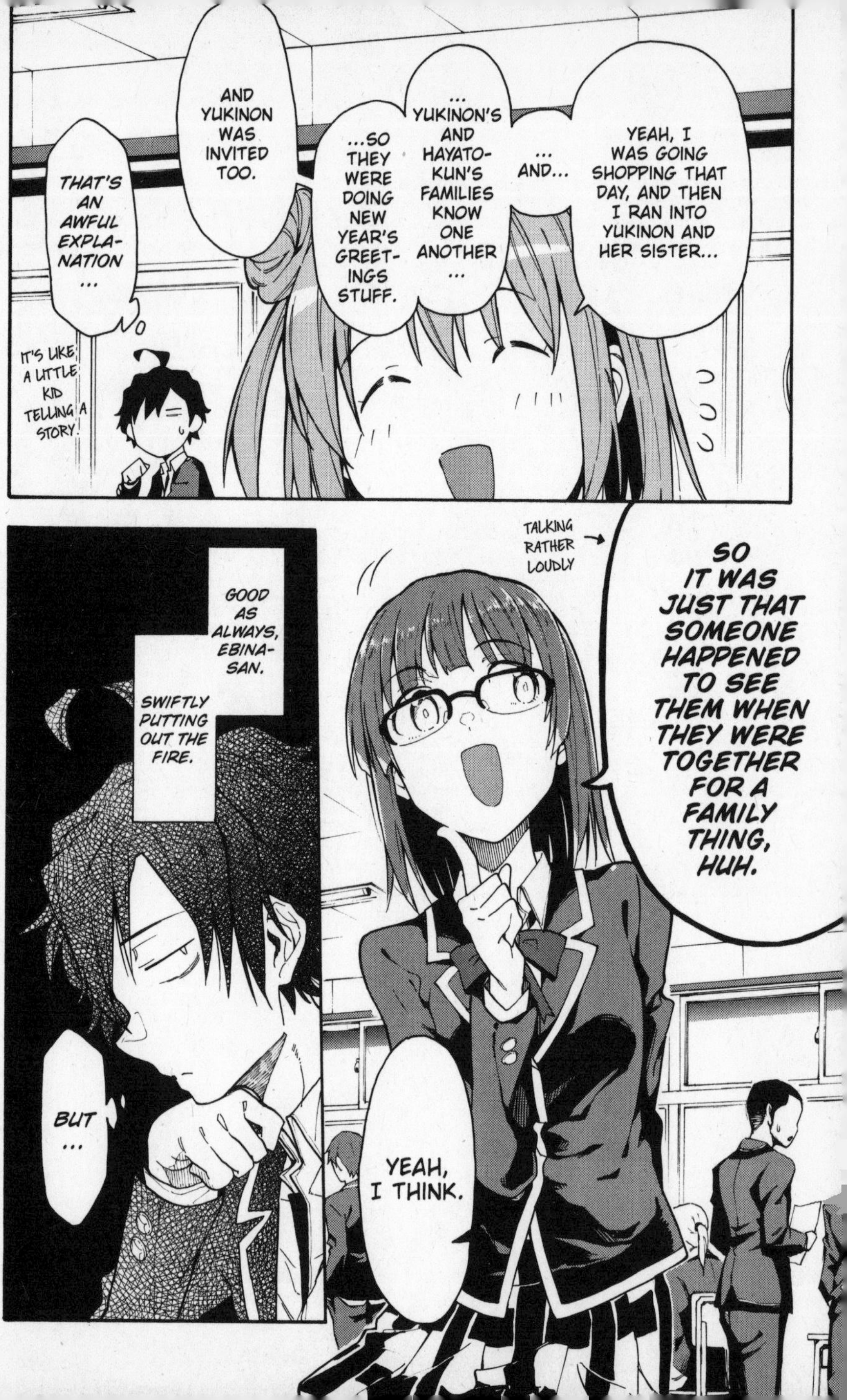
YEAH, I WAS GOING SHOPPING THAT DAY, AND THEN I RAN INTO YUKINON AND HER SISTER...
... AND...
... YUKINON'S AND HAYATO-KUN'S FAMILIES KNOW ONE ANOTHER ...
...SO THEY WERE DOING NEW YEAR'S GREET-INGS STUFF.
AND YUKINON WAS INVITED TOO.
THAT'S AN AWFUL EXPLA-NATION ...
IT'S LIKE A LITTLE KID TELLING A STORY
TALKING RATHER LOUDLY
SO IT WAS JUST THAT SOMEONE HAPPENED TO SEE THEM WHEN THEY WERE TOGETHER FOR A FAMILY THING, HUH.
YEAH, I THINK.
GOOD AS ALWAYS, EBINA-SAN.
SWIFTLY PUTTING OUT THE FIRE.
BUT ...

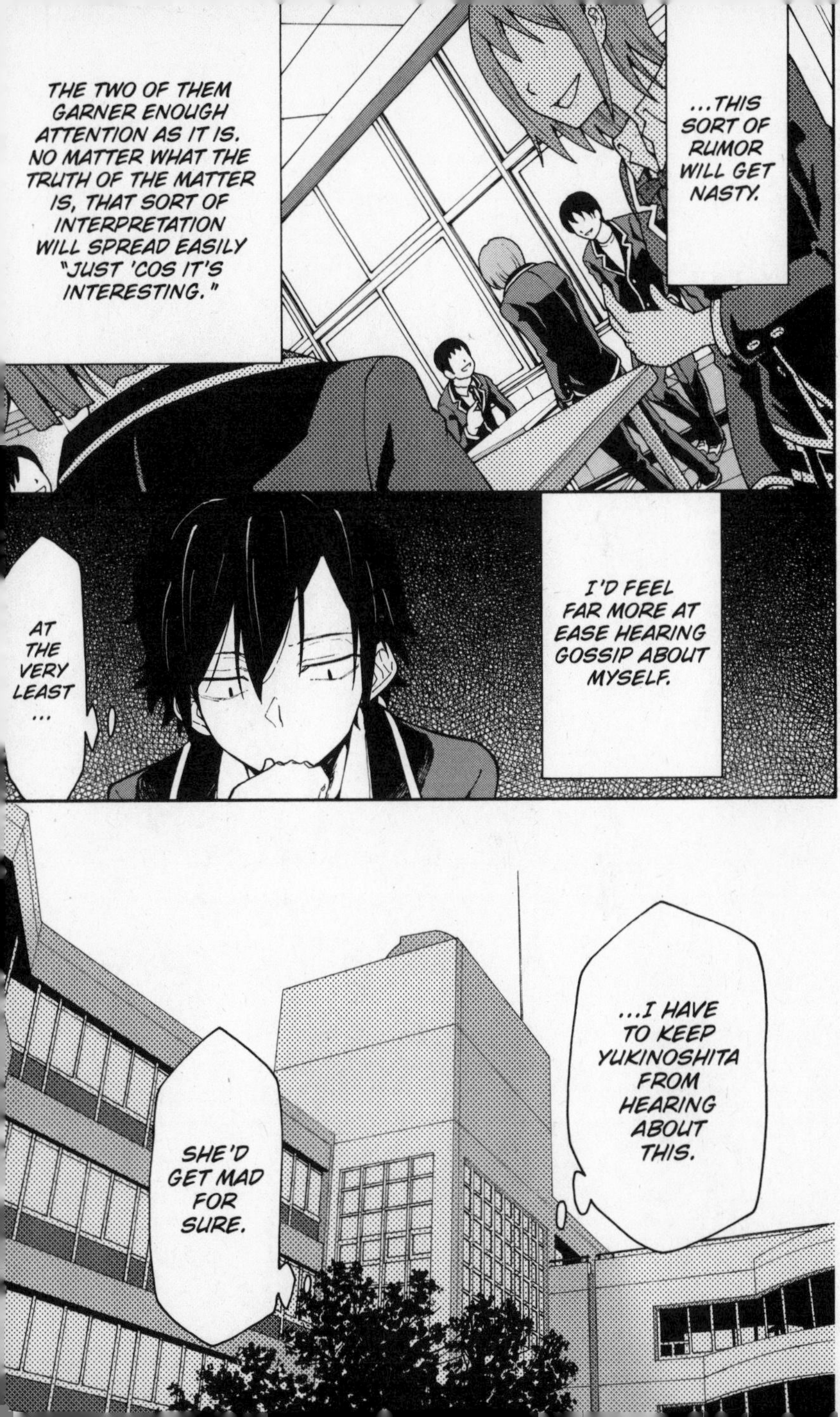
...THIS SORT OF RUMOR WILL GET NASTY.
THE TWO OF THEM GARNER ENOUGH ATTENTION AS IT IS. NO MATTER WHAT THE TRUTH OF THE MATTER IS, THAT SORT OF INTERPRETATION WILL SPREAD EASILY "JUST 'COS IT'S INTERESTING."
I'D FEEL FAR MORE AT EASE HEARING GOSSIP ABOUT MYSELF.
AT THE VERY LEAST...
...I HAVE TO KEEP YUKINOSHITA FROM HEARING ABOUT THIS.
SHE'D GET MAD FOR SURE.

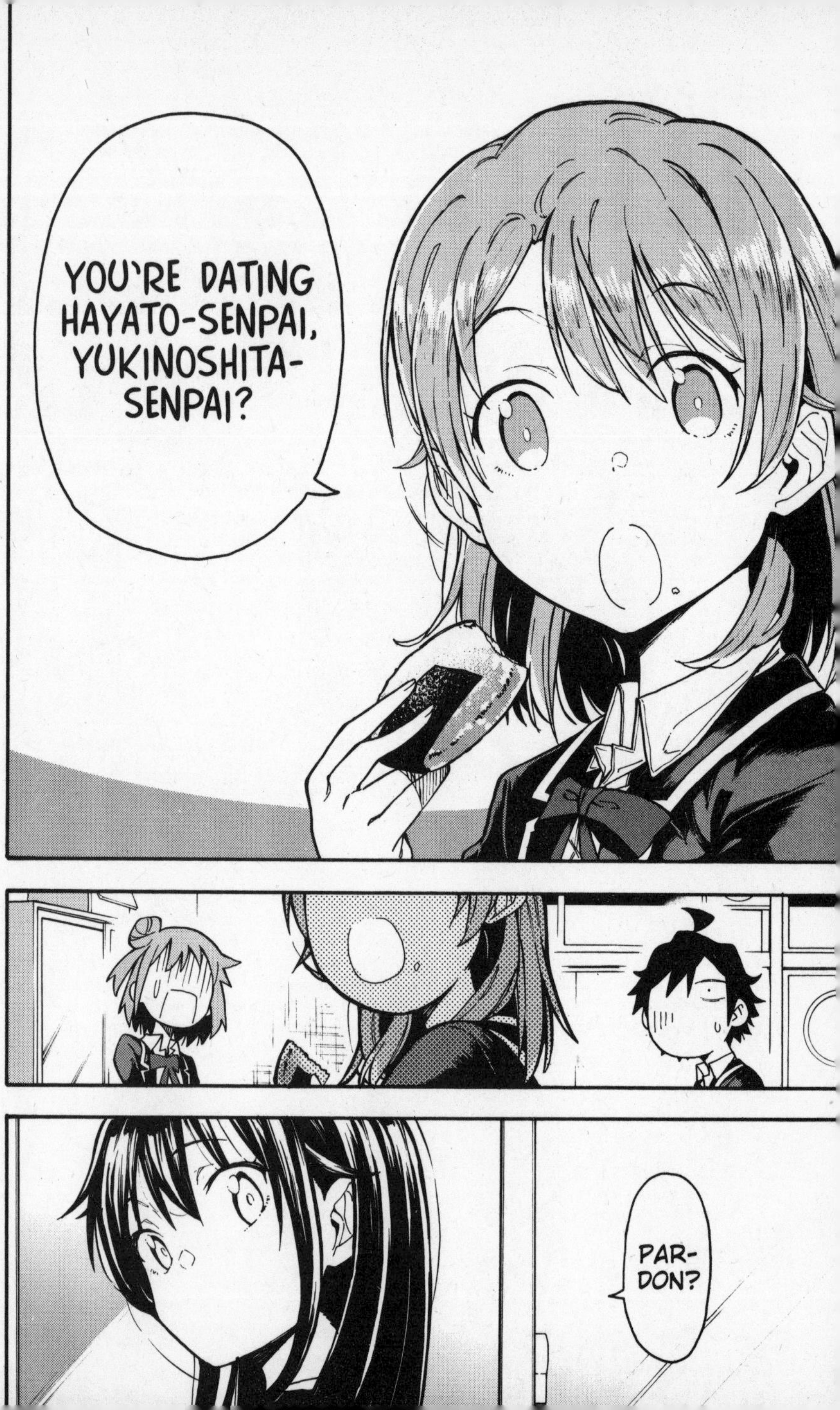
YOU'RE DATING HAYATO-SENPAI, YUKINOSHITA-SENPAI?
PAR-DON?

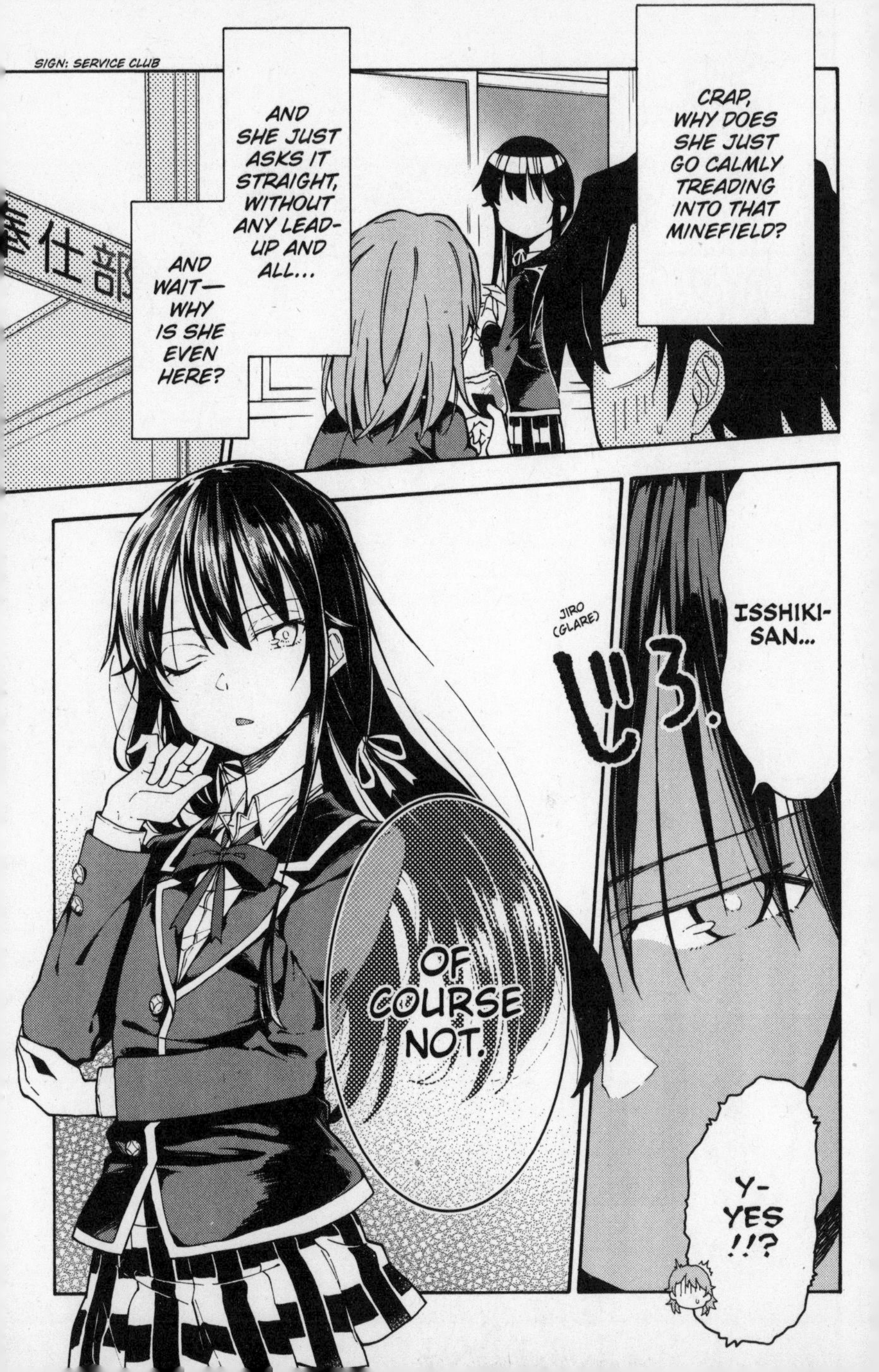
CRAP, WHY DOES SHE JUST GO CALMLY TREADING INTO THAT MINEFIELD?
AND SHE JUST ASKS IT STRAIGHT, WITHOUT ANY LEAD-UP AND ALL...
AND WAIT—WHY IS SHE EVEN HERE?
SIGN: SERVICE CLUB
ISSHIKI-SAN...
JIRO (GLARE)
じろ
Y-YES!!?
OF COURSE NOT.

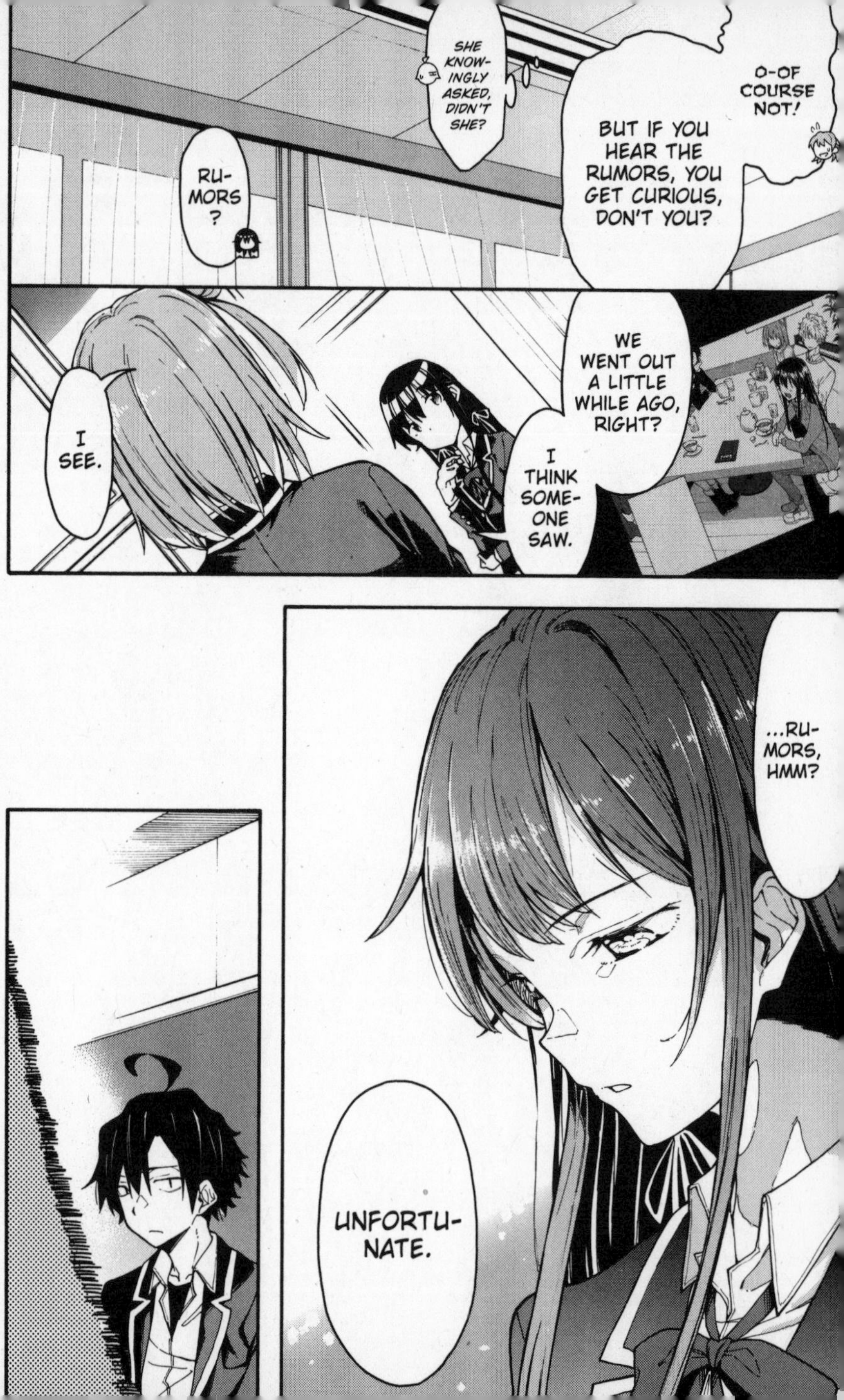
O-OF COURSE NOT!
BUT IF YOU HEAR THE RUMORS, YOU GET CURIOUS, DON'T YOU?
SHE KNOWINGLY ASKED, DIDN'T SHE?
RUMORS?
WE WENT OUT A LITTLE WHILE AGO, RIGHT?
I THINK SOMEONE SAW.
I SEE.
...RUMORS, HMM?
UNFORTUNATE.

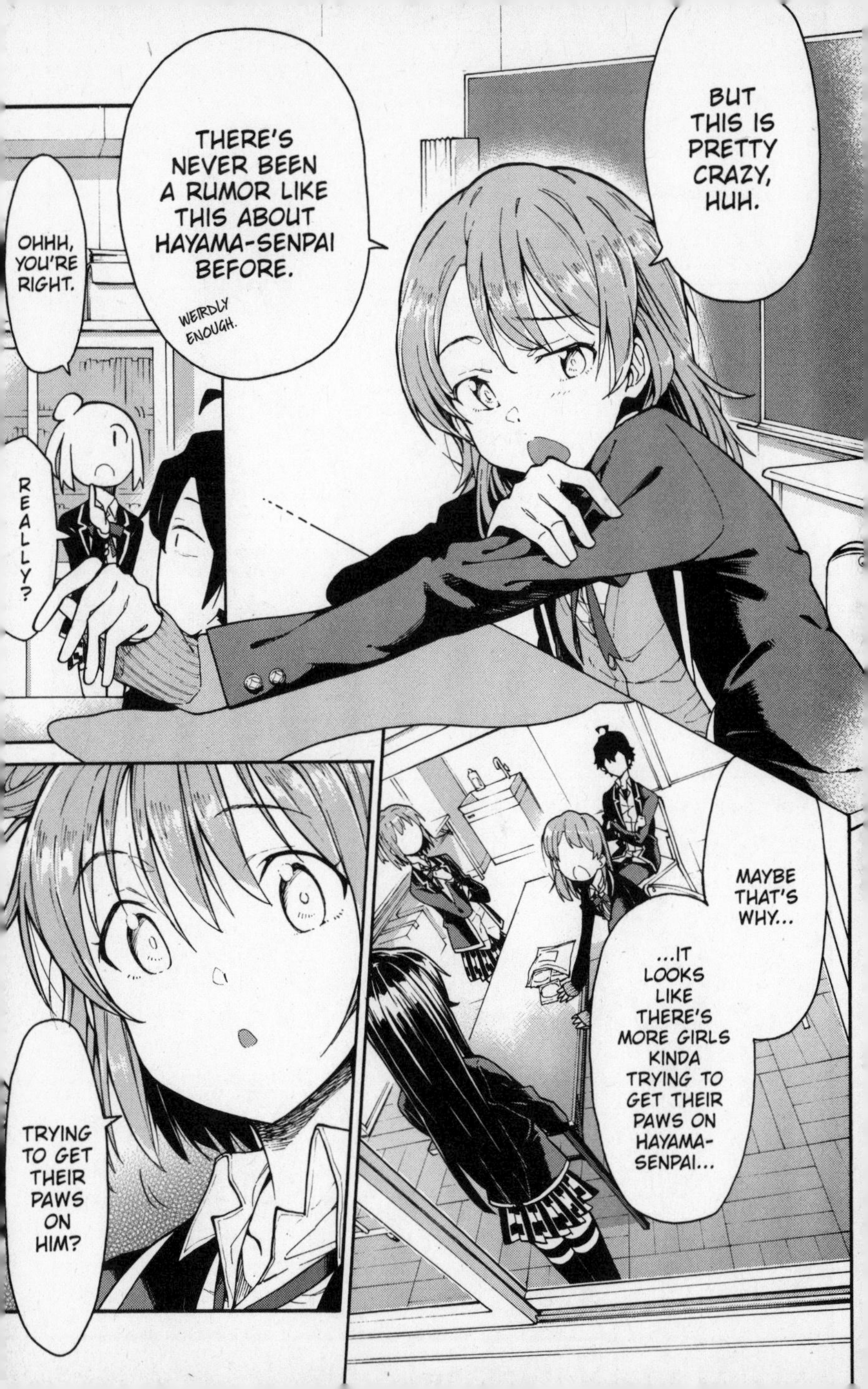
BUT THIS IS PRETTY CRAZY, HUH.
THERE'S NEVER BEEN A RUMOR LIKE THIS ABOUT HAYAMA-SENPAI BEFORE.
WEIRDLY ENOUGH.
OHHH, YOU'RE RIGHT.
REALLY?
MAYBE THAT'S WHY...
...IT LOOKS LIKE THERE'S MORE GIRLS KINDA TRYING TO GET THEIR PAWS ON HAYAMA-SENPAI...
TRYING TO GET THEIR PAWS ON HIM?

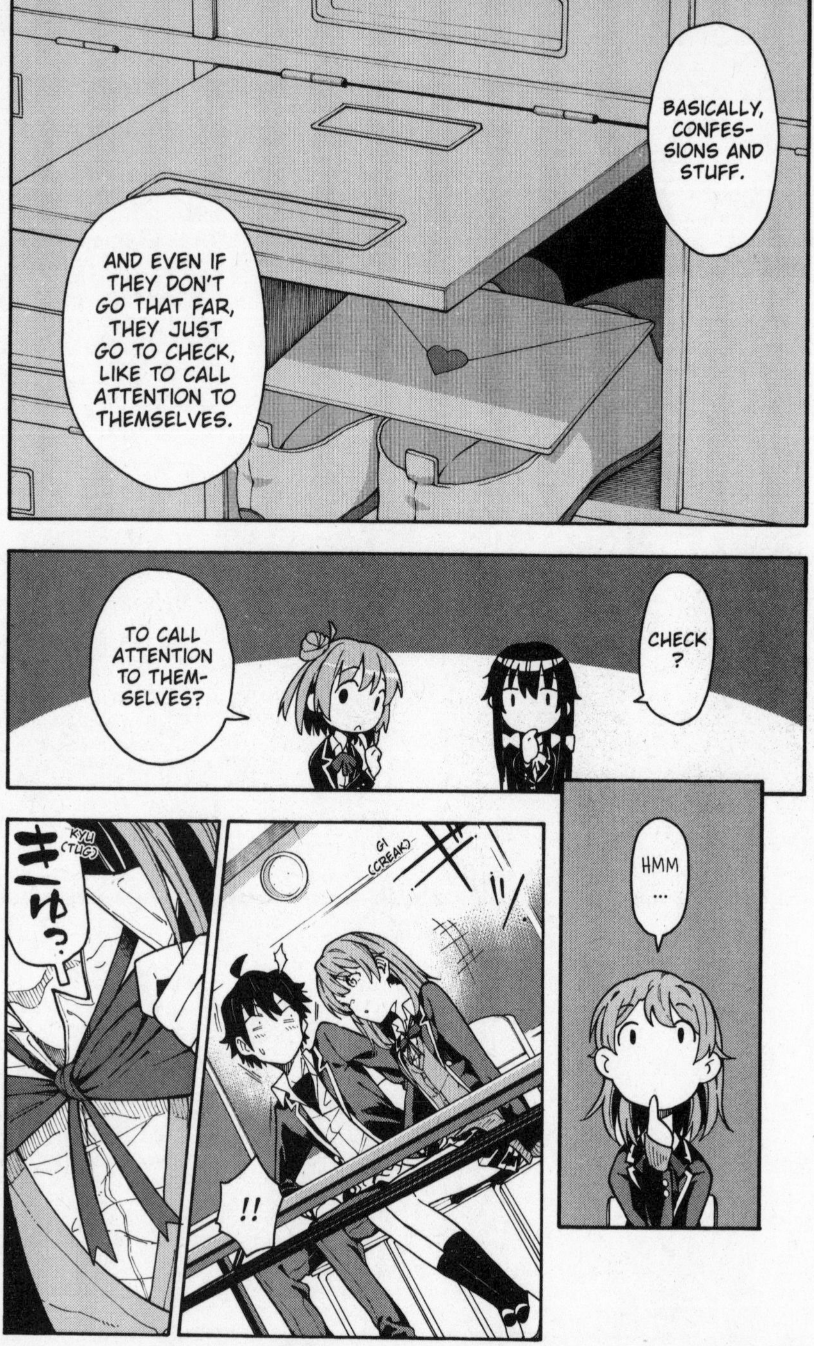
BASICALLY, CONFESSIONS AND STUFF.
AND EVEN IF THEY DON'T GO THAT FAR, THEY JUST GO TO CHECK, LIKE TO CALL ATTENTION TO THEMSELVES.
CHECK?
TO CALL ATTENTION TO THEMSELVES?
HMM...
GI (CREAK)
!!
きゅっ
KYU (TUG)

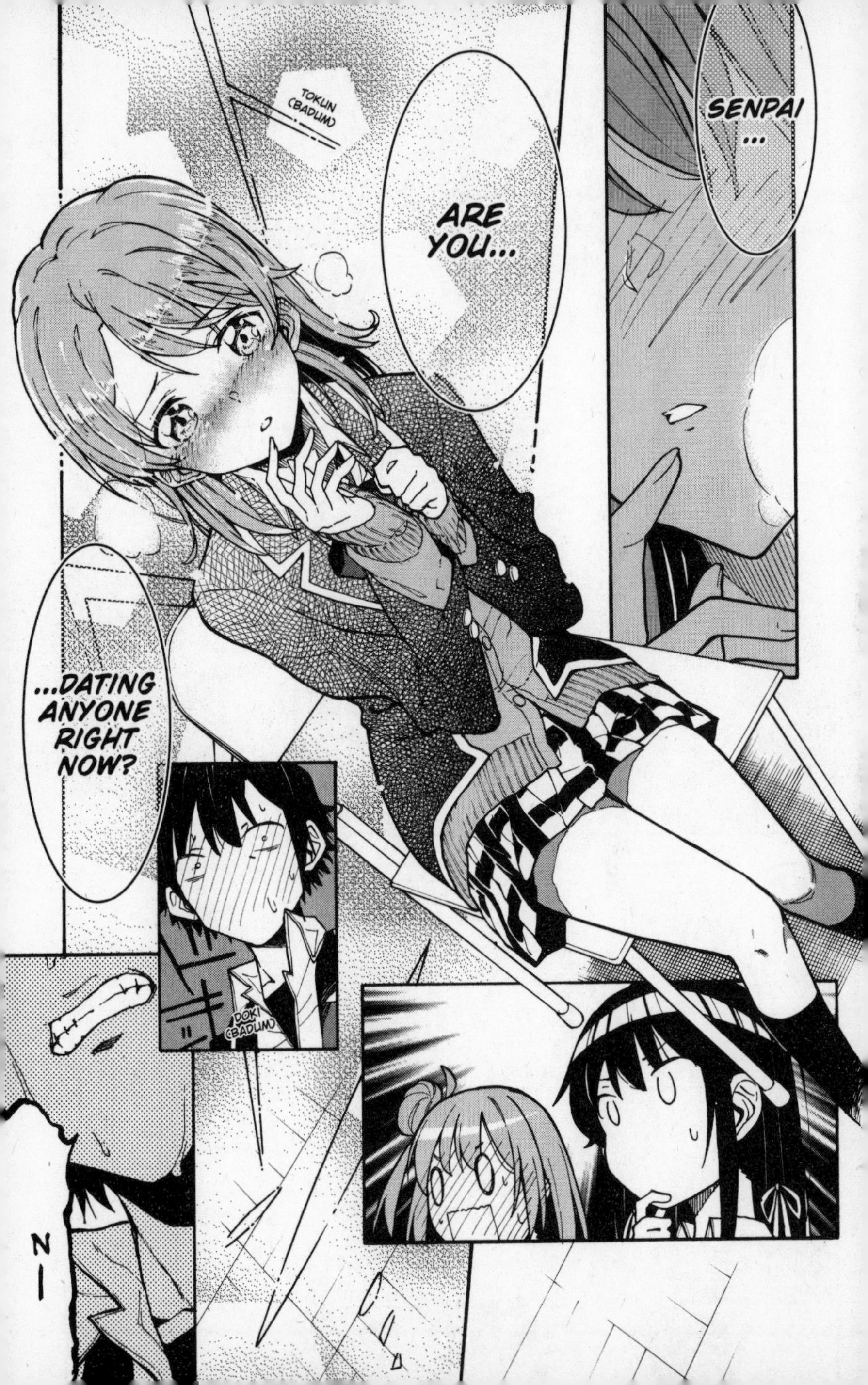
SENPAI...
ARE YOU...
TOKUN (BADUM)
...DATING ANYONE RIGHT NOW?
DOKI (BADUM)

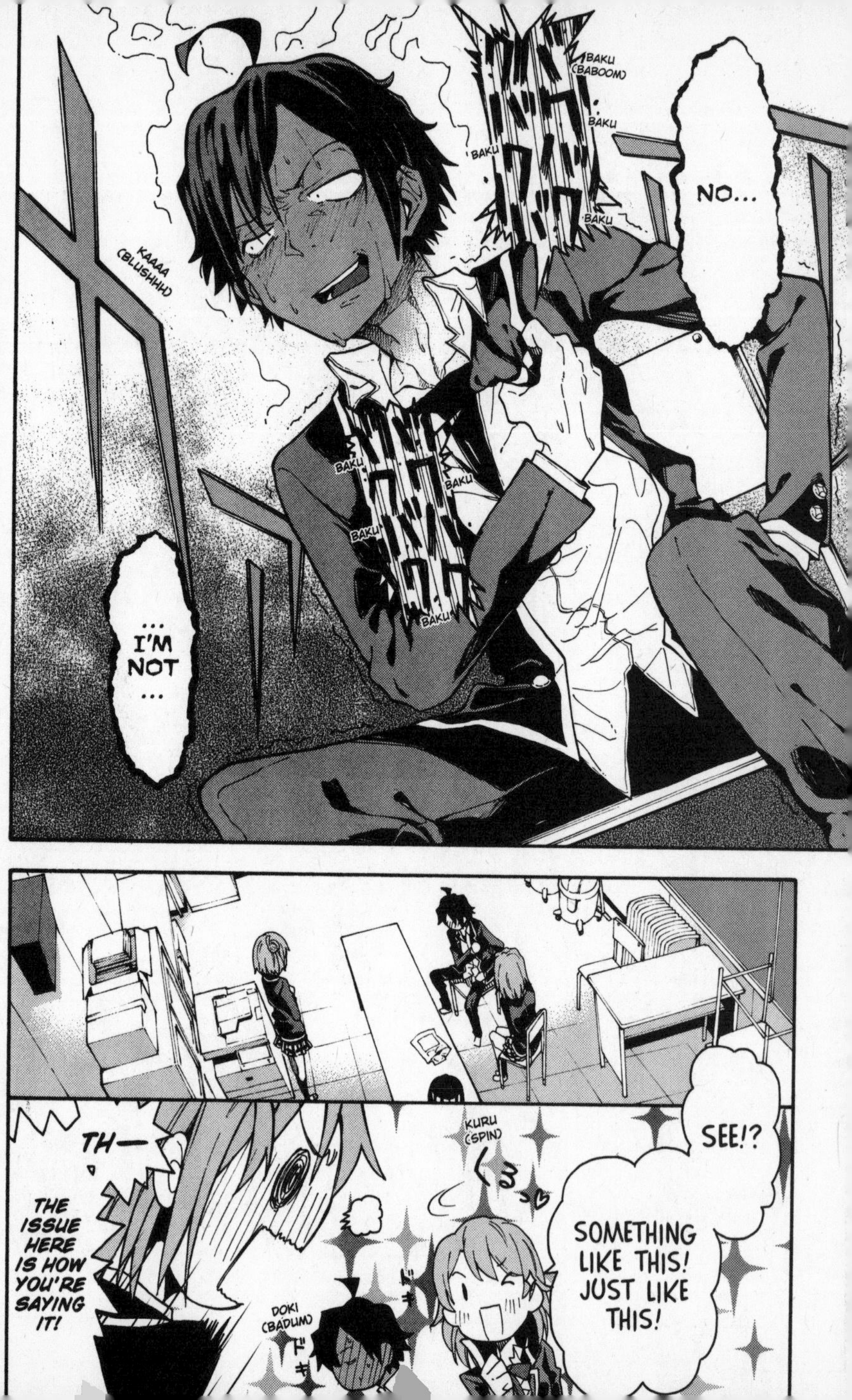
NO...
BAKU (BABOOM)
BAKU
BAKU
BAKU
KAAAA (BLUSHHH)
BAKU
BAKU
BAKU
BAKU
... I'M NOT ...
SEE!? SOMETHING LIKE THIS! JUST LIKE THIS!
KURU (SPIN)
DOKI (BADUM)
TH—
THE ISSUE HERE IS HOW YOU'RE SAYING IT!

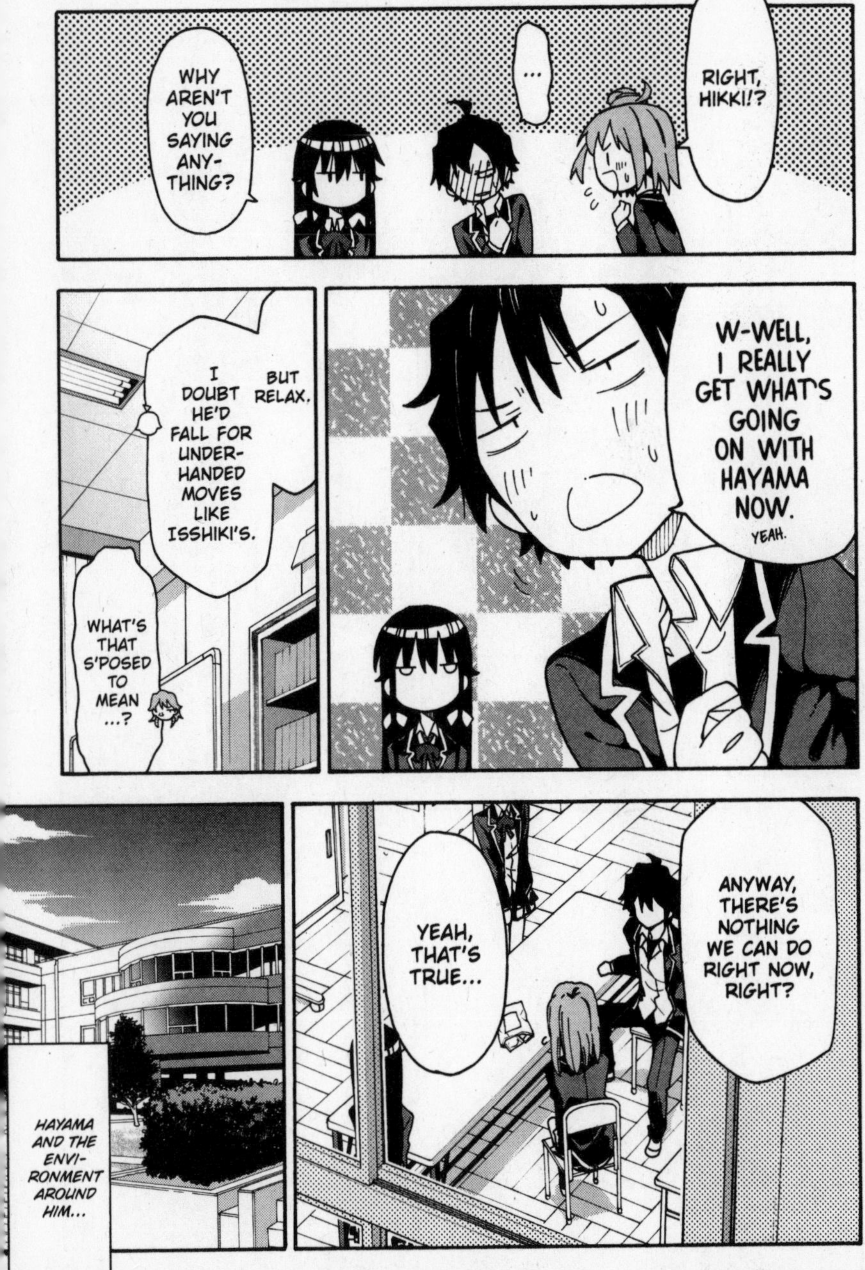
RIGHT, HIKKI!?
...
WHY AREN'T YOU SAYING ANYTHING?
W-WELL, I REALLY GET WHAT'S GOING ON WITH HAYAMA NOW.
YEAH.
BUT RELAX.
I DOUBT HE'D FALL FOR UNDERHANDED MOVES LIKE ISSHIKI'S.
WHAT'S THAT S'POSED TO MEAN...?
ANYWAY, THERE'S NOTHING WE CAN DO RIGHT NOW, RIGHT?
YEAH, THAT'S TRUE...
HAYAMA AND THE ENVIRONMENT AROUND HIM...

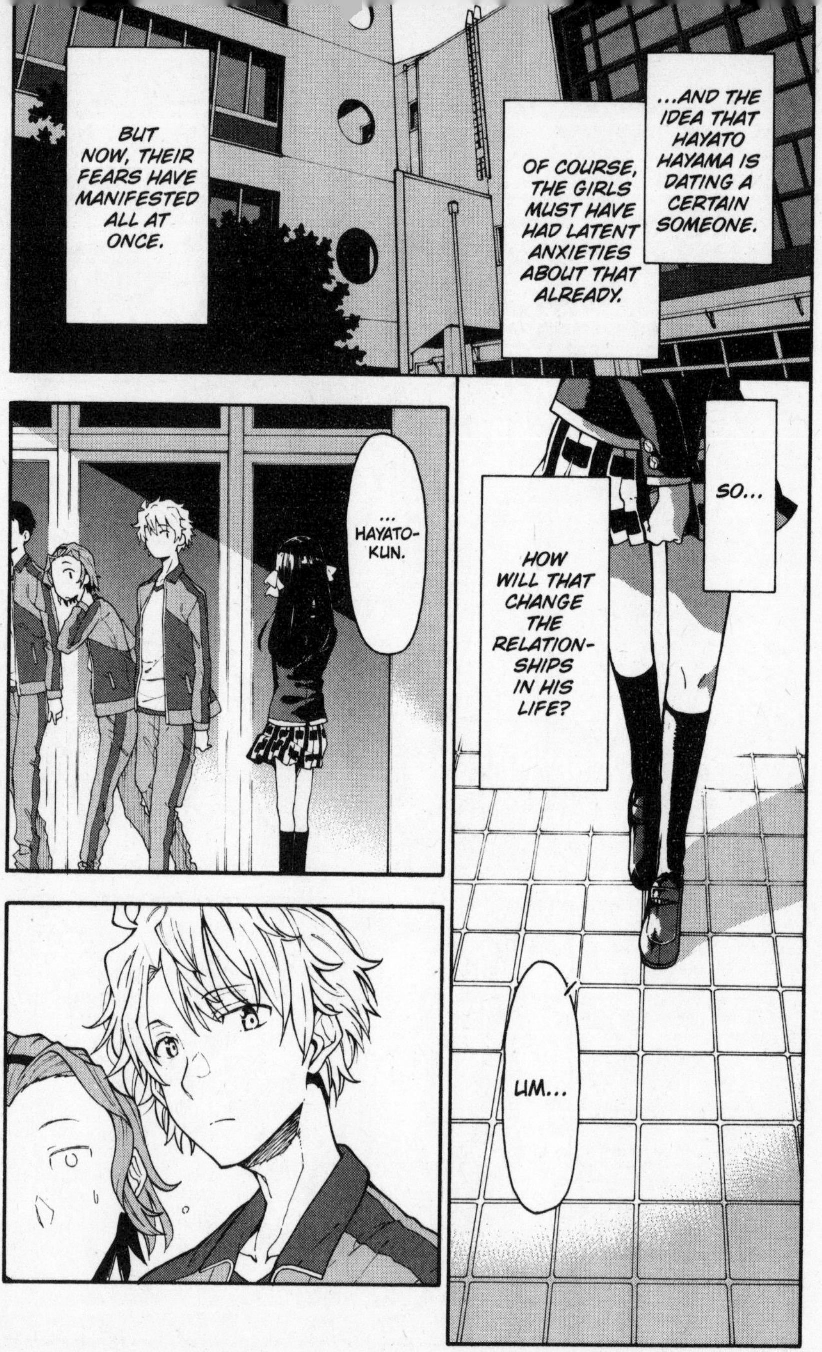
...AND THE IDEA THAT HAYATO HAYAMA IS DATING A CERTAIN SOMEONE.
OF COURSE, THE GIRLS MUST HAVE HAD LATENT ANXIETIES ABOUT THAT ALREADY.
BUT NOW, THEIR FEARS HAVE MANIFESTED ALL AT ONCE.
SO...
HOW WILL THAT CHANGE THE RELATION-SHIPS IN HIS LIFE?
UM...
...HAYATO-KUN.

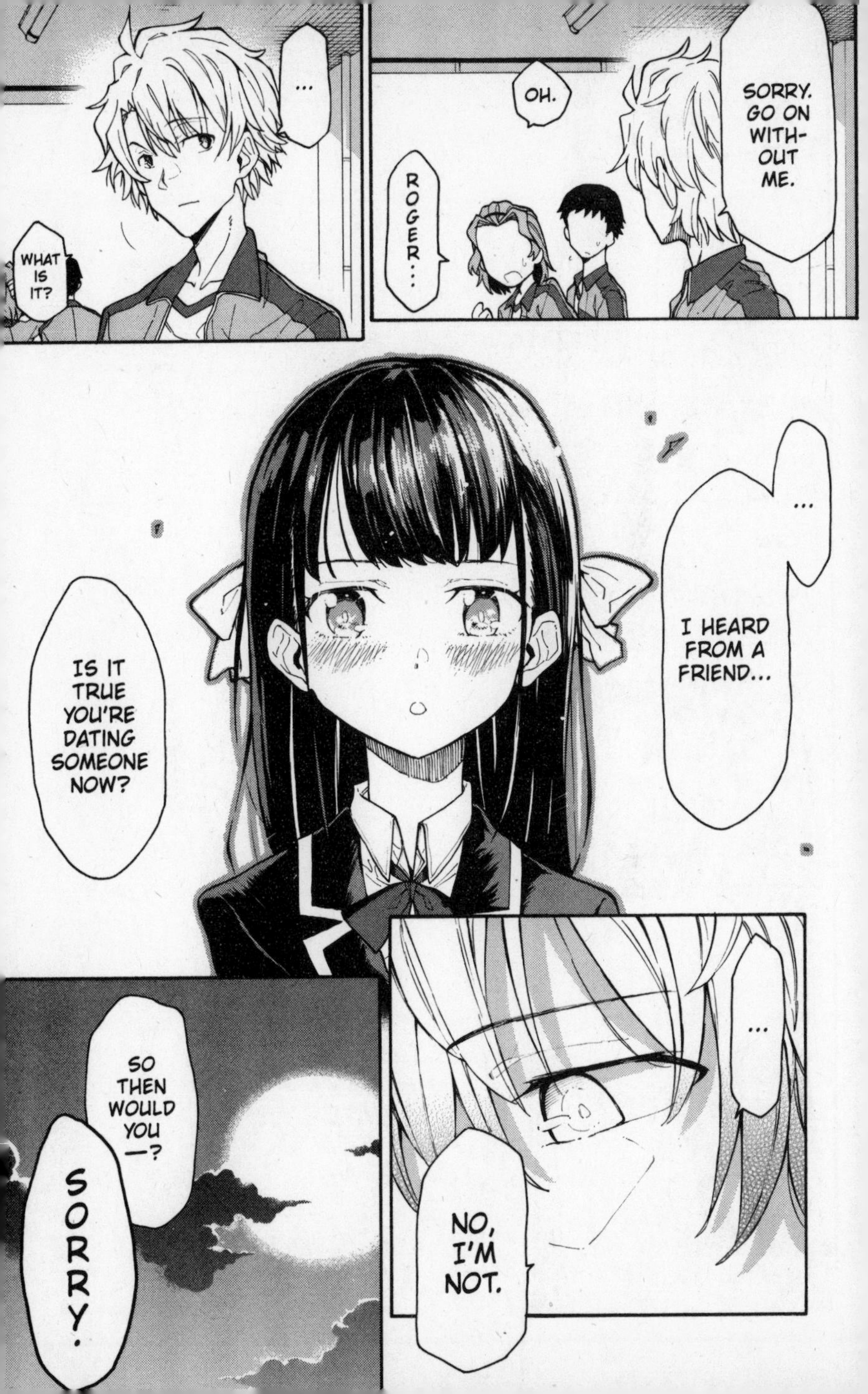
SORRY. GO ON WITH-OUT ME.
OH.
ROGER...
...
WHAT IS IT?
...
I HEARD FROM A FRIEND...
IS IT TRUE YOU'RE DATING SOMEONE NOW?
...
NO, I'M NOT.
SO THEN WOULD YOU—?
SORRY.

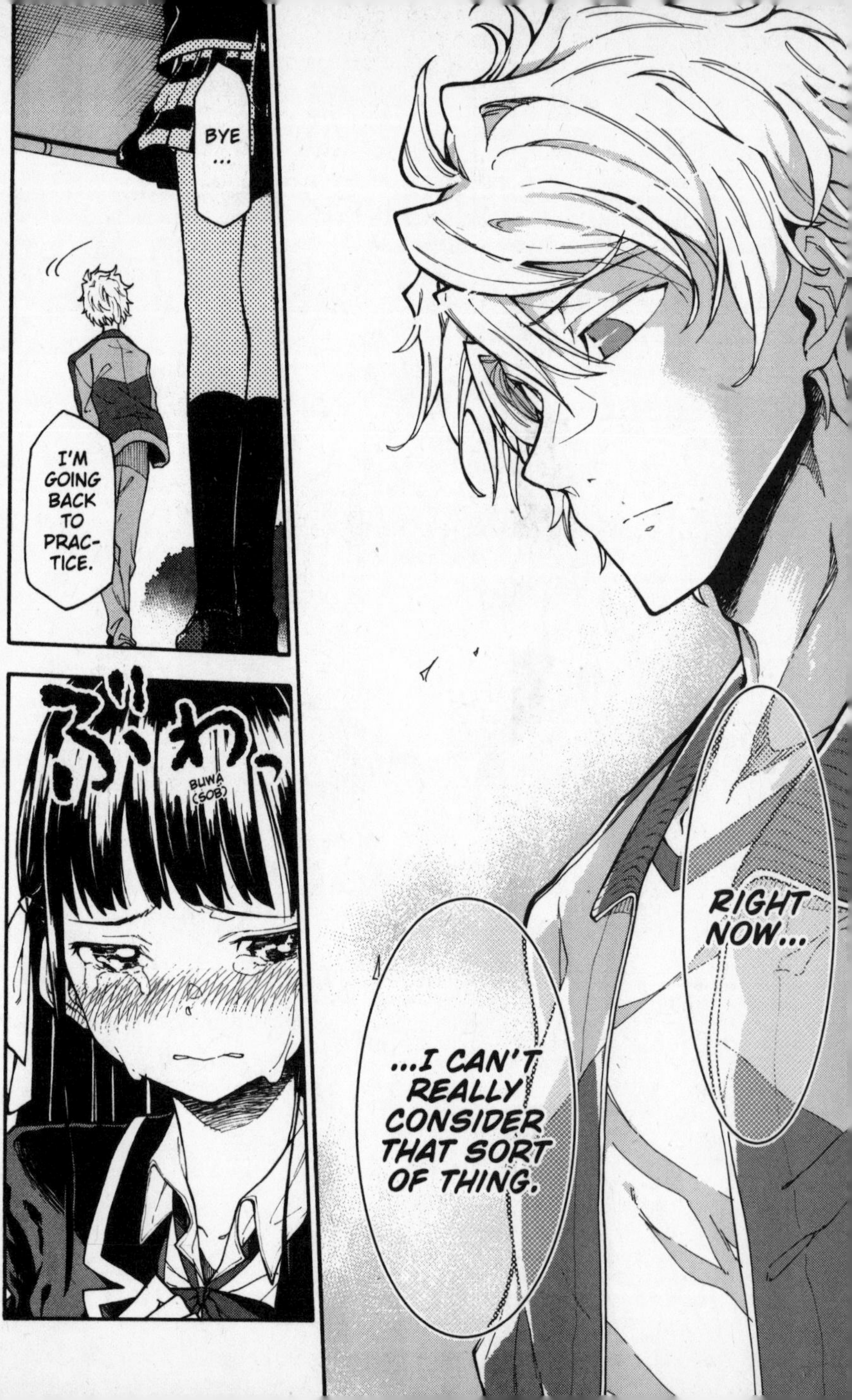
RIGHT NOW...
...I CAN'T REALLY CONSIDER THAT SORT OF THING.
BYE ...
I'M GOING BACK TO PRACTICE.
ぶわっ
BUWA (SOB)

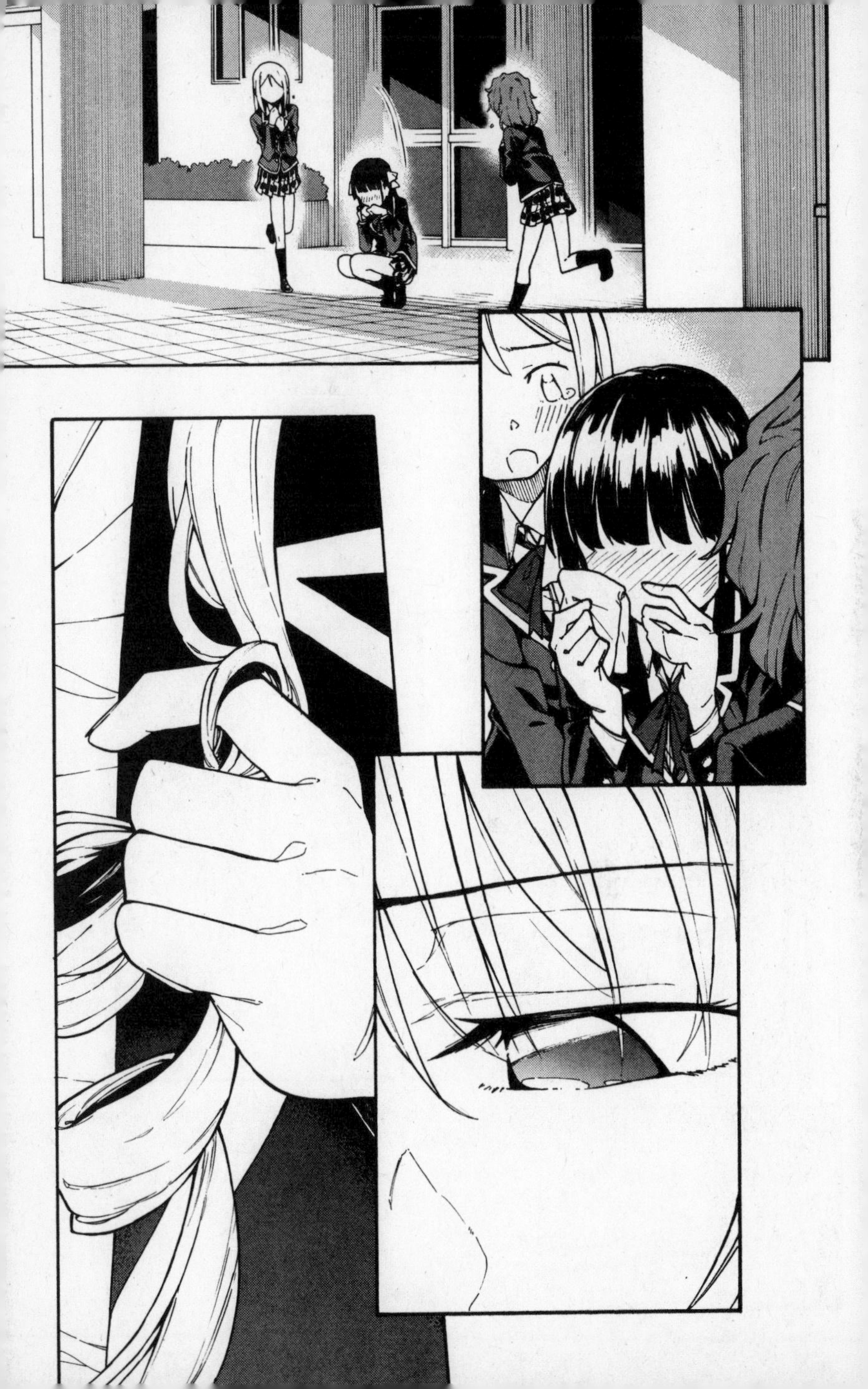

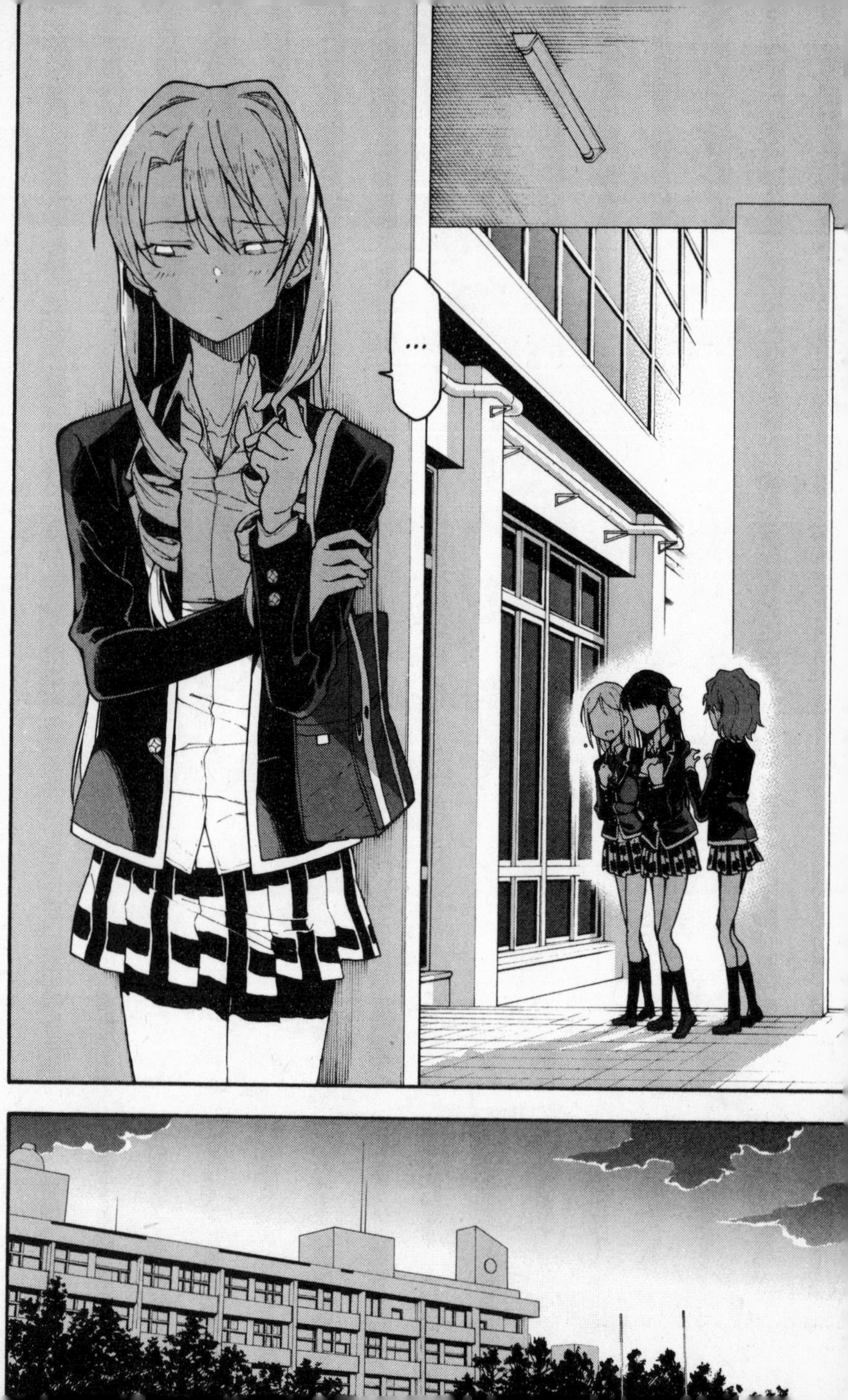
…

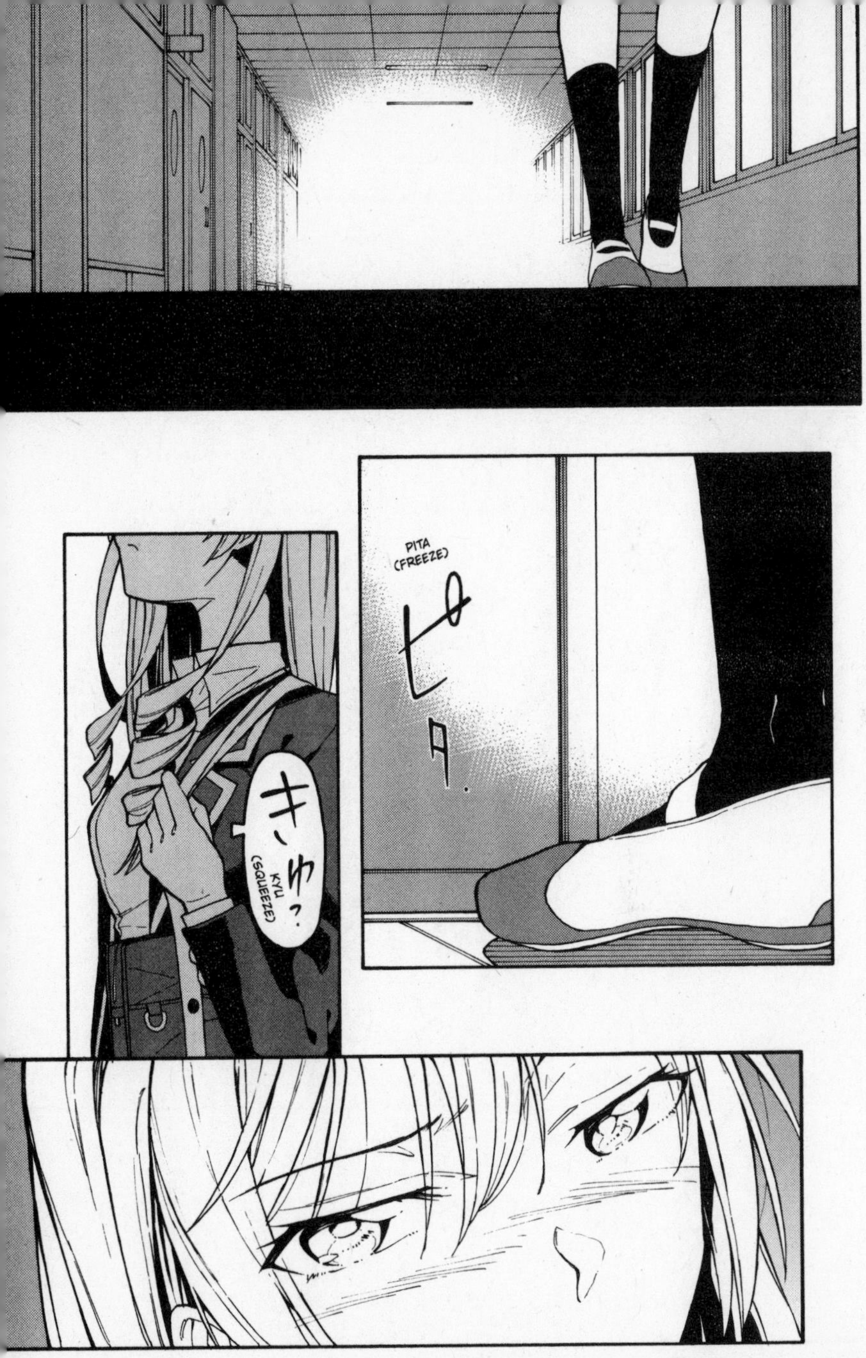
PITA (FREEZE)
ピタ.
きゅっ
KYU (SQUEEZE)

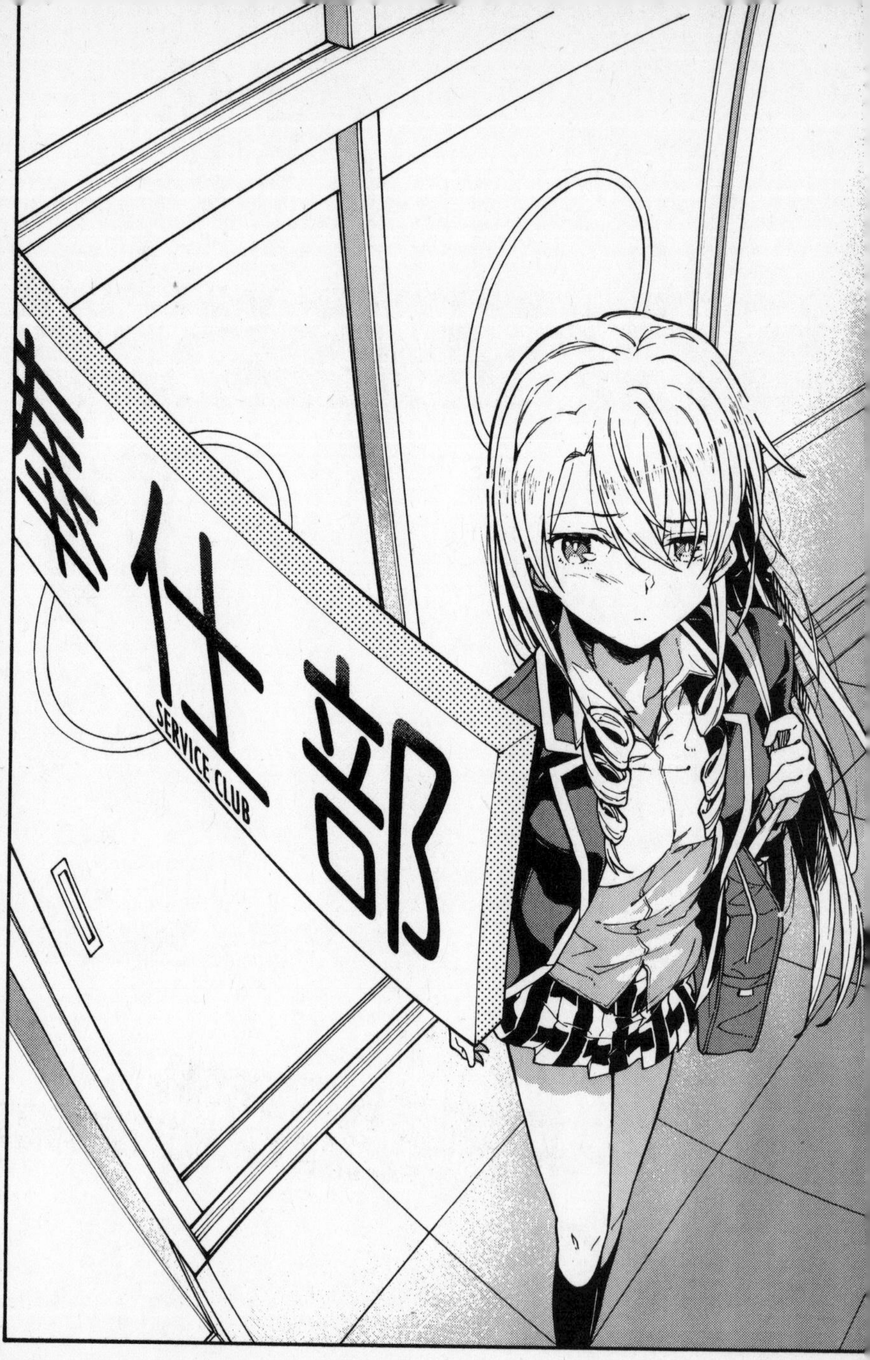
奉仕部
SERVICE CLUB

MY YOUTH ROMANTIC COMEDY IS WRONG, AS I EXPECTE[D]

...To Be Continued

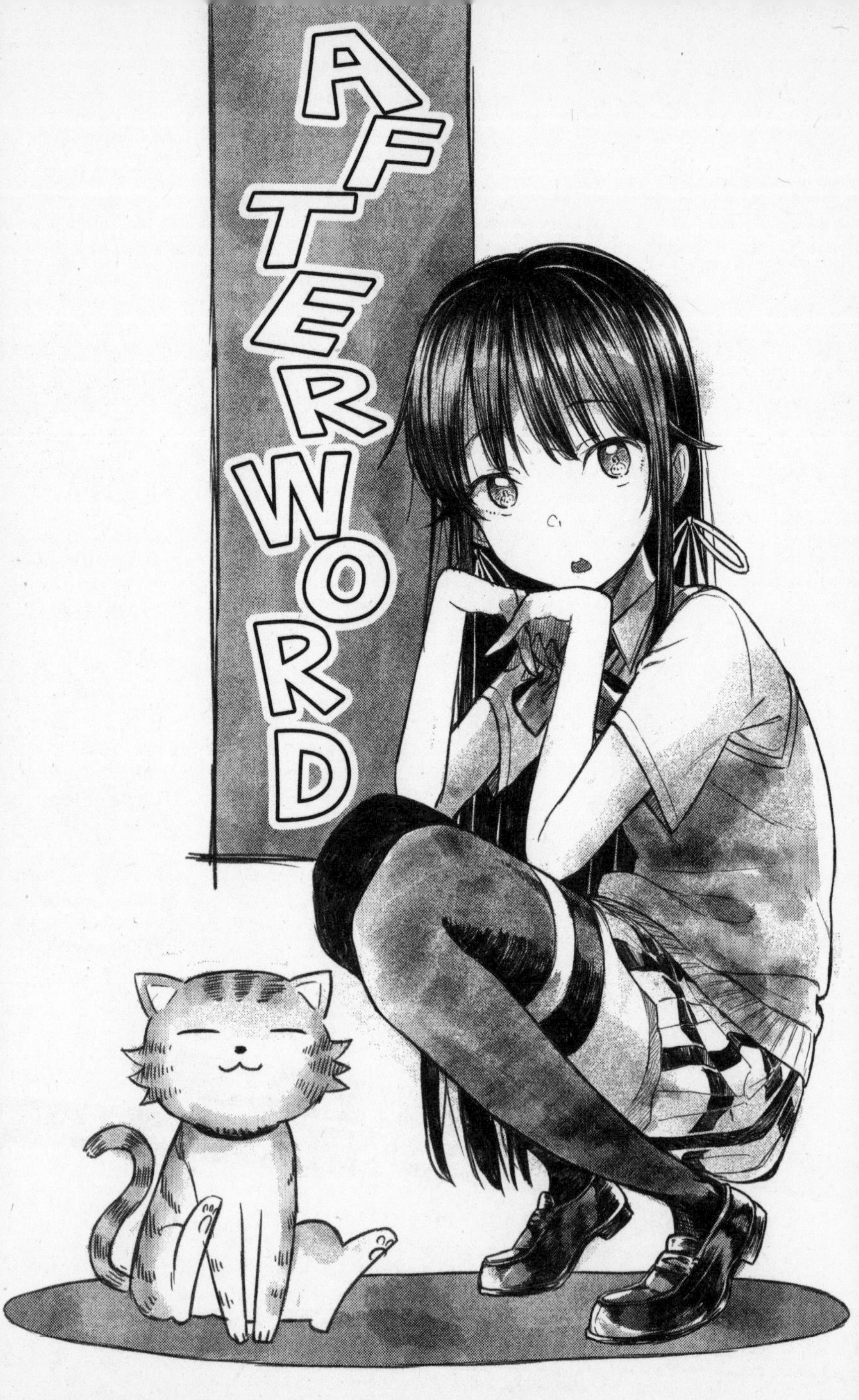
AFTERWORD

CONGRATULATIONS ON THE THIRD SEASON OF THE *MYRC* ANIME!

I did have the vague sense that they were going to do it, but I was really glad when they actually announced it! Now I'm really looking forward to it, and also—hi, I'm Naomichi Io.

All right. So I can't have the @Comic adaptation getting beat by the TV anime, so finally, Volume 13 is out.

This volume, there have been kind of a lot of chapters where Hachiman goes out to various places, so I got to draw lots of his casual clothes on these outings. It's been a lot of fun.

For the casual clothes in this comic, I generally stick to the standard set by the books as much as possible for outfits that are described in the novels, and for other characters, I fantasize about things like "I think this person would buy these kinds of clothes from this kind of clothing store" as I make them.

Since *MYRC* has a decently large cast, quite a lot of the time, just coming up with casual outfits for everyone would take the whole day (sweat), and I found myself thinking on a regular basis that the anime staff must be having a rough time of it coming up with colors on top of that too.

But anyway, I will continue to plug away, doing my best with this manga, so I hope you will please keep on reading it too.

See you next time.

Naomichi Io   2019.4.19

Thanks: Wataru Watari, Ponkan⑧-sama, the Gagaga Bunko editing department, Monthly Sunday GX editing department, Chiba City Location Services

TRANSLATION NOTES

Page 9
Karaoke Master (Karaoke no Tatsujin) is a play on the karaoke chain shop **Karaoke Iron Man** (Karaoke no Tetsujin).

Page 11
Bound2 is a spoof on the Japanese amusement store chain Round1, which also has a presence in the United States.

Page 28
Zuika is a play on the Suica card (the Kanto-region train system's charge card).

Page 49
Gravure is a term that originally referred to a type of photo printing, but in Japan, it refers specifically to risqué soft-core photography, often swimsuit or pinup-style material.

Page 78
The first shrine visit of the year is usually done on New Year's Day, and major shrines are generally packed on that day.

Page 79
"The year's plans are to be made on New Year's Day" is a saying that means if you're going to do anything, planning well ahead of time is a good idea. As usual, Hachiman makes a twisted interpretation of it.

Page 102
"I won't get greedy! Not until victory!" is a 1942 war slogan encouraging the people of Japan to keep a stiff upper lip in the face of austerity.

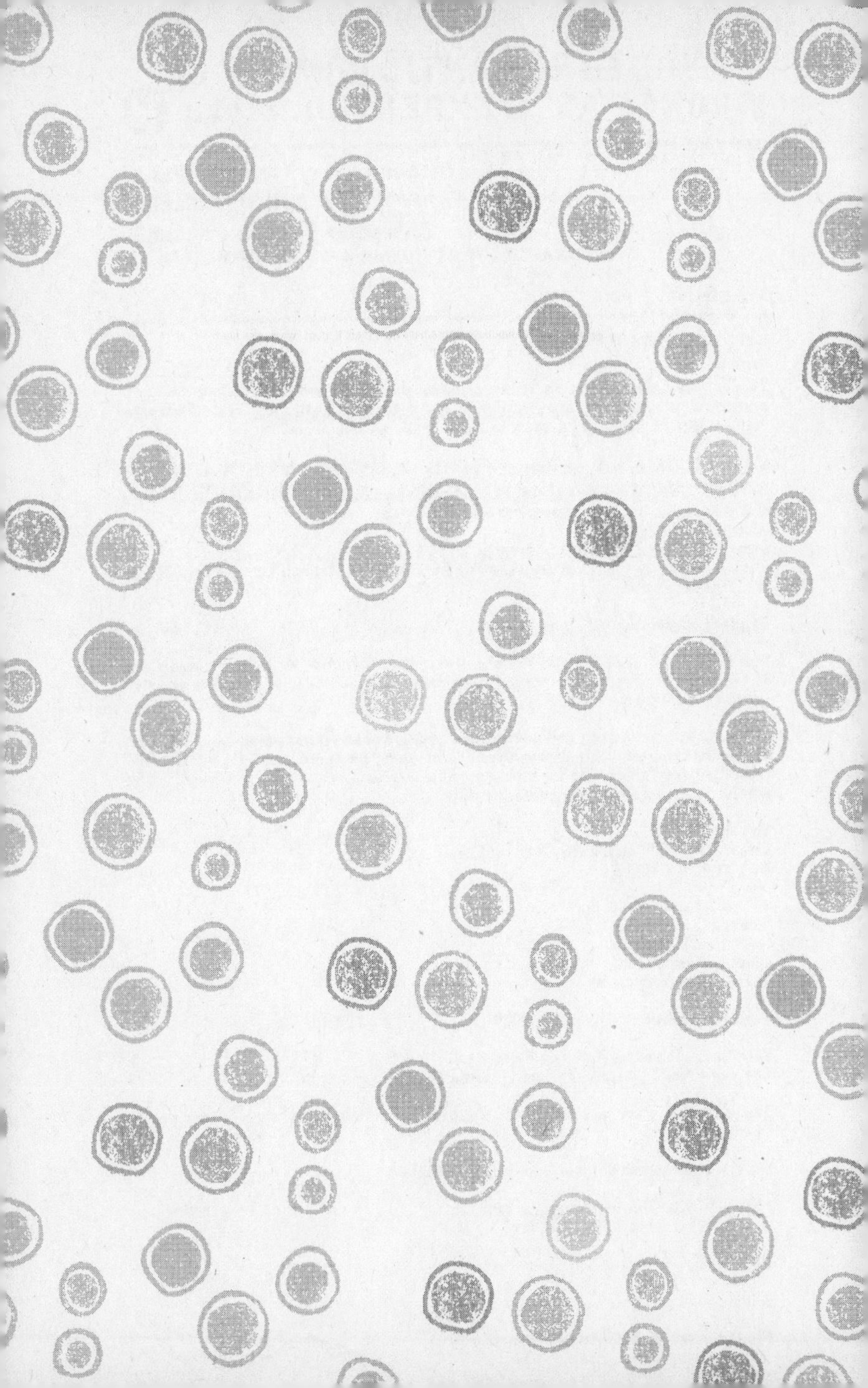

MY YOUTH ROMANTIC COMEDY IS WRONG, AS I EXPECTED @COMIC ⓭

Original Story: Wataru Watari
Art: Naomichi Io
Character Design: Ponkan⑧
ORIGINAL COVER DESIGN/Hiroyuki KAWASOME (Graphio)

Translation: Jennifer Ward

Lettering: Bianca Pistillo

YAHARI ORE NO SEISHUN LOVE COME WA MACHIGATTEIRU.
@COMIC Vol. 13 by Wataru WATARI, Naomichi IO, PONKAN⑧
© 2013 Wataru WATARI, Naomichi IO, PONKAN⑧
All rights reserved.
Original Japanese edition published by SHOGAKUKAN.
English translation rights arranged with SHOGAKUKAN through Tuttle-Mori Agency, Inc., Tokyo.

English translation © 2020 by Yen Press, LLC

Yen Press
150 West 30th Street, 19th Floor
New York, NY 10001

Visit us at yenpress.com
facebook.com/yenpress
twitter.com/yenpress
yenpress.tumblr.com
instagram.com/yenpress

First Yen Press Edition: March 2020

Yen Press is an imprint of Yen Press, LLC.
The Yen Press name and logo are trademarks of Yen Press, LLC.

Library of Congress Control Number: 2016931004

ISBNs: 978-1-9753-9950-4 (paperback)
       978-1-9753-1466-8 (ebook)

10 9 8 7 6 5 4 3 2 1

WOR

Printed in the United States of America